ADVANCING FUTURES

Futures Studies in Higher Education

Edited by James A. Dator

eger Studies on the 21st Century

PRAEGER

Westport, Connecticut
London

Library of Congress Cataloging-in-Publication Data

Dator, James Allen.
    Advancing futures : futures studies in higher education / edited by James A. Dator.
       p.   cm. — (Praeger studies on the 21st century, ISSN 1070–1850)
    Includes bibliographical references and index.
    ISBN 0–275–96945–2 (alk. paper) — ISBN 0–275–97632–7 (pbk. : alk. paper)
    1. Forecasting—Study and teaching (Higher)   2. Twenty-first century—Forecasts—Study
and teaching (Higher)   I. Title.   II. Series.
  CB158.D37   2002
  303.49′071′1—dc21   2001051374

British Library Cataloguing in Publication Data is available.

Library of Congress Catalog Card Number: 2001051374
ISBN: 0–275–96945–2
      0–275–97632–7 (pbk.)
ISSN: 1070–1850

First published in 2002

Praeger Publishers, 88 Post Road West, Westport, CT 06881
An imprint of Greenwood Publishing Group, Inc.
www.praeger.com

Printed in the United States of America

The paper used in this book complies with the
Permanent Paper Standard issued by the National
Information Standards Organization (Z39.48–1984).

10 9 8 7 6 5 4 3 2 1

Contents

Introduction: The Future Lies Behind—Thirty Years of Teaching Futures Studies

Jim Dator

You are holding in your hands a collection of chapters written by twenty-nine people from twelve different countries describing the theories and methods underlying the courses they teach in futures studies (FS) at the university level. Yet the chances are very good that you have never taken a course in futures studies, never met a person who taught it at the university level, teach or study on a campus where futures studies is not offered, and probably associate "futures studies" (if the term means anything to you at all) either with astrology and charlatans or with Alvin Toffler, John Naisbitt, or Faith Popcorn (or, alternatively, with the late Herman Kahn and the late Julian Simon versus the Meadows and the *Limits to Growth/Beyond the Limits*) (Toffler, 1970, 1980; Naisbitt, 1984; Popcorn, 1992; Kahn and Weiner, 1967; Kahn and Simon, 1984; Simon, 1996; Meadows et al., 1972; Meadows et al., 1992) Of these, only Simons and the Meadows were university professors, and they were more nearly arguing for or against one

Most of the chapters in this book were originally published in an issue of the *American Behavioral Scientist*, vol. 42, no. 3, November–December 1998, devoted to "Futures Studies in Higher Education," edited by Jim Dator. I thank Sage Publications for giving me permission to reprint them here.

particular future than primarily concerned with the study of the future, or beliefs about the future per se.

It is also possible that "futures studies" might conjure up images of computer-based mathematical models (such as those of the econometricians or those who would provide disaster early warnings), which attempt or pretend to predict the future with such precision that policy can be confidentially guided by the prediction.

Your own reading about the future is, in all probability, restricted to *Brave New World* and *1984* (if you are of a certain age cohort), and/or to varieties of science fiction and comic books (*Flash Gordon* among a host of others). Your most fundamental images of the future are almost certainly shaped primarily by films and videos you have seen in theaters or on television sets: *The Twilight Zone, The Invasion of the Body Snatchers, It, On the Beach, 2001—A Space Odyssey,* the *Planet of the Apes* series, *Star Trek, Star Wars, Back to the Future, Blade Runner, Brazil, Total Recall, Robocop,* the *Terminator* series, and the various *Mad Max* flicks (perhaps *Buck Rogers*—if you are old enough—or more recently *Twelve Monkeys, Gattaca, Strange Days, Johnny Mnemonic*), or by visits to Disneyland or the Seattle World's Fair (or the 1939–1940 New York World's Fair, if—can I say it again?—you are old enough). Even the recent animated television series *Futurama* is an allusion to the "Futurama" of that New York World's Fair. Some of you (and many among the population at large) have images of the future shaped by Armageddon and other visions derived from the Book of Revelations, perhaps as depicted in the film *The Late Great Planet Earth.*

Statistically speaking, you are unaware of the existence of the World Futures Studies Federation (WFSF), the World Future Society (WFS), or Futuribles International, all of which were created in the mid 1960s, whose members unfailingly read *Future Survey* (a monthly survey—compiled yearly into an indispensable annual—of books, articles, and reports, in English, about or important for the future, and superbly edited by Michael Marien) and routinely publish in this Admantine series, as well as in such journals as *Forecasting, Futures, Futures Research Quarterly, Technological Forecasting and Social Change, Futuribles, Futuribili, Futura, Papers de Prospectiva,* and the *Manoa Journal of Fried and Half Fried Ideas* (. . . about the future) (journals also of whose existence you are unaware, though you might have seen *The Futurist,* published by the World Future Society, in a library). These organizations have held world futures conferences, in the case of the World Futures Studies Federation in Oslo, Norway (1967), Kyoto, Japan (1970), Bucharest, Romania (1972), Rome, Italy (1973), Berlin, West Germany (1975), Dubrovnik, Yugoslavia (1976), Warsaw, Poland (1977), Cairo, Egypt (1978), Stockholm, Sweden (1982), San Jose, Costa Rica (1984), Honolulu, Hawaii (1986), Beijing, China (1988), Budapest, Hungary (1990), Barcelona, Spain (1991), Turku, Finland (1993), Nairobi, Kenya (1995), Brisbane, Australia (1997), Bocolod City, the Philippines (1999), and

Braslov, Romania (2001) (see WFSF Conference Publications, 1967–1996 in the Bibliography).

During the 1970s and 1980s—until the forceful disintegration of Yugoslavia—WFSF offered futures courses every spring through the Inter-University Centre for Post Graduate Studies at Dubrovnik, attracting university students from East and West Europe, as well as Africa, Asia, and North America. With the cooperation of the Center Catala de Prospectiva, the Unesco Centre of Catalunya, the Ministry of Education of Andorra, and the Muncipality of Encamp, the WFSF has also more recently offered futures courses in Andorra. UNESCO has been a major supporter of many of the activities of the WFSF and has sponsored Asia–Pacific Futures Courses in Fiji, Thailand, Malaysia, and the Philippines since 1992.

Presidents of the WFSF have been such highly regarded scholars as Bertrand de Jouvenel (France), Johan Galtung (Norway), Mahdi Elmandjra (Morocco), Eleonora Masini (Italy), Pentti Malaska (Finland), Tony Stevenson (Australia), and Richard Slaughter (Australia). I was first secretary general and then president of the WFSF during much of the 1980s and early 1990s.

Indeed, I have been teaching futures courses since 1967, when I introduced what is sometimes said to be the first undergraduate course on the future that went through the normal channels of faculty and administrative approval while I was teaching for three years in the Department of Political Science at Virginia Tech in Blacksburg, Virginia (Dator, 1971). I had more or less "invented" futures studies during the previous six years (1960–1966) while I was teaching in the College of Law and Politics of Rikkyo University in Tokyo, Japan. But I am thankful to Joseph Bernd, chair of the department, and Leslie Malpass, dean of the College of Arts and Science of VPI, for their active support of my embryonic futures work.

Shortly after I arrived in Blacksburg in 1966, David Greene, a member of the British Archigram Group who was a visiting professor in the School of Architecture and with whom I shared a duplex house near the campus, told me that I "sounded like Buckminster Fuller," who I had never heard of, and showed me a flyer announcing the creation of the World Future Society by Ed Cornish in Washington, D.C. I immediately joined. Shortly thereafter I published my first futures article in *The Futurist* (Dator, 1967). It was an excerpt of a much longer and never fully published essay titled, "Oh, We Belong to a Cybernetic, Post-Money, Situational Ethics Society, My Baby and Me." Recently the journal *Futures*, in its "Second Thoughts" series, republished the old *Futurist* article, with four commentaries by futurists of different age cohorts and cultures (Dator, 1967, 1997; Jones, 1997; Nordberg, 1997; Serra 1997; Slaughter, 1997).

Also while I was at Virginia Tech I compiled an extensive bibliography of books and articles relevant to the study of the future, which the WFS published in the *WFS Bulletin* (the predecessor to the *Futures Research*

Quarterly). This brought me to the attention of John and Magda McHale (then working with Fuller at Southern Illinois University) and Eleonora Masini, who headed the Italian futures group IRADES, which published a quarterly newsletter on the development of futures studies globally, reflective in part of their role in the 1967 Oslo conference convened by Robert Jungk of Austria and Johan Galtung of Norway through Mankind 2000. I thus also was drawn into the circle of futurists who eventually formally established the WFSF in Paris in 1973 (see Some Additional Early Futures Classics in the Bibliography).

In 1969 I went to the Department of Political Science at the University of Hawaii, specifically to teach graduate and undergraduate futures courses, and also to participate in the activities called "Hawaii 2000," which, under the inspiration of Daniel Bell's (1968) U.S. initiative, were beginning under the sponsorship of then Governor John Burns, President of the Senate David McClung, and Speaker of the House Tadao Beppu, and under the main guidance of the editor in chief of the Honolulu *Advertiser*, George Chaplin, and Glenn Paige, a colleague in the Department of Political Science. Chaplin, Paige, and myself attended the 1970 Kyoto Conference of the WFSF, in part to recruit people from the WFSF to participate in the Hawaii 2000 Conference held in 1970, which was, I believe, still the best example of "anticipatory democracy" ever experienced (Chaplin and Paige, 1971; Dator, 1973).

In 1972 the Hawaii State Legislature created the Hawaii Research Center for Futures Studies within the University of Hawaii (eventually within the Social Science Research Institute), which I still direct (http://www.soc.hawaii. edu/future/). The Center does contract and pro bono futures work for public and private groups in Hawaii and the Pacific Island region, as well as throughout the United States, the Asia–Pacific region, and, indeed, worldwide. The Center is best known for work in judicial foresight, which began with the Hawaii State Judiciary in 1971 (under the encouragement of Chief Justice William Richardson and Chief Court Administrator Lester Cingcade). Especially because of funding (1987–1997) from the State Justice Institute (SJI; a federal funding agency), the Center has worked directly and extensively with eleven other American state and territorial judiciaries (Arizona, Idaho, Illinois, Kansas, Florida, Massachusetts, Nevada, Pennsylvania, Puerto Rico, Tennessee, and, most notably, since 1987, with the judiciary of Virginia, which, under the leadership of Chief Justice Harry L. Carrico, Court Administrator Rob Baldwin, and Court Planner Kathy Mays, has elevated judicial foresight to exceptional heights).

The Center has also worked indirectly with all American state judiciaries though futures conferences and workshops sponsored by the SJI, the American Judicature Society, the American Bar Association, and a wide variety of international, national, state, and local judicial, bar, and legal organizations, such as the United Nations Asia and Far East Institute for the Prevention of Crime and the Treatment of Offenders, in Tokyo; the Supreme Court of South Korea; the judiciary of the Federated States of Micronesia and of the State of Pohnpei; the Subordinate Courts of Singapore; the U.S. Federal Judicial Center; the Fourth, Fifth, and D.C. Federal Judicial Circuits; the Congress of State Court Justices; the Conference of State Court Administrators; the Council of Chief Judges; the American Judges Association; the National Association for Court Management; the annual conferences of the American Bar Association; the Western States Bar Assocation; and many more (see Judicial Foresight in the Bibliography).

In 1977 the Department of Political Science instituted a master's degree specialization in Alternative Futures, which has been pumping consulting futurists into the world, at a modest rate, ever since. One of the features of that specialization is a year's paid internship in a futures consulting firm so that students learn how futures studies can usefully be applied in public and private organizations. Students of the Hawaii program have interned at many places, but we have our closest relationship with the Institute for Alternative Futures in Alexandria, Virginia, which was founded in 1976 by Clem Bezold (still the president), Alvin Toffler, Jonas Salk, and myself, among many others (including Newt Gingrich, who was then a futures-oriented professor at West Georgia College).

It would be a big mistake to assume that I am alone in the futures field, as all of the other chapters in this volume will make abundantly clear. It has been an extensive, worldwide activity from the beginning through the present. The national academies of sciences of Finland, China, Russia, Hungary, Bulgaria, and perhaps others have futures studies departments.

And yet you say you have never heard of any of this? It is truly amazing indeed, and I am hopeful that this volume will now lift the veil of unawareness from the eyes of the global academic community, and lure you, and all your colleagues, into this exciting and important area of intellectual and practical endeavor.

WHAT IS FUTURES STUDIES?

So what is futures studies? What are the theories and methods underlying the field? What are its basic concepts and metaphors? How is it related to other academic and practical fields? What is the relationship between teaching and consulting? These are questions that I asked each of the authors in this volume to address. While each responded to them in different ways, and some spent more time discussing some issues and less time on others, an amazing unity emerged within the overall breadth and diversity.

Everyone agreed that futures studies does not try to "predict" the future in the sense of saying precisely what will happen to an individual, organization, or country before it actually happens. However, many of the authors admit that they were originally drawn into futures studies in the hope— indeed, often in the firm belief—that it would be possible to predict the future if one just had the correct theory, methods, data, and, of course, enough funding.

I too had entered futures studies with this belief, having been very much influenced by the 1950s–1960s "behavioral revolution" in political science, with its emphasis on quantitative methods and formal modeling. Indeed, it was because I attended Joe Bernd's National Science Foundation (NSF) summer course in mathematical applications in political science, offered at Southern Methodist University in Dallas, Texas, during the summer of 1965 (Bernd, 1966) that I returned from Japan in 1966 and went with Bernd to VPI to start the new Department of Political Science there.

It was fascinating for me, then, to see that at the same time, in a completely different part of the world, operating under a completely different ideological system, two Hungarian futurists report in their contributions to this collection that they were similarly beginning their work, confident that they too had (or could soon have) the methodological keys that would unlock the ability precisely to predict the future.

Not one of the authors of the chapters assembled here believe in prediction in that sense anymore. Though some feel they have theoretical understandings and rigorous methodologies that enable them to forecast strong tendencies (or even soft predictabilities) with considerable confidence, most of the authors insist (as I do) on the reality of "alternative futures" rather than a single "the future." We have concluded (at least I have) that the future is fundamentally plural and open, an arena of possibilities (which is what the French term, *futuribles* is intended to capture), and not of discernible inevitabilities.

Most futurists therefore forecast a wide variety of alternative futures rather than predicting the future. They also seek to help people (students, clients, community groups, even entire nations) invent and try to move effectively toward their "preferred future," all the time monitoring their progress toward it and reconsidering their preference in the light of new information and experience gained as time goes by. As Bell and Mau (1971) put it, quoting Robert Brumbaugh, "There are no future facts, but there are no past possibilities" (p. 9). These are still among the wisest words a futurist can utter.

Since the future is the arena of the possible and of the preferred, rather than of the foregone and predetermined, it is also the arena of dreams and values. Ethical considerations are central to futures teaching and futures research. There is no pretense of separating considerations of good and bad, right and wrong, beauty and ugliness, and other core values from academic inquiry into (or professional consulting concerning) the future. Values are central, and must be clearly discussed up front and in every stage of futures study and consulting.

One of the continuing debates in futures studies (as everywhere) centers on some kind of ethical and moral absolutism versus various kinds of ethical and moral relativism. Some futurists believe that there is a set of core values underlying all human action across all cultures that must be the basis of all good futures studies and futures consulting. In this collection, the chapter by Wendell Bell comes closest to representing this perspective. Other futurists believe that there is no such common set of values, at least none that rises beyond vague generalities and can be used to require or outlaw specific actions (much less specific beliefs). I hold to that view.

Nonetheless, Bell and I (and all other futurists) believe that ethical discussion—and the professional ethics of the consulting futurist—are extremely important issues that are central to all teaching and consulting in futures studies. There can be no pretense to "truth," "objectivity," or "universality" on the part of anyone teaching or applying futures studies, though each futurist will and should hold certain views and actions to be better than others, and should not only constantly reexamine their own most deeply held values but also challenge the values of their clients as well as their students as a normal part of their futures work.

At the same time, there is a distinction between what is often called "futurism" or "the futures movement," on the one hand, and futures studies or futures research, on the other. Futurism is clearly concerned about the achievement (or avoidance) of one particular kind of future. People who speak of the futures movement or futurism know from the outset what kind of future they want. They seek a Green, sustainable future, or else they favor continued, unrestrained, "free market" economic growth. Or perhaps it is their dream to plunge us all into mining the moon, terraforming Mars, and expanding quickly into the cosmos. Alternatively, they are focused on creating nonviolent, nonkilling local communities. Or forecasting who the next enemy might be and developing the most effective, efficient, and lethal weapons against it. Perhaps they wish to create global governance, or libertarian anarchy. The number of preferred images of the future is endless, and thus is "futurism" and "the futures movement."

Futures studies, on the other hand, is interested not in itself furthering any particular view of the future, but rather in furthering both narrowly professional as well as broadly participative inquiry into the future; understanding the roots and consequences of each of the manifold images of the future that exist in people's minds and in support of people's actions. We are interested in identifying and understanding the many different images of the future that exist, understanding why certain people have certain images rather than others, how their different images of the future lead to specific actions or inactions in the present, and how present actions or inactions themselves create certain aspects of the future.

Thus, for many of the authors in this volume, just as futures studies does not seek to predict things to come, so also futures studies does not try to study "the future," since "the future" does not exist to be studied. What does exist, and what futurists can and often do study, are "images of the future" in people's minds. These images differ between individuals, cultures, men and women, social classes, and age groups. One job for futurists is to identify and study these varying images, to understand their origins and history, to see how they animate individual and group action, and then to anticipate how people, acting on the basis of an image of the future, "push" society into one future or another, just as their images can be said to "pull" them forward.

As various authors will make clear, these images can be optimistic or pessimistic, frightening or ennobling, paralyzing or motivating, weak or robust, unexamined and naïve, or fully researched, articulated, tested, and developed. But these images (from the point of view of futures studies) are not "right" or "wrong." They simply *are*: They exist; they are the empirical "facts" that the futurist studies. I would say that the concept "images of the future" and its corollaries, "forecasting alternative futures" and "inventing preferred futures," in contrast to "predicting the future," is key to understanding futures studies (K. Boulding, 1956; Polak, 1961; Mau, 1968; E. Boulding, 1971; Bell and Mau, 1971).

But the future is not completely open. As important as images and dreams are, you cannot do anything merely by dreaming and wishing it were so. While nothing good or bad will happen without your dreams, "appropriate action" is also necessary to make your dreams come true, and what appropriate action is depends not upon your (or even the collective) will alone, but also upon environmental factors over which you may have little or no control, but which you must understand and deal with successfully. The metaphor I use to illuminate this dynamic interactive relationship between subjective and objective factors is "surfing the tsunamis of change" (Dator, 1992).

The objective factors are a variety of environmental forces with which any image of the future (and struggle toward a preferred future) must contend. These factors cannot be ignored or wished away. They must themselves be identified and studied. Strategies for coping with them must be developed, tested, and used. What those environmental forces are (or are believed to be) depends on one's theory of social change, one's understanding of what "society" is, what causes it to change and what prevents change, what aspects of society change "easily" and what aspects resist change. Different futurists have different theories of social change. One thing I asked each contributor to this volume to do was to spell out their theory of social change. Each did, in varying degrees of detail.

I have concluded that technology is a major agent of social change, contributing significantly to the creation of all of the other "tsunamis" (demographics, global environmental change, political–economic instabilities, cultural transformation, etc.) upon which we all must "surf" (or drown). While it is too long a story for me fully to explicate here, my understanding is captured best by the aphorism of Marshall McLuhan (1967), "We shape our tools and thereafter our tools shape us."

Humans become human, and change their understanding of what it means to be human, by interacting with their environment and themselves through technology. Values, ethics, mores, religious beliefs, and laws are all made in relation to how humans can behave (and what they then come to believe about themselves as a consequence of their behavior). When technology changes, behavior changes, and thus, eventually, self- and social-consciousness changes. New behavior (and new self-awareness), permitted (and/or constrained) by new technology, challenges values and rules engendered by the behavior (and consciousness) permitted by old technologies, and thus society changes.

Learning how past technologies (and the environments they created) helped shape behavior and beliefs, as well as how then-new technologies changed that behavior, challenged prior institutions and beliefs, and thus precipitated social change is a major source of my understanding by analogy how new and emerging technologies might serve as agents of social change for the future. Thus, not only is the study of history extremely important to me as a futurist, but so also are anthropology, cultural studies, and evolutionary systems theories; indeed, they are even more important because those disciplines cover longer and wider stretches of human (and prehuman) experience than does "history."

It is a very complex interrelation about which I continue to learn, unlearn, and relearn more and more (see Technology and Social Change in the Bibliography). In the chapters that follow, some authors share some of my focus on technology, while others develop their theories of social change on entirely other bases.

In addition to technology, I believe the tsunamis upon which the surfer of human agency must ride are also shaped by cycles (especially the Kondratieff Long Waves, which are themselves influenced by the life cycles of technologies) and age-cohort analysis, the movement of what is sometimes called "generations" through their own life cycles. Thus, for example, I see considerable value in the perspective of those (partly informed by Wallersteinian World Systems theory and partly by Jantschian–Prigoginean evolutionary systems theory) who maintain that (in the American case) we members of the "Silent" and "Boomer" generations (the dynamism of the G. I. Generation, which coincided with the peak of the "4th Kondratieff Wave," now completely gone) are more or less "inevitably" wallowing helplessly within the flaccid trough of the most recent Kondratieff Long Wave, while rushing toward us is a new wave of growth and possibility, fueled by emerging technologies, which will swell during the first several decades of the twenty-first century and be surfed, well or poorly, by the cohorts of what are now sometimes called the "Millennial" and "Cyber" generations, who will live in the twenty-first century long after the last "Silents" and "Boomers" are gone (Berry, 1991; Berry and Kim, 1994; Dator, 1999a, 1999b; Jantsch, 1975; Kleinknecht, 1992; Prigogine, 1997; Schlesinger, 1986; Strauss and Howe, 1995, 1997; Wallerstein, 1979).

My teaching of futures studies through the Political Science Department of the University of Hawaii takes place on all levels. I teach an introductory freshman-level course, an advanced undergraduate course, and two graduate courses (one an introduction to the Alternative Futures M.A. Option, and the other a specialized course within it), and chair or sit on futures-oriented Ph.D. dissertation committees within the department and elsewhere.

The freshman course and the introductory graduate course are both similar in basic purpose and design, but quite different in execution. Both are oriented around what I call the "basic paradigm" in futures studies:

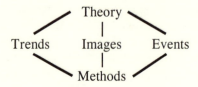

As I hope I have made it clear by now, I consider "images of the future" to be the key focus of futures studies. So I begin my class by discussing the concept and presenting a wide variety of different images of the future from different cultures, classes, and periods of time. I also expect each of my beginning graduate students to get to know the ideas of two different futurists very well, through all of their writing and personal contact where possible (Coates and Jarratt, 1989; Inayatullah, 1996; Marien and Jennings, 1987). I stress that all knowledge, including that about the future, is personal, and so I want them to try to discover why certain futurists believe some things to be true about the future, while others believe something quite different but with equal fervor and certainty. Also, when and why did "their" futurists become futurists? And have they substantially changed their views of the future as they have matured, or not, and why?

While I admit that any attempt to categorize the rich array of images of the future that actually exist does violence to the richness of that array, and while I know that other futurists have come up with different categorization schemes, I have concluded that all images in all cultures that I have encountered can be lumped into one of four major (generic) images of the future:

Continuation (usually "continued economic growth")

Collapse (from [usually] one of a variety of different reasons such as environmental overload and/or resource exhaustion, economic instability, moral degeneration, external or internal military attack, meteor impact, etc.)

Disciplined Society (in which society in the future is seen as organized around some set of overarching values or another—usually considered to be ancient, traditional, natural, ideologically-correct, or God-given.)

Transformational Society (usually either of a "high tech" or a "high spirit" variety, which sees the end of current forms, and the emergence of new [rather than the return to older traditional] forms of beliefs, behavior, organization and—perhaps—intelligent lifeforms) (Dator, 1979, pp. 376–380).

In my teaching and consulting, I try not to favor one category or image over any of the others, nor to assume that one (or more) is "good" or "the most likely" or "the best (or worst) case scenario," terms I think are irrelevant here. While I certainly do have my own "vision" of what I call a "Transformational Society" (Dator, 1974, 1982, pp. 38–45), my interest is primarily in helping students (and clients) understand that there are a wide variety of different (more or less firmly and reasonably held) images of the future in existence, and for them to reflect on what their own image is— where it came from, how "robust" it is—and to test and exercise their image by comparing and contrasting it to the images of their classmates, fellow workers, other people in their community, and the broader world.

In addition, I have found that these four generic alternative futures can serve as the basis for a futures technique I call "deductive forecasting." That is to say, I can forecast the general characteristics, in each of the four alternative futures, of any present role or institution by deducing it from each of these four generic societal images.

So, for example, I can say something useful and coherent about the future of, say, "the family" if the future is one of "continued growth," while "the family" will have certain other characteristics if the future is one of "collapse," or a "disciplined society," or a "transformational society." This is so for any role, institution, or value (Dator, 1981). One of the methods I encourage my students (especially in the Alternative Futures M.A. Option) to learn and then to use in their consulting, as I do in mine, is deductive forecasting.

Another method (among the many which futurists use), which I especially feature in my teaching and consulting, is "emerging issue analysis." This derives from early work done by Graham T. T. Molitor (1977). He observed that all "problems" of the present at one time did not exist (the same is true of all "opportunities" in the present). They each go through a more or less regular life cycle (S curve) of earliest (usually totally unnoticed) emergence, through slow (and barely noticed) growth, then rapid (and more frequently noticed) growth, until they burst, as a full blown (and brimming with popular acclaim or disdain) problem (or opportunity) in the present, whereupon a great deal of time and attention is spent on the problem (or opportunity) until it eventually fades away, either to nothingness or, more likely, until it reemerges yet again, unnoticed, at some point in the future.

Most futurists work not with "emerging issues," but with "trends," at the point where the growth of the problem or opportunity is most obvious to those who are looking ahead, though still not part of the contemporary policy and popular discourse. Futurists often try to get decision makers and/ or the public to be concerned about these trends, pointing out that they will become problems (or opportunities) in the near future, so why don't we deal with them (or take advantage of them) now, while they are more malleable?

Emerging issue analysis is interested in identifying future problems or possibilities at their earliest possible emergence, rather than waiting until they are fully formed and powerful trends. Identifying trends is important, but seeing things in their first emergence is more useful. There are specific techniques involved in learning how to spot emerging issues and then presenting them to decision makers usefully, which are important parts of how we teach (and use) futures studies in what Chris Jones (1992) calls "the Manoa School of futures studies."

Returning now to the content of my introductory undergraduate and graduate futures classes, after discussing various images of the future I introduce various theories of social stability and change, and then various methods for forecasting, inventing, and creating preferred futures (in part as I have indicated them here). I focus more deeply and comprehensively on both theories and methods in the introductory graduate course than I do in the introductory undergraduate course, but it is important that students at all levels get a sense of the theoretical and methodological perspectives underlying futures studies (Fowles, 1978; Godet, 1991; Kurian and Molitor, 1996; Slaughter, 1996a; World Futures Studies Federation, 1986).

I then identify and discuss certain forces (trends) that seem to be looming (or declining, as the case may be) in the future, and also how unexpected "events" often interrupt and redirect the trends. It is here where I introduce things like demographic change; arguments pro and con about "the limits to growth" and "sustainability"; changing and persisting gender and age roles; new and renewed economic and political systems; developments in telecommunications, artificial intelligence and life, genetic engineering, and space settlement; new and renewed cultural forms and beliefs; and the like. I try to consider each of these trends and events in the generic four alternative futures perspective. Examination of these trends and events one by one is a more prominent feature of my undergraduate than of my graduate introductory courses.

In both courses I expect students to develop a comprehensive statement of their preferred future. This is the major focus of both introductory classes. In recent years I have asked students to do this not in terms of their own personal preferences but in terms of what they have determined to be the needs and desires of future generations. "Future generations" are defined as the unborn, not immediately related to you, whose lives you will impact by the way you live your life now, but who you can never know and who can never know you and so can never thank you or criticize you for the world you have given them. The "unborn" can include nonhuman as well as human life (Busuttil, 1990; Kim and Tough, 1994; Kim and Dator, 1995).

Since I am a political scientist, I also teach two courses, one undergraduate and one graduate, which focus on the future of political systems—specifically, the design of new political systems. Proceeding from the realization that society, in sum and in all its parts, is a human invention, I seek to have my students become inventors of new political systems. To do this they must first understand how various political systems were invented and evolved, beginning with the earliest human organizations—hence the importance of anthropology again—and moving quickly through to the present, focusing especially on the design problems encountered and overcome in the invention of the American federal Constitution. At this point we discuss the concept of "constitutionalism" that underlies virtually all government-building attempts, even today. Then I problematize "constitutionalism" by contrasting the "Newtonian" cosmology of the American Founding Fathers with "quantum politics" on the one hand (Becker, 1991; Dator, 1984) and the cosmologies of Confucian, Islamic, and Hawaiian cultures, on the other, as perhaps resulting in different political "design problems" to be overcome, as well as different notions of what are acceptable "solutions." Finally, I ask the students to consider five of the many "complaints" people often have about all current governments, and challenge them to design a political system that overcomes those specific complaints (plus any others that might be of particular concern to themselves), and to do so not only singly but also in relation to the other four (or more) complaints raised against existing systems of governance.

Several years ago, to help my undergraduates rise above their own narrow views of history, the baggage of which they seemed inevitable to carry with them in their political designs, I required that they design their political community on Mars and not on Earth. This turned out to be a fortuitous decision, because very few people in the national or international space community have thought about issues of governance beyond those of the very first explorers and pioneers (who will almost certainly be under a kind of military command system) and of "space law" (which is simply the extension of Earth law into space). Who actual settlers on Mars might be, what their governance preferences might be, how the very different environment of Mars might evoke a different kind of "natural law" for governance, and many other matters unique to extraterrestrial communities somewhat frees their minds to think more creatively and yet seriously in ways that might also be helpful not only for future space settlements but also for new forms of terrestrial governance.

As a consequence of my "Mars politics" course, I have since 1993 been codirector (with Ben Finney of the Department of Anthropology of the University of Hawaii at Manoa) of the Space and Society division of the International Space University (ISU). ISU is headquartered in Strasbourg, France, where it offers a Master's in Space Studies degree. Also, since 1987 ISU has offered a ten-week summer session in interdisciplinary space studies, each summer at a different location somewhere on Earth (so far). At ISU I lecture on futures studies, space governance, and social science and space studies in both the M.S.S. and summer sessions.

Finally, to return to the Alternative Futures M.A. in the Department of Political Science of the University of Hawaii, students are also expected to take two methods courses, choose among several electives, and, as mentioned before, have a year's paid intern experience in a futures consulting firm. I direct the intern graduate seminar that is the academic part of that intern experience.

Both graduate and undergraduate students work on a voluntary or paid basis in the Hawaii Research Center for Futures Studies, which I also direct, and also have access to the resource room of the center, which has one of the most extensive libraries on the history of futures in existence. Magda McHale's Center for Integrative Studies at the State University of New York, Buffalo, which is an exceptionally rich collection of futures material, recently merged with the material in my resource room, and is to be housed in a futures archives created in the Hamilton Library of the University of Hawaii. In Europe, the Robert Jungk Library in Salsburg, Austria, is also exceptional. Additional materials are in the collections of Eleonora Masini in Rome and Pentti Malaska in Turku, Finland.

The following professors within the Department of Political Science of the University of Hawaii have also taught or still teach required or elective courses within the Alternative Futures Option: Ted Becker (democratic theory), Doug Bwy (methods), Dick Chadwick (computer modeling), Kathy Ferguson (administration and feminist theory), Manfred Henningsen (political theory), Deane Neubauer (public policy), Neal Milner (judicial politics), Glenn Paige (nonviolent politics), Fred Riggs (governmental organization), Ira Rohter (Green politics), Rudolph Rummel (peace and conflict studies), Glen Schubert (political behavior), Michael Shapiro (political theory), Carolyn Stephenson (peace studies), Kate Zhou (comparative politics). Outside the department, Dan Wedemeyer and Michael Ogden (Communications Department) teach one of the two required methods courses. Ben Finney (Anthropology), Majid Tehranian (Communications), David Swift (Sociology), and Pat Takahashi (Engineering) also teach frequently chosen courses.

THE CHAPTERS IN THIS BOOK

As I have said repeatedly, I am by no means alone in the area of futures studies. Twenty-eight people responded to my invitation to describe how they teach futures studies and engage in futures consulting. I have arranged their contributions in the following order.

The first six chapters each and together serve as a kind of overview to and history of futures studies. The first is by Wendell Bell of the Department of Sociology of Yale University. Bell has been involved in futures studies for as long as I have (Bell and Mau, 1971), and his story of the struggle to introduce the perspective at Yale is informative, to say the least. Bell has also recently written what is surely the most comprehensive attempt ever made to explain futures studies (Bell, 1997). Anyone interested in finding out more about futures studies should read Bell's two volumes.

Bell's chapter is followed by a chapter by Eleonora Masini, professor of futures studies and of human ecology at the Gregorian University of Rome. Masini is the major academic figure in European futures studies, in my judgement, important not only for her long and influential work at the Gregorian University but also—and perhaps even more important—for her work that led to her 1971 book, and then within the World Futures Studies Federation as secretary general, president, and then chair of the executive council at various crucial stages in the growth and development of the WFSF. Without her, the WFSF would not exist today, certainly not at its high level of international prominence and influence. Several years ago she also wrote a much-needed overview to futures studies (Masini, 1993). In her contribution here she discusses why most conventional academics have ignored and sometimes ridiculed futures studies, and why some futurists have ignored conventional academia to their peril and our embarrassment.

Reed Riner is professor of anthropology at Northern Arizona University in Flagstaff and brings a perspective on futures studies that contrasts nicely with that of Bell and Masini. This is partly because he is an anthropologist and they are sociologists. But it is also because of his different pedagogical modes (using Multiple User Domains, telecommunities, and simulations as well as regular classroom techniques) and his interest in simulated space settlements as sources for anthropological research and theory making. The narrative of his various activities is informative and illuminating. Riner acknowledges the contribution of another anthropologist to futures studies: Robert Textor (1990) of Stanford, whose Ethnographic Futures Research technique Riner discusses. Ben Finney in the Department of Anthropology of the University of Hawaii (and of ISU) is another who should be mentioned again because of his work in future space settlements (and what he calls "the cosmicization of humanity and the humanization of the cosmos").

W. Warren Wagar, our next contributor, is especially important because, as an historian at Binghamton University of the State University of New York, he views futures studies as a natural part of the discipline of history, being simply the history of the futures instead of the past. He very clearly points out that if the past is an acceptable academic endeavor then so must be the futures. The past is as "unknowable" by empirical methods as are the futures. The past is also as contestable and reinterpretable as are the futures. What one believes about the futures, as about the past, strongly influences what one believes about oneself, and how one acts today.

From my point of view (and here also combining a point that Jordi Serra discusses in his chapter), one of the key academic concerns of futures studies is the conception of time. My introductory undergraduate course always opens with a unit titled, "It's About Time!" Here both history and anthropology have much to contribute. Futurists should not naïvely accept their own culture's notions of time, but should problematize the very notion of time itself. Not all cultures speak of "past, present, and future," and it is by no means clear that they—much less only those three categories—"really" exist. The boundary between each is extremely fuzzy. "The future" is far too vague a term—stretching from here to eternity—without obvious demarcation. Futurists need be clear what they are talking about when they refer to "the future(s)." Generally speaking, I mean (for a variety of reasons I will not discuss now) "the next 20–50 years, and usually the next 20–30." When I mean a longer or shorter time period, or when I mean "from now to some period in the future," as I sometimes do, then I must indicate what that is, and why.

What does one mean by saying—as so many commencement speakers do say—that "we must face the future with confidence"? What does it mean to "face the future"? Does the future *really* "lie ahead," and the past "behind" us? Some early Greeks (as well as traditional Hawaiians) believed the reason the future sometimes was so surprising is because we face the past (which we can "see" well until it, too, fades in the distance and over the horizon). But the future "suddenly" appears in our view from in back of us. Could it be that, in fact, "the future lies behind"? Thus, from one perspective, history (and anthropology) and futures studies should combine into a single discipline called, perhaps, "chronology": the study of human ideas about time, and of the beliefs about and interpretation of the evidence of the movement of humans through time, from the earliest emergence of human communities through to the end of "time." In any event, it is quite a mistake to assume that futures studies is opposed to, uninterested in, or ignorant of "history."

Alternatively, just as some historians become experts in some past time and place, so might futurists become experts in one or another future time and place. For several decades, because of George Orwell's famous book, the year 1984 served as a symbol of the future, in this case of a thoroughly dystopic future. Then 1984 finally arrived, with considerable fanfare and discussions—Is 1984 "1984" or not?—and then passed with scarcely a subsequent mention. For far, far too long "The Year 2000" seemed to many to represent all that needed to be said about "the future," though it too finally became the past.

My idea is that some futurists might choose some date (day, year, decade, or era) in the future, collecting all the information they can find beforehand about it, and all the information about the date when it actually happens, and then serving as a source of information about the date when it recedes into the past. That way history and futures studies become more obviously joined, as they should be (Fletchtheim, 1966; Heilbroner, 1960).

Richard Slaughter, a Britisher living in Sydney, Australia, has done more than any single person to describe and develop what he calls "the Knowledge Base of Futures Studies." He has recently edited four important volumes on this issue, and written several books and numerous articles describing what futures studies is in its totality. His contribution to this volume is especially important because it draws upon this impressive body of work

(Slaughter 1992, 1993, 1995a, 1995b, 1996a, 1996b, 1996c, 1996d, Slaughter and Tough, 1997).

Sohail Inayatullah, from Pakistan but currently affiliated with the Queensland University of Technology in Brisbane, Australia, makes it abundantly clear in his contribution that there are many different kinds of futures studies, all legitimate, but some perhaps more valuable in the long run than others. Inayatullah (like Masini) focuses especially on the cultural dimension on the one hand and (like Slaughter) on the critical dimension of futures studies on the other.

Inayatullah, one of the most prolific, learned, creative, and active scholars in the field, also represents a "new generation" of futurists, at least in comparison with myself and the five previous futurists. Other younger futurists featured here include Huston, Jones, Rubin, and Serra, with the rest of the contributors falling somewhere in between the old timers and the new blood. But futurists younger still (representing the views of "Generation X," perhaps) are emerging from graduate schools everywhere and will be represented in a reprise of this volume, should there be one, say, ten years from now.

The next part of this volume I call "Explaining and Defining." Peter Manicas (1987), a philosopher of social science and head of the Liberal Studies Program of the University of Hawaii, discusses the philosophical and theoretical differences between (and similarities in) "explaining" the past and "predicting" the future.

Peter Bishop of the Studies of the Future Department of the University of Houston, Clear Lake, outlines his understanding of social stability and social change, concluding that both "transformational change" (so popular among certain futurists) and slow incremental change (the way most nonfuturist seem to feel) are rare. In contrast to both, Bishop says, change is "sticky"—like plate tectonics—with stability lasting longer than it should and transformation rarely happening, though "jolting" when it does occur.

The next two chapters are especially interesting. The first is written by Erzsébet Nováky and the second by Eva Hideg, both affiliated with the Futures Research Department of the Budapest University of Economic Sciences. They each describe the evolution of futures research from its optimistic and positivistic roots and assumptions in the 1960s and 1970s, through the days of opening and excitement in the 1980s (when I first met the two scholars at what was then called the Karl Marx University of Budapest), through the collapse of the socialist systems and the revitalization of futures research within a Hungary that is now part of the global capitalist world.

These two Hungarian scholars show the importance of evolutionary systems theory to their current work. Mika Mannermaa, who held the chair in futures research of the Finnish Academy of Science and has been for some time a major theorist as well as futures activist, develops that perspective in somewhat more detail, while Jan Huston of the University of Hawaii makes the strongest case of any contributor here that evolutionary systems theory permits—indeed, requires—futurists to understand both the general direction of society and the general process through which all social change occurs. Thus, while "alternative futures" play an important part for Huston, the feasible alternatives are not nearly as numerous and open as many futurists seem to assume. They are carefully bounded and identified by the logic and reality of the theory, he maintains.

A similar statement of a more rigorous and guiding theory and methodology is presented by Kaoru Yamaguchi. His perspective, which he designates FOCAS (Future-oriented complexity and adaptive studies), emerged from discussions he has had over the past several summers with a global network of scholars he has brought to Awaji Island, on the Inland Sea of Japan. Yamaguchi's chapter is interesting not only because of the areas of the future it presently explains, but also because it identifies what new areas of research are most pressingly needed.

The next eleven chapters, grouped under the heading "Courses and Methods," tend to be more or less explicit descriptions of how the authors teach futures studies at the university level. This, of course, is what I asked all the contributors to do, and all did this. These eleven, however, did so in a bit more detail, and thus are, I believe, unusually helpful for people interested in knowing how to get started in teaching futures themselves. It is especially important to note that the authors come from a variety of academic disciplines.

Ikram Azam offers a particularly inspiring as well as illuminating discussion of the wide variety of courses in futures studies at all levels that he and his colleagues offer through the Pakistan Futuristics Institute in Islamabad, Pakistan. Like many other pioneers in futures studies in other parts of the world, the impetus behind futures studies for Azam was his desire to find a venue where a more harmonious world than that of the present could be freely envisioned and actually created. Because of Pakistan's own troubled history and present, especially vis-à-vis India and Bangladesh, Azam intends his courses in futures studies to have the practical outcome of helping create viable conditions for peace and prosperity in the region.

Kuo-Hua Chen presents the most impressive attempt to "futurize" a university that I am aware of. Courses in futures studies are required for graduation of all students enrolled in Tamkang University, Taiwan. Chen describes what this means specifically, and what this requirement has achieved both within the university and the broader community. Yet he also shows that there are limitations, if not indeed drawbacks, to anything that is required of all students.

Markku Sotarauta describes how he teaches "Futures-seeking communicative policy processes" within the Department of Regional Studies and Environmental Policy of the University of Tampere, Finland. In a way reminiscent of the story told by Novaky and Hideg in Hungary, Sotarauta contrasts the assumptions about teaching planning and engaging in planning consulting under the old concept of "the government of uncertainty," which characterized planning in the 1960s and 1970s, with "the governance of ambiguity," which is the concept that best describes the paradigm of planning in the present, he believes.

Graham May, principle lecturer in futures research at Leeds Metropolitan University in the United Kingdom, next tells a hauntingly similar story of his odyssey from geography, to planning, and thence to futures studies, as well. By now we are beginning to see that this is a familiar tale, told by most of the early futurists.

Sam Cole has for a very long time been one of the most productive and quantitatively oriented members of the global futures community. He first burst upon the international scene with a book that examined and challenged the influential book, *The Limits to Growth* (Meadows, Meadows, Randers, and Behrens, 1972), on the methodological instead of the primarily ideological grounds that most other critics fancied. His *Models of Doom* (Cole, Freeman, Jahoda, and Pavitt, 1973) immediately revealed Sam Cole to be a premier methodologist in the futures-oriented wing of the field of urban and regional planning. Cole's contribution to this volume shows that he continues in that tradition. Yet is also reveals the way in which quantitative and qualitative methods can and should be fused with core value orientations in a positive yet thoroughly practical way.

The next four contributors in the "Courses and Methods" section—Christopher Jones (University of Houston, Clearlake), Jordi Serra del Pino (Centre Catala de Prospectiva, Barcelona), Anita Rubin (Futures Research Centre, Turku, Finland), and Paul Wildman (Southern Cross University, Lismore, Australia)—represent the younger generation of scholars for whom overcoming positivism (and modernity) was never an issue. They live in the postmodern, de-reconstructed world, and understand that their students live there even more intensively. They each show how it is necessary to connect to their students (as well as to understand the dynamics of their world) through images of the future in popular culture (a point also made by Huston). While all of the four stress the key role of "images of the future," this is especially the focus of Anita Rubin in her teaching, consulting, and research.

Paul Wildman's chapter is of special importance because it describes how he designed and taught a futures course on the Web. He also indicates that he uses the Web in his consulting in order to involve his clients more directly in the creative process. They (just as his students) are no longer passive "consumers" of futures, but even more clearly active imaginers and creators of their future.

David Hicks is professor of futures education at Bath Spa University College in the United Kingdom, responsible primarily for teaching future teachers how and why to include futures studies in their curricula. Like

Rubin and Gidley, he believes that it is extremely important for the future itself that students at all levels become familiar with the theories, methods, and substantive ideas about the future that futures studies bring. He, along with many others, point out the continued serious social consequences of an educational system and popular culture that are both either mindless of the future or else project negative, indeed paralyzingly apocalyptic, images of it.

This part concludes with a fascinating chapter by Oliver Markley, also of the University of Houston at Clear Lake. He shows the ways in which he uses visionary techniques—"guided cognitive imagery," such as "virtual space travel" and "depth intuition"—to aid his students and his business clients to gain positive control over their futures. He concludes by pointing out that these methods have much in common with those with which most behavioral scientists feel comfortable, however strange they might initially appear to be.

I have titled the final section "Concerns and Issues" because these four chapters come closest to reflecting those of academics who are passionately committed to the achievement of a specific kind of future and/or who focus on a specific kind of student or client in their work and teaching.

Ian Lowe, of Griffith University, Nathan, Australia, is especially concerned about sustainability and countering the pathologies of blindly continued economic growth. He is, of course, by no means unique among the contributors to this book in that respect. It is just that his contribution here is more clearly focused on that concern. It is also important to know that Lowe was executive director of the Commission on the Future, which the Australian federal government created a decade or so ago under the championship of Barry O. Jones (1995), who is an exceptional futurist, as well as politician, in his own right.

Arthur Shostak, professor in the Department of Psychology, Sociology, and Anthropology, Drexel University, Pennsylvania, is probably unique among all futurists in that he works primarily with organized laborers, helping them develop positive images and understandings of the future. He describes here his experiences teaching futures at the AFL–CIO's George Meany Center for Labor Studies in Silver Spring, Maryland.

Ernest Sternberg, a colleague of Magda McHale and Sam Cole at the School of Architecture and Planning of the State University of New York at Buffalo, looks at the changing global economy from an especially fresh and provocative perspective. The "information society" as typically envisioned has come and gone, he argues. Now the world is driven by a new form of capitalism "in which art and commerce collapse into each other, turning commodities into icons and workers into performers."

Finally, William Halal, professor of management at the George Washington University in Washington, D.C., argues that futurists today are the "high-tech equivalent of the ancient prophets" and that it is our job both to announce the end of the old world and to give heart by proclaiming the better world to come. Halal outlines what he believes can and should be the major contours of this better future.

FINAL WORDS

A few final words before I let you loose to savor the ideas that follow. One is that futures studies is a specific academic discipline, with its own theories, methods, journals, conferences, courses, professors, students, funding, and the like. This is both proper and unfortunate. It is proper that futures studies become a normal, widely accepted part of the each university everywhere on the planet and beyond.

It is equally unfortunate if this should happen because futures studies is and must be a profoundly cross-disciplinary (and cross-cultural) activity. A futures orientation should be a specific part of all academic endeavors, and not become a separate discipline. Each academic discipline should become future oriented, as should all other aspects of society, most certainly governance (Kim and Dator, 1999).

Futures studies should not be relegated to some academic departmental ghetto, and should not become just one discipline among many. Indeed, one of the major problems of contemporary academia is clearly its segmentation into departments and specialties that not only no longer make any sense, if they once did, but are also contributing to the demise of the modern university because of the inability of any one discipline to address the pan-disciplinary, future-oriented problems of the world (Wallerstein, 1996). That a certain school of economics is now privileged by decision makers over other social sciences—and that there is no fully integrated applied as well as theoretical future-oriented social science anywhere—is one of the more serious problems of the present, itself contributing to an increasingly unsustainable future. Also, for futures studies now to become a normal and well-integrated part of modern universities is like it becoming just one more proverbial deck chair on the *Titanic*.

The nineteenth- and twentieth-century public university of mass education does not have a bright future. While a handful of largely private elite universities will almost certainly survive into the twenty-first century to serve the children of the rich and powerful, and while myriad "convenience store" virtual, distance, corporate, and campusless training opportunities for the poor and powerless will certainly flourish, the old public, moderately open, "land grant," brick-and-mortar university for which the United States is especially famous (and that finds its counterparts in contributors to this book, especially in Australia and Finland) is about to go the way of the dodo bird, as in many ways it should (Inayatullah, 1998).

Futures studies—which is not a product of this intellectual heritage, but is rather is a harbinger of intellectual perspectives still to come (Dator, 1986, 1996)—should thus not go down with it. That would be the greatest irony of all.

REFERENCES

Becker, T. (Ed.). (1991). *Quantum politics*. New York: Praeger.

Bell, D. (Ed.). (1968). *Toward the year 2000: Work in progress*. Boston: Houghton Mifflin.

Bell, W. (1997). *Foundations of futures studies* (2 vols.) New Brunswick, NJ: Transaction.

Bell, W., and Mau, J. (1971). Images of the future: Theory and research. In W. Bell and J. Mau (Eds.), *The sociology of the future* (pp. 6–44). New York: Russell Sage Foundation.

Bernd, J. (1966). *Mathematical applications in political science, II*. Dallas: Arnold Foundation Monographs, Southern Methodist University.

Berry, B. (1991). *Long wave rhythms in economic development and political behavior*. Baltimore: Johns Hopkins University Press.

Berry, B., and Kim, H. (1994). Leadership generations: A long-wave macrohistory. *Technological Forecasting and Social Change, 49* (1), 1–9.

Boulding, E. (1971). Futuristics and the imaging capacity of the west. In M. Maruyama and J. Dator (Eds.), *Human futuristics* (pp. 29–54). Honolulu: Social Science Research Institute, University of Hawaii Press.

Boulding, K. (1956). *The image: Knowledge in life and society*. Ann Arbor: University of Michigan Press.

Busuttil, S. (Ed.). (1990). *Our responsibilities towards future generations*. Malta: Foundation for International Studies.

Chaplin, G., and Paige, G. (Eds.). (1971). Hawaii 2000. *A continuing experiment in anticipatory democracy*. Honolulu: University of Hawaii Press.

Coates, J., and Jarratt, J. (1989). *What futurists believe*. Mt. Airy, MD: Lomond.

Cole, H., Freeman, C., Jahoda, M., and Pavitt, K. (Eds.). (1973). *Models of doom: A critique of The Limits to Growth*. New York: Universe Books.

Dator, J. (1967, 1997). Valuelessness and the plastic personality. *The Futurist, 1* (4), 53–54. Reprinted in *Futures, 29*, 667–669.

Dator, J. (1971). Political futuristics. In D. Plath (Ed.), *Aware of utopia* (pp. 55–63). Champaign: University of Illinois Press.

Dator, J. (1973). Futuristics and the exercise of anticipatory democracy in Hawaii. In A. Somit (Ed.), *Political science and the study of the future* (pp. 187–203). Hinsdale, IL: Dryden.

Dator, J. (1974). Neither there nor then: A eutopian alternative to the "development" model of future society. In E. Masini (Ed.), *Human futures* (pp. 87–140). London: IPC Science and Technology Press.

Dator, J. (1979). The futures of culture or cultures of the future. In A. Marsella, R. G. Tharp, and T. J. Ciborowski (Eds.), *Perspectives in cross-cultural pychology* (pp. 369–388). New York: Academic Press.

Dator, J. (1981). Alternative futures and the future of law. In J. Dator and C. Bezold (Eds.), *Judging the future* (pp. 1–17). Honolulu: Social Science Research Institute, University of Hawaii Press.

Dator, J. (1982). Loose connections: A vision of a Transformational Society. In E. Masini (Ed.), *Alternative visions of desirable societies* (pp. 25–38). New York: Pergamon.

Dator, J. (1983). Loose connections: A vision of a transformational society. In E. Masini (Ed.), *Alternative visions of desirable societies* (pp. 38–45). New York: Pergamon.

Dator, J. (1984). Quantum politics and political design. In R. Homann (Ed.), *Changing lifestyles as indicators of new and cultural values* (pp. 53–66). Zurich: G. Duttweiler.

Dator, J. (1986). The futures of futures studies: A view from Hawaii. In L. Garita (Ed.), *Futures of peace: Cultural perspectives* (pp. 519–527). San Jose: University of Costa Rica. Also in *Futures, 18*, 440–445.

Dator, J. (1992). Tsunamis of change. In L. C. Lyne (Ed.), *Site world: The 1992 yearbook of global super projects* (pp. 89–94). Atlanta: Conway Data.

Dator, J. (1996). Futures studies as applied knowledge. In R. Slaughter (Ed.), *New thinking for a new millennium* (pp. 105–115). London: Routledge.

Dator, J. (1999a). From tsunamis to long waves and back. *Futures, 31*, 123–133.

Dator, J. (1999b). Return to long waves. *Futures, 31*, 361–372.

Flechtheim, O. (1966). *History and futurology*. Haim: Meisenheim an Glan.

Fowles, J. (Ed.). (1978). *Handbook of futures research*. Westport, CT: Greenwood Press.

Godet, M. (1991). *From anticipation to action: A handbook of strategic prospective*. Paris: Unesco Future-Oriented Studies Programme.

Heilbroner, R. (1960). *The future as history*. New York: Harpers.

Inayatullah, S. (Ed). (1996). What futurists think. *Futures, 28* (6–7).

Inayatullah, S. (Ed.). (1998). The futures of universities [special issue]. *Futures, 30* (6).

Jantsch, E. (1975). *Design for evolution: Self-organization and planning in the life of human systems*. New York: G. Braziller.

Jones, B. (1995). *Sleepers wake! Technology and the future of work* (New ed.). Melbourne: Oxford University Press.

Jones, C. B. (1992). The Manoa School of Futures Studies. *Futures Research Quarterly, 8* (2), 19–25.

Jones, C. B. (1997). Plastic fantastic future? *Futures, 29*, 672–673.

Kahn, H., and Simon, J. (1984). *The resourceful Earth*. New York: Blackwell.

Kahn, H., and Weiner, A. (1967). *The year 2000: A framework for speculation on the next thirty-three years*. New York: Macmillan.

Kim, T.-C., and Dator, J. (Eds.). (1995). *Creating a new history for future generations*. Kyoto: Institute for the Integrated Study of Future Generations.

Kim, T.-C., and Dator, J. (Eds.). (1999). *Co-creating a public philosophy for future generations*. London: Adamantine.

Kim, T.-C., and Tough, A. (Eds.). (1994). *Thinking about future generations*. Kyoto: Institute for the Integrated Study of Future Generations.

Kleinknecht, A. (Ed.). (1992). *New findings in long-wave research*. New York: St. Martin's Press.

Kurian, G., and Molitor, G. (Eds.). (1996). *Encyclopedia of the future* (2 vols.). New York: Macmillan.

Manicas, P. (1987). *A history and philosophy of the social sciences*. New York: Basil Blackwell.

Marien, M., and Jennings, L. (Eds.). (1987). *What I have learned: Thinking about the future then and now*. Westport, CT: Greenwood Press.

Masini, E. (Ed.). (1971). *Social forecasting: Ideas, men, activities*. Rome: Istituto Ricerche Applicate Documentazioni e Studi.

Masini, E. (1993). *Why futures studies?* London: Gray Seal.

Mau, J. (1968). *Social change and images of the future*. Cambridge, MA: Schenkman.

McLuhan, M. (1967). *The medium is the message*. New York: Bantam.

Meadows, D. H., Meadows, D. L., and Randers, J. (1992). *Beyond the limits*. Post Mills, VT: Chelsea Green.

Meadows, D. H., Meadows, D. L., Randers, J., and Behrens, W. W. (1972). *The limits to growth*. New York: Universe Books.

Molitor, G.T.T. (1977, Summer). How to anticipate public-policy changes. *S. A. M. Advanced Management Journal, 42* (3), 4–13.

Naisbitt, J. (1984). *Megatrends: Ten new directions transforming our lives*. New York: Warner Books.

Nordberg, D. (1997). Valuelessness and the plastic personality: A 30-year retrospective. *Futures, 29,* 669–671.

Polak, F. (1961). *The image of the future* (2 vols.). New York: Oceana.

Popcorn, F. (1992). *The Popcorn report: Faith Popcorn on the future of your company, your world, your life*. New York: HarperBusiness.

Prigogine, I. (1997). *The end of certainty*. New York: Free Press.

Schlesinger, A., Jr. (1986). *The cycles of American history*. Boston: Houghton Mifflin.

Serra, J. (1997). The value of valuelessness. *Futures, 29,* 671–672.

Simon, J. (1996). *The ultimate resource 2*. Princeton, NJ: Princeton University Press.

Slaughter, R. (Ed.). (1992). Futures studies and higher education [special issue]. *Futures Research Quarterly, 8* (4).

Slaughter, R. (Ed.). (1993). The knowledge base of futures studies [special issue]. *Futures, 25* (3).

Slaughter, R. (1995a). *The foresight principle: Cultural recovery in the 21st century*. London: Adamantine.

Slaughter, R. (1995b). *Futures tools and techniques*. Melbourne: Futures Study Centre.

Slaughter, R. (1996a). *Futures concepts and powerful ideas*. Melbourne: Futures Study Centre.

Slaughter, R. (Ed.). (1996b). *The knowledge base of futures studies* (3 vols.). Hawthorn, Australia: DDM Media Group.

Slaughter, R. (1996c). The knowledge base of futures studies as an evolving process. *Futures, 28,* 799–812.

Slaughter, R. (Ed.). (1996d). *New thinking for a new millennium*. London: Routledge.

Slaughter, R. (1997). On provocation, youth and dystopia. *Futures, 29,* 673–675.

Slaughter, R., and Tough, A. (Eds.). (1997). Learning and teaching about future generations [special issue]. *Futures, 29* (8).

Strauss, W., and Howe, N. (1995). *Generations: The history of America's future, 1584–2069*. New York: William Morrow.

Strauss, W., and Howe, N. (1997). *The fourth turning*. New York: Broadway Books.

Textor, R. (1990). Methodolological appendix. In S. Ketudat (Ed.), *The middle path for the future of Thailand*. Bangkok: Thai Watana Panich Press.

Toffler, A. (1970). *Future shock*. New York: Random House.

Toffler, A. (1980). *The third wave.* New York: Morrow.
Wallerstein, I. (1979). *The capitalist world-economy.* New York: Cambridge University Press.
Wallerstein, I. (1996). *Open the social sciences: Report of the Gulbenkian Commission on the restructuring of the social sciences.* Stanford: Stanford University Press.
World Futures Studies Federation (Ed.). (1986). *Reclaiming the future: A manual of methods.* New York: Taylor and Francis.

BIBLIOGRAPHY

WFSF Conference Publications, 1967–1996

Oslo 1967

Jungk, R., and Galtung, J. (Eds.). (1969). *Mankind 2000.* London: Allen and Unwin.

Kyoto 1970

Hayashi, Y. (Ed.). (1970). *Challenges from the future* (5 vols.). Tokyo: Kodansha.

Rome 1973

Masini, E. (Ed.). (1973). *Human futures.* London: Butterworths.

Cairo 1978

Abdel Rahman, I. (Ed.). (1978). *The future of communication and cultural identity in an interdependent world.* Bucharest: ILEXIM.

Stockholm 1982

Page, W. (Ed.). (1983). *The future of politics.* London: Frances Pinter.

San Jose 1984

Garita, L. (Ed.). (1986). *The futures of peace: Cultural perspectives.* San Jose: University of Costa Rica Press.

Honolulu 1986

Dator, J., and Roulstone, M. (Eds.). (1986). *Who Cares? and How?* Honolulu: WFSF Secretariat, University of Hawaii.

Beijing 1988

Masini, E., Dator, J., and Rodgers, S. (Eds.). (1991). *The futures of development.* Paris: Unesco.

Budapest 1990

Mannermaa, M. (Ed.). (1992). *Linking present decisions to long-range visions* (2 vols.). Budapest: Research Institute for Social Studies.

Barcelona 1991

van Steenbergen, B., Nakarada, R., Marti, F., and Dator, J. (Eds.). (1991). *Advancing democracy and participation*. Barcelona: Centre Catala de Prospectiva.

Turku 1993

Mannermaa, M., Inayatullah, S., and Slaughter, R. (Eds.). (1994). *Coherence and chaos in our uncommon futures*. Turku: Finland Futures Research Centre/ Turku School of Economics.

Nairobi 1995

Ogutu, G., Malaska, P., and Kojolo, J. (Eds.). (1997). *Futures beyond poverty: Ways and means out of the current stalemate*. Turku: Finland Futures Research Centre/Turku School of Economics.

Brisbane 1997

Inayatullah, S., and Leggett, S. (Eds.). (1999). *Transforming communication: Sustainability, technology and future generations*. Twickenham, England: Adamantine Studies of the 21st Century.

Additional Early Futures Classics

Boulding, K. (1965). *The meaning of the 20th Century: The great transition*. New York: Harper and Row.

Brown, H. (1954). *The challenge of man's future*. New York: Viking Press.

Brown, H., Bonner, J., and Weir, J. (1957). *The next hundred years: Man's natural and technological resources*. New York: Viking Press.

Clarke, A. C. (1962). *Profiles of the future: An inquiry into the limits of the possible*. New York: Harper and Row.

de Chardin, P. T. (1959). *Phenomenon of man*. London: Collins.

de Jouvenel, B. (1967). *The art of conjecture*. New York: Basic Books.

Diebold, J. (1952). *Automation: The advent of the automatic factory*. New York: Van Nostrand.

Dobzhansky, T. (1955). *The biological basis of human freedom*. New York: Columbia University Press.

Dobzhansky, T. (1962). *Mankind evolving*. New Haven: Yale University Press.

Dubos, R. (1961). *The dreams of reason: Science and utopias*. New York: Columbia University Press.

Dubos, R. (1965). *Man adapting*. New Haven: Yale University Press.

Dunstan, M., and Garlan, P. (1970). *Worlds in the making: Probes for students of the future*. Englewood Cliffs, NJ: Prentice Hall.

Drucker, P. (1950). *The new society*. New York: Harper.

Ehrlich, P. (1968). *The population bomb*. New York: Ballantine Books.

Etzioni, A. (1968). *The active society*. New York: Free Press.

Ewald, W., Jr. (Ed.). (1968). *Environment and change; Environment and policy; Environment for man* (3 vols., each subtitled *The next 50 years*). Bloomington: Indiana University Press.

Fuller, B. (1969). *Utopia or oblivion: The prospects for humanity*. New York: Bantam Books.

Furnas, C. (1936). *The next hundred years*. New York: Reynal and Hitchock.

Gordon, T. (1965). *The future*. New York: St. Martin's Press.

Greenberger, M. (Ed.). (1962). *Computers and the world of the future*. Cambridge: MIT Press.

Hahn, S. J. (Ed.). (1971). *Korea in the year 2000*. Seoul: Korea Institute of Science and Technology.

Halacy, D. S., Jr. (1962). *Computers: The machines we think with*. New York: Harper and Row.

Halacy, D. S., Jr. (1965). *Cyborg: Evolution of the superman*. New York: Harper and Row.

Halacy, D. S., Jr. (1968). *Century 21: Your life in the year 2001 and beyond*. Philadelphia: Macrae Smith.

Hayashi, Y. (Ed.). (1970). *Perspectives on postindustrial society*. Tokyo: University of Tokyo Press.

Heilbroner, R. (1974). *An inquiry into the human prospect*. New York: Norton.

Helmer, O. (1968). *Social technology*. New York: Basic Books.

Hiltz, S. R., and Turoff, M. (1978). *The network nation: Human communication via computer*. Reading, MA: Addison Wesley.

Institute of History of Natural Sciences and Technology, the Institute of Philosophy of the Academy of Sciences of the USSR, and the Institute of Philosophy and Sociology of the Czechoslovak Academy of Sciences (Eds.). (1973). *Man—Science—Technology: A Marxist analysis of the scientific–technological revolution*. Prague: Academia.

Ivakhnenko, A. G., and Lapa, V. C. (1967). *Cybernetics and forecasting techniques*. New York: American Elsevier.

Jantsch, E., and Waddington, C. H. (Eds.). (1976). *Evolution and consciousness: Human systems in transition*. Reading, MA: Addison Wesley.

Kahn, H., and Weiner, A. (1967). *The year 2000: A framework for speculation on the next thirty-three years*. New York: Macmillan.

Maruyama, M., and Dator, J. (Eds.). (1971). *Human futuristics*. Honolulu: Social Science Research Institute, University of Hawaii Press.

McHale, J. (1969). *The future of the future*. New York: G. Braziller.

McLuhan, M. (1951). *The mechanical bride: Folklore of industrial man*. New York: Vanguard Press.

Michael, D. (1963). *Cybernation: The silent conquest*. Santa Barbara, CA: Center for the Study of Democratic Institutions.

Michael, D. (1968). *The unprepared society: Planning for a precarious future*. New York: Basic Books.

Peccei, A. (1969). *The chasm ahead*. New York: Macmillan.

Prehoda, R. (1967). *Designing the future: The role of technological forecasting*. Philadelphia: Chilton.

President's Research Committee on Social Trends (Ed.). (1933). *Recent social trends in the United States* (2 vols.). New York: McGraw-Hill.

Theobald, R. (1961). *The challenge of abundance*. New York: C. N. Potter.

Theobald, R. (1972). *Futures conditional*. Indianapolis: Bobbs-Merrill.

Theobald, T. (1968). *An alternative future for America*. Chicago: Swallow Press.

Wells, H. G. (1913). *The discovery of the future*. New York: B. W. Nuebsch.

Judicial Foresight from the Hawaii Research Center for Futures Studies

Dator, J. (1972). A dowager in a hurricane: Law and legal systems for the future. In L. Cingcade (Ed.), *Proceedings of the Conference on the Administration of Justice* (pp. 127–136). Honolulu: Hawaii Supreme Court.

Dator, J. (1978). Beyond a researchable doubt: Some alternative futures for corrections and the criminal justice system in the US. In B. Nanus (Ed.), *The future of corrections* (pp. 1–108). Washington, DC: National Institute of Law Enforcement and Criminal Justice.

Dator, J. (1981). Alternative futures for the adversary system in America. In J. Dator and C. Bezold. (Eds.), *Judging the future* (pp. 86–110). Honolulu: Social Science Research Institute, University of Hawaii.

Dator, J. (1982). Inventing a judiciary for Ponape. *Political Science* (Wellington), *34* (1), 92–99.

Dator, J. (1988). The changing face of America—How will demographic trends affect the courts? *Judicature, 72* (2), 125–128.

Dator, J. (1991). *Culturally appropriate dispute resolution techniques and the formal judicial system in Hawaii: Final report*. Honolulu: Hawaii Research Center for Futures Studies, University of Hawaii. Includes

Barner, B. Cultural pluralism and the future of the judiciary.

Dator, J. Culturally appropriate dispute resolution techniques and the formal judicial system in Hawaii: A report to the Chief Justice of Hawaii.

Jones, C. Exploring alternative dispute resolution techniques in the Asia–Pacific region.

Rodgers, S., and Scheder, J. The use of videotape in analyzing cultural approaches to conflict resolution.

Scheder, J. (producer). Cultural approaches to conflict resolution (2 one-hour videotapes).

Schultz, W. Culture in transition: The changing ethnic mix of Hawaii and the nation.

Dator, J. (1993). American state courts, five tsunamis, and four alternative futures. *Futures Research Quarterly, 9* (4), 9–30.

Dator, J. (1994). The dancing judicial Zen masters: How many judges does it take to see the future? *Technological Forecasting & Social Change, 46* (1), 59–70.

Dator, J. (1994). Judging the future. *Texas Bar Journal, 57*, 748–751, 770–771.

Dator, J., and Halbert, D. (1996). Law and Justice in the 21st Century [special issue]. *Technological Forecasting & Social Change, 52* (2–3).

Dator, J., Inayatullah, S., Borg, B., and Farthing-Capowich, D. (1994). Judicial foresight bibliography. *Futures Research Quarterly, 10* (1), 61–70.

Dator, J., and Rodgers, S. (1991). *Alternative futures for the state courts of 2020.* Chicago: American Judicature Society.

Inayatullah, S. (1985). Challenges ahead for state judiciaries. *Futurics, 9* (2), 16–18.

Inayatullah, S. (1985). The futures of state court administration. *Futures Research Quarterly, 2* (1), 5–18.

Inayatullah, S. (1986). Law school to World Court: Judicial and legal impacts of the Pacific Shift. *Hawaii Bar Journal, 20* (1), 61–71.

Inayatullah, S. (1991). Judicial foresight in the Hawaii judiciary. *Futures, 23*, 871–878.

Inayatullah, S. (1992). Preliminary report of the 1991 Judicial Foresight Congress. *Futures Research Quarterly, 8* (3), 76–90.

Inayatullah, S. (Ed.). (1993, 1994). The futures of state courts (2 vols.). *Futures Research Quarterly, 9* (4), *10* (1).

Inayatullah, S. (1994). Linking the present with the future: The politics of futures research in judicial bureaucracies. *Futures Research Quarterly, 10* (1), 19–30.

Inayatullah, S. (Ed.). (1994). *Proceedings of the 1991 Hawaii Judicial Foresight Congress.* Honolulu: Hawaii State Judiciary.

Inayatullah, S., and Monma, J. (1989). A decade of forecasting: Some perspectives on futures research in the Hawaii Judiciary. *Futures Research Quarterly, 5* (1), 5–19.

McNally, P., and Inayatullah, S. (1988). The rights of robots: Technology, law and culture in the 21st century. *Futures, 20*, 119–136.

Schultz, W., Bezold, C., and Monahan, M. P. (1993). *Reinventing courts for the 21st century: Designing a vision process. A guidebook to visioning and futures thinking within the court system.* Williamsburg, VA: National Center for State Courts. (Includes videotape, *Envisioning justice: Reinventing the courts for the 21st century.* Tampa, FL: Tradewinds Video).

Yasutomi, W. (1983). *Emerging issues analysis in the Hawaii judiciary: Theory and application* (report to the Hawaii Judiciary). Honolulu: Hawaii Supreme Court.

Yue, A. (1983). *The collapse of the Hawaii judiciary* (report to the Hawaii Judiciary). Honolulu: Hawaii State Judiciary.

Yue, A., and Inayatullah, S. (1984). *Information scanning in the Hawaii judiciary* (report to the Hawaii Judiciary). Honolulu: Hawaii State Judiciary.

Numerous internal emerging analysis and trend scanning reports, and the contents of the quarterly newsletter, *Justice Horizons*, are not listed here.

Technology and Social Change

Dator, J. (1982). Loose connections: A vision of a Transformational Society. In E. Masini (Ed.), *Alternative visions of desirable societies* (pp. 25–38). New York: Pergamon.

Diebold, J. (1969). *Man and the computer: Technology as an agent of social change.* New York: Praeger.

Ellul, J. (1964). *The technological society.* New York: Vintage.

Ginzberg, E. (Ed.). (1964). *Technology and social change.* New York: Columbia University Press.

Goonatilake, S. (1998). *Merged evolution: Long term implications of biotechnology and information technology*. Newark, NJ: Gordon and Breach.

Levinson, P. (1999). *Digital McLuhan*. New York: Routledge.

McLuhan, M. (1964). *Understanding media*. New York: McGraw-Hill.

Mesthene, E. (Ed.). (1967). *Technology and social change*. Indianapolis: Bobbs-Merrill.

Mesthene, E. (1970). *Technological change: Its impact on man and society*. New York: Signet Books.

Mumford, L. (1967). *The myth of the machine: Technics and human development*. London: Secker and Warburg.

1

Making People Responsible:
The Possible, the Probable,
and the Preferable

Wendell Bell

I could write a book or two—and probably already did (Bell, 1997)—in response to the five questions posed by Jim Dator, the editor of this book. There is far too much that can be said to fit into this short chapter. Thus, I will limit my answers to a brief account of only a few points, focusing mostly on three of the assumptions underlying futures studies: (1) Humans by their behavior constantly shape their natural and social environments and, in so doing, shape their own future, although not always in ways that they intend or understand; (2) disciplined and valid prospective thinking can help people shape their environments and their future effectively and responsibly; and (3) explicit and objective moral analysis can help people responsibly create desirable futures.

As prologue, let me say that I began teaching a course in futures studies at Yale with some form of "future" in the title (e.g., "futuristics," "futures research," "social change and the future") in 1967. Moreover, I confess that during the last three decades in all the courses that I taught on whatever topic—from "Introductory Sociology" to "Class, Race, and Nation in the Caribbean" and even to "The Logic of Social Research"—I always included some of the principles of futures thinking. I did so at the risk of appearing to be yet another academic imperialist pushing his or her latest intellectual infatuation, because I believed that, despite the existence of a social forecasting industry and the general acceptance of prediction as an indicator of valid scientific knowledge, competent futures thinking was largely missing from the mainstreams of the various social sciences (Bell, 1974). No social science, I believed, could be fully acceptable without a healthy dose of futures thinking.

Have I mellowed over the years and softened this view? Definitely not. To the contrary, I would go further today and make a stronger assertion: No college education is adequate unless it includes some systematic study of the concepts and principles of the futures field. One reason is that self-conscious futures thinking helps people become more responsible for their actions. Another reason is that any understanding of contemporary social change, the nature of the modern social world, and key features of the coming future is dangerously incomplete without the insights provided by futures studies. In this chapter, I try to give a few explanations of why this is so.

THE INDIVIDUAL AND SOCIETY

During my first year in graduate school at UCLA in 1949, I read that it "has been the contention of sociologists from Auguste Comte and Lester F. Ward to [Pitirim A.] Sorokin that the chief justification of sociology is the guidance it can furnish to public officials and private citizens relative to building a better social order" (Barnes, 1948, p. xi). As an aspiring sociologist, I was challenged by these words, imagining a future professional career providing such guidance.

But I was also puzzled. Only two pages earlier in the same book, I had read that different sociologists had "highly contrasting conceptions as to the possibilities of social planning"; that Comte, Morgan, and Ward believed "that the main purpose of sociology is to facilitate planned progress," while "Spencer, Sumner, and Gumplowicz" held an opposite view and that, for them, the great practical service of sociology is to warn about the "danger of the notion that man can facilitate and hasten social progress through deliberate action" (Barnes, 1948, p. ix).

Although this account, I soon learned, is an oversimplification, it nonetheless points to contradictory views, sometimes unacknowledged and even denied, that still exist among sociologists today. Some sociologists—probably the vast majority—view society as shaping the individual, providing him or her with the illusion of having automonous choices, while, in fact, being a system of social control and cultural forces that more or less inevitably determines his or her beliefs, attitudes, and behaviors.

Other sociologists, to the contrary, view society as a product of individual and collective choice and decision. For them, the actions and interactions of purposive individual actors importantly shape and construct the social order itself. Although admitting that there are often unintended and unanticipated consequences that require constant correction, they see social change largely as the result of deliberate action or inaction. They view society as it actually is at any given time as problematic, merely one of many possible outcomes that could have resulted from what individuals, separately and together, might have decided to do.

As stated, of course, these are extreme views. Most sociological works fall somewhere between them, rightly acknowledging some truth in each. Yet even in the most sophisticated writings we can find a preference for one or the other perspective. For example, Vaughan (1996) highlights the causal influences of organizational structures and culture in her explanations of the events that led to the explosion of the space shuttle *Challenger*. As we all know from the extensive media coverage at the time, seventy-three seconds after launch at Cape Canaveral, Florida, on January 28, 1986, the *Challenger* disappeared in a fireball and huge cloud of smoke, then dropped into the Atlantic, killing all seven crew members (Vaughan, 1996, p. 7).

Vaughan (1996, p. xv) directs our attention to "the relentless inevitability of mistake in organizations," to how social determinants systematically shaped the behavior of the individuals involved in the fatal decision to launch. She does acknowledge that at the very top levels of management some individuals could have behaved differently and, thus, could have acted to avoid the disaster. Yet she sees no merit in searching for individual moral responsibility as an explanation of the catastrophe and the deaths that occurred. Even though she recognizes how the work culture had been produced at NASA before the launch decision, in her analysis of the decision itself she views culture as fixed and determinant. For example, she speaks of "cultural scripts" and views people as simply playing roles that have been scripted in advance by social and cultural imperatives. Thus, individuals, in her view, can no more be held accountable for their acts than can puppets.

Others have contested this view. Allinson (1997), in his review of Vaughan's book, points out that things could have happened differently. The explosion resulted because the giant rubber gaskets designed to keep combustible hot gases from leaking out during liftoff, known as O-rings, failed after exposure to the cold weather. But other, better, technology than the O-rings could have been employed in the original design, and, in fact, had been proposed. Given the O-ring technology, the engineers who knew it best recommended against launching, but the flight managers failed to heed their advice. In addition, the flight managers could have informed senior management of the engineers' opposition to launching, but they did not. If the senior managers had been informed, they could have vetoed the decision to launch, as, indeed, they later said they would have. The lives of the astronauts could have been saved, if the *Challenger* had been equipped, as it could have been, with an abort system and parachute descent package.

Also, Vaughan (1996) takes great pains to show that the decision to launch was not a deviant act given the cultural setting of NASA within which it took place. The tragic decision to launch, she contends, was not the result of anyone violating any rules. To the contrary, it was the result of rule-abiding behavior. People were simply doing their jobs as they were supposed to. It was conformity, not deviance, that led to the decision. Therefore, she concludes managers were behaving morally.

Her conclusion is debatable. At least since the Nuremberg trials of Nazi war criminals, we have known that following rules, behaving as ordered, doing what we are supposed to do according to organizational expectations can produce evil consequences. This analogy is invited by Vaughan (1996, p. 407) herself when she likens some of her findings of the banality of organizational life to Arendt's *Eichmann in Jerusalem* (1964). Contrary to Vaughan's view, all of us ought to be held personally accountable for our acts even if we are conforming to organizational rules and common belief systems. It is our moral duty to question such rules and belief systems and to disobey them if obeying would lead to seriously wrongful consequences.

As Allinson (1997, p. 101) makes clear, specific individuals all along the decision stream made decisions "in the light of full knowledge of both the dangerous risk and the horrifying consequences." Such decision makers were not helpless victims of social organization or culture. The *Challenger* disaster was avoidable. It was the direct result of purposive human action and irresponsible moral choice, even though, as in this case, the action conformed to the rules. The wrongful acts of particular, identifiable people caused the explosion.

Let's look at another example of sociological inquiry, but one whose emphasis is placed on planful action, policy design, and implementation. Moskos and Butler (1996) examine how the U.S. Army has dealt with race relations. They describe how top Army decision makers responded to the order to desegregate the Army and the various programs and policies they invented to do so. In a nutshell, they show that Army leaders have been largely successful in achieving racial equality of opportunity by making race relations everyone's responsibility while holding particular people accountable. Army leaders made an absolute commitment to nondiscrimination, while maintaining uncompromising standards of performance at every level and for every person.

At the same time, Army managers took compensatory action aimed at disadvantaged groups by creating paths of opportunity through education, training, and mentoring for both pre- and post-inductees into the Army. The goal of the compensatory action was to remedy educational or skill deficiencies so members of such groups would have a chance to meet the standards of competition based only on the merit of their performance. No quotas were set and no promotions were made because of the color of a person's skin. Army personnel view good race relations not an as end in itself, but as "a means to readiness and combat effectiveness," factors that contribute to the success of the Army's most central mission (Moskos and Butler, 1996, p. 53).

In the final chapter of each book, the respective authors attempt to describe the implications of their research. In "Lessons Learned," Vaughan (1996) gives no practical advice whatsoever, no "do this" or "do not do that" if you want to avoid disastrous decisions in organizational settings. Instead, for example, she conveys a "message about the influence of these preconscious schema on the production, exchange, and interpretation of information in organizations" (p. 405). She shows how this relates to some theory, affirms that, gives a vivid example of the other, demonstrates something else, and so on, but gives no advice about how people could have been or can become more responsible actors.

Why is she of no help? Apparently, because the "effect of unacknowledged and invisible social forces on information, interpretation, knowledge, and—ultimately—action are very difficult to identify and to control" (Vaughan, 1996, p. 416). We are left with the thought that the "scope and interconnectedness of this causal system make mistakes inevitable" (p. 418).

Contrast that with Moskos and Butler (1996). In one chapter, "Army Lessons for American Society," they give a primer on overcoming racial discrimination. They offer guidance, as Comte, Ward, and Sorokin might have done, telling the American people what can and ought to be done to create equal opportunity and racial harmony in twelve assumptions and behavioral maxims that they draw from their research. For example, they recommend the following: "Focus on black opportunity, not on prohibiting racist expression" (p. 132); "Be ruthless against discrimination" (p. 133); "Affirmative action must be linked to standards and pools of qualified candidates" (p. 136); "Recognize Afro-Anglo culture as the core American culture" (p. 140); and so on.

Although both of these works are examples of serious sociological inquiry, the difference between them is striking. Vaughan's (1996) ambitious study of the *Challenger* disaster leaves us facing the future with a sense of futility. Her interpretation focuses on the essential helplessness of people in the face of the powerful imperatives of social and cultural forces and the seemingly inevitable destiny they force upon them. The Moskos and Butler (1996) study, to the contrary, leaves us facing the future armed with suggestions for possible actions. We are empowered and, although we are clearly informed of our embeddedness in organizations and cultures, we are made to understand how we individuals can—and probably ought to—act to change those organizations and cultures themselves for the better.

In my judgment, any adequate theory of society and social change—certainly of large-scale, modern society in which change is the norm—must include people, as Moskos and Butler (1996) do, as active, purposeful, responsible, and creative beings whose future-oriented behavior has consequences for their own lives and for social structures and cultures. Such people may be only partially informed, often misinformed, calculating but sometimes wrong in their calculations, occasionally have fuzzy goals that are only partially consistent with each other, subject to social and cultural pressures, and often too fixated on the short range. Nonetheless, they are accountable for their actions, all of which is precisely why, whether they are top leaders or ordinary people, they often need help in making right choices and taking effective actions. Such help can sometimes be provided by properly designed, future-oriented social research (Bell and Mau, 1971; Etzioni, 1968).

POSSIBLE AND PROBABLE FUTURES

This is not to say, of course, that society and culture have no effect on individuals and their behavior. Of course they do. We are all shaped to some degree by the social capital and cultural traditions available to us and, as we grow and develop, by our personal histories, habits, and obligations. Certainly, we learn the customs of our tribes, but we do not learn or practice them precisely. We deviate, we innovate, we rebel, we cheat, we underconform, and we overachieve, and thus we make changes and help to create a future different from the past. Moreover, people invent new technologies, including social technologies, which in turn drive change as people put them into use, producing new products, new occupations, new styles of life, new patterns of social interaction, and new personal trajectories through time and space.

The determinants of present behavior in modern societies, then, are only partly found in social and cultural backgrounds and present locations of social actors. They are also found—perhaps most important—in anticipation, because people address their behavior to the future. As they travel through time, people orient and guide themselves, more or less self-consciously, using their cognitive maps of the future, their hopes and fears. Thus, understanding those maps, even though they are sometimes wildly inaccurate, is essential to explaining people's behavior. Such maps or images of the future include not only people's intentions, but also their beliefs about what will happen, what might happen, and what ought to happen. Thus, no theory of society and social change is complete if it does not incorporate the idea of the "image of the future."

The image of the future, of course, is a central concept of futures studies. Although the terminology may vary, it can be found in most futurist works, such as, to mention a few examples, D. Bell's (1973) *The Coming of Post-Industrial Society*, Boldt's (1993) *Surviving as Indians*, Boulding's (1956) *The Image*, Dator and Rodgers's (1991) *Alternative Futures for the State Courts of 2020*, Jouvenel's (1964) *The Art of Conjecture*, Kahn's (1960) *On Thermonuclear War*, Kahn and Wiener's (1967) *The Year 2000*, Mau's (1968) *Social Change and Images of the Future*, Polak's (1955) *The Image of the Future*, and Toffler's (1981) *The Third Wave*.

Futurists not only study images of the future held by various people in an effort to understand and explain their behavior, they also investigate the process of image making itself, encourage people to rigorously explore alternative images of the future and construct images of the future themselves. In so doing, futurists aim to help people become more competent, effective, and responsible actors, both in their personal lives and in their organizational and societal roles.

Among other things, futurists work to expand the alternative possibilities that people consider before they decide to act one way or another. Present possibilities for the future are real, but many are often ignored as people go through their daily lives blindly following past routines of behavior. Futurists encourage people to look beyond the familiar and to search for opportunities for themselves and their organizations; to add medium- and long-term visions to their decision making; to use their imaginations to consider things, including social arrangements, that do not now exist; and to plan deliberate actions—solely or cooperatively with others—to achieve more desirable futures. Thus, futurists aim to expand the conscious choices people have so that they can act more intelligently.

Futurists also attempt to forecast the most probable futures given specific situations, sets of circumstances, and particular alternative courses of action. People cannot become competent, effective, and responsible actors unless they know what the consequences of their acts will be. But such consequences, obviously, will occur in the future, and the future, until it becomes the present, is nonevidential and unobservable. Thus, because the future does not yet exist, people face an apparent obstacle in making warranted assertions about probable futures; that is, assertions that they can demonstrate are reliable and valid.

Futurists have written too much about how to make such warranted assertions for me to do justice to their views here. Let me simply say that futurists have appropriated or created many social scientific tools, both methodological and conceptual, to expand the range and to increase the accuracy of people's cognitive maps of the future. Generally, although they focus on the future, futurists use logical deduction and known facts just as other social scientists do (Bishop, 1994). Specifically, the theory of knowledge known as critical realism, based importantly on Karl Popper's fallibilism, can be used to warrant assertions about the past, present, and future, as I have explained elsewhere (Bell, 1997).

Futurist methods include extrapolation of time series, cohort-component analysis, standard survey research, the Delphi method, cross-impact analysis, simulation and computer modeling, gaming, monitoring and scanning, content analysis, technology assessment, issues management, relevance trees, contextual mapping, participatory futures praxis including future workshops, social experiments, ethnographic futures research, and, most important, writing scenarios (Bell, 1997, vol. 1, chap. 6).

Impressed with the uncertainty and openness of the future, futurists also have developed a variety of strategies, perspectives, and concepts to improve people's futures thinking. They include preparing for improbable as well as probable future events, especially if the improbable possibilities would be of great moment if they occurred, just as pilot training incorporates rehearsals of all kinds of emergency situations that will probably never occur. They also include increasing the chances of surprise-free futures by systematic efforts to uncover the unintended consequences of proposed actions and otherwise hidden or unanticipated consequences. And they include constant monitoring, updating of forecasts, and reviewing of policy choices in the light of new information, and making responsive policy corrections.

In addition, they include the concept of self-altering predictions (Bell, 1997; Henshel, 1978). Because a prediction about the future, once made, may enter into the situation as a causal factor itself, predictions may turn out to be self-fulfilling or self-denying. For example, if supporters of candidate Y learn of a major network news prediction that candidate X will win the coming election in a landslide, then they may decide that it is a waste of time for them to vote; if enough of them fail to vote, then candidate X may indeed win in a landslide, precisely because so many supporters of candidate Y did not vote. In this case, the reactions to the prediction reinforce it and tend to make it self-fulfilling. The classic case of the self-fulfilling prophecy, of course, is the example of a presumptively false rumor that a (perfectly sound) bank will fail, which leads people to rush to the bank to withdraw their money and, in turn, leads to the actual failure of the bank and the terminal truth of the initially false rumor.

An example of a self-denying prediction can be seen in a situation in which members of a school board learn from a study that they have commissioned that their city schools will be unable to accomodate all of the students expected five years from now. As a result of the prediction, the school board convinces the city council to build more schools. Thus, five years later there are ample school places to accomodate all of the eligible children.

The conceptual distinction between *presumptively true* and *terminally true* assertions about the future is important in evaluating both the utility and truth of predictions. For example, the prediction that in five years the schools will be unable to accomodate all the students, if based on reliable and valid population projections, is presumptively true at the time it is made. It is useful in making a decision and designing appropriate social action. Because the city council does decide to build more schools, the original prediction turns out to be self-denying and terminally false. Thus, it is much too simple to evaluate a prediction by whether or not the prediction turns out to be true or false in the end. Predictions can be useful precisely because they lead to action that negates them.

Almost all predictions contain a variety of contingencies and assumptions. Such contingencies and assumptions, futurists have learned, need to be made explicit and examined for their cogency. "If current demographic trends continue as they are . . . ," or "if we do not build more schools . . . ," or "if we do not do thus and so . . . ," then the schools will be unable to accomodate all the future students. Anticipation includes taking such contingencies and assumptions into account. Doing so, people become more effective in shaping the future.

Differences of opinion about probable futures—"What will happen *if* we do—or do not do—this or that, or thus and so?"—are often the focus of intense debate and acrimonious social conflict. Will government regulations that reduce the emission of carbon dioxide and other greenhouse gases result in the loss of American jobs and damage the American economy or not? Will such regulations slow global warming and the disastrous consequences that have been predicted if nothing is done? Will the decriminalization of marijuana result in more drug addicts, more deaths, higher health-care costs, and a further breakdown of control over illegal drugs? Or will it result in alleviation of pain among some ill people, reduce the caseloads of police departments so they can focus on more serious crimes, relieve prison crowding, and permit more adequately funded antidrug educational programs?

Questions about future outcomes go on and on. Reliable and valid answers to them are crucial to making wise decisions, some of which are important and far-reaching enough to affect all of our future lives and those of our children and grandchildren. Yet public debates about many such questions are often filled with outrageous, self-serving, biased, partisan, venomous, emotional, and groundless assertions. Thus, one turns to members of the social science community to join more fully into public discourse and, thus, to raise both its civility and its intellectual content. More social scientists are needed to make a professional commitment, as have their futurist cousins, to improving the theories and methods of making sound assertions about the future.

PREFERABLE FUTURES

To become competent, effective, and responsible, then, people need to know what alternative actions they can possibly take and what the probable consequences of their particular acts will be. But they need to know more. They also need some reasonably accurate way of judging the *desirability* of those probable consequences, both intended and unintended. They need some set of values that can be used as a standard of judgment to help them decide what they ought to do.

It was not desirable, for example, to act in ways that led to the explosion of the *Challenger* and the death of its crew. It is desirable to act in ways that lead to equal opportunity, racial harmony, high morale, and combat readiness in the Army. Although most of us take such value judgments for granted, how do we really know if they are the ones that we ought to make? What reasons can we give to convince ourselves and skeptics that our judgments are morally right? How can we justify judgments about what we ought to do in an objective and scientific way?

Unfortunately, neither the futurist nor the social science literature provides fully satisfactory answers to such questions. The futurist literature dealing with the subject rests in part on studies of the preferences of some set of respondents. For example, in Delphi studies respondents are often asked whether or not some possible or probable development would be good or bad (Linstone and Turoff, 1975). Thus, preferable futures can be constructed based on an analysis of the value judgments of the respondents. Also, it rests in part on little else than an explicit statement of the author's values without any serious effort to justify them, even in some of the most sophisticated futures research (Meadows, Meadows, and Randers, 1992).

In addition, because a considerable number of futurists work as consultants, it rests in part on the goals and values of the clients who hire them. Such goals and values may deal with almost anything conceivable. To take just a few examples from my own work, they include wanting to sell a new toy (six, later twelve, understuffed, soft baby animals designed for both girls and boys that are inherently high touch and nonviolent as opposed to high tech, violent toys); trying to improve the global awareness of American college students; evaluating the future probable environmental and other costs and benefits of supersonic commerical air transportation and if it ought to be subsidized by the U.S. government (which it was not); attempting to reform American prisons in the next decade and beyond; planning how to safely store military radioactive wastes for the next 10,000 years; evaluating efforts to increase culturally appropriate dispute resolutions in the Hawaiian judiciary; helping to prepare U.S. foreign service officers for their future Caribbean assignments; lecturing to a variety of groups on the uses of futures thinking (such as to midcareer officers at the Air Command and Staff College at Maxwell Air Force Base and Air University, "Force 2025"); and serving as a gubernatorial appointee of the Commission on Connecticut's Future that included reviewing future plans of state government agencies ranging from agriculture and transportation to prisons and education.

Beneficially, consulting futurists generally encourage their clients to reexamine their own goals and values as part of any consulting arrangement. And sometimes clients are willing to do so. Thus, goals and values can be clarified, explicitly examined, consciously reevaluated, and changed if desired.

Although the study of respondents' preferences, explicit statements of the researchers' values as they bear on the issues under investigation, and clarifying and reevaluating clients' goals are useful steps in giving direction to both futures research and decision making, they fail as adequate assessments of the relevant values and goals themselves. Wise and moral decisions about what the future ought to be need to be informed not only by what people *believe* is right and what is clear and explicit; they depend also on knowing what really *is* right.

Turning to the social science literature, we find some help. The applied and policy-oriented side of all the social sciences have some definitions of the good and desirable, such as nearly full employment and real growth in GNP in economics or democratic governance and the protection of public liberties in political science. All have codes of ethics that define morally proper professional behavior. All contain some research whose empirical results support behavioral maxims of right and wrong, such things, to mention only a few, as altruism (Batson, 1991; Collard, 1978; Eisenberg, 1986), cooperation (Axelrod, 1984), educational innovation (Clark, 1970), justice (Walster et al., 1978), mental health (Myers and Bean, 1968), and trust (Barber, 1983).

Also, we know from the work of social scientists that near-universal human values exist and that they are not arbitrary (Brown, 1991); that cultural and ethical relativism, however beneficial they may have been in combating ethnocentric bias, have been discredited (Edgerton, 1992; Washburn, 1997); and that the recent academic fad of postmodernism, despite its beneficial corrections of the arrogant certitudes of positivism, ultimately leads to the dead end of nihilism (Rosenau, 1992). Moreover, Edgerton's (1992) evaluation of the anthropological literature shows the way to an objective analysis of human values and culture by asking whether or not they contribute to the survival and flourishing of a society's population, to the physical and mental health of its members by satisfying their needs, and to their life satisfaction and happiness. Societies differ in how well they meet these basic, universal criteria: There are good societies that pass these objective tests to one degree or another and sick societies that do not.

Although there remains much that we do not yet understand, these and other examples of social research suggest that there are core human values that are widely shared. They derive from the nature of human beings (e.g., if humans were immortal, there would be no need to have an injunction against murder), the preconditions of social life (e.g., values such as honesty and trust are necessary for much learning from others to take place), and the nature of the containing physical environment (e.g., gravity, the nature of air, fire, and water, and mundane things as objects sharing length, weight, volume, etc.) that limits the number of possible solutions to similar problems faced by basically similar beings.

Some values and practices contribute to the surviving and thriving of human beings and some do not. Generally, what is moral makes social life possible and contributes to the well-being of human societies; what is immoral does not. Standards of morality appear to be long lasting, nonarbitrary, and amenable to objective tests regarding their contribution to human well-being. But some values and practices that made a positive contribution to human well-being in the past may no longer do so in the the future (e.g., values supporting high rates of human reproduction). Thus, to find the right values (i.e., our criteria for deciding what we ought to do) for the changed conditions of the coming future is a challenge not only to futurists but to all social scientists.

Many social scientists do not respond to such a challenge because they remain in the grip of the widespread belief that making value judgments objectively is impossible. It remains the current orthodoxy among scientists generally that moral propositions, unlike factual statements, cannot be shown to be true or false by scientific methods. Thus, assertions about what is good or what is bad regarding society and culture have largely been banned from mainstream social science.

There is, however, agreement that, as scientists, we can use a means–ends model (if given an end or a goal, we can find efficient and effective means of achieving it) or a commitment–deducibility model (if we make a commitment to some value statement, then we can deduce what acts would be consistent or inconsistent with it). But in the last analysis these approaches are unsatisfactory, because they are limited. Scientists, the argument goes, cannot objectively assess the worth of either the end or the commitment themselves. Thus, they must be accepted on extrascientific grounds.

Although it has not proceeded very far as yet, I believe that this view has been eroding among social scientists (Boulding, 1985; Habermas, 1973; Phillips, 1986). We may yet see the day when the tools of social science are routinely used to answer questions about the good, including what is a good future, just as they are used today to answer questions about what is true.

Although some philosophers are as prone as some social scientists to accept the dogma that value judgments cannot be objectively shown to be true or false, other philosophers have demonstrated ways of doing so (Baumeister, 1991; Gert, 1988; Gewrith, 1978; Midgley, 1993; Sprigge, 1988). Particularly useful are Lombardi (1988) and Lee (1985). Lombardi justifies two sets of criteria by which to objectively evaluate human behavior and societies, human welfare and freedom. What is good contributes to welfare and freedom. What is bad does not. Lombardi's analysis provides philosophical support for Edgerton's (1992) empirical research on sick societies. Lee gives a method that she calls "epistemic implication." It is based on Popper's fallibilism and is compatible with the critical realist theory of knowledge. Using epistemic implication, one can develop a consistent, coherent, rational, and objective morality. Moreover, it is well adapted to answering questions of how people ought to behave and what is a good society.

The underlying logic is straightforward. It is simply that prescriptive statements contain or rest upon some descriptive contents that can be tested. Thus, if such descriptive contents can be shown to be false, then they provide no grounds for belief in the prescriptive statement. Contrariwise, it is reasonable to believe in prescriptive statements whose grounds have been put to test and were not falsified.

Lee (1985) gives five criteria that have to be met for the grounds or evidence supporting a value proposition to be accepted. The evidence must be *serious* (not mere personal preference or supernatural belief, but public external features of the situation referred to in the value assertion), *referentially relevant, causally relevant, causally independent*, and *empirically true*. I won't try to explain or illustrate these criteria here, but I refer the reader to Lee's work and to my discussion (Bell, 1997, vol. 2). I have made a few elaborations of epistemic implication, mostly to explicitly take into account the prospective aspect of assessing values as they are used in decision making and taking action, and explored them in relation to religion, law, and a variety of other approaches to deciding what is the right thing to do.

TEACHING, RESEARCH, AND ACTION

Of course, I use the principles of futures thinking in my teaching, research, and participation in decision and policy making. When I first started teaching, though, I did not know what I now know about such principles. Nor did I know much then about the nature of morality and the values that ought to be used to define and evaluate a meaningful life. I wish I had. I could have done a much better job. It is a tragic irony that so many young people who have health, nearly a lifetime ahead of them, and endless choices for their own futures so often fail to take advantage of them. They are occasionally blind to what is truly possible for themselves, show little genuine concern for the well-being of their own future selves and much less for that of future generations, do not engage in effective planful action or do not persist in it when they do, and understand only too late what is truly valuable in life and worth striving for. Sometimes they squander their chances to fulfill their potential and to live satisfying and purposeful lives.

This might be understandable among, for example, some inner-city Afro-American children exposed to a subculture that self-destructively condemns achievement, even trying to do well in school, as "acting white" and being traitorous to one's race. But even at a place like Yale, where students are highly selected and among the most motivated and talented in the country, many students desperately need instruction in making good life choices. Over the years I found that, among other things, I could help undergraduates by emphasizing three things in my teaching:

1. Showing them how to search for possible and probable futures, their own as well as those of groups, societies, and the entire human community, and why it is important to do so; teaching them how to more accurately forecast the future outcomes of their own actions and inactions.

2. Showing them how to select preferable futures; teaching them the importance of moral judgments and how to put them to objective test.

3. Demonstrating the importance of critical discourse, of open and free discussion and exchange of views; emphasizing the use of reason and a willingness to change one's mind when warranted by the evidence.

Teaching graduate students is quite another matter, although these three considerations still ought to be honored in mentoring relationships. As a teacher of graduate students, I accepted the obvious commitment to help prepare students to become professionals and thus to teach about professional ethics, history, theories, methods, and the substantive content of their field; to help prepare them to add to knowledge and thereby to contribute to human freedom and welfare; and, of course, to help them get jobs.

For nearly four decades I made the additional commitment to trying to improve sociology itself by adding more futures thinking and objective moral discourse to the field. This commitment largely came down to two things. The first was to encourage students to select topics for investigation, especially for their doctoral dissertations, that were socially significant, so that their findings would bear on the design and implemention of social policy. Such topics, which pretty much describe the subjects of my personal research projects, included studies of democracy, social participation, public leadership, decision making, nation-building, the nature of futures thinking, the causes and consequences of images of the future, perceptions of inequality, attitudes toward social justice, racial segregation, alienation, the achievement of life goals, changing cultural identities, and human values. Throughout, of course, I invited students with whom I worked, although not always successfully, to look at people as future-oriented and value-driven decisional systems and to look at society as a product of their behavior.

The second thing was to encourage students to do their work in societies other than their own, which during my first full-time teaching job at Stanford University meant getting students off the campus and into some of the wealthiest and poorest neighborhoods in San Francisco. After that, it mostly meant getting American students to go abroad to do their research.

Such field experience, often a year or two working in another country, helped to expand students' visions of the range and possibilities of the human condition and their understanding of both the differences and similarities of people and their societies. Also, whether working among Haitian market women, Jamaican leaders or slum dwellers, Antiguan managers and workers, Canadian Indians, residents of London neighborhoods, Swedish socialists, Mexican decision makers, international black intellectuals, or white South African elites, students helped to elaborate a decisional theory of human behavior and social change, to explain how people act to try to control their own future, and to show how people can act to do so more effectively.

Happily, today, American sociology is less parochial than it was several decades ago and has become more cosmopolitan, incorporating more of the totality of world experience. Unhappily, sociology today has not yet adequately incorporated those other "foreign countries," futures thinking and objective moral discourse.

In my own small efforts to change the world along these lines, I organized and directed training programs for graduate students that took them abroad: the West Indies Study Program at UCLA and the Comparative Sociological Training Program at Yale. Moreover, at Yale I worked closely with the Yale Center for International and Area Studies, and, among other things, served several terms on the Council on Latin American Studies. As chairman of the Yale Department of Sociology, I focused much of my department-building efforts on expanding departmental expertise in comparative sociology, foreign and international studies, and political and social change. Also, I supported the preexisting medical sociology training program at Yale, which was addressed to an important human value, health, and at least partly dealt with the future by investigating how to improve health delivery services.

Yale itself was in transition. When I first joined the Yale faculty in 1963, Yale College students were all male (and in most other social ways were unrepresentative of the American youth population of the day). During the next several decades the campus was in turmoil, besieged by conflict and political struggles, the protest against the Vietnam War being only one of many issues. Various members of the Yale faculty and administration sought to transform Yale to include women and minority undergraduates; to add members of minority groups to the Yale faculty through an affirmative action program; to establish a new business school and an Institute for Social and Policy Studies; to create new programs in Afro-American studies and, eventually, women's studies; and to set up many other interdisciplinary centers and programs, from studies of the environment to AIDS. Furthermore, despite the existence of a variety of area-studies programs, including the historic Yale-in-China program, Yale at the start of the 1960s was largely a national university; by the 1990s it had been transformed into an international university.

I should add, given the topic of this book, that in the late 1960s Harold D. Lasswell and I cofounded the Yale Collegium on the Future, which, unfortunately, no longer exists. Lasswell was a pioneering futurist at least a generation ahead of his time, who greatly influenced me. He moved much of his own futures thinking into defining and developing the policy sciences, which are, at least through the Lasswell connection, first cousins of futures studies (Lasswell, 1971; Lerner and Lasswell, 1951). At the time, some members of the Yale community opposed almost all of these changes. In addition to advocating new courses in futures studies, I was personally deeply involved in several of them (e.g., bringing women to Yale College, and, especially, starting the Afro-American Studies Program and making affirmative action work for both students and faculty). Of course, during the struggles to control Yale's future, one could observe the usual political ploys. Past favors and obligations were called in to get support, deals were made (e.g., "you support X and I'll support Y"), friendships were imposed upon, some timid souls always agreed with the powerful while a few perennial rebels always pushed a verbal clenched fist into a dean's face, and a few faculty members revealed hidden talents for demagoguery. In the end, although it was sometimes entertaining, I doubt if any of this mattered very much.

What mattered was something quite different. In addition to patience, persistence, and polite diplomacy, the usually effective means in such situations, what worked was constant explanation, over and over again, and yet again and still again, explain! Moreover, constant listening to people with different views was also necessary, over and over again, and yet again and still again, listen! There were, of course, some exceptions (like the meeting dealing with the status of the Yale R.O.T.C. unit during the Vietnam War), when emotions raged out of control, wrong decisions were made, and right decisions had to await another day. But, generally, the system of faculty governance worked just about as it was supposed to.

Generally, one had to discuss what would happen if the proposed change was or was not made ("Oh my God," one Yale historian wailed, "if women are admitted to Yale College, then instead of graduating a thousand potential national leaders a year we will only graduate five hundred! What a loss to the country!" The thought that women, too, could become national leaders was apparently inconceivable to him). And one had to discuss why supporting the proposed change was a better moral choice ("For God, for country, and for Yale") than opposing it. And both the prediction of the consequences and the moral judgment had to be justified by giving reasons for which one could plausibly claim objective truth and logical correctness. Usually, it was only then that a decision for or against a proposed change might be certified by a faculty majority as being "responsible."

CONCLUSION

In this chapter, I look at how social scientists understand the nature of social order and change and how they can help people become more effective and more knowingly responsible for the future outcomes of their actions and inactions. The most useful and the most accurate understanding of modern societies comes from investigating the effects of deliberate social action on the part of individuals and groups, asking how people create their own social worlds and how their actions are causes of social change. Some variables that ought to be taken into account are people's images of the future, their possible choices, their decision-making processes, and their moral judgments. In such a social analysis, people are held accountable for their behavior and its consequences, both intended and unintended. They can be shown to be liable for the things that they do.

Theoretical explanations using concepts of impersonal social forces or cultural imperatives that are viewed as inevitably compelling people to behave in certain ways, as in Vaughan's (1996) analysis of the *Challenger* disaster, ought to be considered incomplete social analysis. They are shorthand ways of describing social situations, but, if accepted as full and complete understandings, they tend to obscure more than they reveal about who is doing what to whom for what purpose and with what consequences. Also, because they tend to absolve people of being concious and controlling agents of their own actions (and inactions), such explanations encourage irresponsible behavior ("The social system made me do it"). Moreover, they give little help to people who try to improve human performances in the future.

An example of social scientists profitably bringing people into their depictions of social realities as active, purposeful, future-oriented, and creative policy makers is the Moskos and Butler (1996) study of combatting racial discrimination in the Army. Such a study contributes both to holding people accountable and to giving guidance to improve the effectiveness and morality of future behavior.

People can be taught to become more effective and responsible by their knowing and following some of the principles of futures thinking, for example, by more fully investigating present possibilities for the future, by rejecting the idea that "what is" must be as it is and is all that can be or could be, by more accurately forecasting probable futures (especially the future outcomes of their own acts), by preparing for improbable as well as probable future events, by creating surprise-free futures through exploring the unintended and otherwise unanticipated consequences of particular actions and inactions (including their own), by understanding the functions and utility of self-altering prophecies, and by making a distinction between presumptively true (or false) and terminally true (or false) predictions as conceptual tools in decision making.

Of course, knowing what futures are preferable is as essential for making competent, effective, and responsible decisions as knowing what futures are possible and probable. But what is a preferable future? How do we know? Both futurists and social scientists deal with making judgments of what is desirable (e.g., surveys of the attitudes of various respondents, clarification of goals, using the means–ends and commitment–deducibility models, etc.). But these methods are ultimately inadequate, because in the end they depend on unfalsifiable beliefs about what is good.

Recently, some promising progress has been made toward constructing methods for making objective tests of value judgments, both in social science and in moral philosophy. Alternative possibilities for the future, different choices of courses of action, even entire societies can be judged as good or bad by using criteria dervied from considerations of human freedom and welfare. Particularly useful is the method of epistemic implication proposed by Lee (1985), by which even ends such as human freedom and welfare can be justified. Clearly, we have reached a point where social scientists should open-mindedly reconsider the possibility of objective methods of testing value judgments and of enlarging their concerns to encompass an empirically grounded moral discourse.

In conclusion, I realize that I have not been able in this brief chapter to adequately answer all of the questions posed by Jim Dator, especially his question concerning my vision of a plausible, preferred future. Elsewhere (Bell, 1997, vol. 2), I have given a detailed image of the future and I won't attempt to summarize it here. But I would like to say something specifically related to this chapter.

My positive, ideal image of the future for the twenty-first century includes the spread of futures studies into colleges and universities, not only as centers and institutes but also as new, mainstream Departments of Futures Studies, composed mostly of interdisciplinary faculty appointments with other university departments. It includes, further, the spread of futures thinking into other departments, bringing a prospective component to most social research on whatever topic it is focused. And it includes bringing objective moral discourse into the social sciences as a legitimate and rigorous concern.

Thus, the systematic and rigorous study of the possible, the probable, and the preferable would be joined to create a growing and widely followed science of social action to help people become more responsible. It would help people participate as informed, effective, and moral beings in the critical discourse about how they ought to act to create a desirable future, both for themselves and others, for presently living people and for as yet unborn future generations.

NOTE

I wish to thank Charles C. Moskos and Albert J. Reiss for their helpful comments on a draft of this chapter.

REFERENCES

Allinson, R. E. (1997). [Review of the book *The Challenger launch decision: Risky technology, culture and deviance in NASA*, by D. Vaughan]. *Society 35*, 99–102.

Arendt, H. (1964). *Eichmann in Jerusalem: A report on the banality of evil.* New York: Viking Press.

Axelrod, R. (1984). *The evolution of cooperation.* New York: Basic Books.

Barber, B. (1983). *The logic and limits of trust.* New Brunswick, NJ: Rutgers University Press.

Barnes, H. E. (1948). Preface. In H. E. Barnes (Ed.), *An introduction to the history of sociology* (pp. vii–xi). Chicago: University of Chicago Press.

Batson, C. D. (1991). *The altruism question*. Hillsdale, NJ: Lawrence Erlbaum Associates.

Baumeister, R. F. (1991). *Meanings of life*. New York: Guilford Press.

Bell, D. (1973). *The coming of post-industrial society: A venture in social forecasting*. New York: Basic Books.

Bell, W. (1974). Social science: The future as a missing variable. In A. Toffler (Ed.), *Learning for tomorrow: The role of the future in education* (pp. 75–102). New York: Random House.

Bell, W. (1997). *Foundations of futures studies*, 2 vols. New Brunswick, NJ: Transaction.

Bell, W., and Mau, J. (1971). Images of the future: Theory and research strategies. In W. Bell and J. Mau (Eds.), *The sociology of the future* (pp. 6–44). New York: Russell Sage Foundation.

Bishop, P. C. (1994, September). *Knowing the future*. Paper presented at the Workshop on Futures Intelligence Methodologies, Joint Military Intelligence College, Washington, D.C.

Boldt, M. (1993). *Surviving as Indians: The challenge of self government*. Toronto: University of Toronto Press.

Boulding, K. (1956). *The image: Knowledge in life and society*. Ann Arbor: University of Michigan Press.

Boulding, K. (1985). *Human betterment*. Beverly Hills, CA: Sage.

Brown, D. E. (1991). *Human universals*. Philadelphia: Temple University Press.

Clark, B. R. (1970). *The distinctive college: Antioch, Reed & Swarthmore*. Chicago: Aldine.

Collard, D. (1978). *Altruism and economy*. New York: Oxford University Press.

Dator, J., and Rodgers, S. (1991). *Alternative futures for the state courts of 2020*. Chicago: American Judicature Society.

de Jouvenel, B. (1964). *The art of conjecture*. New York: Basic Books.

Edgerton, R. B. (1992). *Sick societies: Challenging the myth of primitive harmony*. New York: Free Press.

Eisenberg, N. (1986). *Altrustic emotion, cognition, and behavior*. Hillsdale, NJ: Lawrence Erlbaum.

Etzioni, A. (1968). *The active society*. New York: Free Press.

Gert, B. (1988). *Morality: A new justification of the moral rules*. New York: Oxford University Press.

Gewirth, A. (1978). *Reason and morality*. Chicago: University of Chicago Press.

Habermas, J. (1973). *Theory and practice* (J. Viertel, Trans.). Boston: Beacon Press.

Henshel, R. L. (1978). Self-altering predictions. In J. Fowles (Ed.), *Handbook of futures research* (pp. 99–123). Westport, CT: Greenwood Press.

Kahn, H. (1960). *On thermonuclear war*. Princeton, NJ: Princeton University Press.

Kahn, H., and Wiener, A. (1967). *The year 2000: A framework for speculation on the next thirty-three years*. New York: Macmillan.

Lasswell, H. D. (1971). *A pre-view of policy sciences*. New York: Elsevier.

Lee, K. (1985). *A new basis for moral philosophy*. London: Routledge and Kegan Paul.

Lerner, D., and Lasswell, H. D. (Eds.). (1951). *The policy sciences*. Stanford, CA: Stanford University Press.

Linstone, H. A., and Turoff, M. (1975). *The Delphi method: Techniques and applications*. Reading, MA: Addison-Wesley.

Lombardi, L. G. (1988). *Moral analysis: Foundations, guides, and applications.* Albany: State University of New York Press.

Mau, J. (1968). *Social change and images of the future.* Cambridge, MA: Schenkman.

Meadows, D. H., Meadows, D. L., and Randers, J. (1992). *Beyond the limits.* Post Mills, VT: Chelsea Green.

Midgley, M. (1993). *Can't we make moral judgements?* New York: St. Martin's Press.

Moskos, C. C., and Butler, J. S. (1996). *All that we can be: Black leadership and racial integration the Army way.* New York: Basic Books.

Myers, J. K., and Bean, L. L. (1968). *A decade later: A follow-up of social class and mental illness.* New York: John Wiley and Sons.

Phillips, D. L. (1986). *Toward a just social order.* Princeton, NJ: Princeton University Press.

Polak, F. (1955). *The image of the future* (2 vols.). New York: Oceana.

Rosenau, P. M. (1992). *Post-modernism and the social sciences.* Princeton, NJ: Princeton University Press.

Sprigge, T.L.S. (1988). *The rational foundations of ethics.* London: Routledge and Kegan Paul.

Toffler, A. (1981). *The third wave.* New York: Bantam.

Vaughan, D. (1996). *The Challenger launch decision: Risky technology, culture, and deviance at NASA.* Chicago: University of Chicago Press.

Walster, E., Walster, G. W., and Berscheid, E., in collaboration with Austin, W., Traupmann, J., and Utne, M. K. (1978). *Equity: Theory and research.* Boston: Allyn and Bacon.

Washburn, W. E. (1997). *Against the anthropological grain.* New Brunswick, NJ: Transaction.

2

A Sociologist's Experience

Eleonora Barbieri Masini

For decades futures studies has been very much separated from social sciences and specifically from sociology, the area I know best and in which I received my training. Sociology has been an accomplished and recognized scientific field for more than one hundred years. Futures studies, as an area of research and training, can be traced back about fifty years, both the United States and France being the initial points of thinking. It is not my intention to describe the history of either of these disciplines. Rather, I wish to underline what has been lost by their developing separately, and indicate what could and, in some cases has, made their contact intellectually and empirically fruitful.

Further, I will show how these contrasts have in some way informed, and at the same time, challenged and enriched my research and my teaching. Both activities have been my concern for over thirty years and hence my experience may, I hope, be useful to those younger than myself searching in the two still-separate areas of intellectual and practical endeavor that both disciplines, like most other sciences, share.

SOCIAL SCIENCES, SOCIOLOGY, AND FUTURES STUDIES

Apart from some pioneers, such as William F. Ogburn (in W. Bell, 1997, vol. 1, pp. 7–8), Harold Lasswell (in W. Bell, 1997, vol. 1, pp. 47–56), John McHale (1969), Daniel Bell (1967), and Wendell Bell himself (W. Bell and Mau, 1971), all in the United States, few early social scientists showed an interest in a future perspective.

Other pioneers in the area of futures studies with a social science background are to be found in France: Gaston Berger (1958), Bertrand de Jouvenel (1967), Pierre Massé (1967). These are all social scientists, with the exception of the creative Gaston Berger, who was originally a philosopher but gave incredible impulse to future thinking not only in France, but in Europe as a whole and later in Latin America and Africa.

There are some later examples of social scientists engaged in future thinking or in futures studies, specifically those who were or are active members in the World Futures Studies Federation. This federation was founded in Paris at UNESCO in 1973 and connects scholars in different fields who have a future orientation or who use futures theories and methods professionally, as recognized futurists or as members of other academic communities. Among these there are social scientists, such as the sociologists Elise Boulding, Johan Galtung, and Hidetoshi Kato; Yehezkel Dror and Jim Dator, both political scientists; as well as Donald Michael, social psychologist. The economist Kenneth Boulding also was decidedly future oriented. Still earlier, the contribution to the development of futures studies by the philosopher Fred Polak and the historian Ossip Flechteim was enormous. In this regard it is interesting to note that the Polish school of future studies, which contributed greatly to the whole field of future studies, especially in the 1960s and 1970s, was grafted onto the thinking of social scientists and specifically sociologists, such as Andrej Sicinski and Jan Strezelecki. In this specific case the critical approach of the excellent Polish school of sociology was probably the spur toward futures thinking. This is not to say that there have not been other social scientists with a future orientation outside of the WFSF. I am just mentioning some the few who have to be considered special cases of social scientists particularly attentive to change in society, because the fact still remains that the majority of social science schools and institutional studies have not been open to future thinking, as Wendell Bell in his recent book also makes clear.

The interest by social scientists in futures studies, and by futurists in the social sciences, emerged mainly in the 1960s and 1970s. It then diminished in the late 1970s and 1980s, with some indications of renewed interest in the 1990s. The decline in the 1980s might be because economic elements have in some way superseded the earlier social emphasis. Futures studies, on the other hand, developed in the 1960s and 1970s especially in areas related to strategic studies (in the United States this was the case, especially in the

1960s), then in connection to systems analysis and mathematics, and later still in such areas as environmental studies. The link with conventional social sciences is therefore quite recent (the exceptions previously indicated notwithstanding).

Indeed, for decades a certain disinterest or even contempt characterized the attitude of the academic world (social scientists included) toward futures studies. I can document this personally with the history of RC07, the Future Research Committee of the International Sociological Association (ISA). The committee was founded in Varna by the very distinguished French social scientist, Bertrand de Jouvenel, in the late 1960s at a world conference of ISA. I followed de Jouvenel as president of the committee for many years and have recently passed the chair to Reimon Bachika, a sociologist from Bukkyo University in Kyoto, who was elected in late 1997.

The attitude of social sciences, and especially sociology, is changing as social scientists and sociologists are to some extent forced to look at changes taking place in society, in addition to analyzing and studying social systems, actions, structures, and so on.

On its part, futures studies has failed to show much interest in the social sciences, in part because of the latter's reluctance to look ahead and also because of a certain disdain for established disciplines on the part of some futurists. This attitude prevented futurists from understanding the importance of sound field social research and indeed even made them unaware of what is actually happening in social dynamics and to people as members of societies.

The consequences of this approach—namely the lack of social research in futures studies—has been especially damaging in the developing countries where futurists, mainly from industrialized countries, have often assumed situations from their standpoint as futurists from the developed world, rich in technology and human resources. Fortunately this approach was offset by the many positive contributions from organizations and scholars from the developing world who sought to reach a better understanding of the real situations in developing countries.

Examples of the latter are the Indian Centre for Developing Societies in Delhi, where social scientists such as Ashis Nandy (1987) and Rashni Kothari (1974) have shown, not only in their writings but also in their action-oriented field work, what is really happening in such countries. In Africa, Mahdi Elmandjra (1986), as a political scientist, has also shown the importance of social sciences for futures studies and the need, at the same time, for social sciences to have a broad worldview as well as a long-term perspective to better understand the dynamics of the world as a whole in social terms.

These are some brief indications of the dynamics between futures studies and social sciences through the years. We have seen that they have been mainly negative, but that they now seem at last to be finding new ways of understanding because of mutual needs and the rapidity of change in society.

REFLECTIONS ON THE DICHOTOMY BETWEEN SOCIAL SCIENCES AND FUTURES STUDIES: DIFFICULTIES AND INTELLECTUAL ENRICHMENT EMERGING FROM AND IN MY TEACHING AND MY RESEARCH

On and in My Teaching

I have been teaching for many years in the Faculty of Social Sciences of the Gregorian University, a university that enjoys great prestige at the international level. It was the first university founded by the Jesuits as far back as 1551. The Faculty of Social Sciences was founded in 1951 and has therefore reflected both the difficulties and the conquests of social sciences in the last forty years, operating within a highly intellectual, Roman Catholic environment. Since 1976 I have been teaching what is called "Social and Human Prospective Studies" ("Prospective studies" might be said to be futures studies that takes the past and the present into account and develops alternative futures as well as indicating possible choices for the future. The definition is based on the thinking of the French school in the area). Since my faculty is within a university that has students from 116 countries, of which 20 percent are women, this means that each year at least twenty students belonging to many countries have gone back to their countries with a basic understanding of what is called futures studies. Moreover, each year about four of these twenty students choose to write a major thesis in futures studies, and one or so will go on to write a doctoral thesis. This means that many young people, not only from Western and Eastern Europe, but also from Latin America, Africa (there have been many Africans in the last decade), and less so from Asia now have an understanding of futures studies. The university and the faculty are international, intercultural, and interdisciplinary, as many courses are open to the other faculties.

The Faculty of Social Sciences is composed of three disciplines: economics, sociology, and the social doctrine and ethics of the Catholic Church (hence, the faculty is also interdisciplinary in itself). There are also students from other religions, such as Buddhists and Moslems. I teach a group of students with the tools of social and economic research. I have had to adapt my course, or rather enrich it, with the capability of understanding social and economic reality from a futures perspective. I do this with a course that covers the following:

1. The accepted principles of futures studies, such as the following: The future is not subject to positivistic, empirical modes of analysis. The future is not singular. Rather, there are many alternative futures that depend on present choices, enriched by the understanding and interpretation of the past. The future is the only area on which the human being can have an influence, since the past can only be interpreted and the present is in most ways already decided by events and actions in the recent or distant past.

2. Other information more grafted on the social sciences: the concept of time and space in futures studies, our responsibility for the future, and the impact of actions and choices not only on our future but also on the social future of many others (a point I stress greatly in my teaching).

3. Critical analysis of major futures studies from a social science perspective.

4. Futures studies methodologies (extrapolative and normative), such as Delphi, cross-impact matrix, strategic management, environmental management, global models, and so on. There is a special emphasis on scenario building that requires, in my view, considerable input from social sciences in an interdisciplinary way.

Hence, I try to combine futures studies and social sciences—and specifically sociological analysis and sociological empirical research—as a basis of alternative futures scenarios. I also have an experimental period of scenario building to which all students contribute. Last year it was on the future of the European Union; this year on vocational training and technical schools in Italy.

My teaching experience, not only at the Gregorian University but also at the International University Centre (IUC) in Dubrovnik for over ten years (1975–1989), at the University of Trieste in Italy, and in the United States for one semester as a visiting professor at St. Cloud State University in Minnesota, is that students grasp very well the need for futures studies to be based on social sciences with the contribution of rigorous empirical analysis. They come to see that futures studies gives social sciences the possibility of going beyond simply "photographing the present," instead using a motion picture camera that not only captures change but even shows indications of different possible futures.

On and in My Research

My research has been mainly in developing countries or with international groups and organizations working in developing countries. This type of research requires a great deal of social science analysis as well as future-oriented methods. An example of my work is a ten-year research project, conducted for the United Nations University in Tokyo, on the impact that major socioeconomic and even political events have had on women in eight developing countries (Argentina, Colombia, Chile, Brazil, Sri Lanka, China in two provinces [Sichuan and Jiangsu], Kenya, and Ivory Coast) (Masini and Stratigos, 1991). The research was interdisciplinary, as it was conducted with demographers, sociologists, historians, anthropologists, and statisticians. All the participants came from the countries involved in the research, with the exception of myself as coordinator and some consultants. The second objective of the research was more future oriented, in that it aimed at studying the impact that women and changes in the family can be expected to have in the countries considered. Here my experience in futures studies was particularly important.

Another research program has been to help produce scenarios in developing countries (Barbieri Masini, 1995). There was a first extended phase based on a great deal of social science analysis of the socioeconomic and political situation, mainly carried out by local researchers with my guidance. In the second part, scenarios were developed with local researchers and decision makers. I strongly support participatory scenario building where experts and decision makers in the area are present and take part in the actual building of the scenarios, once the lengthy preparatory process of collecting quantitative and qualitative data has been completed. In this way the creative and alternative phase of the research is done with the people who might be able to make the scenarios realizable. The topics covered for this research were different levels of education and changes in agricultural planning as carried out in developing countries, mainly Latin America.

The scenario building I have done with international religious groups stems from the need that such groups have to make decisions and important changes given the major social changes occurring in the contexts in which they operate. In this case the preparatory phase of search for data is usually very long, as such groups operate in many parts of the world. The first phase was therefore similar to the cases already described, requiring at the same time social science analysis on structures, management, and internal organization, as well as analysis of the objectives and activities of the groups. Much of the work was done through electronic mail and the like. I was present during the final phase, which was generally organized in Rome or in some other major location of the groups. This phase differed in duration.

The results of this kind of futures research, conducted with the support of social sciences, have been as follows:

- to clarify the interconnections between different aspects of the different areas (for example, the source of funding for education in Latin America might have influenced the systems and structures of education more than was apparent at the start).

- to educate people who make decisions to think in a futures-oriented way and in the awareness of the many interactions at play.

- to educate people to look into the future in terms of alternatives rather than in linear terms, even to the point of considering the unexpected best and worst possibilities (for example, that a religious order has to close, that there may be a coup d'état in a given country, that the religious order might become so large that it has to be divided into many groups, or that the reform of education in Latin America might be sponsored by some impartial source). Of course, other more feasible alternatives are also considered.

- to increase the sense of responsibility for present decisions and of building the future with a greater amount of awareness.

- to decrease the level of uncertainty of decision making in situations of great complexity.

My experience is that scenarios are time and energy consuming but that the balance is positive in relation to the previously indicated results.

MY EXPERIENCE WITH THE
WORLD FUTURES STUDIES FEDERATION

Over and beyond the previous activities, I have been involved for twenty years in the World Futures Studies Federation. I was secretary general for five years, president for ten years, and finally chair of the executive committee for three years.

In the minds of its founders—such as Robert Jungk, Johan Galtung, and John McHale—the aim of the WFSF was from the very start to emphasize the human side of futures thinking. This also accounts for the number of social scientists and humanists I have mentioned previously. In this emphasis, the need for the contribution of future-thinking people in the whole world, and not only in the Western world, was very strong. This is indeed another distinction of futures studies as visualized by the WFSF in contrast with most of the social sciences (especially the institutional social sciences), where the emphasis is Western even if there are excellent social scientists in the rest of the world. Hence, in the WFSF for many years a great effort has been made to identify and involve future-oriented scholars or others in what are now called the countries in transition as well as in Latin America and Africa. In this period, Johan Galtung, Mahdi Elmandjra, and myself were presidents. The efforts continued with Jim Dator and Pentti Malaska as presidents, and it will hopefully continue in the future with Tony Stevenson and beyond.

The importance of the contribution of different ways of thinking about the future, in cultural, political, or other terms, was what I was committed to in the belief that there are many future alternative possibilities and that they have to be unveiled, to the extent of our capacity, and at the same time respected. The idea that there is only one view of the future is not only incorrect in the face of empirical evidence offered by the past and very strongly in our present times, but is also a very powerful manipulatory tool that futurists must avoid. Futures studies in this understanding represents one expression of a moral responsibility that each and all human beings have about the future and the futures of all others.

CONCLUSION

I therefore advocate closer cooperation and reciprocity between futures studies and the social sciences. This closer cooperation requires overcoming difficulties of a theoretical and practical nature, both in teaching and in field work. Enhanced cooperation is important for strengthening the foundations of futures studies (W. Bell, 1997) and looking ahead, in terms not only of understanding social mechanics, but also mainly social change, at the same time acknowledging the human responsibility toward the future of scholars in all socially related areas.

REFERENCES

Barbieri Masini, E. (1995). Institute for Prospective Technological Studies (Ed.), *Two scenarios implemented in the social area*, pp. 80–85. Seville: Institute for Prospective Technological Studies, European Commission.

Barbieri Masini, E., and Stratigos, S. (1991). *Household , gender and age*. Tokyo: United Nations University.

Bell, D. (Ed.). (1967). Toward the year 2000: Work in progress. *Daedalus 96* (3).

Bell, W. (1997). *Foundations of futures studies* (2 vols.). New Brunswick: Transaction.

Bell, W., and Mau, J. (1971). *The sociology of the future*. New York: Russell Sage Foundation.

Berger, G. (1958). L'attitude prospective. *Prospective No. 1*. Paris: Presses Universitaires, de France.

de Jouvenel, B. (1967). *The art of conjecture*. New York: Basic Books.

Elmandjra, M. (1986). Africa's needs for futures studies. In World Futures Studies Federation, Association Internationale Futuribles, Association Mondiale de Prospective Sociale (Eds.), *Reclaiming the future: Manual for African planners*. London: UNDP, Tycooly International.

Kothari, R. (1974). *Footsteps into the future: Diagnosis of the present world and a design for alternatives*. Delhi: Orient Longman.

Massé, P. (1967). *Le Plan ou l'anti-hazard*. Paris: Collection idées, Gallimard.

McHale, J. (1969). *The future of the future*. New York: George Braziller.

Nandy, A. (1987). *Traditions, tyranny and utopias: Essays on the politics of awareness*. Bombay: Oxford University Press.

3

The Future as a Sociocultural Problem: A Personal Ethnohistory

Reed D. Riner

A QUEST FOR PATTERN

I woke up to the future in the winter of my seventh-grade year of public school, 1953–1954, while reading a collection of alternative futures, short stories in the paperback edition of A. E. Van Vogt's (1952) *Destination Universe*. The future was, from then on, the only thing I really wanted to study, but serious scholarship excluded both science fiction and the future. I continued through high school and two universities. I collected, more by accident than intent, a generalist's major in "distributed humanities." Then I enlisted in the Navy, still searching for some singular perspective that would integrate everything I had learned about human activities and my continuing, closeted passion for the future. The community and technology systems of ships—and the hands-on proximity to the fire-control systems that had started the cybernetic revolution—were fascinating, but the hierarchical command structure of warships at sea was not the explanatory perspective I was seeking. I was searching for a discipline more ecumenical than sociology, but more systematic, scientific and processual than history, and by accident I found it, in 1966, in a book called *Anthropology* (Kroeber, 1948). Here was the holistic social science that embraced all people in all places and times, that included all of human experience, back even to before we were human, and promised that it could reach just as far into the future. For thirty-one years I have been working to extend that reach.

As a graduate student I taught four years as the anthropology representative in yoke with peers from each of the other social sciences—economics, political science, justice, psychology, and sociology—in an interdisciplinary social science undergraduate preteacher education program.[1] Often we graduate assistants and our faculty argued about what it is that defines a social science, what are the distinguishing central concepts, and so on, where any one of our disciplines left off and its neighbor began, if the social landscape really changes hue from green to pink when one crossed one of these interdisciplinary boundaries, and if a unified social science, as proposed by Kuhn (1975) was feasible and desirable. I learned to explain the role of the science of culture—and anthropology's model of multilinear and punctuated evolution of "whole sociocultural systems" (Miller, 1978)—among her elder sister social sciences, and to defend anthropology in her inductive, participant-observation methods against critics who suffered from physics envy and claimed that only the deductive, experimental pursuits can be "scientific." Privately I sought to answer how the study of the future could be developed as a cumulative, self-critical, self-correcting, and systematic discipline wherein practitioners could generate independently replicable results.

I took this motivation forward between two real-world parameters. On one hand, I have worked in an academic rather than a practitioner environment, where highest priorities are accorded to disciplinary integrity and pedagogical responsibility, within the limits of institutional pragmatics. But this department has been, on the other hand, an anthropology department with a strong and explicit "applied" (hence, real-world) problem-solving orientation. This has fostered the opportunity and the support to work on a variety of different kinds of projects, which have spanned, and often merged, the categories of teaching, research, and service to both the profession and the community. I will discuss five of these projects in detail to illustrate how working between these complimentary perspectives has contributed to my own integration of methods, theories, and applications in both classroom and research–consulting–service areas of futures studies, and to my own image of a preferable future.

CULTURAL FUTURES RESEARCH: PATTERNS IN DISCIPLINES

In the years 1970 to 1974, Magoroh Maruyama and Arthur Harkins organized, hosted, and published the preconference volumes of papers for a series of symposia presented at the annual meetings of the American Anthropological Association (AAA) (Maruyama, 1970, 1971, 1972, 1973; Maruyama and Harkins, 1975). These sessions brought persistent attention to the future by a community of scholars whose interests were traditionally in the past and the present, although typically the ethnographic present, which is safely frozen in the past and not subject to ongoing change into the future. Two strains of interest continued beyond this series of symposia and publications. Robert B. Textor facilitated the organization of permanent special interest groups, the Cultural and Educational Futures Committee in the Council on Anthropology and Education (CAE) of the AAA (1978), and the Cultural Futures Research Network in the Society for Applied Anthropology (SfAA) (1979). The former committee initiated a quarterly refereed journal, *Journal of Cultural and Educational Futures*, edited by Marion L. Dobbert, Arthur M. Harkins, and Robert B. Textor, from April 1979 through 1981. Beginning from discussions in November 1974, Carol Motts, Elizabeth Bjornen, and Darlene Thomas had founded a journal that became *AnthroTech* under Thomas's editorship and was published quarterly until the summer of 1981. In the summer and fall of 1981 I consolidated the two journals into *Cultural Futures Research* (CFR), a refereed quarterly recognized as the official journal of the futures interest groups in the AAA, the SfAA, and the Futurology Commission of the International Union of Anthropological and Ethnographic Sciences (IUAES). CFR was published until the summer of 1983.[2]

I had entered the field of anthropological futures research during a decade of high interest. Beginning in 1975, I wrote a regular commentary for *AnthroTech*, was active in the AAA and SfAA interest groups, organizing symposia for both, and finally editing CFR. These various service activities over seven years provided me with an overview of the kinds of contributions that anthropology as a discipline could make, and that anthropologists could be persuaded to make to the study of the future. The final issue of *AnthroTech* (Spring–Summer 1981), guest edited by Albert Bergeson, featured a collection of papers about the future considered in the Wallersteinian Capitalist World-System paradigm (Bergesen, 1981). Subsequently, CFR published papers addressing the emergence and foreseeable characteristics of a supranational level of sociocultural integration; that is, a world civilization (Wolfe, 1982; Kurth-Shai, 1983; Lewellen, 1983; Preston, 1983), the foreseeable characteristics of settlements in space (Williamson and Chandler, 1983; Thompson, 1983; Stoddard, 1983; MacDaniel, 1983), methods and case studies that revealed patterns in culture that had potential for anticipating the future (Bergesen, 1982a; 1982b; Guilmet, 1982; Roy, 1982; Eldredge, Oliver, Sanders, Yatim, and Textor, 1983; English, 1983; Kirk, 1983; Klass, 1983; Morozas and Alger, 1983; Nash and Withlam, 1983; Smith, 1982), and the future of human communication and cognition (Agrawal, 1983; Brown and Greenhood, 1983; El-Shall and El-Alfy, 1983; Guilmet, 1983; Tyzzer, 1983). Viewed in retrospect, *Cultural Futures Research* helped to focus attention on four general themes that had not concerned futurists with a practitioner background: (1) the multidisciplinary approach that integrates human biology, material culture ("technology"), social systems of individuals, and the shared values and beliefs—the culture—that characterizes that society; (2) the evolutionary perspective, multilinear and punctuated, that seeks to provide a materialist, causal, nomothetic, maximally long-term and contexting explanation for these kinds of systems (Harris, 1979); (3) a cross-cultural and culturally relativist comparative method that recognizes a range of variation in behavior and belief comparable to the range of human diversity exhibited by the 5,000 to 15,000 remaining languages, diminishing yet currently spoken by the members of the crew of spaceship Earth; and (4) the notion that alternative futures, however we apprehend them, are only images produced, like language, art, and science, out of a cultural dialogue, that they are "cultural things" and therefore greatly determined and biased by the configuration of the culture that has produced them, and are appropriate objects of study for the methods and theoretical perspectives of anthropology.

CONTACT: PATTERNS IN IMAGINATION

In 1981 I received a letter inviting me to participate in a proposed conference that would bring together anthropologists and other social scientists, science fiction writers and artists, futures and NASA research scientists to collaborate in discussion and exploration of longer-range futures for humanity. Jim Funaro proposed to use play to explore situations in the future that could not be worked on experimentally. The venue would be a weekend conference that would include the expected scholarly symposia on topics of mutual interest. The program was as follows:

The Science Fiction–Anthropology Connection
    Reed Riner—"Materialists and Mentalists"
    Paul Bohannan—"Premises and Science Fiction"
    Larry Niven—"Specifics"

Science Fiction as Creative Ethnography
    Michael Bishop—"Fictional Mirrors of Contemporary Human Societies"
    C. J. Cherryh—"Regul: Case Study in Alien Creation"
    Mischa Adams and Ruby Rohrlich—"In Search of Utopia: Mavericks and
       Mythmakers"

Monkey Bodies and Others
    Robert N. Tyzzer—"Biological Factors in Species Contact"
    Richard D. Johnson—"Looking Forward"
    Paul Preuss—"Stranger Than We Can Imagine"

Monkey Minds: Theory and Method
    Jerry Pournelle—"Data and the Voodoo Sciences"
    Jim Funaro—"Science and Other Magick"
    Charles F. Urbanowicz—"Culture, Anthropology and Science Fiction"

But the piece de resistance would be a Bateson Project. Inspired by the writings and mentoring of the late Gregory Bateson (Bateson, 1972, 1979; Bateson and Bateson, 1987), Funaro proposed to divide conference participants into two teams. Members of the "Alien Team," including artist and anthropologist Joel Hagen and science fiction writer Larry Niven, both veterans of the prototypic world-building "Thrax Project" (Hartman, 1982), would collaborate in designing and describing a scientifically plausible other planet, with ecology, sentient species, and culture. The members of the "Human Team" would precess contemporary human culture up to that future point of contact. The first encounter between humans and aliens would be—indeed was—improvised and dramatized in a kind of guerrilla theater during Sunday brunch, and was stunning beyond expectation.

CONTACT has reconvened every year but one since that first conference in 1982, and celebrated its eighteenth anniversary on the traditional "first weekend in March," 2001. Proceedings have been published for many of the years (Funaro, Riner, and McDaniels, 1985; 1987; 1988; 1989; Loritz, McDaniels, and Riner, 1989; Nordley, 1996; Speakman, 1997; Speakman and Sisson, 1996); a middle-school curriculum version of the human-meets-aliens exercise, "Cultures of the Imagination—coti.jr," has been developed and disseminated; and the strategy of using play and role-playing—the essence of a Bateson Project—has been successfully applied to the collaborative development of scenarios Vision 2020 (1988) and Southwest 2039 (1989), to explore likely consequences of success in the Search for Extraterrestrial Intelligence (SETI) project, SimSETI, and in a three-year exercise in alien culture-building, the Epona Project (http://www.io.com/ ~ stefanj/82Eridani/index.html). In addition, CONTACT has inspired university-level courses at California State College at Los Angeles, Elizabeth Viau's Edit 490, Parts I and II of World Builders (http://www.calstatela.edu/academic/builders/index.html) and Northern Arizona University (NAU) Solar System Simulation (http://www.nau.edu/ ~ anthro/solsys).

CONTACT is unique in two respects. It constitutes a sort of "Leftcoast Futures Society," a compliment to the World Future Society, in that it brings together anthropologists and other social scientists—almost all of them involved full time in higher education—science and science-fiction authors and graphic artists, NASA and Federal Research Lab scientists (applied and research scientists), and many students, with an emphasis placed on the participants' active and self-critical involvement in building and critiquing images of alternative, scientifically plausible futures. Thus, the CONTACT conference creates an ambiance very different—more playful, scholarly, egalitarian, and scientific—than meetings of the WFS. In addition, CONTACT has developed a distinctive method of futures research, the Bateson Project, that has been applied to diverse futures "problems," and is successful in secondary and postsecondary education and potentially in strategic planning processes with educational and other kinds of organizations.

FLAGSTAFF TOMORROW: PATTERNS IN MACROHISTORY

"The individual or nation which has no sense of direction in time, no sense of a clear future ahead is likely to be vacillating, uncertain in behavior, and to have a poor chance of surviving" (Boulding, 1961, p. 125). "A community or society without a clear image of what it wants to get is hardly likely to end up wanting what it does get" (Textor, Bhansoon Ladavalya, and Prabudhanitsarn, 1984, p. 1). "The community's posture toward images of the future would not merely reflect its notion of knowledge, but would be that knowledge, and would determine the image's utility value in community planning, development of best-case and worst-case scenarios, and the like . . . an image is plausible when it stimulates dialogue within the community, forces us to lay aside old and attempt new languages, and opens us to seeing new and different possibilities for the future" (Denton, 1986, p. 60).

I began, during the fall semester of 1984, to teach a course on the methods and premises of futures research, a graduate research seminar called "The Study of the Future." The members of my department were, at that time, involved in a process of reflection, strategic planning, and program redesign that produced, over the next years, a master's program in applied anthropology that continues to receive highest professional recognition. I was concerned that this course would, in the spirit of our program redesign, involve the students actively in using the methods of futures research in an applied context, and that the course would provide a complement to more traditional courses on ethnographic research methods, culture change, development, and applied anthropology in the core of our program. The course would bring together theory and epistemology with research methods, ethnography with futures, and gown with town (that is, the university with its host community).

I taught ANT-547, "The Study of the Future," four times during a period characterized by a rise of local interest in the future, in fall 1985, spring 1986, spring 1988, and spring 1990. In each instance the research took a twenty-five year horizon, hence Flagstaff 2009/10, -11, -13, and -15. Each iteration was organized as a team project, intending to discover how different type-groups of people in our community thought about, envisioned, and imagined the future of Flagstaff, Arizona, where NAU is located. Among the thirty-seven individual research projects over these six years, the majority employed the distinctively anthropological research method called the Ethnographic Futures Research (EFR) method (Textor, 1990, pp. xxiii–xlvii; McKeown, 1988, 1990). In these instances each student-ethnographer selected a group of informants (a.k.a. consultants, respondents) who had some important occupational or lifestyle feature in common. That is, they were all health-care providers, or all policemen, or all psychics, or all long-term, permanent residents of the near South side. Each ethnographer then identified eight to fifteen people of this kind, and conducted lengthy, semistratified but open-ended and confidential interviews to elicit how the members of this group imagined that Flagstaff would look—at its best, at its worst, and at its most likely—twenty-five years hence.

The complete research process can be summarized as follows: elicit > clarify > analyze > interpret > critique > feedback, and repeat, with the caveat that the process is potentially recursive at every step. The seminar devoted one session to the close examination of each of these processes. The EFR papers presented distillations and critiques of the images of alternative futures for Flagstaff as those images are shared among the citizens.

Despite the public attention to the future, the images of the future entertained by the local citizenry were characterized by shallow time depth, little detail, a lack of internal connectedness among topics, and negligible differentiation among alternatives of best case, worst case, and most likely. A few of the student researchers used other methods, such as Delphi Polling and trend extrapolations, alternative research methods that project different kinds of images of Flagstaff's possible futures and provide both check and contrast, and independent grounds for the critique of the EFR papers. The research team reported their findings back to their consultants and the community at large in public symposia as the culmination of the class.

The period from fall 1984 through fall 1991 was characterized by the rise and fall of local interest in the future. In the summer of 1985, the university, at the behest of the Arizona Board of Regents, initiated the design phase for a strategic planning process. In the spring of 1987, the community of Flagstaff conducted its first Town Hall Meeting, and the city adopted the "Growth Management Guide 2000" (GMG2000). In October 1987 the Arizona Department of Transportation sponsored a two-day futures symposium. I have written about these events and the opportunities they provided to involve my students and myself in achieving the objectives I set for the course (Riner, 1986, 1987). This period of rising interest was exciting, and I have written about it optimistically up to the point at which "Two Roads Diverged in the Yellow Wood of Incrementalism" (Riner, 1988).

The Town Hall Meeting made recommendations for transportation corridor beautification, downtown revitalization, and (tourist) destination development, to be paid for by a "bed, booze and board tax," an agenda that, after considerable rediscussion, was adopted by the city. The city adopted GMG2000, a comprehensive plan, but a synoptic, or "rational" sort of plan that focused overwhelmingly on the infrastructure without addressing issues of image and values, and without specifying processes that would lead the city beyond its heritage of incrementalist planning. My personal involvement in the university committee, the Town Hall Meeting process, and critical review of GMG2000 taught me two things: first, that "futures methods" can be discriminated into the categories of "research methods" and "implementation" or "process" methods. The research methods enable a person or team to collect and analyze a set of futures images in a replicable manner. The process methods enable a person or team, in leading members of a group or employees of an organization, to discover their shared image of a preferred future, and to develop value commitments toward accomplishing or realizing that image. Second, I developed an abiding interest in "the metabolism of organizations," focusing on the tempos at which things get done (the last billboards on downtown Route 66 finally came down in May 1997, ten years and two months after the initial mandate), the extent to which the component processes are or are not synchronized, and the extent to which the organization has institutionalized any "foresight circuitry," and so deals with its images of alternative futures in a newly recurrent, systematic, and replicable manner.

In the winter of 1987–1988, city government made decisions regarding urban development that indicated that the tradition of incrementalist planning would continue, in no way encumbered by GMG2000. The steering committee for the second Town Hall Meeting began work toward an agenda of issues that offered participants a smorgasbord of concerns, rather than a focus on one, and so rendered this process structurally and permanently disabled. In the spring of 1989 the university accepted the internally generated design for the strategic planning process that had been mandated by the Board of Regents, dismissed the committee, shelved the report, and continued with the familiar crisis-to-crisis, micromanaged style of management. These depressing events were offset by three personal "baccalaureate" events. In the spring of 1988 I was asked to review and critique the source materials that were being prepared for the Arizona Board of Regents own strategic planning process, an opportunity to view from a more general level what I had been immersed in at a local level. That summer I was asked to help a midwestern town clarify its image of a preferred future and organize itself for realization (Riner, 1991b). In late 1989 I participated in a symposium (WFS) and workshop (AAA) with my EFR mentor Bob Textor, in which we had the opportunity to reflect on and share what we had learned from doing EFR research over the last several years.

Some practical lessons came out of this demise of local interest in futures. I learned experientially what Charles W. Taylor would later set to numbers: The majority of people selected to do future visioning and strategic planing are temperamentally ill-suited to the task: 52 percent being the "ISTJ" (Introverted, Sensing [concrete], Thinking [logical], Judgmental) and "ESTJ" (Extroverted, Sensing, Thinking, Judgmental) types in the Meyers–Briggs Temperamental Indicator scheme, with all other six types accounting for the minority (Taylor, 1990, p. 6).

I was persuaded that knowledge of the content of images of the future and knowledge of organizational dynamics are not sufficient to a complete discipline of futures research, but that two additional factors—an understanding of the cultural and individual constructions of the experience of time, and an understanding of the values and the attached "affects" (feelings that are formative in these images)—are essential. The images of alternative futures are formed within the parameters of a particular conception of time, and organizations deliberately—or unwittingly—apply these images in navigating through time as they conceive it. I had brought the anthropological key concepts of "culture" and "worldview" to a central position in my thinking and teaching about the future, and began to discuss the role of the image of the future in social action (Riner, 1991a).

After a hiatus of four years, I taught ANT 547 again in the fall of 1994; the students published the set of ten papers produced by this renewed round of research (Head and Lee, 1995). In 1995, seven local citizens met to create "Friends of Flagstaff's Future," and in October convened the first session of an eighteen-month visioning process on behalf of the community (Flagstaff 2020, 1996a, 1996b). In June 1996 and March 1997, the Social Science Research Laboratory of the university took random samples of 500 community members regarding the visioning process (Solop and Nelson, 1997). During the spring semester of 1997, a colleague of mine taught a small research seminar doing an intensive ethnography on this community process during that semester. And in the fall semester of 1997 I taught the most recent installment of "The Study of the Future" as "Flagstaff Tomorrow: Flagstaff 2022," a multimethod impact assessment of the "Vision 2020" process.

Students conducted extensive exploratory data analysis of materials already collected, performing a "factor, then cluster" analysis on the two survey databases, applying ethnographic depth analysis on the thirty interviews of Visioning Process participants, conducting EFR interviews in three groups of nonparticipants in the process, and constructing a time line, supported by newspaper articles, of the process supplemented by in-depth interviews with the reporters who had covered the story, and made this news, of "Visioning Process: Flagstaff 2022." The papers reporting the findings of this research are in preparation for conference presentation and subsequent publication.

NAU SOLAR SYSTEM SIMULATION: PATTERNS IN FUTURE HISTORIES

In March 1989, following CONTACT-VI, my colleague Mel Neville, who had participated in the conference, came to me with a proposal: "Why don't we do one of those [Bateson Project] things here?" This led to our offering, in the spring semester of 1990, a pair of "yoked" honors courses, one for social science credit, the other for natural or "hard" science credit, in which students were challenged to collaborate in building an historically and scientifically plausible working model of the first permanent human settlement on Mars. In that pilot semester, two of our students proposed that the instructors and the class use e-mail and the newly introduced Multiple

User Domain (MUD) software to expand the model-building activity into cyberspace and to enable communication with teams at other sites. (NAU was connected to the Internet in the fall of 1989, and the first installment of "The Mars Course" was taught the following spring semester.) We adopted the new technologies and began to explore their potentials. In the process, we transformed the MUD, which had been a relatively low-tech, popular, "everyman's" sort of virtual reality, by turning it from recreational to pedagogical and social science–futures studies research ends; in other words, we turned a playroom into a laboratory and learning center.

In installments subsequent to the pilot, from 1991 to 1997, classes–teams and individual students were recruited and participated, usually for university credit, from Cabrillo College (California), the New School University of Florida, the University of Dayton, the University of Texas–Austin, Hamilton College (New York), Issaquah High School (Washington), the University of Hawaii, Eastern Oregon University, and Stanford University. In addition to anthropology, the participating departments have included, computer science engineering, political science, communications, and honors. The NAU Solar System Simulation is not a disciplinary-dependent project, but rather is intended to serve learning objectives in as many disciplinary areas as possible. Universities in Sweden (communications), England (engineering), Israel (education), and Australia (futures studies) have expressed interest and are prospective participants. Each year corrective feedback has been elicited from students and faculty, and has been applied in refinement and further development of the potentials of the simulation medium.

The NAU Solar System Simulation (SolSySim) provides a holistic, general-purpose environment that includes a theme, general objectives, and resources, but does not dictate a particular curriculum. The theme is the relatively near future of exploration and human settlement of nearer, sub-Jovian space; the date is set arbitrarily at "the establishment of the first permanent settlement on Mars." The general objectives are to build working models of communities that are historically and scientifically plausible, ethically and aesthetically desirable, and sustainable, and to establish and maintain mutually beneficial communication and simulated exchange among these communities. The resources include traditional library resources and local resources, such as, in Flagstaff, Lowell Observatory and USGS Planetary Data Facility, but also Internet resources and disciplinary experts who have volunteered their time to the simulation. Northern Arizona University provides the primary infrastructure and intersite coordination for the simulation. Each instructor determines the specific learning objectives, assignments, and evaluations appropriate to his or her course.

In the current form of the simulation, each class–team elects a site in their shared Solar System contemporaneous with the establishment of the first permanent settlement on Mars; at NAU, "Mars Is Ours!" Each team has to design its site and explain the history of that site within the limits of scientific and historical plausibility. Plausibility is refereed by members of the simulation's Board of Virtual Consultants in the role of Plausibility Police.[3] As local site identities begin to develop, teams must begin to communicate with each other to share design ideas and to negotiate a common scenario for their collective future. Communication among the teams is facilitated by former students who have developed great enthusiasm for the course, are familiar with course expectations and dynamics, and who return year after year to help enrich the experience for students in their first encounter with simulation-based learning (Neville and Riner, 1993; Riner and Clodius, 1995; Riner, 1996b).

The significant features of the NAU Solar System Simulation, a thoughtful application of anthropology and futures research, are the following:

- the use of text-based virtual reality as a laboratory environment.
- the successful and effective use of a play paradigm rather than a work paradigm for course organization.
- the students' sustained and self-critical identification with plausible situations in a desirable future, resulting in developing positive attitudes toward space development and the space program.
- the effective integration of collaborative learning, inquiry learning, interactive instruction, computer networking, virtual classrooms, and distance learning into an organized whole before many of these practices were labeled and discussed in educational practice and theory.
- the generation of student enthusiasm such that alumni from each year of the simulation return voluntarily to help with subsequent iterations.

Assessment of the NAU Solar System Simulation has had to go beyond the conventional question, "What have students in this class produced?" Individually, the students have produced writing portfolios increasingly more sophisticated in their visual illustrations, dynamic description, and critical analysis of their creation. But collaboratively, each team of students has created a community together with its culture, and all the teams together have created a supraplanetary sociocultural system, a synergetic thing greater than the sum of its parts, a fabric of virtual traditions and real interpersonal affections that continues into the present. Traditional assessment strategies do not address these supraindividual, system-level, and longer-term kinds of phenomena. The simulation uses feedback to learn from its own experience, and traditional methods were not adequate to assess this kind of learning. I have treated each year's iteration as a case and applied the method of controlled comparison in order to discover the similarities among and the differences between the several iterations. Three similarities are conspicuous and illustrative. In composing and negotiating the timeline(s), students invariably "undershoot," trying to pack too many events in too few years, and at the last minute have to insert another decade or score of years or more to accommodate events. More striking, perhaps, is that all the Mars teams, unaware of preceding class products, have posited that the first permanent human settlement on Mars will be established in 2075–2085. Finally, it takes two-thirds of the semester for undergraduate students to learn how to organize themselves into a smooth-working team, and to realize how much more efficient it would have been to have adopted a relaxed version of Robert's Rules of Order at the outset. The differences have had much to do with class size and events in the surrounding "real" world, and it has been from the differences that we have learned where more structure can be imposed in the process, moving decisions along more expeditiously without stifling student creativity. *Cresit eundo*—It grows as it goes.

TIMELINES: MORE THAN TRENDS AND CYCLES— PATTERNS IN MACROHISTORY

The flow of ideas between futures studies and anthropology has been, for me, reciprocal. While I was, on one hand, importing social scientific, particularly anthropological, concerns about epistemology, theory, and method into my futures work, I was simultaneously importing futures methods and content into my teaching of anthropology. This interdisciplinary transfer of knowledge took two conspicuous forms: (1) the introduction of interactive exercises for the students, an influence from CONTACT, SolSySim, and the process methods of futures studies generally, and (2) the development of a unit for my world ethnography course that attempts to explain the emergence of the modern world-system and its likely course into the future. The catalyst for the "Timeline Project" occurred in this latter context, specifically when I recognized that the reason my students cannot write persuasive scenarios is because they seem to have no sense that there are patterns in history and that such patterns can be extrapolated with reasonable confidence. The existence of these patterns belies the fact that there are regular and "universal" processes by which history is caused. But my students, overwhelmingly, do not understand this—either intuitively or practically— and I have had to draw them a picture, in the most literal sense.

This "picture" is now a chart, two feet tall and nine feet long. It identifies events of human history from 1450 to 2150. I have divided the scroll into strata according to the cultural materialist paradigm (Harris, 1979): Events illustrating the environment and its exploration are at the bottom; inventions and technology rest on that; the division of labor and economy rests on that; warfare and colonialism resting on that; political activity resting on that; and science, philosophy, religion, and art crowding the upper margin, all with the expectation that as relevant events accumulate, their distribution will belie the underlying processes that are the causes of particular events. I map events into this organizing scheme, so in fact, my timeline is in perpetual revision as new information is incorporated and implicit patterns are made explicit. The Capitalist World-System model has helped greatly in making primary economic and political processes apparent (Erickson, 1985; Bergeson, 1982a, 1980; Bergesen and Schoenberg, 1980; Wallerstein, 1980, 1979; Graham, 1973). More recently, incorporation of the growth-curve patterns exhibited by the introduction of technologies is helping to clarify connections between technology and the systems of political economy (Modis, 1992).

This kind of compilation of the events of history reveals and illustrates trends and cycles as qualitative, structural features, which helps better to situate and understand singular events in their structural context. It also illuminates patterns larger than cycles and trends. Most conspicuous among macropatterns are the qualitative transformations of the European-cum-World-System by the mechanical revolution of the Middle Ages, the Industrial Revolution in the mid-eighteenth century, and the current polynymic revolution that I refer to as a concurrent "TelElectronic–BioGenetic CoRevolution" (Riner, 1991a). Each of these revolutions, like the human, biological, and agricultural revolutions preceeding, are transformations characterized by significant changes, fundamentally by increases in the amount of energy harnessed through new modes of production into sociocultural systems, resulting in changes in the structure and quality of the systems that cannot be anticipated by quantitative extrapolation.

This fact of the qualitative transformation of sociocultural systems in the emerging Capitalist World-System calls attention to Alvin Wolfe's hypothesis that we are witnessing, indeed living through, the greatest sociocultural revolution, the emergence of a supranational level of sociocultural integration (Wolfe, 1977, 1963; Riner, 1991a). Wolfe develops his idea in the context of the Steward (1955)–Service (1978) model of levels of sociocultural integration; that is, of band, tribe, chiefdom, simple state, empire, nation-state, and by pointing specifically to "the rapid expansion of international economic activity and especially the organization of production on a world scale through institutions of multinational enterprise" (Wolfe, 1963, p. 155). I described the emergence of one aspect of this system, focusing specifically on the pattern over time of interlocking directorates among the largest corporations and other large organizations that had adopted the corporate form (Riner, 1981).

Work on the timeline has reinforced my confidence in the cultural-materialist, evolutionary paradigm, but simultaneously has led to my recognition of a pattern of events that potentially challenges the sovereignty of an exclusively cultural-materialist paradigm in explaining the whole system. The events in this pattern are all innovations in how we humans have represented our experiences to ourselves. This is a very substantial part of our worldview, that field of personal information in which we represent and evaluate experience and make decisions. As the "rules of representation" change, so the "representation of reality" or experience changes, and the evaluations and decisions change accordingly. In other words, some kinds of innovations change how we represent experience or reality to ourselves. They act directly on and through worldview to change culture, our shared representations of experience, along with the attached values, thence changing our social and material systems. These kinds of innovations may or may not simultaneously effect change along the material vector through patterns of labor, division of labor, and so on. This sequence of perceptual revolutions includes the invention of writing, providing for the extrasomatic and potentially permanent storage of culture as part of the agricultural revolution; the introduction of phonetic writing in the Mediterranean; the introduction of perspective illustration, the printed book, and the globe in Europe at the climax of the mechanical revolution (1445–1492); and, most recent, "electronic" representation, culminating—currently—in the about-to-go-wholly-digital Internet. We are beginning to see already the implosion of the diversity of electronic technologies into a single system, itself an evolutionary process like we have never before witnessed in the history of technology, which has up to now been characterized by differentiation rather than integration. Aspects of these revolutions in representation were discussed by McLuhan (1962, 1964), but take on added significance considered in the timeline context.

I have a particular pedagogical concern in drawing out this picture so that I can show a graphic model of the past and present and of "history as system." This kind of model provides an antidote to the annecdotalist presentations of history, humanities, and all the "studies" topics that sprouted in the 1960s: black studies, Indian studies, Latino studies, women's studies, futures studies, and, nationwide, the public school endorsement of "social studies" to the exclusion of social science. The hallmark of anecdotal presentation of any topic is that it avoids dealing with the fact that history is caused, and so can be systematically understood, anticipated, and manipulated. To deny this has both intellectual and mundane political consequences, both of which bear importantly on the trajectory of futures studies over the next several years. Generally, the "studies" programs flourished as long as a charismatic leader was at the helm, but failed when they were forced to reply on discipline rather than authority for their leadership: Is this fate inevitable for futures studies?

CONCLUSIONS: PATTERNS MERGING

The issue of anecdotalism versus a causal model of history as system brings us full circle back to the question of the study of the future as a social science: Does it have what it takes? We have arrived on familiar ground, that ground I described graduate students stomping on in the 1960s, the common ground beneath these two issues: "What criteria define a kind of discipline, such as the social sciences?" I have examined a succession of five projects to illustrate how the study of the future has developed the characteristics of a potentially autonomous social scientific discipline.

In the case of Cultural Futures Research, anthropology, as a discipline and a professional community, illustrated for me a relationship that the study of the future has, or can have, with every one of the social sciences, a complementary exchange of epistemological, theoretical, and methodological ideas raising broad-scale themes and issues transcending the particulars of practitioners and of topical content. The future should be an integral part of the content in every one of the social sciences, and futures studies has enriched itself immeasurably as it has developed its disciplinary potentials. The study of the future has developed a much more sophisticated, self-critical, and multi- or interdisciplinary image of itself, most recently and masterfully articulated and integrated by Wendell Bell (1997a, 1997b). The CFR perspective on interdisciplinary relations also raises the practical, real-world, organizational question of whether the study of the future can have both disciplinary identity and integrity and a home of its own, have a potential home in every traditional social science department, or have both.

The case of CONTACT is another case of interdisciplinary collaboration around the theme of the future, only the collaborators are somewhat different in kind: the science fiction connection, placing stronger emphasis on the arts and literature and addressing generally a wider-ranging, longer-term perspective than other gatherings of futurists. The Bateson Projects demonstrate a new method in futures research, and provide a method for getting futures thinking into schools (and getting students into futures thinking) and onto the Web, as well as into strategic planning processes of all other kinds of organizations.

The Flagstaff Tomorrow project illustrates some of the kinds of roles that can bring the study of the future into practical applications—and professional careers—in communities and universities, and, by extension, all human organizations. It focuses attention on issues such as the metabolism of organizations—how people think about the future—and it raises new questions for research, the opportunity to do "predesigned," hypothesis-testing research in addition and supplement to problem-solving, applied research. This project also illustrates that human values and feelings are unavoidably a part of the content and context of futures studies.

The NAU SolSySim is a case where the teaching of futures and the uneven arrival of the future, in this instance the Internet, collided and mutually impacted each other, changing what was taught (curriculum), how it was taught (methodology), what was learned (content), and how learning by students and by process was assessed. This case also illustrates the kind of change in context and content that foreshadows the world, at least the campus-based part of the world, that the study of the future is emerging into, and how it can adapt to that situation.

The Timelines Project, as a method, offers a qualitative and structural approach to forecasting: a third polar alternative to ethnographic elicitation at one extreme, and quantitative, projective modeling at the other. It presents a statement of empirical data from history and the humanities in such a way that it can be seen as the result of a causal system which is potentially understandable and manipulable. As such it emphasizes that history does not "just happen" with priorities established by authority figures, as the anecdotal approach assumes. The scientific approach on the one hand assumes that "nature out there" is the final authority, while anecdotalism on the other attributes authority to certain individuals and organizations with far-reaching political consequences.

I have sought to illustrate in these examples that in futures studies of this kind we have a nascent social science, one that satisfies six criteria of disciplinary organization by having specified the following:

- An empirical unit of study: the world community, or the human community, wherever it be found, and any and all of the component organizations within that community.
- A central concept: "the future," comparable in its role to the concept of "personality" in psychology and "culture" in anthropology.
- A model of "human": holistic, empirical, and open ended.
- A primary method of data collection: a multimethod approach, including methods of both projection and the elicitation of images of the future, in which scenario-building is a central feature.
- A primary method of data analysis: prohibited from experimentation by moral, ethical, and political considerations, the study of the future will continue to develop primarily as a naturalistic and inductive science, relying on methods of controlled comparison to develop generalizations that can be tested by observation if not by experimentation.
- A primary strategy of explanation: a kind of evolutionary–whole-systems theory that incorporates the discoveries and insights of the day.

These criteria are supported by a developed and self-critical sense of its own origins, history, and organization, and a real-world organization of students of the future, ranging nearly seamlessly from practitioners to scholars, from praxis to theory, and providing for their own self-governance. These features together provide for an enterprise that can collect images of the future, clarify them, analyze them, interpret them, critique them, and provide feedback into decision-making processes at all levels, from individual to global. These increasingly well-considered images of the future introduced into decision-making processes will result in our "getting the kind of future that we do want."

NOTES

1. Undergraduate Preservice Teacher Education Program (UPSTEP), Lawrence Senesh, Director, University of Colorado, Boulder.

2. Four other events are significant in this timespan. Marcus Young Owl organized in 1978 the CSU–LA Conference on Extraterrestrial Anthropology. That same year the collected papers of the Futurology Commission sessions of the Ninth World Congress of the IUAES were published (Maruyama and Harkins, 1978). The World Future Society sponsored its first World Conference ("Thinking Globally, Acting Locally") in 1981. And in the late 1970s and early 1980s, Robert B. Textor (Textor, Bhansoon Ladavalya, and Prabudhanitsarn, 1984) codified his Ethnographic Futures Research method.

3. The members of the NAU Solar System Simulation Board of Virtual Consultants are professional scientists and educators in full-time employment, seven federal employees and eight civilians, who have been sufficiently interested in the simulation to volunteer their time and talent. Board membership has included Christopher McKay, Michael Simms, Carol Stoker, and Don M. Scott (NASA Ames), John Spencer and William Buckingham (Lowell Observatory), Jeff Kargel (USGS Planetary Data Center), Todd Satogata (Brookhaven National Labs), Steve Howe (Los Alamos National Labs), Steve Gilette (University of Nevada–Reno), Jerome Glenn (American Counsel, United Nations University), Joel Hagen (CSU–Stanislaus), Cathy Wittbrodt (Home.Net), Robert Neal Tyzzer III (San Diego State University), and Jennifer Clodius (SolSySim Administrator).

REFERENCES

Agrawal, B. C. (1983). Education and development through satellite communication: An anthropological study of site. *Cultural Futures Research, 7* (2), 7–21.

Bateson, G. (1972). *Steps to an ecology of mind: Collected essays in anthropology, psychiatry, evolution, and epistemology*. New York: Chandler.

Bateson, G. (1979). *Mind and nature: A necessary unity*. New York: E. P. Dutton.

Bateson, G., and Bateson, M. C. (1987). *Angels fear: Towards an epistemology of the sacred*. New York: Macmillan.

Bell, W. 1979a. *Foundations of future studies*. Vol 1. New Brunswick, NJ: Transaction.

Bell, W. 1979b. *Foundations of future studies*. Vol 2. New Brunswick, NJ: Transaction.

Bergesen, A. (1980). Cycles of formal colonial rule. In Terence K. Hopkins and Immanuel Wallerstein (Eds.), *Processes of the world system: Vol. 3 of Political Economy of the World-System Annuals*. Beverly Hills, CA: Sage.

Bergesen, A. (Ed.). (1981). The future in world-system perspective [Special issue]. *AnthroTech: A Journal of Speculative Anthropology, 6* (34).

Bergesen, A. (1982a). Economic crisis and merger movements: 1880's Britain and 1980's United States. In E. Friedman (Ed.), *Ascent and decline in the world-system: Vol. 5 of Political Economy of the World-System Annuals*. Beverly Hills, CA: Sage.

Bergesen, A. (1982b). Patterns of fatal violence during the 1980 Miami race riots. *Cultural Futures Research, 7* (1), 23–30.

Bergesen, A., and Schoenberg, R. (1980). Long waves of colonial expansion and contraction, 1415–1969. In A. Bergesen (Ed.), *Studies in the world-system* (pp. 231–277). New York: Academic Press/Harcourt Brace Jovanovich.

Boulding, K. (1961). *The image: Knowledge in life and society*. Ann Arbor: University of Michigan Press.

Brown, J. C., and Greenhood, W. (1983). Paternity, jokes and song: A possible evolutionary scenario for the origin of mind and language. *Cultural Futures Research, 8* (2), 7–53.

Denton, D. E. (1986). Images, plausibility and truth. *Futures Research Quarterly, 2* (2), 53–62.

Eldredge, S., Oliver, D., Sanders, J. H., and Yatim, D., with Textor, R. (1983). Silicon images: An assessment of the future cultural implications of the computer revolution. *Cultural Futures Research, 7* (3), 17–34.

El-Shall, M., and El-Alfy, S. (1983). The concept of future time in the definition of culture: An analysis and proposal. *Cultural Futures Research, 7* (3), 7–16.

English, J. A. (1983). Millenialism in the holistic health movement. *Cultural Futures Research, 8* (1), 29–43.

Erickson, S. W. (1985). The transition between eras. *Futurist, 19* (40), 40–44.

Flagstaff 2020. (1996a). *Flagstaff 2020: Community profile—Where are we now? Where are we going? What issues do we face?* Flagstaff, AZ: Flagstaff 2020/ Kwik Kopy.

Flagstaff 2020. (1996b). *Flagstaff 2020: Community values survey—Final report*. Flagstaff, AZ: Flagstaff 2020/Kwik Kopy.

Funaro, J. J. (Ed.). (1991). *Anthropology for the future: CONTACT—Cultures of the imagination*. Cabrillo, CA: Contact.

Funaro, J. J., and Riner, R. D. (Eds.). (1989). *Proceedings: CONTACT VII*. Capitola, CA: Contact.

Funaro, J. J., Riner, R. D., and McDaniels, G. (Eds.). (1985). *Proceedings: CONTACT III*. Capitols, CA: Contact.

Funaro, J. J., Riner, R. D., and McDaniels, G. (Eds.). (1987). *Proceedings: CONTACT IV*. Capitola, CA: Contact.

Funaro, J. J., Riner, R. D., and McDaniels, G. (Eds.). (1988). *Proceedings: CONTACT V*. Capitola, CA: Contact.

Funaro, J. J., Riner, R. D., and McDaniels, G. (Eds.). (1989). *Bateson projects CONTACT III & IV, 1985, 1987*. Capitola, CA: Contact.

Graham, A. K. (1973). The long wave. *Journal of Business Forecasting, 1* (5), 82.

Guilmet, G. (1982). Defining the resource utilization and the resource technologies of the low entropy society. *Cultural Futures Research, 6* (1), 17–45.

Guilmet, G. (1983). Impact of the computer revolution on human cognition. *Cultural Futures Research, 8* (1), 45–56.

Harris, M. (1979). *Cultural materialism: The struggle for a science of culture*. New York: Random House.

Hartman, W. E. (1982). A "what-if" world comes to life in Los Angeles. *Smithsonian, 12* (12), 86–95.

Head, M. S., and Lee, E. K. (Eds.). (1995). *Flagstaff Tomorrow IV: Flagstaff 2019*. Flagstaff, AZ: Reed D. Riner and Northern Arizona University.

Ketudat, S., and Textor, R. B. (1990). *The middle path for the future of Thailand: Technology in harmony with culture and environment*. Chiang Mai, Thailand: Faculty of Social Sciences, Chiang Mai University; Honolulu: Institute of Culture and Communication, East–West Center.

Kirk, R. C. (1983). Micro-electronics and change: New wave or tidal wave. *Cultural Futures Research, 7* (3), 35–42.

Klass, M. (1983). The little man who wasn't there: Transformations of the robot in science fiction. *Cultural Futures Research, 7* (3), 43–48.

Kroeber, A. L. (1948). *Anthropology: Race, language, culture, psychology and prehistory*. New York: Harcourt, Brace.

Kuhn, A. (1975). *Unified social science: A system-based introduction*. Homewood, IL: Dorsey Press.

Kurth-Shai, R. (1983). Unity in diversity: A cross-cultural approach to the study of global citizenship. *Cultural Futures Research, 7* (4), 27–45.

Lewellen, T. C. (1983). Telectronics in the Wallersteinian world capitalist system. *Cultural Futures Research, 8* (1), 9–19.

Loritz, S., McDaniels, G., and Riner, R. (Eds.). (1989). *Bateson Project: 2020 Vision*. Capitola, CA: Contact.

MacDaniel, W. E. (1983). Niagara University Space Settlement Studies Project. *Cultural Futures Research, 6* (2), 36–37.

Maruyama, M. (Ed.). (1970). *1970 American Anthropological Association Cultural Futurology Symposium: Pre-conference volume*. Minneapolis: Office for Applied Social Science and the Future, University of Minnesota.

Maruyama, M. (Ed.). (1971). *1971 American Anthropological Association Experimental Symposium on Cultural Futurology: Pre-conference volume*. Minneapolis: Office for Applied Social Science and the Future, University of Minnesota.

Maruyama, M. (Ed.). (1972). *1972 American Anthropological Association Experimental Symposium on Cultural Futuristics: Pre-conference volume*. Minneapolis: Office for Applied Social Science and the Future, University of Minnesota.

Maruyama, M. (Ed.). (1973). *1973 American Anthropological Association Experimental Symposium on Cultural Futuristics: Pre-conference volume*. Minneapolis: Office for Applied Social Science and the Future, University of Minnesota.

Maruyama, M., and Harkins, A. M. (Eds.). (1975). *Cultures beyond Earth: The role of anthropology in outer space*. New York: Random House/Vintage Books.

Maruyama, M., and Harkins, A. M. (Eds.). (1978). *Cultures of the future*. The Hague: Mouton.

McKeown, C. T. (1988). *The future of science: Young scientists at the International Institute for Applied Systems Analysis*. Unpublished doctoral dissertation. Northwestern University, Evanston, IL.

McKeown, C. T. (1990). The future of science: The human context of scientific expectations. *Futures, 22*, 46–56.

McLuhan, M. (1962). *The Gutenberg galaxy*. Toronto: University of Toronto Press.

McLuhan, M. (1964). *Understanding media*. New York: McGraw-Hill.

Miller, J. G. (1978). *Living systems*. New York: McGraw-Hill.

Modis, T. (1992). *Predictions: Society's telltale signature reveals the past and forecasts the future*. New York: Simon and Schuster.

Morozas, B. A., and Alger, L. (1983). Applications of remote sensing technology in monitoring rapid culture change. *Cultural Futures Research, 8* (1), 21–27.

Nash, R. J., and Withlam, R. G. (1983). Futures-oriented archaeology. *Cultural Futures Research, 7* (4), 9–16.

Neville, M. K., and Riner, R. D. (1993). The Mars course: A technological and societal simulation. In D. Hartman (Ed.), *Proceedings: Attracting and keeping the best.* Flagstaff, AZ: American Society of Engineering Education, Pacific Southwest Section.

Nordley, G. D. (Ed.). (1996). *Proceedings: CONTACT XII.* Capitola, CA: Contact.

Polak, F. (1961). *The image of the future* (2 vols.). New York: Oceana.

Preston, J. (1983). World civilization: An anthropological perspective. *Cultural Futures Research, 7* (4), 17–26.

Riner, R. D. (1981). The supranational network of boards of directors. *Current Anthropology, 22,* 167–172.

Riner, R. D. (1986, March). *Flagstaff 2010: Multi-Methods Futures Research.* Paper presented at the forty-sixth annual meeting of the Society for Applied Anthropology, Reno, NV.

Riner, R. D. (1987). Doing futures research: Anthropologically. *Futures, 19* (3), 311–328.

Riner, R. D. (1988). Two roads diverged in the yellow wood of incrementalism. *City and Society, 2* (1), 19–29.

Riner, R. D. (1991a). Anthropology about the future: Limits and potentials. *Human Organization, 50* (3), 297–311.

Riner, R. D. (1991b). From description to design: Ethnographic futures research methods applied in small town revitalization and economic development. *Futures Research Quarterly, 7* (1), 17–30.

Riner, R. D. (1995). Six years in Cyberia: Impacts of the new information technology on the Academy. In G. Nordley (Ed.), *Proceedings: CONTACT-XII.* Milpitas, CA: Contact.

Riner, R. D. (1996a, March). *A positive view of a long-range future.* Paper presented at the CONTACT-XIII annual conference, Milpitas, CA.

Riner, R. D. (1996b). Virtual ethics—Virtual reality. *Futures Research Quarterly, 12* (1), 57–70.

Riner, R. D., and Clodius, J. D. (1995). Simulating future histories: The NAU Solar System Simulation and Mars Settlement. *Anthropology & Education Quarterly, 26* (1), 95–104, with editorial commentary by E. Jacob, Teaching anthropology: An opportunity to apply our discipline and to research that practice, pp. 105–111.

Roy, B.B.K. (1982). Discussion on the future of selected institutions: Futurology Commission, IUAES. *Cultural Futures Research, 6* (1), 29–30.

Smith, R. W. (1982). Alternative futures in American education: Some fundamental changes and changes in fundamentals. *Cultural Futures Research, 7* (1), 31–45.

Solop, F. I., and Nelson, T. L. (Eds.). (1997). *Flagstaff 2020 Vision Validation Survey: Executive summary.* Flagstaff, AZ: Social Science Research Laboratory, Northern Arizona University.

Speakman, R. J. (Ed.). (1997). *CONTACT XI: Conversations from the forum.* Capitola, CA: Contact.

Speakman, R. J., and Sisson, E. (Eds.). (1996). *CONTACT XIII: Conversations from the forum*. Capitola, CA: Contact.

Stoddard, E. R. (1983). Subsistence societies—Earthside and space communities: The convergence of cultural anthropology and sociology. *Cultural Futures Research, 7* (2), 27–35.

Taylor, C. W. (1990). *Creating strategic visions*. Carlisle Barracks, PA: Strategic Studies Institute, U.S. Army War College.

Textor, R. (1980). *A handbook on ethnographic futures research* (3d ed., Version A). Stanford, CA: School of Education and Department of Anthropology, Stanford University.

Textor, R., Bhansoon Ladavalya, M. L., and Prabudhanitsarn, S. (1984). *Alternative sociocultural futures for Thailand: A pilot inquiry among academies*. Chiang Mai, Thailand: Faculty of the Social Sciences, Chiang Mai University.

Thompson, S. I. (1983). The L-5 society as a revitalization movement. *Cultural Futures Research, 7* (2), 17–20.

Tyzzer, R. N., III. (1983). Genetic engineering and cultural futures. *Cultural Futures Research, 7* (4), 47–50.

VanVogt, A. E. (1952). *Destination universe*. New York: New American Library and Signet Books.

Wallerstein, I. (1979). The rise and future demise of the world capitalist system: Concepts for comparative analysis. In I. Wallerstein, *The capitalist world economy* (pp. 1–36). Cambridge: Cambridge University Press.

Wallerstein, I. (1980). The future of the world economy. In T. K. Hopkins and I. Wallerstein (Eds.), *Processes in the world system* (pp. 167–180). Beverly Hills, CA: Sage.

Williamson, R. A., and Chandler, P. P. (1983). The promise of space and the difference it makes: The quest for the golden age. *Cultural Futures Research, 7* (2), 11–42.

Wolfe, A. (1963). The African mineral industry: Evolution of a supranational level of integration. *Social Problems, 11* (2), 153–164.

Wolfe, A. (1977). The supranational organization of production: An evolutionary perspective. *Current Anthropology, 18*, 615–636.

Wolfe, A. (1982). Sociocultural integration above the level of the state. *Cultural Futures Research, 7* (1), 9–22.

—————————————————————— 4

Past and Future

W. Warren Wagar

E. H. Carr (1964) said it well: "Good historians, I suspect, whether they think about it or not, have the future in their bones. Besides the question: Why? the historian also asks the question: Whither?" (p. 143). As Keith Jenkins (1995, pp. 58–59) notes, Carr's interest in the future probably stemmed more from his High Church Marxist faith in progress and human perfectibility than from his life-long career as a professional historian. Be this as it may, all one can say is that historians, even nonbelievers in progress, should have the future in their bones. They do not, by and large.

As one of the few practicing historians with credentials as a futurist, I encounter a fair amount of suspicion on the part of my colleagues, not to mention resentment at the large enrollments in my futures studies courses, which steal departmental resources (and, God forbid, students) from offerings in "real" history. Nevertheless, I persist because I believe in the laws of physics. There is, after all, no difference between past and future except the position in time of the observer. The space–time continuum is seamless, unidirectional, and unforgiving. Things happen in one way and no other, in a context as vast as the universe itself. They always have and they always will. A specialist in the study of the past should, therefore, be a specialist in the study of the future as well.

At one time, of course, in the golden era of "scientific" history that began with the followers of the great Leopold von Ranke in nineteenth-century Germany, it was imagined that the past could be literally recovered. Ranke's dictum that the task of the historian was "to show what actually happened" became the watchword of historians everywhere (Stern, 1972, p. 57). One settled down in the archives, read all the primary sources, connected the dots, and voila! The result was a well-documented narrative that reconstructed the past objectively and scientifically. True, the discovery of new evidence might compel rewriting the narrative at some later time—nothing should be chiseled in stone—but the method itself was more or less foolproof. In 1935 the American historian Theodore Clarke Smith referred reverentially to Rankean methodology as "that noble dream" and deplored all efforts by skeptics and polemicists such as Charles Beard to shatter it (Novick, 1988, p. 259). Beard and his confederate from Cornell, Carl Becker, did manage to shake the faith of some professionals for a few years, but at least until the early 1970s it remained essentially intact. The past was a Humpty Dumpty that could, indeed, be put back together again by piecing together its evidentiary traces.

It followed that the future was terra incognita. By definition, the future had produced no primary sources. There were no archives to ransack. So the future could not be studied, at least not by professional historians.

Then came the postmodernist revolution, with its debunking of the definitive and its deconstruction of the document. Michel Foucault, Michel de Certeau, and many others unmasked a great array of previously unquestioned assumptions about the past as read by historians. Hayden White (1973), in his epochal text *Metahistory* and several other works, dismantled the whole project of objective history. Historians, he said, like novelists, were storytellers. They made rather than found their stories. Jenkins sums up the postmodern understanding of historiography as "a verbal artifact, a narrative prose discourse . . . constructed by present-minded, ideologically positioned workers . . . operating at various levels of reflexivity." The work they do "can be seen as taking place entirely in the present." The cogency of that work, moreover, "can be admitted without the past per se ever entering into it—except rhetorically" (pp. 178–179). In short, historians infected by postmodernist theory acknowledge that what they do is create texts about texts, which can be read in infinitely different ways but can in no sense recover or reconstitute the real past. The real past happened, but is now gone, every nanosecond of it. Hence, the past is just as inaccessible as the future.

I had more or less figured all this out for myself long before I knew what a postmodernist theory was, with the help of Beard and Becker, the Austro-English logical positivists, the existentialists, and such major forerunners of postmodernism as Friedrich Nietzsche and Benedetto Croce. But the postmodernists (whose abominable obscurantist jargon I dislike as much as any of their reactionary critics) have surely sharpened my thinking on the issues at stake. More to the point, they have sold a good part of their message to a good part of the current crop of professional historians. All that remains is for these newly enlightened historians to grasp that the future now belongs as much—and as little—to them as the past.

From the Rankean perspective, postmodernism seems to divest historians of the possibility of doing anything worthwhile at all. If historians cannot reconstruct the past, what use are they? If documents cannot restore the dead to life, why read them? The answer, of course, is that we here and now are alive, and we are curious about the past, and we enjoy discourses about the past. The tropes and plots and other devices we employ to engage the past may not give us the past, but they help us define ourselves and others in uniquely human ways. Discourses that engage the past comprehensively and inquiringly engage our interest. We need them. We need historians, just as we need the faculty of memory. As long as we do not reify and deify the discourses we produce, they can help us live fuller and perhaps even wiser lives.

But all this is just as true of the future. We here and now are alive, and we are curious about the future, and we enjoy discourses about the future. Remember, the future is the same as the past, not in the sense that history repeats itself, but in the sense that the space–time continuum is seamless. The future does not branch off in many directions at some critical juncture we call the present. There will be only one future, one future for humankind, for the Earth, for the galaxy, for the universe, just as there was only one past, unscrolling moment by moment along an ever-moving line of time. Scholars who are in the habit of telling stories about the past are especially well positioned to tell stories about the future. They cannot predict the future, any more than they can recover the past. Their stories of the past tell us bits and pieces of what might have happened, as we today are empowered and conditioned to construe it. Their stories of the future tell us bits and pieces of what might still happen, but not what did happen and what will happen. The mood of the verb here is all important. Both history and futures studies are not, speaking strictly, cognitive discourses.

I cannot, however, stop there. Historiography has much more to offer futures studies than its deep sense of movement in time and its understanding of the relative and contingent nature of human knowing. The old classic objective historiography was blind to two other realities about the human condition, what I might call the vertical and the horizontal dimensions of the totality of experience. Rankeans wrote mostly political history, and not just any political history, but the political history of the states of Europe and North America. In the twentieth century we were able to move on from this narrow base of operations to the whole experience of the human race. From the New History of James Harvey Robinson and the History as Synthesis of Henri Berr through the Annales school in France, the rise of world history in the work of William H. McNeill and many others, the new social history, the new intellectual and economic and gender history, all the way to the world-system theory of Immanuel Wallerstein and his colleagues, wave after wave of "new" histories have transformed the nature of the historian's task almost beyond recognition. Politics is no longer foregrounded. Europe is no longer foregrounded. Nothing at all is foregrounded, at least by the profession as a whole. In Peter Novick's (1988) phrases, every group is now its own historian, the center does not hold, and there is no king in Israel (titles of chs. 14–16). Chaos appears to reign, but it is a fertile chaos.

I call the realities addressed by these waves of change both the vertical and the horizontal dimensions of totality. That is, the awareness that politics is not the sum and essence of human life opens up to us the possibility of seeing all the activities of Homo sapiens as relevant to the historian and, for good measure, thickly intertwined. This is the vertical dimension of human reality: We are not just political animals, but thinking reeds, players in markets, children and parents, class strugglers, sexual predators, all this and much more, at one and the same time.

The horizontal dimension, of course, runs the width and circumference of the planet. As Andre Gunder Frank has argued, all the continents except the American have flourished in continuous interaction for at least 5,000 years (Frank and Gills, 1995). In the past 500 years the American continents have been drawn into the ecumene as well, and there has arisen what Wallerstein (1974–1989) calls the "modern world-system," a single global capitalist economy existing side by side with a network of sovereign states and a plurality of cultures. To follow Benjamin Barber (1995), a ding-dong battle is now in progress between that same monolithic economy and that same politicocultural diversity, or, as he puts it, between "McWorld" and "Jihad." Each is a formidable contender, and if we knew which (if either) would ultimately prevail, and how, we would probably know what is most important to know about the twenty-first century.

My point is simply that historians today are concerned, as a profession, with all kinds of events in all parts of the world at all times in the past, right up the last second. Futurists must similarly be concerned with all kinds of events in all parts of the world at all times in the future, from the next second forward. Like the past, the future will consist of people in all their complexity and many-sidedness interacting with other people in all of theirs on a planetary scale along a single continuous line of time. For the sake of convenience we may write about the future of the United States or the future of women or the future of biotechnology, but in fact our highest and ultimate subject matter is the future of humankind on (and beyond) Earth. In the final analysis, no smaller subject will do. Does anyone seriously imagine that discourse about the future of the United States, for example, can be cogent without considering the future of China, and Russia, and Latin America, and all the rest? Can women's future be chemically separated from the future of men? Can we explore the future of biotechnology without exploring the future of biology and technology, and science in general, and the economy that sustains scientific inquiry, and the systems of governance that regulate economies, and so forth and so on until we have taken everything human into account? I think not.

In short, the study of the future is, for me, the history of the future, and for the past twenty-five years I have tried with modest success to import my ideas into the classroom at Binghamton University. More recently I have also written two books that illustrate and expand on these ideas, books that I inflict (with due but not excessive reluctance) on my students (Wagar, 1991, 1992).

The first of these courses, introduced in 1974, is entitled simply "History of the Future." I have taught it every year but one since then. In its various editions it has enrolled more than 6,000 undergraduate students. The second, introduced in 1983, was first given as "World War III" and in these post–Cold War days is known as "War: Past and Future." Offered in most years, it has attracted some 2,600 students. The third, which dates from 1978 but is scheduled less frequently, is my senior research seminar, "Alternative Futures," an opportunity for alumni of the other courses to study a futures topic of their choice in depth. I have recounted my experience with these courses in my recent article, "Teaching the Future: A Memoir" (Wagar, 1996).

One aspect of my teaching not seriously addressed in that article, however, is the methodology of futures inquiry that I stress in the classroom. In what follows here I shall try to repair the omission, showing the link between my concept of futures studies and my pedagogical praxis.

Let me be quite direct. I entertain no hope, no hope at all, that futures studies can become another member of the family of the so-called social sciences. I have great respect for the brave efforts of Wendell Bell (1997) to enlist futures studies in that family, but I fear he is just wrong. His courage reminds me of the courage of Don Quixote: noble, pure, but unavailing. For all the reasons and considerations I have already suggested, we cannot know the future. It is not here (yet). Like the past, which is not here (anymore), it eludes our grasp. We can talk about it, play with it, speculate, muse, build theories and models, assemble quantitative data that may bear upon it, but we do not have knowledge of the future.

By the same token, we can imagine any number of alternative pasts, tell our story a thousand different ways, but never be able to reconstruct the past as it "actually happened." Even if every soul who ever lived had left a documentary record of everything he or she ever did or said or thought, which no one ever has or could have, we should still not be able to know the past as a thing in itself. The future is much the same, except that our documentation is skimpier. There is documentation, of course, because everything that will happen will undoubtedly be shaped to some degree by what has already happened, which can be engaged by scholars in the form of still-existing documentary and artifactual evidence, what White (1973) calls "traces." But the problem of recovery and the problem of anticipation are at heart the same problem. We cannot know, strictly speaking, what happened, or how or why; we cannot know, strictly speaking, what will happen, or why or how.

The pedagogical corollary of this assumption about the limits of futures inquiry is that no teacher should attempt to predict the future in the classroom or encourage students to predict the future. All the methods called upon by futurists reduce, in my judgment, to just one: the construction of multiple scenarios, whether by computer models or by hunches, by trend extrapolation or by historical analogies, by cyclical theory of history or by world-system theory, whatever we like, but always the construction of multiple scenarios. Furthermore, such scenarios become more cogent (not more true) the broader their scale in space and time, in both the vertical and the horizontal dimension. So what I attempt to provide in my classroom, and what I train my students to invent for themselves, are alternative images of plausible world futures. The more, the merrier. The more holistic, the wiser.

Let me illustrate. In "History of the Future" we begin by sorting the anticipations of futurists into three rough categories, depending on their ideological underpinnings. The first is what I call the "technoliberal" paradigm, encompassing both so-called liberal and so-called conservative futurists who put their faith in market economics, representative democracy, and the wizardry of high tech. The second is the "radical" or "Marxist" paradigm, committed to democratic socialism. The third is the "countercultural" paradigm, espoused by thinkers who reject both capitalism and socialism in favor of a new global culture that will assign the highest priority to community self-governance, attunement with nature, and a sustainable economy.

My reason for stressing these normative foundations is my belief that all futurists, even Wendell Bell, approach the future with ideological baggage in hand. We are never just scientists exploring future prospects, as, for example, an entomologist might peer into an ant hill. I am myself, among other things, a Marxist. Not a Marxist like my Canadian friend Bryan Palmer (1990), who inveighs against the "descent into [postmodernist] discourse" on behalf of a closely reasoned historical materialism, but simply someone who finds Marxist explanations cogent, without for a moment crediting their pretensions to comprise a "science." At any rate, there are surely Marxist futurists. There are also capitalist futurists and futurists who adhere to one or another rapturous countercultural ideology. Beyond these three camps, there are also the fundamentalist Christian and Muslim futurists, the technocratic futurists, and so on, but in my course we focus on just the three already identified. Throughout, I challenge my students to detect the ideological inspirations informing every text they read and every lecture they hear from the podium.

But ideology is not everything. I also try to show how people, even of similar persuasions, can arrive at wildly different images of the future depending on what evidence they choose to consider and how they assess its weight. Different theories and selected bodies of evidence yield different futures. In most of my lectures—although I make no secret of my personal predilections and biases—I offer students, with as much conviction as I can muster, multiple scenarios of the global future. The point is not for students to spot the scenario that is "right," but to stimulate dialogical play, to foster both irony and openness to unforeseeable twists and turns.

For just one example, in my lecture on the future of women and the family, I narrate three scenarios: the "extrapolation" model, in which current global trends proceed with few interruptions to a world in which the playing field for men and women is level and Jessie Bernard's hope for "shared-role" marriages prevails; the "beyond-the-cash-nexus" model, where a rich variety of connubial options are available, accommodating both straights and gays; and the "backlash" scenario, where socioeconomic and environmental stringencies force a return to the patriarchal model of family life, imagined by Margaret Atwood (1986) in her novel, *The Handmaid's Tale*, and in Volker Schlondorf's eponymous movie, which has become a regular part of my film series for the course. I do not ask or wish my students to swallow any of these scenarios hook, line, and sinker, but I hope they are provoked to think and make choices for themselves.

The books for the course are also scenarios or can be taught as such. I like to make extensive use of novels, which, as White (1973) would remind us, are put together very much like the narratives of historians. We read Ernest Callenbach's (1990) *Ecotopia* as a scenario of the best imaginable future from the perspective of a countercultural futurist, and Aldous Huxley's (1946) *Brave New World* as a scenario of the worst imaginable future from a similar perspective. Other novels of the future I have used through the years include Walter M. Miller's (1959) *A Canticle for Leibowitz*, John Brunner's (1968) *Stand on Zanzibar*, and Stanislaw Lem's (1974) *The Futurological Congress*. Whenever possible, the nonfiction texts selected supply contrasting readings of the same issues: for example, a liberal environmentalist preaching sustainability (such as Lester Brown or Paul Kennedy) versus an open-throttle advocate of economic growth (such as Herman Kahn or Julian Simon). My own book, *A Short History of the Future* (1992), contains three scenarios, one assuming the triumph of Barber's (1995) *McWorld*, one exploring the vicissitudes of a socialist world commonwealth formed in the aftermath of thermonuclear Armageddon, and one imagining a world consisting of thousands of self-governing intentional communities.

At examination time, my teaching assistants, who do most of the grading, are encouraged to keep their minds open and their ideological preferences suspended. We owe all our students a fair hearing. In the 1997 edition of my course, when we solicited student opinion near the end of the semester, one student wrote, and I quote verbatim, "Prof. Wagar's effort to abstain from dominating the lectures with his own political ideals is greatly appreciated. Currently I have another prof who is so caught up with his own viewpoint that he obscures and distorts all texts that we read to fit his own agenda. Thanks, Prof. Wagar, for being a teacher and not an ideological dictator."

I have never received a more welcome comment in twenty-five years of teaching the future. The great lesson of postmodernity is humility. As I make abundantly clear in *A Short History of the Future*, I could wish nothing better for my species than the eventual empowerment of a democratic socialist world republic. But I do not have the authority to impose this vision on my students. I do not know that such a republic is even possible or that it would create the kind of civilization I devoutly desire. Who could know? For we know in part, and we prophesy in part, and we see through a glass, darkly.

REFERENCES

Atwood, M. (1986). *The handmaid's tale*. Boston: Houghton Mifflin.

Barber, B. R. (1995). *Jihad versus McWorld*. New York: Times Books.

Bell, W. (1997). *Foundations of futures studies* (2 vols.). New Brunswick, NJ: Transaction.

Brunner, J. (1968). *Stand on Zanzibar*. New York: Ballantine.

Callenbach, E. (1990). *Ecotopia*. New York: Bantam.

Carr, E. H. (1964). *What is history?* New York: Knopf.

Frank, A. G., and Gills, B. K. (Eds.). (1995). *The world system: Five hundred years or five thousand?* London: Routledge.

Huxley, A. (1946). *Brave new world*. New York: Harper. (Original work published 1932.)

Jenkins, K. (1995). *On "what is history?" from Carr and Elton to Rorty and White*. London: Routledge.

Lem, S. (1974). *The futurological congress*. New York: Seabury.

Miller, W. M., Jr. (1959). *A canticle for Leibowitz*. Philadelphia: Lippincott.

Novick, P. (1988). *That noble dream: The "objectivity" question and the American historical profession*. Cambridge: Cambridge University Press.

Palmer, B. D. (1990). *Descent into discourse: The reification of language and the writing of social history*. Philadelphia: Temple University Press.

Stern, F. (Ed.). (1972). *The varieties of history from Voltaire to the present* (2d ed.). New York: Meridian Books.

Wagar, W. W. (1991). *The next three futures: Paradigms of things to come*. New York: Praeger.

Wagar, W. W. (1992). *A short history of the future* (2d ed.). Chicago: University of Chicago Press.

Wagar, W. W. (1996). Teaching the future: A memoir. In Howard F. Didsbury, Jr. (Ed.), *Futurevision: Ideas, insights, and strategies* (pp. 78–87). Bethesda, MD: World Future Society.

Wallerstein, I. (1974–1989). *The modern world-system* (3 vols.). New York: Academic Press.

White, H. (1973). *Metahistory: The historical imagination in 19th century Europe*. Baltimore: Johns Hopkins University Press.

5

Futures Studies as an Intellectual and Applied Discipline

Richard A. Slaughter

Nearly a quarter of a century ago the CIBA Foundation (1975) published a book called *The Future as an Academic Discipline*. I remember approaching the book with eager anticipation, then recoiling in disappointment as I read the turgid prose, the lacklustre analysis. If, at that time, the title had been posed as a question, then the answer would have been "no." But now, nearly twenty-five years later, the answer is a definite "yes": Futures studies has come of age during this time. This chapter begins by tracing some of the reasons for that transition. My own journey into FS has paralleled its emergence from obscurity to a growing preeminence on the world scene. The chapter continues with a review of how I taught Critical Futures Studies in three universities before leaving academia to work as a full-time, independent futurist. Finally, it considers some of the significant links between the intellectual foundations of FS and an increasing number of highly significant practical applications in organisations of all kinds.

To most people "the future" is an abstraction, an empty box. Standing unconsciously within an empiricist frame, even highly educated people will ask questions like, "If it doesn't exist, how can you study it?" or "Can futurists predict the future?" Such questions are more revealing of the questioner than of FS because they display typical unexamined assumptions. The fact is that, yes, the future does exist: It is a profoundly vital component of the present (however defined) or, more fundamentally, a principle of present action or present being (Slaughter, 1996d). But, no, the future cannot be predicted. It can be understood, explored, mapped, and created, but not predicted. This is because human beings are agents of history and their freedom of action means that the future cannot, in principle, ever be predetermined.

It is easy to show in theory, practice, and also experientially that this domain that we call the future is not an abstraction, not an empty box, and not without a host of immediate implications and applications across the board. The future is important to people because it serves to support and enable the entire spectrum of their hopes and fears, their plans, purposes, goals, and intentions. Remove these and you don't have people, you have robots. The future is important to organizations because if they don't take it into account, the powerful forces it contains will undermine them and consign them to history. The future is important to human cultures and societies because the success of the industrial period has progressively undermined the capacity of the planet to support life and thrown up historically new forces and dilemmas that cannot be resolved by fatalistic "wait and see" responses. The future is important to education because it provides principles and practices that are largely absent from present systems and structures but that hold out numerous options for development and renewal. So, far from being a fad, a fallacy, or merely a lowly perspective, FS actually represents a paradigmatic turning point in the production and use of knowledge. It provides the tools for human beings to grasp their historical predicament, respond to it, and move on to new stages of civilized life. In other words, it is a sine qua non of a livable future. While not everyone will need to become an official paid-up futurist, everyone does need, and will need, the understandings, skills, and competencies that emerge from it.

Properly understood, FS provides an evolving view of the "big picture" from a number of viewpoints and at a number of levels of analysis. In my opinion, mastering the forward view—that is, creating it, sustaining it, and using it effectively—is the single most critical goal that any organization can aim for. It may come as a surprise to some, but FS is grounded in ways that make it far stronger, more useful, and more durable than is yet widely realized. As such, it makes perfect sense to regard it as an emerging discipline. The next quarter century will see it permeate all relevant fields and stimulate the development of a huge range of emerging futures professions.

STARTING POINTS

My most early influence was reading science fiction. I saw very clearly that the future was not an empty space. Many futures were possible; however, most of those I encountered in fiction were pretty bleak. So as a teenager I found myself asking, "Why does the future look so bad?"

That question led me to search more widely. When I was training to be a teacher (1965–1968) I came across Edmund Leach's (1968) book *A Runaway World*. It was the first nonfiction futures-related book I had ever read. It made clear that a whole layer of reality was missing from the curriculum. Soon after that I went to live and work in Bermuda. I came to see that this tiny country had simply drifted into its future, which was looking increasingly bleak. Here I wrote (and photographed) my first book, *Birds in Bermuda* (Slaughter, 1975). It allowed me to explore the way that the natural features of the islands were being overwhelmed by the postwar development process. Behind the postcard tourist image was a very different story, one of materialism, commercial greed, and short-term thinking. I felt that this was not a viable model.

So when I left in 1975 I entered the University of Lancaster through an "independent studies" program, which allowed me to design two-thirds of my bachelor's degree. The result was a multidissertation program called "Science, Technology and the Human Future," which was completed in 1978, and for which I received First Class Honors. This gave me the chance to begin to explore the futures literature. From there I went on to do a Ph.D., which set out the foundations of critical futures study and explored some of the rich links between futures and education. During this time I found work by Lewis Mumford, Fritz Schumacher, Hazel Henderson, Robert Jungk, and many, many others illuminating. But the real turning point was the so-called First Global Conference on the Future in Toronto in 1980. It was here that I first met some of the people whose work I had been reading, and also teachers with direct practical experience of teaching futures in schools and universities. Both gave me the confidence to continue and finish my Ph.D.

In summary, the key influences were as follows. First, outrage at the highly negative futures portrayed in science fiction. Second, a dawning awareness that key features of the social and global context were being overlooked by mainstream education, media, politics, and so on. Third, the intense experience of living in a social laboratory (Bermuda) that demonstrated some of the costs of ignoring the future. Finally, immersing myself in the futures literature, going to many meetings, and eventually "joining in the conversation" with colleagues around the world. Since that time, critical futures study has proved to be a well of inspiration. Each year is a delight and a surprise, as new insights emerge and new challenges and opportunities arise.

THE NATURE OF CRITICAL FUTURES WORK

My main concern is to participate in and help create an advanced futures discourse. In my view it is this above all else that nourishes the raw human capacity for foresight. Beyond this, futures methods and tools, and what I call "institutions of foresight," constitute "layers of capability" that enable a societywide foresight capacity. Foresight is highly relevant to education, but it is also intimately related to social learning. So I use the concepts, some methods, tools, literature, and close contacts with colleagues, to progressively develop my understanding of the near-future context: the "future landscape." The insights so gained provide many vital insights into our times, giving us new choices and a measure of what Habermas (1971) calls "steering capacity."

I do not see the future as an abstraction, but as a multifaceted reality that affects human life and culture in many powerful ways. I also believe that the Western industrial worldview is profoundly defective. Hence, I use a multileveled approach. At one level, I consider empirical trends; at another, laws, regulations, and procedures in society; finally, at a deeper level, I consider epistemology, meaning, and paradigm commitments. I don't think we can come to grips with our reality without some kind of "layered causal analysis."[1] A clear diagnosis emerges that helps us discern a basis for a less catastrophe-prone civilization. A foresight (or far-sighted) culture, based on certain ethical and humanistic foundations, would be a huge step in the right direction. It irritates me to see the instrumentalities of science and technology constantly overidentified with the future.

In summary, I work with an evolving diagnosis of what has gone wrong in Western culture and an evolving view of what this means for the future. My output is in the forms suggested here: lectures, seminars, papers, books, and so on. In order that I may teach I always attend to my own learning. With a focus on understanding, discourse, paradigms, and frameworks of meaning, I have little use for quantitative methods. However, I will happily use the output of such methods (e.g., forecasts). For the reasons given, a "critical futurist" regards critique as a central methodology. The essential point is "probing beneath the surface" (of social reality), or "looking more deeply." So my focus is on understanding our historical predicament, renegotiating cultural commitments, empowering myself and others to induce this overheated culture to change course away from the "overshoot and collapse" mode it has been in for a long time. The essential goal of futures study is to help us make the transition from one type of culture to another while there is still time to do so.

DRIVERS OF CHANGE, POINT OF INFLUENCE

My list of key drivers of change include technical dynamism coupled with scientism, materialism, commercial exploitation (profit-driven organizations such as the transnationals, banks, etc.), nationalism (the military–industrial complex), colonialism, greed, short-term thinking, ego, fear of death, and defects in the Western industrial worldview, particularly short-term thinking and the hegemony of instrumental rationality.

Western industrial culture certainly contains some desirable features (e.g., ideals of social justice, technical skill, high material standards of living), but it is fundamentally antilife, having lost its collective "soul" during the industrialization process. By this I mean it read out of its world picture key areas such as myth, ritual, connectedness, spirituality, and the numinous. This diagnosis, far from being merely "negative," helps us to locate the grounds of the global problematique in what I call the "metaproblem." In brief, a defective worldview is constantly creating the social world and progressively destroying the natural one. Social movements and some non-governmental organizations (NGOs) have to some extent moderated the dynamic of global deterioration, but far, far more needs to be done.

The trends I want to encourage include all those social innovations that break away from the industrial fantasy and reconnect us to each other and the earth. This means revaluing native cultures, ending exploitation, and embracing "the other." I also want to encourage people to feel symbolically powerful; that is, capable of redefining their reality and actively responding to their own deeper needs and those of their children and future generations. I therefore want to see the growth of foresight and wisdom in all the world's cultures. I want to see them implemented in every organization and built up to the social and global levels. I also want to see morality and ethics become much more widely understood and applied. Otherwise I believe that technology or ecocatastrophe will overrun us, much as science fiction writers have depicted.

Unlike some of my futurist colleagues, I don't believe that aliens will visit us or that the human race is merely a transitional species that should make way for so-called intelligent machines. Rather, it is a species capable of endless self-transformation, vertical (qualitative) growth, and development. As a humanistic and transpersonal futurist, I will always regard science and technology as derivative and secondary. I look for a growing awareness of the different layers of being (in people and the world) and the progressive development of cultures toward shared transpersonal ends. The two writers I have found most helpful in this key area are Ken Wilber (1981) and Duane Elgin (1993).

INTELLECTUAL FOUNDATIONS OF (CRITICAL) FUTURES STUDIES

The term "critical" is often misunderstood, particularly in the United States. However, it does not simply mean "to criticize." Nor does it signify a negative or derivative stance. It is not threatening and should not be construed as such. Rather, it signifies a range of methods and tools through which we may look "beneath the surface" of social reality in order to realize the full potential of futures work (Slaughter, 1989). Critical futures study does recognize the partiality of traditions, cognitive frameworks, and ways of knowing. It is therefore possible to problematize aspects of the existing social and economic order and to explore some of their contradictions. Why is this a constructive enterprise?

An unproblematic status quo is one that is accepted without question; one that embodies certain quasitranscendental goals that are to be progressively realized now and in the future. Such goals could include "health, wealth and prosperity for all humankind." Others might be "racial equality," "steady growth of GNP," and "peaceful international relations." These all sound highly attractive, but given the real substantive character of ideologies, assumptions, systems of exploitation, repression, and destruction now in place, they may not be realizable. Like the advertisements for women's fashions or impossibly perfect holidays, they have little substance.

I take the view that regardless of its very many impressive technical achievements, late industrial culture is the most rapacious, self-centered, humanly and environmentally destructive system yet seen upon the Earth. It presides over numerous wars, the repressive exploitation of many Third World populations (and their underprivileged equivalents in Western countries), and the implacable destruction of the world's life-support systems. Given this context, conventional sanguine views of the future have a flat, unconvincing, and, indeed, blatantly spurious quality. The standard Western worldview, far from leading to universal peace and prosperity, actually leads directly toward the abyss. It holds out no possibility whatsoever of sustainable human futures. Hence, in the extraordinary conditions of the late twentieth century, business-as-usual outlooks are positively dangerous. These uncomfortable facts tend to be missed by the conventional discourses of dominant social institutions, which, on the whole, are locked into short-term thinking and remain preoccupied with industrial-era priorities such as those of status, power, and control.

Hence, there is value in looking in depth at this culture and asking some penetrating questions. This is exactly what critical futures study attempts to do. Calling the bluff of anodyne views of futures (or overly negative ones) helps us to isolate aspects of our present culture and way of life that urgently require critical attention. No one should doubt that this is a responsible and constructive task.

Let me be clear: If it were not possible to interrogate the received wisdom of industrialized cultures, then we would most certainly be set on an irreversible path toward global catastrophe. If we were not able to understand our situation and act with informed foresight to avert the worst dangers, we would be committed to social learning by the crudest of experiences. We would have to experience catastrophe in order to prevent it. This is clearly unacceptable. The price of crisis learning becomes too great in an over-stressed and endangered world (Milbrath, 1989). Critical futures study therefore aligns with other critical and interpretive initiatives to explore the possibility of productive discourse about the character, assumptions, and likely directions embedded within the dominant culture, as well as some laying beyond it (Macy, 1991). The following are some key propositions of this approach:

1. Discourse is not neutral. It is grounded in particular traditions and speech communities that cannot, by definition, be "objective." Intersubjectivity is universal but only partly rational.

2. It is helpful to adopt a reflexive posture; that is, one in which the observer does not simply observe (speak, act, etc.), but is aware of the active, shaping character of these processes.

3. A presumption is made in favor of what Habermas (1971) called "the human emancipatory interest," or, simply, the fundamental interest of all persons in freedom, self-constitution, and unconstrained conditions of life.

4. It is suggested that "progress" is no longer a term that can be used without irony. It has much less to do with tools, techniques, and the external conditions of life than with understanding the breakdown of the "industrial" synthesis at the epistemological level and recovering the ability to discern a basis for qualitatively different futures.

5. Technologies are not regarded merely as neutral tools but as cultural processes embodying specific ideological and social interests. The most notable features of technologies are often invisible and intangible (which is why they are overlooked by empiricist approaches).

6. Stories are regarded as powerful explanatory devices. They are not "mere fiction," because they model human reality in novel and useful ways. They can therefore be used to explore some aspects of human futures in ways not accessible to reason, analysis, or the techniques of futures research (such as forecasting).

7. There is an explicit focus on the negotiation of meanings (such as work, leisure, defense, health, etc.). This gives access to some of the most important shaping processes involved in social and cultural change, including those associated with cultural editing.[2]

The origins of these propositions lie in a number of related fields. They include the following:

1. The interpretative perspective, itself emerging from critical practice, hermeneutics, the analysis of discourse, and semiotics.

2. The sociology of science and technology; science as a social product, technology as cultural text.

3. The critical theory of society; cognitive interests, Habermas's theory of communicative action, and the like, and Foucault's analysis of power.

4. Speculative writing; stories that comment with awareness on past, present, and a wide range of futures.

5. Environmental scanning and strategic planning; techniques of futures research applied in organizations.

To this account should be added a number of others. For example, a masterly paper by Jay Ogilvy (1996) called "Futures Studies and the Human Sciences: The Case for Normative Scenarios" elaborates the perspective upon which this account is based. He demonstrates with great skill and clarity how FS should not be "knocking on the door" seeking academic approval, so much as the fulfillment and culmination of certain key developments across the entire humanities. A different approach is provided by Wendell Bell (1997) in his two-volume opus, *Foundations of Futures Studies*. Here he sets out a detailed account of the origins and purposes of FS, and its assumptions, methods, and a epistemology based on "critical realism." For Bell, FS is a social science with a great deal to offer. Volume 2 considers questions of values and the search for the "good society." Overall, it is a welcome contribution to the grounding of FS in durable theories, perspectives, and practices.

These cultural and symbolic resources provide futures study and research with the kind of foundations necessary for any viable discipline. In turn, they contribute to an advanced futures discourse and support a number of powerful metatheoretical and applied tools.

THE KNOWLEDGE BASE OF FUTURES STUDIES (KBFS)

The KBFS emerged in response to a felt need for a more widely shared account of what the field actually is and how the different parts of it reinforce each other. A special issue of the journal *Futures* in 1993 set out a provisional model and provided a number of commentaries on various aspects of FS (Slaughter, 1993a). The issue received wide support and was subsequently developed into a substantive series of books (Slaughter, 1996b). The first three volumes contain work by some fifty authors from around the world. The significance of the KBFS is that, first, we now have a collective statement about what the core elements of FS are. Second, and unlike earlier formulations, this account is not merely "Western." Rather, it includes the work of people from many different cultures, east and west, north and south. Third, it incorporates notions of dissent and critique, the latter being seen both as a core methodology and as a part of the field's own provision for quality control.

The present model is based on the following elements. These subheadings are those from the subsections of the three existing KBFS books:

Volume 1: Foundations

      Part 1: Origins

      Part 2: Futures concepts and metaphors

      Part 3: The Futures literature

      Part 4: The foundations of Futures Studies

Volume 2: Organizations, Practices, Products

    Part 1: Futures organizations

    Part 2: Futures methods and tools

    Part 3: Images and imaging processes

    Part 4: Social innovations and futures

Volume 3: Directions and Outlooks

    Part 1: New directions in futures thinking

    Part 2: The outlook for the new millennium

    Part 3: The long view

Volumes 1 and 2 provide a systematic overview of core elements of FS, elements that enhance and reinforce each other. Volume 3 samples some of the high-quality interpretative knowledge that emerges from FS. It is significant for the role of FS within the wider community that such knowledge arguably cannot be derived from any other source. However, it is essential to note that the KBFS is not "foundational" in the sense of constituting a set of monolithic, unchanging certainties. Rather, it will develop and change over time as a result of at least four processes:

- Critique—the elimination of redundant aspects.
- Innovation—the incorporation of new ideas, methodologies, and so on.
- New voices—the emergence and participation of those from non-Western contexts.
- Synthesis—new developments based on combinations of new and older elements (Slaughter, 1996c).

Hence, what is considered "foundational" now will not be the same as that in times to come. Nevertheless, the existence of this knowledge base provides a powerful stimulus to the further development and application of FS as a discipline in many fields, not the least of which is education. Here there are a number of direct applications, which include the following. The KBFS provides

- an authoritative reference source.
- a source of methods, ideas, and frameworks of inquiry.
- a foundation for new futures modules, units, and courses.
- a basis for in-service and professional development work.

The availability of these and the other resources mentioned clearly signal the emergence of FS as a maturing field of inquiry and action.

CRITICAL FUTURES STUDIES AND RESEARCH
AT THE TERTIARY LEVEL

Futures studies has been taught successfully in a number of universities around the world for over twenty-five years, but it must be said most universities have been abysmally slow to take up and apply this fascinating discipline. My own experience at three universities in the United Kingdom and Australia suggests that students find it a very attractive option, but that university administrations are not aware either of its academic standing or its many successful applications in, for example, business and industry. Within the educational realm I have seen a vast but latent demand on the part of practitioners everywhere. The demand is latent because of what I call the "threshold problem." That is, in order to find out what FS offers, people need to reach the threshold of the discipline and begin to explore for themselves what lies beyond it. Unfortunately, all too few people get the opportunity, so FS tends to remain out of sight, unexplored, and unappreciated.

However, the failure of most established academic institutions to foster and develop FS does have real consequences because the means to do so are now flowing around them and taking other forms. They are springing into life across the Internet, which will soon support a range of distance offerings that will outflank the built institutions entirely. Still, the experience gained from teaching FS in conventional universities will certainly help to inform what is attempted in other media and in other contexts. The following is derived mainly from the five years I spent at the University of Melbourne, Australia, teaching a number of FS units within an Institute of Education (Slaughter, 1992).

Critical futures study can be defined as the application of critical futures concepts, ideas, and theories to futures problems. Teaching it is first and foremost a matter of providing an introduction to the conceptual and methodological aspects of a futures discourse. It is about helping students to learn the language, engage with the literature, clarify understandings, and join a global conversation with peers. The outline syllabus for an introductory postgraduate course I offered on critical futures studies included elements such as an introduction to the futures field, building blocks of the approach, case studies, analysis of the industrial worldview, cultural innovation and the recovery of meaning, imaging futures, and futures study in education.

Specific foci for critical futures study are many and varied. The courses I offered touched on themes such as the following:

- critical analysis of discourse and ideological interests.
- the critique of worldview assumptions and practices.
- the reconceptualization of "world problems."

- analysis of person–person, person–nature, and person–machine relations.
- dealing with fears and concerns about futures.
- the design and implementation of futures curricula.

From even this brief outline, Critical Futures Study is clearly seen as a scholarly and applied activity. It is not social science (which I take to be past and present oriented), and it certainly does not search for laws (which are inapplicable in the futures domain). As noted, it is certainly not concerned with prediction, nor even forecasting (though it may use, or refer to, forecasts, trends, and the like). It has nothing to do with the so-called futures market, and nothing whatsoever to do with crystal balls and the latest commentaries on Nostradamus. Such activities belong to vastly different traditions of inquiry.

Rather, CFS seeks to provide a critical purchase on our historical predicament. It attempts to develop and refine tools of understanding that, on the one hand, reveal processes of cultural formation and cultural editing, and, on the other, reveal options for intervention and choice. It seems to me that when this work is successful it has a number of outcomes: a new (or renewed) ability to diagnose where we are historically, to clarify what is at stake, to reconceptualize the "global problematique," and to redirect human effort through self-constitution and cultural innovation. In educational contexts these outcomes mean that the most significant defects in existing systems can be overcome: Teaching and learning can be reconnected to "the big picture," the wider world, and the actual social and personal prospects with which the young are faced.

In this view, CFS is not social science, though again, it may use some of the tools of the latter. It is not "owned" by a professional elite, though it is certainly aided by practitioners and futures organizations. It is both a cultural formation (because it incorporates some elements of the futures-related social innovation movements) and an academic discipline. However, the academic "backbone" is essential: If FS could not satisfy the very necessary criteria of substance and quality that apply at the highest levels of inquiry, we could not expect it to be taken seriously elsewhere. Hence, CFS flourishes where it has access to the skills and other resources (such as libraries, researchers, and communications systems) that constitute the normal infrastructure of scholarship. As a relative newcomer that questions existing paradigms and historically validated knowledge formations, it also requires political and organizational skills within organizations. In addition, a range of humanistic competencies are expressed in futures workshops and other facilitative milieux where people are actively engaged in futures visioning, design, and implementation.[3]

In summary, critical futures study combines rational intelligence with intuitive and visionary abilities to provide a forward-looking context in which some of the "big questions" can be posed and answered: Where are we going? How do we get there? What problems need to be solved? Why take this path rather than another? Such questions tend to be obscured in most fields of inquiry, but they are central to FS and vital to the well-being of society. They go well beyond the questions asked in related fields, such as history, environmental studies, cultural studies, and sociology. So, more than anything, the emergence of FS can be seen as a widely felt response to the deepest human and cultural needs of our time.

Critical futures research emerges from this. A working definition would perhaps see it as the attempt to generate new knowledge about the constitution of human futures. Obviously, such knowledge cannot be limited to particular domains. It will routinely cross existing disciplinary boundaries and often challenge settled norms and procedures. Like critical futures studies, this approach to research differs from futures research per se in that it is not primarily concerned with using and applying the standard methodologies (such as scenarios, matrices, Delphi, and the like). Rather, these are used sparingly and more commonly seen as part of the subject matter. Critical futures research has a number of characteristic foci, which include the following:

- research into the social construction of temporality.
- the formation, negotiation, and significance of images of futures.
- the clarification of social learning processes and the application of social inventions.
- the evolution of postmodern outlooks and worldviews.
- the reformulation and representation of knowledge for global and futures-oriented uses.
- the development of an ethical basis for acknowledging responsibilities to future generations.
- the study and implementation of foresight.

While, as noted, critical futures studies and research cannot be completely separated, it can be seen that the latter assumes a mastery of the former and is applied to more extended and demanding areas. For example, while critical futures studies may merely survey and/or critique young peoples' fears about futures, critical futures research moves on to consider the grounds of systemic solutions within a renewed worldview and culture. These are demanding areas and they require a high level of intellectual and applied capacity. So it is as well that the methodologies involved in critical futures research are thoroughly grounded in the critical and hermeneutic skills and metatheoretical perspectives outlined here (Belsey, 1980; Slaughter, 1989). They include the study of different types of futures discourses, paradigm phenomena, and foresight contexts, and the conscious design of postmodern worldviews (Slaughter, 1995a).

FROM THEORY TO IMPLEMENTATION

If the claim that FS is not just a minor theoretical development but a broad spectrum and paradigmatic one is true, then it will be applied in ubiquitous ways. Two examples of this are environmental scanning (ES) and strategic foresight (SF). Both illuminate some of the powerful links between academic inquiry and practical applications in other contexts, such as business and consulting.

Environmental Scanning

The global environment is constantly emitting an infinite number of "signals" about many, many processes. No individual or organization can pay attention to more than a tiny fraction of them. In addition, the early signals of potentially influential phenomena are usually small, indistinct, and hard to separate from the background "noise." Yet the earlier they can be detected, the longer is the lead time available to respond. So the central task of environmental scanning is to reconcile sensitivity to new and significant information with careful, systematic selection criteria. Given the turbulence of the early twenty-first-century environment, the dysfunctions embedded in social, economic, and some technical systems, and the rapid pace of change, ES promises to be one of the most widespread industries of the near future. It is quintessentially an information- and knowledge-based activity. It will become ubiquitously necessary as organizations at all levels struggle to find their feet amidst the turbulence to create viable strategies for moving forward.

There is a human and a technical aspect to ES. The human side is primary because the skills involved demand high-order cognitive skills. This is where futures work based on humanistic, critical, and cultural sources comes into its own. From this perspective it is understood that all cultures contain nonrational elements, that values, institutions, and traditions are socially constructed, and that language and meaning are far more subtle and open ended than earlier scientific and empiricist views allowed. So to carry out ES well requires an in-depth immersion in cultural understanding and the humanities. In this view, the most productive insights about the emerging future are less available through standard methodologies such as trend analysis and forecasting than from immersion in a high-quality futures discourse and the subsequent development of reflexivity, judgment, and discrimination.

That said, the technical side of ES is also important. One of the earliest tasks for an organization setting up an ES system is to create its own particular "scanning frame." This is a device for paring away 99.99 percent of reality in order to focus on the signals and processes that have a direct bearing on the present and future functioning of the organization. The scanning frame acts as a dynamic filter to screen out unwanted material, but in so doing it may miss new and significant information. Hence, the frame must be constantly reassessed and revised to take account of the new, the novel, the "lone signal" that may herald entirely novel phenomena. Entire books have been written on how to set up an ES system within an organization (Choo, 1995). They contain all the basic knowledge needed: the key purposes, the operational requirements, the information systems needed, and the uses to which the products of ES may be put by decision makers. These technical and organizational issues must be resolved on a case-by-case basis. There is no one "right" way to set up an effective ES system.

Overall, it seems to me that high-quality environmental scanning will necessarily become a core competence within a wide range of organizations. The informal, CEO-led ES of the past, which depended solely on a personal, idiosyncratic reading of the external environment, is now as useful as a paper hat in a hurricane. The torrent of change we are all immersed in will certainly overturn many industrial-era assumptions and the organizations based upon them. We can already see this happening with schools, government departments, and many, many businesses. In each case the imperatives operating within organizations are increasingly "out of sync" with those of the wider world. So, like the human capacity for foresight in general, ES is a necessary innovation that serves to protect from anticipated dangers and also alert us to whole new areas of opportunity.

Strategic Foresight

Strategic foresight is the ability to create and maintain a high-quality, coherent, and functional forward view and to use the insights arising in organizationally useful ways; for example, to detect adverse conditions, guide policy, shape strategy, and to explore new markets, products, and services. It represents a fusion of futures methods with those of strategic management. As indicated, most organizations operate primarily on the basis of priorities and principles laid down in the past, within a taken-for-granted worldview. They modify their underlying past orientation with inputs from the current environment, such as market information, economic signals, and government regulations. Few attempt to bring these factors from the past and present into a coherent relationship with the forward view.

Strategic foresight is needed for a number of reasons. At the broadest, or "macro" level, SF provides a number of ways of coming to grips with what I term the "civilizational challenge"; that is, the exhaustion of aspects of the Western worldview and the industrial ideology that went with it. Though essentially superseded, this ideology remains strong. It includes such elements as the denial of limits, the single-minded pursuit of material (economic) growth, the commodification of human needs, the reduction of natural entities to the status of mere "resources," exploitive trade practices, and future discounting. Such elements have contributed to what has been termed the industrial "flatland," which, in essence, is an overly empirical and hence "thin" and eventually self-defeating view of the world.[4] My own reading of the forward view suggests that the continuation of "flatland" leads inexorably to a world that no sane person would want to live in, much less pass on to their children. It is a world that is impoverished, mined out, polluted, stripped of (nonhuman) life, and overwhelmed by increasingly powerful technologies.[5] Strategic foresight provides a way out of this cultural trap. It does so by helping organizations to grasp some of the major "big picture" concerns about human purposes, cultural evolution, and sustainability. Since the wider implications of such concerns lie "in the future," they have been glossed over by mainstream economists and defocused by conventional empiricist, short-term, bottom-line thinking. But SF brings them directly into the decision-making arena.

Second, strategic foresight must be of direct use to organizational policy and practice on a day-to-day basis. While organizations will have to face the long-term issues eventually, their immediate priority must be to remain viable in the short- and medium-term present. Here, SF brings into play a new range of factors and possibilities. As noted, environmental scanning can alert an organization to "signals" in its operating environment that herald challenges to its business, new opportunities, and the identification of new products and services. Again, the careful use of scenario-building techniques can provide a range of high-quality insights into the near-future environment. Armed with this "foreknowledge," a variety of strategies can be explored under different assumptions and conditions. As a result, the organization is not only alert to "signals of change," it can grasp opportunities to develop a range of possible responses. Hence, reaction time is reduced. Decisions can be made in a broader context and with greater confidence because the near-term future ceases to be an abstraction. It becomes a highly significant part of the immediate operating environment.

Third, an extension of this argument is that strategic foresight can be developed to the point where it opens out what Hamil and Prahalad (1994) call "future competitive space." This means that organizations do not have to wait for the promptings of competitors or the mythical call of "market demand." Instead, they can decide what they want to do and then put in place the means to achieve it. This sounds unexceptional until it is realized that the forward view contains many novel and unconventional possibilities. It is only by giving that view due attention that the latter can be understood or recognized. Here are insights into new industries, new ways of solving old problems, new sources of impact-free wealth creation, and the grounds of new business and civil cultures. Clearly, the forward view is a significant resource that can contribute to management and strategy in a number of ways.

To sum up, the underlying rationale for strategic foresight is that the world is changing rapidly. The forward view tells us that there are a number of very real dangers to avoid and an equally impressive number of opportunities to be taken up and developed. This pattern of dangers and opportunities is highly relevant to everything that an organization attempts to do, even in the short-term present. Organizations that attempt to move into this turbulent, challenging future without SF will find themselves overwhelmed by forces that were indeed visible for some time but were overlooked. On the other hand, while no futures method can imitate history and foresee all eventualities, organizations that routinely employ SF will find that they are better equipped to negotiate the turbulent conditions ahead. They will prosper and develop because they have understood the structure of the near-future context. In essence, a well-crafted forward view reduces uncertainty and reveals the grounds of otherwise unavailable strategic options.

In both of the cases I have discussed we are clearly not just dealing with technical issues. Rather, these examples are representative of the wide range of emerging futures-oriented knowledge professions that require the development of high-level human cognitive capacity, ethical judgment, discrimination, insight, and in-depth understanding of complex issues and systems.

The development of these high-level human abilities constitutes a new disciplinary platform and opportunity for futures practitioners who are themselves willing to put in the time and effort to master new forms of theory, discourse, and practice. In other words, the skills of Critical Futures Studies have ceased to be esoteric and have finally become practical. As such, they will be increasingly used, not just in schools and universities but also in government departments, businesses, and, indeed, all organizations that wish to weather the turbulence that so clearly lies ahead (Dator, 1995).

CONCLUSION

This chapter has argued that futures studies in general, and Critical Futures Studies in particular, have come of age. That is, FS can now be regarded as a viable discipline with multiple uses and applications. I also suggested that critical futures work taps deeper sources than the still-dominant empiricist American tradition and, in so doing, provides access to a range of powerful new tools and options. If this is correct, then we will witness the further emergence of FS onto the world stage in both practical and applied ways. This would clearly enhance the prospects for humankind to weather the storms ahead and move on to a truly post–postindustrial civilization.

NOTES

1. For an early expression of "layered analysis," see Slaughter (1993b). For a later development of this idea as a methodology, see Inayatullah (1996).

2. Many of the concepts in this chapter are explored in Slaughter (1996a). Also see Slaughter (1995b).

3. For an introduction, see Ziegler (1991).

4. For a masterly critique of the "flatland" concept, see Wilber (1996).

5. This future is powerfully evoked by Broderick (1997).

REFERENCES

Bell, W. (1997). *Foundations of futures studies* (2 vols.). New Brunswick, NJ: Transaction.

Belsey, C. (1980). *Critical practice*. London: Methuen.

Broderick, D. (1997). *The spike: Accelerating into the unimaginable future*. Melbourne, Australia: Reed Books.

Choo, C. (1995). *Information management for the intelligent organization: The art of environmental scanning*. Medford, NJ: ASIS/Information Today.

CIBA Foundation. (1975). *The future as an academic discipline*. Amsterdam: Elsevier.

Dator, J. (1995). *Surfing the tsunamis of change*. Paper presented at the Futures of Construction Conference, Espoo, Finland.

Elgin, D. (1993). *Awakening Earth*. New York: William Morrow.

Habermas, Jurgen. 1971. *Toward a rational society*. London: Heinemann.

Hamil, G., and Prahalad, C. K. (1994). *Competing for the future*. Cambridge: Harvard University Press.

Inayatullah, S. (1996). Methods and epistemologies in futures studies. In R. Slaughter (Ed.), *The knowledge base of futures studies: Vol. 1. Foundations* (pp. 186–202). Hawthorn, Australia: DDM Media Group.

Leach, E. (1968). *A runaway world*. London: BBC.

Macy, J. (1991). *World as lover, world as self*. Berkeley, CA: Parallax Press.

Milbrath, L. (1989). *Envisioning a sustainable society*. Albany: State University of New York Press.

Ogilvy, J. (1996). Futures studies and the human sciences: The case for normative scenarios. In R. Slaughter (Ed.), *New thinking for a new millennium* (pp. 26–83). London: Routledge.

Slaughter, R. (1975). *Birds in Bermuda*. Hamilton: Bermuda Bookstores.

Slaughter, R. (1989). Probing beneath the surface: Review of a decade's futures work. *Futures, 22*, 447–465.

Slaughter, R. (Ed.). (1992). Futures Studies and Higher Education [special issue]. *Futures Research Quarterly, 8* (4).

Slaughter, R. (Ed.). (1993a). The knowledge base of futures studies [special issue]. *Futures, 25* (3).

Slaughter, R. (1993b). Looking for the real "Megatrends." *Futures, 25*, 827–849.

Slaughter, R. (1995a). *The foresight principle: Cultural recovery in the 21st century*. London: Adamantine.

Slaughter, R. (1995b). *Futures tools and techniques*. Melbourne, Australia: Futures Study Centre.

Slaughter, R. (1996a). *Futures concepts and powerful ideas*. Melbourne, Australia: Futures Study Centre.

Slaughter, R. (Ed.). (1996b). *The knowledge base of futures studies* (3 vols.). Hawthorn, Australia: DDM Media Group.

Slaughter, R. (1996c). The knowledge base of futures studies as an evolving process. *Futures, 28*, 799–812.

Slaughter, R. (1996d). Long-term thinking and the politics of reconceptualization. *Futures, 28*, 75–86.

Wilber, K. (1981). *Up from Eden*. London: RKP.

Wilber, K. (1996). *A brief history of everything*. Melbourne, Australia: Hill of Content.

Ziegler, W. (1991). Envisioning the future. *Futures, 23*, 516–527.

6

Pedagogy, Culture, and Futures Studies

Sohail Inayatullah

FUTURES STUDIES IN SEARCH OF A DOXA

In traditional disciplines, even as postmodernity undoes defining and organizing narratives, there is a doxa: certain classic texts that must be read and
must be adhered to. Futures studies does not yet have these boundaries. It is
transdisciplinary, in search of an interpretive community, its knowledge
base just being defined.[1] Who the futurists are is still in contention.[2] Is
futures studies a science? An appendage to strategic planning? Should futures studies be technical, concerned with forecasting, or culture-based,
concerned with recovering the futures from the instrumental rationality of
modernity? Or is futures studies primarily a movement, an attempt to keep
futures pluralistic, to keep the future open, less concerned with academic
treatises, and more with social action? Or should futures studies be specific
in its orientation, as in "future generations studies," which seeks to sustain
and transform social conditions on behalf of the rights of future generations
(humans, animals, plants, as well as metaphors)? Or should futures studies
primarily be concerned with deconstructing hegemonic images of the future
held by the powerful, thereby creating the spaces for the emergence of authentic
alternative visions and social designs? That is, should futures studies essentially be about decolonizing dominant views of time–space and perspective?

While there have been many attempts to map the field, it still remains contentious, with no hegemonic paradigm defining it.[3] In earlier articles, among other mapping schemes by thinkers such as Linstone, Masini, Gillwald, Sardar, Amara, and Bezold, I have divided futures studies into three overlapping research dimensions: empirical, interpretive, and critical.[4] Each dimension has different assumptions about the real, about truth, about the role of the subject, about the nature of the universe, and about the nature of the future.[5] My own preference has been approaches that use all three, that contextualize data (the predictive) with the meanings (interpretive) we give them, and then locate these in various historical structures of power or knowledge: class, gender, *varna*, and episteme (the critical).

In the *predictive–empirical*, language is assumed to be neutral; that is, it does not participate in constituting the real. Language merely describes reality, serving as an invisible link between theory and data. Prediction assumes that the universe is deterministic so that the future can be known. By and large this view privileges experts (planners, policy futurists, economists, and astrologers). The future becomes a site of expertise and a place to colonize. In general, the strategic discourse is most prevalent in this framework, with information valued because it provides lead time and a range of responses to deal with the enemy (a competing nation or corporation). Linear forecasting is the technique used most. Scenarios are used more as minor deviations from the norm instead of alternative worldviews.

In the *cultural–interpretive*, the goal is not prediction but insight into difference, with the hope of creating unity. Truth is considered relative, with language and culture both intimately involved in creating the real. Through comparison—examining different national or gender or ethnic images of the future—we gain insight into the human condition. This type of futures studies is less technical, with mythology as important as mathematics. Learning from each model in the context of the search for universal narratives that can ensure basic human values is the central mission for this epistemological approach. While visions of the future often occupy center stage in this interpretive view, the role of identity is also important, whether based on class, gender, or other categories of social relations.

In the *poststructural–critical*, futures studies aims neither at prediction nor at comparison, but seeks to make the units of analysis problematic, to undefine the future, to seek a distance from current understandings and epistemological agreements. Of concern in this perspective is not forecasting, say, the futures of population, but how the category of population has become valorized in discourse. Why "population" instead of "community" or "people"? we might ask. The role of the state and other forms of power in creating authoritative discourses is central to understanding how a particular future has become hegemonic. Critical futures studies asserts that the present is fragile, merely the victory of one particular discourse or way of knowing over another. The goal of critical research is to disturb present power relations through making problematic our categories and evoking other places, other scenarios of the future. Through this distance, the present becomes less rigid, indeed, remarkable. The spaces of reality loosen, the grip of neorealism (of the bottom line, of the predictive approach) widen, and the new is possible. Language is not symbolic but constitutive of reality. While structures are useful, they are seen not as universal but as particular to history and episteme (the knowledge boundaries that frame our knowing).

Ideally, one should try to use all three types of futures studies. If one makes a population forecast, one should then ask how different civilizations approach the issue of population. Then one should deconstruct the idea of population itself, defining it, for example, not only as an ecological problem in the Third World, but relating it to First-World consumption patterns as well. Empirical research then must be contextualized within the science of the civilization from which it emerges, and then historically deconstructed to show what particular approaches are missing and silencing.

TEACHING FUTURES STUDIES

My own pedagogy in the area of futures studies has focused on the interpretive and critical. I have been particularly concerned with decolonizing the future, examining how we buy other's used futures and how we disempower ourselves by accepting the futures of others as ours. But once the purchased future is deconstructed, it is equally essential to offer alternatives. In my own work I ask, What are alternative imaginations of the future? How can we learn from those who have suffered? What are the images of the future of those we consider outside history? What are other ways to "time" the world instead of the dominant scientific model, such as women's, spiritual, or cyclical time. Thus, crucial to a liberation pedagogy is a concerted effort to identify dissenting authentic images of the future.

My own inspiration to engage in alternative futures has come from classical Tantra as redefined by P. R. Sarkar, from indigenous Pacific islander's visions of time and family, and from the range of social movements—the spiritual, the environmental, the womanist—all dedicated to creating a global *ohana*, being part of a global *samaj*, a planetary civilization.

Teaching and learning about the future, then, is centrally about understanding the human condition, what it has become, and how we can participate in changing it (and understanding the structural limitations of change; i.e., the deep cycles and trends of history that create our own subjectivities).

My own experience in the last fifteen years has been in conducting workshops for university administration and departments, nongovernmental organizations, corporations, local governments, research institutes, international organizations, and advocacy groups; participating in international courses in futures studies (usually sponsored by the World Futures Studies Federation and UNESCO); and more formal teaching at the University of Hawaii (wherein I used a futures perspective to frame the topic being taught, Hawaii politics in this case), and public lectures at numerous universities and institutes throughout the world (Yugoslavia, Greece, Denmark, Pakistan, Hungary, India, and Australia, to mention a few).

The style that I use in formal courses is to have students–participants search for alternative ways to define the past, present, and future. Not only is the future considered probable and makeable, but so is the past and present. The idea is to open up the present, to give different readings of political events and trends. In one course, a student developed scenarios of Hawaii's future by rewriting history. He asked, What if Captain Cook had never landed on the Hawaiian Islands? What if contact with the West had been on the terms of the Islanders? This historical questioning led to the creation of scenarios in which Pacific islands—instead of a history of disunity and imperialism—unite, recognizing that they are a liquid continent, and creating something akin to the Federated Cultures–Regions of Oceania.

In conducting workshops—where I work with a specific group aiding in the development of their vision or strategy for the future—my own method has been to first create a shared identity, to explore why each person is at the workshop and what history they bring with them, and then I seek to open up the workshop. The opening-up process occurs through methods such as emerging issues analysis—which identifies areas of sudden transformation, of unexpected futures—and what-if questions, which again call into question the present and projected future.

This is followed by a sorting of positions in vertical layers, from the most obvious litany to the deeper metaphorical layers: the method of Causal Layered Analysis (CLA), which is explored in more depth later in this chapter. Information from these methods is used to create alternative scenarios, pictures of possible and probable futures.[6] From these scenarios, agreement is often reached on a vision of the future. This can occur through small working groups or strategic questioning, in which the elements of the group vision emerge. In strategic questioning I ask selected individuals to imagine—in detail—a day in their life in their desired or plausible future. I ask questions like, What do you see out the window? How do you get to work? Do you walk, use virtual technologies, or whatever? Do you work? What do you eat during the day?

These stories create shared meanings among participants and they legitimate the future, since imaginations are owned by the individuals relating them. Detail is crucial here, as this forces participants to select, from a range of possibilities, what they desire or believe will occur in the future. Thus, from individual scenarios of the future, a shared vision comes to be articulated.

The final stage is backcasting, deriving strategy by going backward from the future and asking individuals to remember the historical events and trends that created the present. At this stage, with the contours of the future already agreed on, the issue is remembering the past, not engaging in debates about whether a particular future could or could not have occurred. Backcasting can result in a strategic plan or, even better, a range of organizational experiments with real funding and faces behind who does what, when, and with whom.

While this is a general model, there are, of course, many variations depending on the local culture of the participants, their worldview, and how they imagine the future. Being sensitive to local perspective on the future, I believe, is a crucial skill in teaching futures studies. Listening to the language others use to talk about the future is also essential. Finally, while it is important to honor others' views of the future, thinking about the future, as Dator has argued, is an unnatural act: It requires years of training. The teacher should not be shy about prodding others toward more imaginative, creative, and plausible futures. Thinking about the future is more than fantasy fulfillment. There are real rigorous methods, from the most to the least mathematical, that can aid in this process.

Finally, as in all pedagogical situations, there is a process of politics. This includes conventional understandings of the politics of planning: the role of participation and hierarchy, of who gets to speak and who listens, who is expert and who is lay, as well as more subtle issues as to the appropriateness of using futures studies for organizational learning and transformation.

What follows are case studies of workshops and courses selected to illustrate these concepts.

EXPERTISE AND UNCERTAINTY

While one would normally expect expertise to be one of the most important criteria in determining the success of a workshop, in a day-long visioning workshop for an Australian university we found that the most important determinant in the workshop's success was our own uncertainty as to how to run the workshop.[7] Deans, professors, and administrators were initially resistant to participate in a visioning workshop. They feared that the workshop would be used by management to gain points over labor. They were also uncertain of the academic respectability of futures studies.

Our first goal was to ensure commitment from top management.[8] Our second goal was to locate futures within macrohistory, within the large patterns of social and civilizational change. This was important in that the future was seen less as fantasy and more as part of a knowledge base. Our third goal was to keep the workshop fluid, to constantly change directions as our perception of participants' needs changed. This fluidity on our part was central to allaying fears that we had a hidden agenda (for management). The result was that since we were unsure of ourselves, the future ceased to be an authoritarian space. Rather, it became an open space that could be shared, where expert knowledge had not colonized alternatives.

Academics agreed afterward to continue the visioning process in their own departments. Earlier, they had worried that we would be crystal-ball gazers, but the issues we raised at some level fit their worldviews but also challenged them. For example, we asked them to explore the challenge of multiculturalism in the university (not just in terms of better and equal opportunity for minorities but of using non-Western models of knowledge and of the university to define their future), to explore the end of the university because of the Web, to explore a more corporatized university (as current globalization trends suggest), and to explore a return to core values. These issues later emerged in scenarios and shared agreement was reached in the visioning part of the workshop (i.e., the desirability for a more mentoring role than a strict "I am smart and you are not" role and faculty having concurrent contracts with different universities). The ideas that came forth most likely would not have emerged if the day had been spent discussing current issues—matters of office space, of access to better computers, of labor contracts—all critically important, but all reinscribing the present instead of creating or even imagining alternative futures.

Thus, while technically the workshop was problematic (miscues, and, in general, a trial-and-error learning process), in terms of its outcomes—a shared vision, a shared backcast, and a shared strategy of transformation, as well as an openness toward the process of creating alternative futures—the workshop was highly successful. Besides our tentativeness, central to this success was an opening speech by the university president in which he showed his commitment to the process, as well as vigorous participation by hard-headed academics once they saw that we were not there to "workshop" them or to con them. This latter point is crucial, since futures studies, even while it has grown by leaps and bounds in academia, still remains for many a "pop" consulting tool (i.e., as change management or a manipulative device).

MULTICULTURAL FUTURES

More satisfying and challenging than conducting workshops for specific organizations or institutes have been international futures courses sponsored by WFSF (often with seed money from UNESCO).[9] Whether in Dubrovnik, Andorra, Thailand, or the Philippines, these courses begin with cultural difference and conclude with cultural difference. While introducing futures studies, these courses usually also have specific themes, such as the futures of development, communication, ecology, and policy making and education.

These courses are challenging to teach in that not only does one have to teach a new field of knowing—futures studies—but one has to do so in ways that make sense to how individuals from different cultures know the world. Not only is the future constructed differently, but there are a range of diverse expectations of pedagogical style. Some prefer more formal lectures, others prefer informal small-group sessions. Some expect that information about the future should be given to them, while others believe that any fantasy about the future is an appropriate scenario. Some resist the idea that the future is at some level open. For example, they may be committed to religious worldviews in which the future is God given. Others believe that the future should be explored only through statistical-modeling methods and not through "softer" metaphorical approaches.

Teaching futures is already challenging; more so is teaching futures in cross-cultural contexts, wherein the knowledge, style, and forms of presentation are all open (or not) for negotiation. What I have found most noteworthy is that futures studies must be localized in the language of participants, in their ways of knowing and experiences.

Some years ago, Draper Kauffman developed an exercise, widely used since by some futurists, which asks people to say whether they think the future is more like a roller coaster ride, paddling down a river in a canoe, sailing on an ocean, or throwing dice in a game of chance (as in the American board game, "Monopoly"). People who choose roller coaster or game of chance are considered to have restricted, fatalistic images of the future, while those who say river have a more open image, with ocean being the most optimistic and "can-do" image of the future of the four.

During a presentation of these four images to students at a futures workshop held in Islamabad, Pakistan, in March 1995, one student responded, "But who would want to live in a future which was entirely open." She added, "An ocean has no direction." She proceeded to offer the daily Muslim prayer while facing toward Mecca as an appropriate metaphor for Islam and the future: united and facing in one direction.

Earlier in a UNESCO–WFSF–sponsored workshop on the futures of education held in Suva, Fiji, in 1993, Pacific islanders had offered two metaphors they believed more adequately represented their traditions. The first was a coconut tree. One had to work hard to climb up the tree, but at the top were ample rewards. This was clearly the influence of Protestant Christianity on the islands, the participants agreed. The second image they offered was of being a passenger in a car driven by a man with a blindfold. This of course represented the islands' interaction with modern Western capitalism, a perception that they were not in control of their own destiny.

In contrast to these metaphors, an Indian participant at the second WFSF Bangkok Asia–Pacific futures course in 1993 suggested the onion as a more appropriate image. Reality, in this view, has many layers. Our task as humans is to peel away the layers, discovering new levels of reality, until all is revealed, and the empty infinity of the *atman* is revealed to us. A Filipino participant suggested a less spiritual metaphor, the coconut. A coconut is hard on the outside (in response to the cruelty of the world) but soft on the inside (our inner tender spiritual selves). The coconut also has many uses: It can be eaten, its juice drunk, and its husk used and recycled for a variety of agricultural and industrial purposes. It was a metaphor for all seasons, all futures.

Staying within the ecological discourse, an Australian participant at a Southern Cross University–WFSF course in 1995 suggested the seed. For her, the seed was most appropriate for expressing future generations and the future since it embedded alternative futures within an organic unity. As with children, the seed needs nurturing but as it grows it can provide nourishment for others. Once it is a tree, there are many branches—alternative futures—all arising from our common humanity (the trunk). Finally, the seed privileges ontology over epistemology, being over knowing.

These and other examples have made it clear to me that our language, our metaphors of the future, are culture and gender bound. To only use the models found in Western futures educational books is severely limiting.

At a 1994 futures visioning workshop in Penang, Malaysia, these limitations were further exposed.[10] The dice, while adequately representing randomness, misses entirely the role of the transcendental as a type of superagency. The roller coaster, while appearing to represent predestination, does not capture the importance of the group or larger community Asians and Africans are embedded in. The ocean, while representing unbounded possibilities, misses the role of history and deep social structures, of fate and power. While the image of river with its dangerous submerged rocks represents well the need for information and swift decision making to avoid risks and take advantage of opportunities, it does not provide metaphorical entry for guidance from others: leadership, family, or God. Surprisingly, the metaphor that did emerge from discussion with Malay Muslims was the "snakes and ladders" game; that is, life's ups and downs are based on chance, and when one goes up, one should be ready to fall at any moment. While appearing to be fatalistic, the resolution of this metaphor of the future was faith in Allah as the deeper reality on which one must rest one's self.

In this workshop, participants had little interest in the future until we asked them to think of the future in their own cultural categories. Once this question had been asked, there was an abundance of discussion. Participants searched within their own civilizational history to imagine the future. They took their future-oriented metaphors from their recent agricultural past and sought to understand if these still made sense within Malaysia's new role in the world economy. This led to the creation of new types of future imaging and a call for Malays and Muslims constructing futures and futures studies.

They thus sought to decolonize the future and make it their own. Myths and metaphors were the central tools of empowerment that they used in this process. However, not neglected were issues of social design, of articulating futures that dealt with the realities of the world economy; nonetheless, they did so in the context of Islamic economics, devising and creating new financial instruments that did not violate Islamic ethics.

As mentioned at the outset of this essay, my view of the best futures studies would ideally bring in all these different perspectives, being able to move in empirical, interpretive, and critical frames, all the time touching on theory, data, and values while being sensitive to the different ways we learn from each other and know the world. One method that is exemplary in this regard, in moving in and out of different types of meaning, is causal layered analysis.

CAUSAL LAYERED ANALYSIS

Causal layered analysis takes as its starting point the assumption that there are different levels of reality and ways of knowing.[11] Individuals, organizations, and civilizations see the world from different vantage points, horizontal and vertical.

The first level is the "litany"—quantitative trends or problems, often exaggerated or used for political purposes (overpopulation, for example)—usually presented by the news media. Events, issues, and trends are not connected and appear discontinuous. The result is often either a feeling of helplessness (What can I do?) or apathy (Nothing can be done!) or projected action (Why don't they do something about it?). This is the conventional level of futures research that can readily create a politics of fear. This is the futurist as fearmonger, who warns, "The end is near! But if you believe my prophecy and act as I tell you to, the end can be averted."

The second level is concerned with social causes, including economic, cultural, political, and historical factors (e.g., rising birthrates or lack of family planning). Interpretation is given to quantitative data. This type of analysis is usually articulated by policy institutes and published as editorial pieces in newspapers or in not-quite-academic journals. If one is fortunate, then the precipitating action is sometimes analyzed (e.g., population growth and advances in medicine or health). This level excels at technical explanations as well as academic analysis. The role of the state and other actors and interests is often explored at this level.

The third deeper level is concerned with structure and the discourse or worldview that supports and legitimates it (e.g., population growth and civilizational perspectives of family, lack of women's power, lack of social security, or the population–consumption debate). The task is to find deeper social, linguistic, or cultural structures that are actor invariant. Discerning deeper assumptions behind the issue is crucial here, as are efforts to revision the problem. At this stage one can explore how different discourses (the economic, the social, the cultural) do more than cause or mediate the issue, but constitute it; how the discourse we use to understand is complicit in our framing of the issue. Based on the varied discourses, discrete alternative scenarios can be derived here. These scenarios add a horizontal dimension to our layered analysis.

The fourth layer of analysis is at the level of metaphor or myth. These are the deep stories, the collective archetypes, the unconscious dimensions of the problem or the paradox (e.g., seeing population as nonstatistical, as community, or seeing people as creative resources, as life). This level provides a gut or emotional experience to the worldview under inquiry. The language used is less specific and more concerned with evoking visual images, with touching the heart instead of reading the head.

Causal layered analysis asks us to go beyond conventional framings of issues. For instance, normal academic analysis tends to stay in the second layer, with occasional forays into the third, seldom privileging the fourth layer (myth and metaphor). CLA, however, does not privilege any one particular level. Moving up and down layers we can integrate analysis and synthesis, and horizontally we can integrate discourses, ways of knowing, and worldviews, thereby increasing the richness of the analysis. What often results are differences that can be easily captured in alternative scenarios; each scenario in itself, to some extent, can represent a different way of knowing. However, CLA orders the scenarios in vertical space.

For example, taking the issue of parking spaces in urban centers can lead to a range of scenarios. A short-term scenario of increasing parking spaces (building below or above) is of a different order from a scenario that examines telecommuting, a scenario that distributes spaces by lottery (instead of by power or wealth), or one that questions the role of the car in modernity (a carless city?) or deconstructs the idea of a parking space, as in many Third World settings where there are few spaces designated "parking."[12]

Scenarios, thus, are different at each level. Litany-type scenarios are more instrumental. Social-level scenarios are more policy oriented, while discourse–worldview scenarios intend to capture fundamental differences. Myth–metaphor-type scenarios are equally discrete but articulate this difference through a poem, a story, an image, or some other right-brain method.

Finally, who solves the problem or issue also changes at each level. At the litany level, it is usually others: the government or corporations. At the social level, it is often some partnership between different groups. At the worldview level, it is people or voluntary associations, and at the myth–metaphor level it is visionaries or artists.

These four layers are indicative; that is, there is some overlap between the layers. Using CLA on CLA, we can see how the current litany (of what are the main trends and problems facing the world) in itself is the tip of the iceberg, an expression of a particular worldview.[13]

USING CLA AT A UNESCO–WFSF COURSE

I have used CLA in a variety of situations. One notable example was at the 1993 UNESCO–WFSF workshop in Thailand on the futures of ecology, where the issue of Bangkok's traffic problem was explored. CLA was pivotal in breaking out of a conventional understanding of transportation futures.

At the litany level, the problem was seen to be Bangkok's traffic and related pollution. The solution was to hire consultants, particularly transportation planners at local and international levels.

At the social-cause level, the problem was seen as a lack of roads, with the solution being that of building more roads (and getting mobile phones in the meantime). If one were doing scenarios at this stage, these would be based on where to build alternative routes and which transportation modeling software to use.

At the worldview level, it was argued that the problem was not just lack of roads but the model of industrial growth Thailand had taken. It is the Big City Outlook that had come down through colonialism: The city is better, and rural people are idiots; wealth accumulation is only possible in the city, especially as population growth creates problems in the rural area. The solution then becomes not to build more roads but to decentralize the economy and create localism, where local people control their economy and feel they do not have to leave their life and lifestyle. Psychologically it means valuing local traditions and countering the ideology that West is best and that bigger is better. New leadership and new metaphors on what it means to be Thai emerged as the solutions.

The key methodological utility is that CLA allows for research that brings in many perspectives. It has a fact basis, which is framed in history and then contextualized within a discourse or worldview, and then located in pre- and postrational ways of knowing, in myth and metaphor. The challenge is to bring in these many perspectives to a particular problem, to go up and down levels and sideways through various scenarios.

Like all methods, CLA has its limits. For example, it does not forecast the future per se and is best used in conjunction with other methods, such as emerging issues analysis (which even while it offers forecasts of nascent issues, disturbs the present through its exploration of the absurd) and visioning.

KNOWLEDGE AND WAYS OF KNOWING

Teaching futures studies or conducting futures workshops has numerous challenges. The process must be sensitive to each individual's cultural framework, to skepticism about the appropriateness of studying the future, as well as to a failure of imagination in thinking about the future, not to mention the complex ways we know the world. For example, Paul Wildman argues that there are at least five ways of knowing: (1) practical, technical knowledge, skills development; (2) scientific theoretical knowledge, knowledge to explain the world; (3) experiential knowledge to change myself or the world around me; (4) metaphorical knowledge or insight, deeper understanding of self and others (at heart and head level); and (5) relationship knowledge, knowledge so as to better relate to others, be they lovers, friends, God, or the environment.[14] A course or workshop thus must find methods and processes that meet these various ways of knowing. Those focused on relationship often prefer small-group exercises, where they can share perspectives and directly learn from others. Those concerned with metaphorical knowledge might prefer personal stories about how one has done futures studies or what one has learned from years of experience or conversations with elders and children. An experiential-knowledge type would be far more concerned with ensuring that the time spent at a workshop would help change the world: Making a difference is far more important than the accumulation of information. Those focused on scientific knowledge might prefer technical descriptions of forecasting. Finally, individuals representative of the first knowledge cluster focused on practical knowledge might want to learn how to do the workshop themselves or would be engaged in a cognitive assessment to discern if these workshops could be applied to their day-to-day work.

For a presenter, the task is certainly challenging. At issue is not just the particular academic text on the future, but how each human learns about others, how each person imagines his or her own role on the planet, and what he or she intends to do about the problems facing humanity. As Martha Rogers argues, teaching and learning about the future raises issues of the heart, head, and soul: All three combine to create powerful forces of discomfort, and individual and social transformation.[15]

One of the great strengths of futures studies is its openness toward its self-definition. Futures studies fortunately has a rapidly evolving knowledge base, thus allying fears that it is merely about fantasy or steeped in nonrigorous discourses. It is transdisciplinary, having a leg in scientific analysis and a leg in cultural studies. This perhaps gives it an advantage. Its lack of institutionalization allows it to remain undomesticated. One can both be expert and student; one can lecture and can create spaces for participatory workshops. Whereas a traditional academic would need to feel that the lecture was perfect, for the futurist there is more space for making mistakes, for laughter, for play, for experimentation, and thus for authentic and successful pedagogy. Indeed, that the future is not immediate and thus less urgent allows creativity to be explored. That the future is about alternative futures and not fixed history allows different interpretations, thus opening futures studies to more participation.

Finally, those who actively participate in teaching the future exist in global educative space, as futures studies is one of the few global disciplines, living and flourishing outside of conventional national and international boundaries of state and knowledge. The "how" of teaching the future then forces one into many academic, cultural, and historical frameworks. This is enriching for practitioners, and problematic, since all certainties are undone by the varieties of frames that create the process of what it is that is taught and learned.

To conclude, engaging in futures-oriented pedagogy requires sensitivity to the different ways women and men, civilizations, classes, people with disabilities and those without—among other conditions—know the world. While all teaching situations have these concerns as well, in futures studies the question of what you (as individual or as representative of your civilization) desire the future to be like is pivotal. This is especially so if one wishes to explore layers of responses, decolonize dominant visions of the future, and create authentic alternative futures. If this is all too much, there is always statistics and other fantasies to fall back on.

NOTES

I would like to thank Dr. Levi Obiifor of the Communication Center for his editorial assistance in the preparation of this chapter.

1. Through efforts such as R. Slaughter, ed., *The knowledge base of futures studies* (3 vols.) (Hawthorn, Australia, DDM Media Group, 1996). Volume 4, titled *Futurists: Visions, Methods and Stories*, is published as a CD Rom in 1998. See also R. Slaughter, The knowledge base of futures studies as an evolving process, *Futures, 28* (1996): 799–812.

2. For one effort at identifying the full range of futurists and what they think, see the special issue of *Futures*, titled What futurists think, *6* (1997).

3. The most recent effort is G. May, *The future is ours* (London: Adamantine, 1996). See, in particular, his section on futures workshops (pp. 194–199). See also W. Bell, *Foundations of futures studies* (2 vols.) (New Brunswick, NJ: Transaction); and G. Kurian and G. Molitor, *Encyclopedia of the future* (2 vols.) (New York: Macmillan, 1996).

4. See, for example, H. Linstone, What I have learned: The need for multiple perspectives, *Futures Research Quarterly, 1*, no. 1 (1985): 47–61. He divides futures into the technical, organizational, and personal. See also E. Masini and K. Gillwald, On futures studies and their social context with particular focus on West Germany, *Technological Forecasting and Social Change 38* (1990): 187–199. They take Linstone's model and apply it historically to Europe and the United States, seeing futures as going through technical, organizational, and personal phases. See also Z. Sardar, Colonizing the future: The "other" dimension of futures studies, *Futures, 25* (1992): 179–187. Sardar argues for a colonization–decolonization dialectic. The classic map of futures studies remains Roy Amara's division into preferred, possible, and probable. See R. Amara, The futures field: Searching for definitions and boundaries, *The Futurist, 15*, no. 1 (1981): 25–29; R. Amara, The futures field: How to tell good work from bad, *The Futurist, 15*, no. 2 (1981): 63–71; R. Amara, The futures field: Which direction now? *The Futurist, 15*, no. 3 (1981): 42–46. See also C. Bezold and T. Hancock, *An overview of the health futures field* (Washington, DC: Institute for Alternative Futures, 1993). Bezold adds the plausible to Amara's three categories. See also S. Inayatullah, Deconstructing and reconstructing the future: Predictive, cultural and critical epistemologies, *Futures, 22* (1990): 115–141.

5. S. Inayatullah, From "who am I" to "when am I?": Framing the time and shape of the future, *Futures, 25* (1993): 235–253.

6. The method I use to make the scenario more real is called "nuts and bolts." This is a strutural–functional analysis of the organization. If, for example, a current

function of an organization, say, the courts, is to resolve disputes, I ask, What are some other ways to resolve disputes? What are some other sites instead of court buildings? If currently judges resolve disputes, what are other ways to resolve them? This method forces one into very specific structural–functional changes.

7. Some of this material is drawn from "Teaching futures workshops: Leadership, ways of knowing and institutional politics," *Futures Research Quarterly, 14*, no. 4 (1998): 29–36.

8. I was working with Dr. Paul Wildman, fellow in futures studies, International Management Centres, Pacific Region.

9. Some of this material is drawn from S. Inayatullah and P. Wildman, Communicating futures in cross-cultural pedagogical environments (Paper presented at the Conference on Teaching and Learning about Future Generations, OISE, University of Toronto, October 1995).

10. See S. Inayatullah, Futures visions for southeast Asia: Some early warning signals, *Futures, 27* (1995): 681–688.

11. This material is drawn from Causal layered analysis: Poststructuralism as method (Research paper, The Communication Centre, Queensland University of Technology, 1998).

12. In Pakistan, for example, parking spaces are rare. Parking as a regulatory discourse is not active there.

13. Most policy thus merely reinscribes the modern capitalist worldview. However, noticing how a particular litany is shaped by a particular worldview allows us to enter alternative worldviews and articulate different policy statements based on them. At the same time, CLA in itself is part of a worldview, one committed to methodological eclecticism but in the framework of a layered, post–postmodern view of reality. It thus not only challenges the "totalizing nature of the empirical paradigm" (to use Paul Wildman's phrase) but also the horizontal relativism of postmodernism.

14. See P. Wildman and S. Inayatullah, Ways of knowing, culture, communication and the pedagogies of the future, *Futures, 28* (1997): 723–740.

15. M. Rogers, Learning about the future: From the learner's perspective, *Futures, 29* (1997): 763–768.

7

Explaining the Past and Predicting the Future

Peter T. Manicas

On the evening of November 9, 1989, a number of us, part of small group of social scientists attending an international meeting at the Wissenschafts-zentrum Berlin fur Sozialforschung, were on the last bus from Kreutzberg, what had become a largely Turkish neighborhood in West Berlin. We came by Checkpoint Charlie. There were large numbers of people, surely enough activity to cause us to wonder what was going on. The bus driver dismissed the crowd as "another demonstration of some sort." That seemed right to us. We returned to our hotel and went to bed. The next morning we discovered that the Berlin Wall had been breached.

No one in our group (which included among others, Tony Giddens, Peter Wagner, Bjorn Wittrock, Richard Whiteley, Hans Joas, Johan Heilbron, and Keith Tribe) had predicted this "dissolution," the title of Charles Maier's (1997) very good book on the subject. Nor do I think that anyone could have. Yet Maier explains the event very well. Indeed, looking back, it seems now almost inevitable. The reasons for apparent paradox help us to see both the promise and limits of futures research.

Providing the reasons will require a brief foray into philosophy of science and into what is sometimes called philosophy of history. Neither are usually explicit features of inquiry, but it is not that inquirers lack commitments to either, for there can be no way to do social science without both.

THE ASYMMETRY OF EXPLANATION AND PREDICTION

It is (still) widely believed that (1) science searches for "laws" (or more weakly, "explanatory generalizations"); that (2) these are of the form, "Whenever F, then G," or (more weakly) "Usually, when F, then G"; and (3) that accordingly, explanation and prediction are symmetrical. That is, explanation and prediction proceed via "a covering law." We can illustrate this by considering Skocpol's (1979) much discussed *States and Social Revolutions*. Summarizing her summary (p. 153),

If a state organization susceptible to administrative and military collapse is subjected to intensified pressures from developed countries abroad *and* there is widespread peasant revolt facilitated by agrarian sociopolitical structures, then there will be a social revolution.

In 1789, France was subjected to such pressures and had an agrarian social structure which facilitated widespread peasant revolt.

Hence, France in 1789 had a social revolution.

The first premise is the "explanatory generalization." We can replace China or Russia for France in the second premise and thus also "explain" their social revolutions.

The argument is a perfectly valid deduction, but if the conditions are not sufficient, the first premise is false. Indeed, it is not clear whether any such explanatory generalization could be true without being trivial. However, we should ask whether any scientific explanation proceeds in this fashion. While the covering law model is a defining attribute of "empiricist" (positivist, neopositivist) understandings of science, there is now a substantial critical literature that has subjected this assumption to fatal criticisms (Scriven, 1959, 1962; Harre, 1970, 1986; Dretske, 1977; Bhaskar, 1975, 1979; Salmon, 1978, 1984; Achinstein, 1981/1993; Aronson, 1984; Woodward, 1984/1993; Lewis, 1986; Kim, 1987/1993; Manicas, 1987, 1989).

First, "laws" that subsume instances (still less "mere" generalizations) cannot explain, since "entails" is the wrong relationship. Thus, says Dretske (1977), "The fact that *every* F is G fails to explain why *any* F is G" (p. 262). While at least a true universal maintains the hold on the individual case, anything less makes the main point vivid. Perhaps 67 percent of people exposed to Herpes I contract it, but why did Sam contract the disease (and why didn't Harry, who also was exposed)? Third, it is easy to construct counterexamples where valid "explanatory arguments" with true premises are just plain silly:

Nobody who takes birth control pills regularly becomes pregnant.

John took his wife's pills regularly.

Hence, John did not become pregnant.

The foregoing criticism suggests that something deeper is amiss; roughly, that explaining the particular case requires something more and other than laws understood as empirical regularities.

First, scientific laws are not best understood as of the form, "Whenever this, then that." Rather, they are best described as statements about the causal powers of "things." I use the word "things" advisedly. Ordinary experience knows that water can dissolve salt and that it can also rust iron. This was known well before modern science. But with modern science, we also know why. We know that ordinary water is mostly H_2O, a theoretical but real "thing," and that ordinary salt is mostly NaCl, another real theoretical thing.[1] Molecular chemistry is a powerful theory that generates a deep understanding of the generative mechanisms (causal powers) of the "things" that constitute its domain. Roughly, by virtue of their atomic structure, hydrogen and oxygen combine to form a molecule that by virtue of its structure has a host of powers: all the things that it can do in interaction with all the other "things" in the universe. Indeed, if the theory is true, we can say that, ceteris paribus (CP), NaCl *must* dissolve in H_2O: It is a law of nature.[2] Of course, we also know that salt doesn't always dissolve in water, just as we know (but usually ignore) that if any particular amount of salt is to dissolve in water, many other things must also happen: Somebody, for example, has to put the salt into the water.

Two issues are involved. First, concrete outcomes are always the outcomes of many causes working conjunctively. Second, the "necessity" regards *only* relations of the theoretical things identified by the law. Thus, not only is ordinary water not only H_2O, and ordinary salt is not only NaCl, but the necessity between H_2O and NaCl holds *only if* other things are in fact equal. They never are, hence the fact of contingency.

On the other hand, it may be that they are equal enough so that we have a reliable generalization: Salt will generally dissolve in water.[3] In some of the physical sciences, we can spell out in some detail the CP clause and we can then experiment. Spelling out the conditions of the CP clause amounts to spelling out the conditions of experimental closure. We try to make everything else equal and see if what was "predicted" (by the theory) to happen does in fact happen. If it doesn't, we can still hold to our theory. We can dismiss the experiment on grounds that we didn't achieve closure.[4] There is, as I hope is clear, an enormous difference between prediction in conditions of (approximate) closure and prediction in open systems, where all sorts of unaccounted-for causes will be working conjunctively to produce outcomes.

This last, of course, is the key point. It is a huge confusion to say that the goal of science is prediction.[5] In open systems, almost anything might happen. This does not mean that there are not laws of nature, nor that they are "violated" (which is why we said *almost* anything might happen). It means, rather, that we best think of the world as a containing both necessity and contingency, the consequence of the fact that the universe is not a closed system. Likely, those who fail to see this take celestial mechanics as their paradigm. For most practical purposes, the solar system is closed: It is not likely that some gigantic mass will enter it and throw off our predictions (calculations) as regards the future space and time coordinates of the planets and other masses in the system.

It is now easy to see what is going on when we seek explanation. To explain, one needs to show what events and mechanisms contingently combined to produce the outcome. Indeed, the presumed limitations of the human sciences are rooted in both fundamental misunderstandings of science and, as Weber saw, our dominating interest in the human sciences in explaining the concrete.[6] The logic of explanation is the same. Explaining revolutions, like explaining the crash of TWA 800, requires a narrative that identifies the causes open-systemically at work in the world, where perhaps none are either necessary or sufficient conditions. In none of the sciences can we hope to find a "complete explanation," since there will always be yet-to-be-identified bits and pieces in the unique causal history of any event. Generally, in fact, we are content when we have identified among the complex of causes—of which most are taken for granted—the cause or causes that seem to us to have made the difference. It is the failed circuit breaker that gets our attention, not the ubiquitous presence of oxygen.

THE ONTOLOGY OF SOCIETY

There is a sense in which providing causal explanations in the human sciences is both easier and harder. It is easier in that human action is absolutely critical to what happens in history. But it is more difficult for two reasons: First, there are immense (theoretical) difficulties in identifying the "conditions" that enable and constrain actors, a consequence of the absence of the capacity to construct system closure, to experiment. Second, because these conditions (viz., social structures are the "products" of human action), the conditions are themselves continually undergoing change. That is, unlike the objects of study in natural science, the objects of study in social science—institutions, social structures, social relations, and the like—do not exist independently of us. They are real, but concept and activity dependent.

Nature exists independently of us. Society does not. This has puzzled thinking about the human sciences from the beginning. Some writers have insisted that society does not exist at all, that only individuals exist. This is true in one obvious sense: We cannot "see" society. We only see persons acting and interacting in various ways. On the other hand, it seems sensible to talk of "social facts," that is, as Durkheim put it, "ways of acting or thinking with the peculiar characteristic of exercising a coercive influence on individual consciousness." What we do is surely "influenced" by "social facts." Otherwise, it is hard to see how there could be any patterns in social life at all or why these patterns do differ from society to society and from time to time.

We can solve the puzzle in this way. Let us say that social structures are incarnate in our activities, that they have a "virtual existence" in that they do not exist independently of human activity. We do not "see" social structures; we see only patterned activities: teachers teaching, employers and workers engaged in production, clerks and consumers buying and selling, males and females marrying and raising families. As Giddens (1979) writes, "Structure enters simultaneously into the constitution of the agent and social practices and 'exists' in the generating moments of this constitution" (p. 5).

Insofar, structure is both medium and product of conscious, intentional activity. Structure is medium in the sense that it is "material" used, both enabling and constraining. For example, a person knows a language and thus can speak. He or she creates sentences with the "materials" of the language; he or she uses it to describe, protest, explain, and so on. On the other hand, he or she is also constrained by language. To be understood, he or she must conform, more or less, to the "rules" of that language (even if these "rules" are mainly tacit and unacknowledged by speakers). Some sentences make no sense. Sometimes he or she strains to communicate his or her meaning, perhaps by creatively employing a metaphor. And some things simply cannot be said.

These features are fully generalizable. Everything we do involves socially available materials: institutions, cultural practices, modes of production. When we work, we work with "materials," language and all the particular "rules," "relations," and "tools" that make up that work activity. Thus, there are bosses who can fire us, tasks expected of us, and ways to accomplish these. We work with a computer, files, telephones, and so on. On the other hand, social structures are products in the sense that, as an unintended consequence, when we speak, we give reality to the language, reproducing it in time and space. Similar to all other activities, our work activity realizes the rules and relations that are incarnate in that sort of work activity.

But since structure depends on activity and people are not automata, structures change. That is, in acting we both reproduce and transform structure. A dead language is frozen in the grammar books; a living language changes. It remains English or Spanish but because it is used, it changes. And so with all social structures: There is both continuity and change. The family of Victorian England is not the typical contemporary American family. Both are families, even while nurturing practices and role relations in families have changed—rather dramatically.

Because social structures do not exist independently of human activity, there are differences between the physical sciences and social science, but these do not entail differences in the nature of either theory or explanation. Two differences demand our attention.

First, as in all the sciences, since scientists must communicate with one another about "the world," they are engaged in interpretation. That is, in order to build a consensus about claims made, they must continually seek mutual understanding about such claims, the standards employed, the evidence adduced, and so on. The social scientist must also build a consensus about claims and theories, so social scientists are similarly engaged in interpretation. But unlike the natural scientist, "the world" that the social scientist is describing, communicating, and seeking consensus about is itself a meaningful world being reproduced (and transformed) by human activity. Activity is meaningful in that human action involves concepts, rules, norms, and beliefs. Accordingly, all social research is characterized by what Giddens (1980) has called "a double hermeneutic." Social scientists must interpret what are already ongoing "interpretations" by members whose activities constitute social structure.

But, critically, although human action involves rules, norms, and beliefs, and competent actors "know" enough to carry on activities, there are both unacknowledged conditions for this action and unintended consequences of it. Sweatshop Asian workers making shoes for Nike may lack an understanding of the structures of global capitalism, and they do not work in order to reproduce it. Owners of four-wheel-drive vehicles may also lack an understanding of global warming, and they do not own these vehicles in order to avoid the pollution restrictions that are imposed on conventional automobiles.

Paralleling the aims of physical science, it is a fundamental goal of social science to provide an understanding of these conditions and their lawful consequences. By abstracting from the concrete, Marx showed that a theoretical convincing consequence of capitalist reproduction is a tendency for the profit rate to fall. This is a "law" of the system exactly parallel to the law of inertia, and like it, the product of abstract theory.[7] Gravity, of course, prevents planets from going off in an infinite straight line and causes, in conjunction with inertia, an elliptical path. Similarly, if we look at historical capitalism we see fluctuations in the profit rate and often long-term increases in it (as recently). This does not falsify the theory, since in the concrete real world there are always other causes at work: politics, wars, natural disasters, temporary advantages of innovation, and so on. Indeed, the recognition that the imperative to lower costs, itself a consequence of the system, will reduce the profit rate unless prevented, is precisely what leads capitalists to seek remedies; for example, monopoly.

Second, social science is inevitably historical and concrete. But since there are no historical laws (versus Whiggism, eschatological versions of Marxism, and evolutionary theory), if we want to understand present practices we must acknowledge that they are contingent historical products that could have been otherwise. There is radical contingency in history, and time (as current complexity theory emphasizes) makes a difference: What happens has effects on what will then happen, and so on. This means that although we can explain these different trajectories, there was nothing inevitable about any of them. To be sure (as with the laws of nature), while not everything is possible and existing ensembles of social structures foreclose some possibilities, actual outcomes are always contingent.

FUTURES RESEARCH

What then of futures research? Scientifically defensible futures research depends upon having an understanding of present arrangements, of the conditions and consequences of action. Thus, if we have an adequate theory of global capitalism (which will likely involve some complex considerations regarding politics and culture), we can understand the activities of the Nike corporation and their Vietnamese workers. We will understand both the unacknowledged conditions for that activity and at least some of the unintended consequences of it. Similarly, if we have an understanding of global warming and an understanding of political economy (along with some complex considerations regarding politics and culture), we can understand the unacknowledged conditions and at least some of the unintended consequences of the increases in the purchases of oversized vehicles by Americans. Given this, we can then say that if these structures are more or less reproduced, the future will likely be thus and so. But for the same reasons that in history not everything was possible and nothing was inevitable, there will be no way to determine actual futures. More than this, because action is structured, not all "scenarios" are equally possible. Massive structural change will be required for some to be realized; for others, perhaps smaller changes could have significant consequences. This is not a matter of speculation but of fact, depending on the adequacy of our understanding of present arrangements.

There is no effort here to predict events, nor, critically, is the claim made that these structures will be more or less reproduced. I take it that the whole point of futures research is to argue that some of them at least must be changed if we are to preclude consequences that no one intends. This then is the real merit of futures research. The idea is not to spin out a series of possible scenarios. Rather, the idea should be to identify what, given present arrangements, are the most appropriate political strategies to intervene positively. To offer scenarios that are politically impossible, or even remote, is to be utopian in the worse sense. The future is not yet made; but whatever it comes to be will be the way it is because of what we do (and do not do).

As noted, theory is critical, for it alone can help us to grasp the dynamics of structures and their relations. Critical here, as well, is the fact that participants, who need not be cognizant of these conditions and consequences, may well have false or distorted beliefs that are essential to the reproduction of practices. Social science is potentially emancipatory in precisely the sense that it can show that, unwittingly, persons may well be acting in ways that are, in point of fact, contrary to their interests, contributing to their own oppression, and, perhaps, to the destruction of the planet as well. Indeed, intended change requires that members have a grasp of the conditions of their activities and their consequences. This is, of course, only the first step, but it is an absolutely essential first step.

NOTES

1. I say "real" here also advisedly, so as to be clear that on the present (realist) view, we trust in theory because theoretical terms "represent" realities that (versus empiricisms) may or may not be "given in experience." See Harre (1986).

2. Everybody recognizes that good correlations need not be causal (even while, given their Humean presuppositions, all our texts flounder in helping us to know when we have a cause and not a "mere" correlation). But we reject the Humean account: A causal relation presupposes a nomic and necessary connection. We need not balk at this. Indeed, Jaegwon Kim (1987/1993) is prepared to say that "most philosophers will now agree that an idea of causation devoid of some notion of necessitation is not our idea of causation—perhaps not an idea of causation at all" (p. 234).

3. Sometimes considered a law of nature, the statement, "gold is yellow," is a generalization that is explained in terms of a host of (true) laws of nature, including physical laws regarding light, pretty well understood, and optical and psychological laws that explain human perception, which are not at all well understood.

4. That is, falsification and confirmation are symmetrically vulnerable.

5. As the foregoing suggests, the primary goal is understanding: achieving a grasp of the causal powers of things. Once this is achieved, of course, we can design technologies and intervene effectively.

6. For Weber, see Manicas (1987, pp. 127–140). The so-called pure sciences (or, for Weber, "abstract sciences") are never sufficient to explain events. Practitioners do not even try. We might say that such sciences can explain generalizations (e.g., that salt generally dissolves in water or that gold is yellow). Even so, it might be better to say that these sciences allow us to understand why such a generalization is true. Providing such an understanding ought to be a goal of science education in our schools.

7. That is, Marx's theory of capitalism stands to historical capitalist societies as molecular chemistry stands to the concrete world of ordinary "things."

REFERENCES

Achinstein, P. (1993). Can there be a model of explanation. In D.-H. Ruben, (Ed.), *Explanation*. Oxford: Oxford University Press. (Reprinted from *Theory and Decision, 13*, 1981.)

Aronson, G. (1984). *A realist philosophy of science*. New York: St. Martin's Press.

Bhaskar, R. (1975). *A realist theory of science* (2d ed.). Atlantic Highlands, NJ: Humanities Press.

Bhaskar, R. (1979). *The possibility of naturalism*. Atlantic Highlands, NJ: Humanities Press.

Dretske, F. (1977). Laws of nature. *Philosophy of Science, 44*, 248–268.

Giddens, A. (1979). *Central problems in social theory*. London: Macmillan.

Giddens, A. (1980). *The constitution of society*. Berkeley and Los Angeles: University of California Press.

Harre, R. (1970). *The principles of scientific thinking*. Chicago: University of Chicago Press.

Harre, R. (1986). *Varieties of realism*. Oxford: Basil Blackwell.

Kim, J. (1993). Explanatory realism, causal realism and explanatory exclusion. In D.-H. Ruben, (Ed.), *Explanation*. Oxford: Oxford University Press. (Reprinted from *Midwest Studies in Philosophy 12*, 1987.)

Lewis, D. (1986). Causal explanation. In D. Lewis, *Philosophical Papers*. New York: Oxford University Press.

Manicas, P. T. (1987). *A history and philosophy of the social sciences*. Oxford: Basil Blackwell.

Manicas, P. T. (1989). Explanation and quantification. In B. Glassner and J. D. Moreno (Eds.), *The quantitative–qualitative distinction*. Oxford: Basil Blackwell.

Maier, C. (1997). *Dissolution: The crisis of communism and the end of East Germany*. Princeton, NJ: Princeton University Press.

Salmon, W. (1978). Why ask "why?" [Presidential address]. *Proceedings and Addresses of the American Philosophical Association, 51*, 663–705.

Salmon, W. (1984). *Scientific explanation and the causal structure of the world*. Princeton, NJ: Princeton University Press.

Scriven, M. (1959). Truisms as ground for historical explanations. In P. Gardiner (Ed.), *Theories of history*. New York: Free Press.

Scriven, M. (1962). Explanations, predictions and laws. In H. Feigl and G. Maxwell (Eds.), *Minnesota studies in the philosophy of science* (vol. 3). Minneapolis: University of Minnesota Press.

Skocpol, T. (1979). *States and social revolutions*. Cambridge: Cambridge University Press.

Woodward, J. (1993). A theory of singular causal explanation. In D.-H. Ruben, (Ed.), *Explanation*. Oxford: Oxford University Press. (Reprinted from *Erkenntnis, 21*, 1984.)

8

Social Change and Futures Practice

Peter Bishop

SOCIAL STABILITY

Social stability is the ability of a group to persist and retain its traits through time, even as its members come and go. I see three forces that give social groups their stability: biology, culture (beliefs, values, norms, customs, etc.), and agreements (law, policy, procedure, etc.). The substrate for social stability is the biological organism, with its capabilities and limitations. The human organism is capable of many animal functions along with the unique human capabilities of language, thought, consciousness, and the ability to imagine nonexistent states, such as the future.

The biological endowment also imposes its limitations. Humans cannot naturally fly or breathe underwater. They perceive only parts of the electromagnetic or auditory spectra. They have a hard time imagining more than three dimensions or time flowing backward. They are often driven by emotion rather than thought. They cannot comprehend realities that transcend their experience: the nature of matter or the universe, a perfectly moral, selfless life, or supernatural phenomena, even if they exist. Language itself seems to contain deep structures across all cultures that constrain our views of the world.

In short, the human biological organism is good for some things and not good for others. Many of the patterns of social groups are designed to make use of the capabilities and compensate for the limitations. For instance, while cooperation among humans is common, people are also naturally self-interested. Society uses that trait in capitalism but must also limit it in law.

The biological organism does change, but the rate is so exceedingly slow that it can be considered constant for any time period shorter than geological.

Culture, the second force for stability, is unique among animal species and changes much faster than biology. Culture includes a people's beliefs about itself and the world, values, norms of conduct, customs, and manners. Culture is tradition, the repository of that people's experience: what works, what to avoid, how to survive and prosper in the world. Culture in most societies and at most times is implicit, unconscious, obvious. As such, it is rarely challenged and stays the same over long periods of time. Cultures do change, but only on historical time scales of centuries or sometimes decades.

The third category of stability are the agreements that people explicitly make with each other. Agreements come in the form of constitutions and laws (governments), charters and contracts (economics), and policies and procedures (organizations). Agreements that are made by humans can be changed by them, but the arduous process of coming to agreement creates an unwillingness to change and an inertia that keeps agreements in place for long periods of time. While faster than biology or culture, agreements do persist and stabilize human activity over time.

Other sources of stability include the following:

- The natural environment, which provides resources and contains threats for human society at particular places and times. Since those resources and threats persist over time, they shape human behavior over that same time.

- Technology is the way humans manipulate the natural environment (and themselves) to provide basic necessities and higher qualities of life. Each technology requires an infrastructure and set of behaviors to be effective. Since the technology persists, so does the behavior.

- Until recently, human populations have rarely changed their size or composition (gender, age, etc.) These persisting demographic traits stabilize the behaviors associated with them.

- Political power is the ability of one or more people to influence or coerce the behavior of others. Since power tends to remain in the same hands or to be passed on to a narrow range of followers, the constraints accompanying that power also persist.

SOCIAL CHANGE

With such an array of forces for stability, it is a wonder that societies change at all. (Of course, starting with the forces for change would leave the impression that societies would never be stable.) In many ways, however, the forces for stability and for change are the same. Forces promote stability when they themselves are stable, but they induce change when they change. Stability and change are therefore a continuum regulated by the degree of stability and change in these forces.

Another perspective on change is what induces the forces themselves to change. Why does society not come to rest like a pendulum and remain the same forever? The question contains an assumption about the nature of society. Most if not all would agree that society is a system, a set of interacting components that relate through feedback. But the type of system is often misunderstood. The image of the mechanical system has dominated the discussion throughout the industrial age, with the clock (or the computer) as the quintessential machine. Structural–functionalism, popular in sociology and other social science disciplines after World War II, illustrated this view. A newer view is that human groups are organic rather than mechanical systems. No one made that distinction until recently, however, because organic systems were also thought to be just complicated machines.

The difference between mechanical and organic systems is the difference between top-down control and bottom-up emergence. Norbert Weiner and John von Neumann, respectively, proposed these concepts of systems in the 1940s. Weiner's concept of cybernetics (top-down control) prevailed and became the basis for systems engineering, which in turn produced the many technical marvels of our world today: rockets, computers, automobiles, and so on.

Von Neumann's concept of automata (bottom-up emergence) was not as useful in building systems, but more useful in understanding those that occur in nature. As opposed to a machine, the development of an organism requires no blueprint, no master builder, no "controller." The developmental sequence is not encoded like a computer program, but rather like the capabilities contained in the cell. Given a certain local environment, the cell develops into bark or leaf, skin or organ, tissue or blood. Using the top-down analogy, people assumed that the brain controls the organism, like the manager controls the department, by giving orders. The new concept is that the brain, at least in nonconscious species, is more like the Internet, passing chemical or electrical messages among independently acting organs. Consciousness is a thin veneer over the multitude of autonomic and unconscious messages that pass through the brain and the spinal cord.

Another property of organic systems is their ability to self-organize. Machines can only change in two ways: They can deteriorate through the action of entropy or they can be improved by some outside force. Machines cannot improve themselves, but organisms can. A system going through the critical transition of transformational change usually dies. Only once in while does it come out of that transition better (or more organized) than it was before. Even computer simulations can demonstrate the principle of self-organization. Many tiny computer programs interact with each other, forming an ecology or organic system. Over time, many of the traits of biological species, including speciation, extinction, parasitism, even cooperation emerge, spontaneously with no outside intervention. The result is emergence, the trait of a system that emerges from the action of "lower-level" interactions. The shape of an organism is emergent, it is based on DNA encoding, but nowhere in the cell is there a picture or a blueprint or a plan of that shape.

If human groups are not top-down machines with master controllers, but rather bottom-up colonies of interacting entities, they can self-organize into novel, even better forms and their properties are emergent and not dictated by some dominant controlling force. The forces of creativity and novelty prevent an organic system from lapsing into static equilibrium. The interacting entities, pursuing their individual interests and goals, keep the pot boiling as long as external resources are available to sustain the system.

So much for why there is change. But what causes some changes to occur and others not to? The basic mechanism is natural selection. Natural selection is actually a misnomer because it identifies only half the process. It should be called natural variation and selection. An organic system (a set of interacting entities) presents a range of variation (a "menu," if you will) to an environment, and the environment selects which of those variations will survive based on its fitness for that environment. Some variations may be equally fit, in which case they survive equally. Some may be below some minimum fitness, in which case they disappear. The process is repeated generation after generation.

If that were all there was, however, the system would quickly converge to the most fit examples and eliminate the variation. Change would stop. Two things prevent a static equilibrium from occurring. One is the tendency of an organic system to create spontaneous variation. In biological systems, it's called mutation; in human systems, invention (of things or ideas). Most mutations and inventions fail, but those that survive provide an endless source of variation.

The second thing that prevents static equilibrium is that the environment itself is not static. The environment of any biological or human system consists, in part, of other biological and human systems. They are changing just as the target system is changing, mutually adjusting to each other in an endless dance of variation and selection. In the process, the standard of fitness is also changing, presenting the system with a "moving target" and the need continuously to find a better solution to the new problem. Thus, the system never comes to rest. Endless variation and adjustment keeps changing even in the presence of the forces of stability.

Characterizing systems this way also displays the property of self-similarity, a trait first recognized in fractals. Self-similar systems look the same at every level. A graph of the stock market, for instance, is self-similar. One cannot distinguish by the graph alone whether the values vary over minutes or hours or days or months or years. The peaks and valleys, noise and trend all look the same.

Similarly, describing change as the variation proposed by a system of interacting entities and selected by an environment composed of other such systems is actually to describe another system, a system at the next level. Thus, cells interacting with their environments (chemicals, hormones, neurotransmitters, etc.) form organs; organs interacting with their environments form organisms; organisms interacting with their environments form species; species interacting with their environments form ecologies; ecologies interacting with their environments form the global, planetary system. Each level emerges from the behavior of the previous level. If the organisms are human, then an additional emergence occurs. Human individuals interacting with their environments form groups (families, work groups, etc.); groups interacting with their environments form organizations and communities; organizations and communities interacting with their environments form societies; societies interacting with their environments form the global society.

Stability in human society then rests on lower-level stability (biological) and on culture and agreements that capture the successful variations of the past. Change in human groups and societies then arises from spontaneous variation (invention), from change in their environments (consisting of natural ecologies and other groups and societies), and from change at different system levels (biological to global).

TEACHING AND CONSULTING

My understanding of stability and change has consequences for my work. It provides me a set of assumptions about the future that I believe are more often correct than not.

The forces of stability support three important assumptions about the future. The first is that transformational change is rare. Futurists emphasize the possibility of the transformational—that's our business. We emphasize it because other views of the future make too little of how rapid, systemic change can overwhelm us as individuals or our organizations and societies. The occupational hazard, however, is that we may believe that transformational change is more likely than it actually is, believing, perhaps, that it is almost as likely as the amount we talk about it. That's probably wrong. Futurists will be the most surprised people around if the world fifty years from now is substantially the same as the world today. But some things have survived the last 50 or 100 or 200 years, and some things are likely to survive that long into the future. In my work, therefore, I try to put the possibility of transformational change in the proper context; that is, it probably won't happen in the short or medium term.

A second assumption from the forces of stability is that they prevent natural, incremental change, thereby setting up the conditions for cataclysm. Were we able to respond immediately and appropriately to invention or external change, we would deal with the forces of change in small increments rather than in large doses. Large-scale change is sticky; biology, culture, and agreement sustain the current system longer that it should. The forces overplay their role as guardians of tradition, maintaining the status quo beyond its useful life. The result is punctuated equilibrium, a term derived from evolutionary biology. As opposed to the gradualism of Charles Darwin, most eras of geological time show little biological change. These eras are separated, however, by short periods of massive shifts in the destruction and creation of species. Significant change, when it does come, usually comes swiftly with devastating consequences for the status quo. This assumption then balances the first. Even though transformational change is unlikely, prudent people consider it in their estimate of the future because the risk of being surprised is too great.

The final assumption arising from the forces of stability is that human intention and action, though the single most powerful force in the world today, is still not as powerful as the unconscious and unknown forces of biology, culture, and long-lasting agreements. Stephen Jay Gould makes the same point when he chastises humankind for overrating its power. We focus on ourselves as conscious and intelligent, but in his view, bacteria still run the world. While I am not a biologist, his argument makes some sense. The consequences for futures studies is to accept the world with some degree of humility: Whatever we do, a lot will happen anyway. The other is to point out to our students and clients that they alter that unknown world at their peril.

So my personal approach to the future and the approach I teach and preach is informed by what I know about how social systems cohere and remain stable over long periods of time. But the future does change, and for that, the forces of change provide three more important assumptions.

The first is that change is most often, if not exclusively, nonlinear. "Nonlinear" is one of those words that has been appropriated to mean anything that is unusual, surprising, or out of the ordinary. I use the term in its mathematical sense. Linear change follows the path of a straight line on a graph. Linear causality means that causes produce effects in proportion to their size. We learned (were indoctrinated into) both of these concepts in school: $y = mx + b$ is the change and $F = ma$ is the cause.

On the other hand, natural change rarely if ever follows a linear path. In fact, straight lines hardly ever occur in nature. Astronauts looking down on the Earth know that straight lines (contrails, wakes, roads, power lines, farms) are always human. Linear causality does occur in machines, but humans and their societies are organic, not mechanical systems. Resting on the bedrock of physics and chemistry is the nonlinear world of biology, where DNA controls the actions of organisms millions of times their size, where viruses sweep through populations and bring down empires, where a contraceptive pill changes the mores of advanced societies. I assume and teach that small events can produce large consequences. Thus, we need to be aware of even the most insignificant finding in a system that is ripe for transformational change.

The second assumption is that emergent, self-organizing systems are capable of creativity and novelty. Brand-new futures are as rare as transformational change, but they do occur. When they do, they introduce a whole new order of reality, a new arrangement that persists for a long time. In the biological realm, life is the ultimate example of self-organization. Multicellular life then continues the long trains of innovation leading to human consciousness. In the human realm, language is the seminal invention, leading to human society and complex forms of cooperation. The creativity of the past gives me hope that we will see more creativity in the future, that we will be pleasantly surprised about how things turn out. Thus, I can encourage people to dream their dreams and work toward their visions. Though I can hardly guarantee them success, amazing things have happened before; why not now?

The final assumption is that context is always important and generally ignored or underrated. For some reason, we are drawn to explanations that treat a target system as closed, independent of the forces of its environment. But that is never true. More often the explanation is a balance of action and environment in which the target system and its environment adjust and react to each other in a dance of change. The dance involves a hazy notion to us: reciprocal causality, two things mutually causing changes in each other. We refer to it as "the chicken or the egg," suggesting the simple notion that one had to come first. That view may be okay for children, but it hardly describes how the world really works.

Another way of stating this assumption is that every system (person, group, organization, society) is ultimately accountable to some outside force, the selecting environment. Even the most powerful people, companies, or nations ultimately rise or fall on their ability to meet the requirements of that environment. Power is the ability to work one's will against resistance, but power is only temporary. It is a brief interlude, holding back the forces of the environment for a time. Sooner or later, the environment wins out and the waters again flow over the spot. It is a gloomy picture to many, because change and progress are not permanent. Nevertheless, we can still celebrate what we have while we have it. It even makes the having more precious because it will ultimately fade.

My view of the future is then simultaneously surprising, creative, and realistic. The nonlinear effects of the unknown and unconscious world will continually surprise us as they create novel inventions and arrangements. The novelty, however, is always accountable to a strict environmental criterion. Wishing will not make it so; the new arrangement must ultimately submit to the harsh discipline of the selecting environment. It survives for as long as it satisfies that environment and disappears a short time after it fails to do so. The balancing of spontaneous innovation with environmental selection in a nonlinear system is as close as I come to a description of how the future progresses. Since current images of the future (over)emphasize tradition and permanence, intentional action and control, and linear causality, my mission is to prepare people for the possibility of novelty springing from unknown areas and to encourage them to create their own novelty in the time they have.

It is a lofty mission, to be sure, perhaps too much so. The forces of stability, permanence, tradition, and the status quo are strong. But the forces of change are equally strong, balancing the tendency to come to rest in some changeless future. The forces are well-matched, neither gaining the upper hand forever. They exhibit the ceaseless balancing of reciprocal forces that changes but does not destroy the underlying stability: variations on a theme. The future is like the past, only different. Or as Mark Twain said, "History does not repeat itself, but it rhymes." That's the future to me.

9

Permanent Development of Futures Research Methodology

Erzsébet Nováky

THE BEGINNINGS

The beginnings of futures research in Hungary date back thirty years to the Budapest University of Economic Sciences (called the Karl Marx University between 1948 and 1990). At the time when the Club of Rome was founded, Géza Kovács, the father of Hungarian futures research, and the futures research team rallying round him strove from the very beginning to make futures research fulfill both research and educational tasks as well as to provide answers to questions arising in practice. This complex objective has, to date, characterized futures research in Hungary.

Hungary had a socialist planned economy when Hungarian futures research emerged. Futures research hitched on to enhance the reality and complexity of the plans. We used prognoses elaborated for several areas of the economy to examine the future effect of the plans, and outlined a long-term complex and normative image of the future to reinforce the social aspects of the plans.

Futures research took root in no time in the training of economics students as well. The undergraduates turned with interest toward the relatively more open approach of futures research, which differed from the blinkered attitude of planning and recognized the role of long-range social aspects as well. Being able to form an opinion concerning the big questions of the future also struck them as something new.

In a matter of no more than ten years, futures research became an independent discipline in Hungary, a feat acknowledged by the Hungarian Academy of Sciences through the creation of the Futures Research Committee in 1976. The university research team played a significant role in this process by placing utmost emphasis on studying the problems of theory and methodology, and by meeting constantly changing social challenges. The department provided an excellent intellectual frame for creative work and scientific cooperation.

CHANGES

In the 1970s, futures research was closely connected with the system of the socialist planned economy, constituting its so-called outer circle. In the 1980s, an independent futures research started to unfold, and attention was increasingly directed to elaborating possible futures. At that time, we also began establishing mutually productive relations with the international vanguard of futures research. The 1990s boosted alternative ways of thinking and paved the way for a change of paradigms in futures research. We started to include researchers of varying professions in order to make our research methods more multifarious. Permanent change and reactions in keeping with the new challenges surfaced in education and in structural transformations as well. The independent Futures Research Department, with myself as the head, was established at the Budapest University of Economic Sciences in 1992.

CHANGES IN THE IMAGE OF THE FUTURE

The differing characteristics of the three time periods are conspicuously present in our work concerning the image of the future, which constitutes the main profile of the department. Each is based on different theories or philosophies, and vary in their methodological foundations too.

Our first long-range complex image of the future, elaborated in the early 1970s, was meant to look ahead to the year 2000. The focus of our survey was the net national product per capita, whose desired level we forecast for the turn of the millennium at $4,000, the lowest threshold for a postindustrial society. We then sought to specify the social and economic structure adequate for this level, which surpassed even the level of the United States at the time. We used the so-called top-down approach, applying both the philosophical tenet that macroprocesses can be broken down into microprocesses and the assumption that the level of economic development greatly determines all other (social, technical, technological, and ecological) processes.

Our second long-range complex image of the future, elaborated in the mid-1980s, focused on the 2020s. Our approach concentrated on the individual's basic needs (such as food, home, health, education, and the environment), and we looked into how the increasing set of needs could be satisfied. Using a bottom-up approach, we applied the philosophical tenet that the economy has to strive to satisfy the needs emerging in society.

We are currently working on the elaboration of our third complex image of the future. The need for this elaboration stems from the fact that fundamental changes have taken place since the late 1980s in the conditions of making forecasts. Changes have taken place in the relations of the socialist countries, falling like dominoes, to the industrialized West and the globalizing world, in the progress of Hungarian society's democratization process, and in the more assertive voicing of individual aspirations and ways of looking at things.

The new image of the future differs from the elaboration of the first two images mainly in the following:

- Our forecasting is worked out amid unstable conditions and is parallel to a change of paradigms.
- We attribute a greater role to the individual, not so much as a human resource but more as a biopsychosocial being that enters into direct contact with the future and, on becoming aware of a wide range of futures alternatives, demands greater freedom to choose and to decide.
- Relations between humans and nature surface from a new aspect. We scrutinize less relations between humans who cause environmental pollution and the environment, and focus more on the needs, perchance harmony, of humans living in a changing natural environment. To use Prigogine's words, this is the "New Testament" of the relationship between individuals–society and nature (Prigogine and Stengers, 1986).
- Humanity is beset by a growing number and variety of conflicts, dangers, and catastrophes from society, nature, and the economy, and yet has to surmount the circumstances of future shock and meet the demands of the future by adapting to them in newer and newer ways.
- The need arises to outline a society organized in keeping with a new system of social values, where modernization and social security, as well as economic growth, social innovation, and the linking of social–individual adaptation are all indispensable.
- Both economic growth and the economy play a "service" role in working out new types of relations between society and nature and society and the individual.
- We attach less importance than before to the analysis and forecasting of the conventional macroindicators (e.g. GDP, net national product [NNP]), and devote more scrutiny to new, frequently nonnumerical gauges that better reflect the interests and values of people in society, such as net economic welfare, the human development index, the pace of socioeconomic innovation, or the index of social satisfaction.

The fundamental dilemma in elaborating an image of the future for "after tomorrow" is that if a probable (or the most probable) version of the future is impossible to predict amid today's circumstances, then what should the image of the future contain and what structure should it have? Consequently, an image of the future composed via the third synthesis can be obtained in a particular way, through combining the top-down and the bottom-up philosophical approaches. Within this we systematically juxtapose versions of the future, one made possible by the economic conditions and the other desired by society and its members, and seek the accomplishable or realizable alternatives.

CHANGES IN THE METHODS, COMBINATIONS OF METHODS, AND THEIR APPLICATIONS

The methodology of futures research has manifestly renewed, even amid our circumstances in Hungary, and we have kept adapting new methods and further developed others for our forecasts for Hungary.

In the 1960s and 1970s, recognizing and forecasting the trends prevailing unchanged was the focal point of futures research. Therefore we integrated forecasting methods based on mathematical–statistical techniques into the methodological treasury of futures research in Hungary to work out the probable (and among them the most probable) futures alternatives. Underlying our investigation was the supposition that the nature of change would continue to be more or less the same as it was at the present or during the recent past. The prevailing methodological view emphasized the examination and extrapolation of existing trends. Time-series examinations as well as correlation and regression calculations proved to be appropriate methodological means for forecasting an essentially unchanged future. For the elaboration of reliable forecasts, it was primarily the (linear, exponential, and hyperbolic) functions without turning points, which express increase or decrease, that provided the basis. We solved simpler forecasting tasks with the help of analogy, morphology, and relevance-tree methods.

Futures research in Hungary was also searching for new methods for understanding alternative views emerging in the second half of the 1970s. In the course of the 1980s our concern was with how to forecast qualitative changes and how to elaborate "manageable" alternatives. From among mathematical–statistical methods, we adopted in our research parabolic functions that contain a turning point or turning points, and logistic curves as well as the envelope curve methods (Besenyei, Gidai, and Nováky, 1977). These helped to make it possible to describe processes of varying growth rates and of limited change, and to examine levels of saturation. Envelope curve calculations provided a basis for the analysis of successive technologies, with the dynamic branches generating economic growth, and for the investigation of breakthroughs.

Methods based on consulting with groups of experts also began to emerge. Using the Delphi method, we examined changes in education technology in Hungary (Nováky, Benedek, and Szucs, 1985) given the new framework of socioeconomic progress. Among modeling methods, we paid particular attention to the cross-impact method (Nováky and Lorant, 1978) during the further development of which we endeavored to make the algorithm easier to follow and adopted a new approach to the quantification of interrelations between events and trends and to estimating the limits of probability zones. We used the cross-impact method to forecast the expected direction and pace of economic growth in Hungary and, moreover, worked out a successful forecast concerning the future of a company that distributed servicing devices. In that period we paid particular attention to interpreting the reliability of forecasts and the methods that can measure the reliability of forecasts (Besenyei, Gidai, and Nováky, 1982).

In the 1980s our greatest undertaking was to examine the interrelationship of the economic and environmental subsystems in Hungary and to forecast their mutual impacts. Through this multidisciplinary model analysis (Nováky, 1991) we sought to find the answer to the question whether there was a forecast version that was equally favorable both for the Hungarian economy and for the environment. We found no such version amid our conditions in Hungary, alas, which meant that a desirable strategy for both the economy and the environment could not be worked out simultaneously unless a radical change took place in their relationship. This also indicated that sweeping changes were needed in the future in the economy, in society, and in the technological structure, all of which futures research must forecast.

We examined changes in the Hungarian environment also by adapting to our Hungarian conditions Forrester's (1971) world model elaborated through a system dynamics process. By further developing the method, we came up with an interactive model (Nováky and Cserhati, 1996), and made it applicable and interesting in a multimedia form.

One of the lessons we learned from the Eleventh World Conference of the World Futures Studies Federation, "Linking Present Decisions to Long-Range Visions," held in Budapest in 1990, was that forecasts for varying time ranges cannot be dissociated from one another, and that the roots of perspective pictures of the future must inevitably be connected to the present, otherwise the members of society will be unable to partake in bringing about that image of the future. This also played a part in launching empirical research, which brought to the surface Hungarian society's future orientation (Nováky, Hideg, and Kappeter, 1994), and the demand (from students, parents, and employers) to further develop professional training in Hungary, as well as the opinions of teachers in vocational schools (Hideg, Kappeter, and Nováky, 1995). By investigating the expectations for the future of nonexperts we began to involve them in making forecasts.

In the late 1980s and early 1990s futures research was looking for a new philosophy and methodologies to interpret the new types of conduct emerging within dynamic systems, and to forecast the future state of such systems. The future state of unstable systems is impossible to forecast (Gordon and Greenspan, 1988) in the sense that their future state is not predictable;

that is, cannot be seen precisely in advance. Therefore, scientific prediction, the exact forecasting of the new state and future conduct of the system, is impossible amid unstable conditions. In chaotic and/or slightly chaotic systems the need (and opportunity) to work out the only (most probable) version of the future must be discarded and, instead, elaborating a number of alternative scenarios must be given priority.

Chaos theory gave us a new outlook and means as to how possible future courses of development could be generated systematically (Nováky, Hideg, and Gaspar-Ver, 1997). We succeeded in applying our method for the analysis of the chaotic behavior of some forty Hungarian economic and social macroindicators and for the forecasting of their future courses of development.

Connecting different methods and constructing them with one another was at all times one of our customary means in order to enhance the reliability of our forecasts. We particularly favored mathematical–statistical methods, linking methods based on asking groups of experts and nonexperts (the Delphi method and the cross-impact method), as well as constructing the cross-impact method and chaos calculations in reference to each other.

CHANGES IN EDUCATION AND SUBJECTS

At first, teaching futures research played an important role only in the training of undergraduates who were future teachers of economics. The original idea was to familiarize those who would spend their lives teaching future generations with the theories and methods of looking into the future. Later, however, teaching futures research became more and more closely linked to the economics of special subjects, while today, futures research is recognized as a subject of methodology at the university (which gives it a certain prestige, too). The students are primarily fascinated by working out and further developing a variety of forecasts, in the course of which they can gain practical experience. We, the staff, are not always too keen to meet these demands, however, as it is our belief that at the university level the theoretical–methodological aspects of futures research are just as important as the practical components.

In keeping with the demands of this day and age we have introduced, beside our basic subject, called futures research, new subjects analyzing special new problems (such as economic forecasting, socioeconomic forecasting, social forecasting, boom research, enterprise prognostics, education and the future, and forecast training). We have also launched a postgraduate course called "Futures Research, Forecasting (Visionary Management)." Beside the Budapest University of Economic Sciences, futures research is taught in the same spirit at provincial universities in graduate and Ph.D. courses. We also endeavor to satisfy company managers' growing interest with our subject by a course called "Thinking about the Future."

Our knowledge base, published as teaching material such as our university notes (called *Futures Research*), our Futures Studies Series, and our handouts, partly convey standard knowledge and partly develop the undergraduates' practical ability to forecast.

Futures research seminars are conducted in the form of intellectual think-tanks and we employ a number of futures workshop techniques. Our undergraduates often get a chance to take a critical approach toward their former forecasts and to try to replicate their forecasts. We also make use of the method of systematic future generation: The students outline possible futures in theory, control them with the help of models, and check their implementation on the computer. We use the method of participative forecasts in examining future orientation when we try to establish young people's images of the future. Thus, computer modeling and multimedia education, through which undergraduates may generate differing versions of the future, are gaining ground in teaching futures research.

Our novel examination methods serve to gauge undergraduates' performance. On the one hand we have introduced group exams, and on the other hand students have to answer comprehensive theoretical–methodological questions and render an account of their practical knowledge of futures research as well as their analytical–critical abilities. With this we can measure students' ability to form their own opinions and to synthesize.

WHAT'S THE WAY AHEAD?
THE TASKS FACING US IN UNIVERSITY TEACHING

The research and teaching work hitherto carried out in the field of scientific futures research, as well as the national and international successes we have scored in working out practical forecasts, both signal that it is time futures research "became a profession." That is to say, futures research should be recognized as an independent discipline in Hungary as long as the people teaching the courses have the necessary combination of knowledge and abilities. That futures research and forecasting should be more closely linked to economics and its fringe areas, and that analysis and forecasting should organically be constructed on each other, are preconditions to this within our current university circumstances. I believe, furthermore, that we have the human and material conditions for futures research to become a major subject in the management Ph.D. program of the Budapest University of Economic Sciences within the next three to five years.

In order to achieve the conversion of futures research into a major subject, the following need to be implemented:

- diversifying and reinforcing university teaching of futures research on all levels of training.
- the scientific deepening of our study courses and their amplification on the basis of international equivalency.

- making computer modeling and multimedia solutions an integral part of education.
- creating distance teaching and developing our materials and methods along those lines.
- preparing for the twenty-first century, for life in the postindustrial (probably information technology) society (scientifically exploring humanity's role as a biopsychosocial being in building a future-oriented, creative society; reinforcing the future-oriented outlook; exploring the changed role of technology foresight; making more organic relations between forecasts of different time ranges; strengthening ties between prognoses and images of the futures).
- enhancing efforts to answer the questions raised by Hungarian reality; to this aim, establishing closer ties with practice, in the framework of a consulting company.

To achieve these aims, we must involve young people all the more in the modernization of teaching futures research. Graduate assistants and Ph.D. students must, therefore, be increasingly drawn into the department's teaching and research work. It is desirable that they, though maintaining their independence and creativity, acquire up-to-date professional, linguistic, computer technology, and communication skills on their way to a higher level of practicing futures research and to mastering the selective and synthesizing outlook that is so indispensable for a complex vision.

Cooperation with young people paves the way for working out and trying out new educational methods, and may constitute a basis for the renewal of the educational practice of futures research in Hungary over the next thirty years.

REFERENCES

Besenyei, L., Gidai, E., and Nováky, E. (1977). *Practice of future research and forecasting: A handbook of methodology*. Budapest: Kozgazdasagi es Jogi Konyvkiado. (In Hungarian).

Besenyei, L., Gidai, E., and Nováky, E. (1982). *Forecasting, reliability, reality*. Budapest: Kozgazdasagi es Jogi Konyvkiado. (In Hungarian).

Forrester, J. W. (1971). *World dynamics*. Cambridge, MA: Wright-Allen.

Gordon, T., and Greenspan, D. (1988). Chaos and fractals: New tools for technological and social forecasting. *Technological Forecasting and Social Change, 34* (1), 1–25.

Hideg E., Kappeter, I., and Nováky, E. (1995). *Vocational training at the crossroads*. Budapest: Munkaugyi Miniszterium. (In Hungarian).

Nováky, E. (Ed.). (1991). *Developing environmental strategies through future research*. Budapest: Ministry for Environment and Regional Policy.

Nováky, E., Benedek, A., and Szucs, P. (1985). *Technological development in education*. Veszprem: Orszagos Oktatastechnikai Kozpont. (In Russian).

Nováky, E., and Cserhati, I. (1996). *Interrelationship between Hungarian economy and environment with system dynamics approach*. Budapest: Jovotanulmanyok 8, BUES. (In Hungarian).

Nováky, E., Hideg, E., and Gaspar-Ver, K. (1997). Chaotic behaviour of economic and social macro indicators in Hungary. *Journal of Futures Studies, 1*, (2), 11–31.

Nováky, E., Hideg, E., and Kappeter, I. (1994.). Future orientation in Hungarian society. *Futures, 26*, 759–770.

Nováky, E., and Lorant, K. (1978). Method for the analysis of interrelationships between mutually connected events: A cross-impact method. *Technological Forecasting and Social Change, 12* (2–3), 201–212.

Prigogine, I., and Stengers, I. (1986). *La nouvelle alliance: Metamorphose de la science* [The new alliance: Metamorphosis of science]. Paris: Gallimard.

10

The Transformation of Futures Research in Hungary

Eva Hideg

MY WAY TO FUTURES RESEARCH

I began to deal with futures research in the middle of the 1970s. Being a Hungarian and having reached adult awareness amid the conditions of Central Eastern European socialism, I first approached futures research through the perspectives of socialist planning. Having read macroeconomic and social process planning at the Budapest University of Economic Sciences, the idea of directing social and economic development in a conscious and preplanned way appealed to me. Becoming familiar with socialist planning, however, I realized that it lacked a sufficient scientific basis, since it merely explored the past and then projected the future based on the Marxist–Leninist image of communism. This closed and somehow preordained nature of the future bothered me in particular. I refused to accept it, and thus turned to futures research. I believed that a more scientific exploration of the future could significantly boost socialist planning. At that stage, of course, I still thought that futures research, and the study of trends and their turning points, could significantly enhance the efficiency and scientific foundation of socialist planning.

MY RESEARCH AND TEACHING ACTIVITIES

During the twenty years I have spent investigating and lecturing about futures research, I have striven, in unison with my colleagues, to make the kind of futures research that applies the achievements and methods of science accepted as a science and as a profession, and to teach it as part of the Hungarian university course of economics and social politics. In spite of some failure, my work has been successful in as much as I have been able to connect self-education, the development of science, the practical testing of new ways of thinking, and working methods with the teaching of new knowledge and skills. At first my motivation lay in the joy of variety, but later success also played a part. This turned out to be a key advantage of futures research. It requires that one be open-minded and aware of novelty and change, and thus constantly renewing oneself and challenging one's previous beliefs and perspectives.

By the end of the 1970s, as a result of almost twenty years of investigation in Hungary, the theory, methodology, and methods of futures research crystallized and molded into teaching material that conformed to the criteria of classical science. I myself was an active participant in this development. It used to be evident to me that the future is something that will eventually materialize and that futures research should deal with this kind of future by obtaining preliminary knowledge of it in the present. During that time I focused on the theoretical and methodological questions of getting knowledge of the future of social processes. I believed that such knowledge would lead to the discovery of relevant development tendencies and their turning points. I also sought to discover the difference between social forecasting and scientific prediction undertaken by the various social sciences. I came to the conclusion that the movement of social processes could be revealed in all their complexity and mutual technical–technological and economic relations. This complexity is what distinguished social forecasting from scientific prediction in the different social sciences, I concluded. I used to think that by connecting futures research to socialist social planning it would be possible not only to forecast but to shape the future of our society. From this perspective I participated in developing different futures images for Hungary and believed I could forecast tendencies and direct changes in social mobility, housing needs, and all other similar social variables in Hungarian society.

However, by the middle of the 1980s I began to notice that these futures images and social forecasts in fact did not influence Hungarian society. While they were known, they were not used in socialist planning. I reluctantly came to the conclusion that futures research could not be connected to socialist planning. I overcame my disappointment at this by turning to teaching activities. I thought that if more university economic students became acquainted with the approach, methodology, and methods of futures research through forecasts and futures images in different fields of reality, then the utilization of these forecasts and futures images would be improved. At that time I developed new courses on "Possibilities of the Future" and "Forecasting Analysis."

The change of regime in the late 1980s, and the years since then, have considerably altered my view of the future, the way the future can be influenced and society directed, and many aspects of futures research itself. By now I have come to realize that obtaining preliminary knowledge of the future amid unstable circumstances is possible only through the further development of the methodology of futures research. The collapse of the authoritarian society has made me see, moreover, that "the future" means not only what will eventually or possibly materialize but also the human consciousness and psychic content that people today have of the future, which affects their activities in the present, and thus the future itself. In a society becoming more democratic and free, the future orientation of people and their institutions is a dimension of the future at least as important as the traditional dimension of the future depicted through conclusions drawn by scientific reality studies of probable and possible futures. As a futures researcher, I have had to come to grips with this new realization.

How futures research can be further developed in the new circumstances is what preoccupies me now. At present I think the following paths are open for futures research in Hungary:

- a redefinition of the notion of the future.
- further developments in the methodological investigation and elaboration of possible futures amid circumstances of instability.
- further developments in teaching futures research.

Redefining the notion of the future is needed because future orientation is not part of most people's consciousness yet. The forecasting activities on the rise in our region still operate on the notion that the future can be predicted by identifying the most important likely trends of development. Planning, which has lately returned to the center of attention, urges the elaboration of action programs. Both perspectives lack the open dimension of the future inherent in the concept of future orientation.

"Future orientation" is a human ability, consciousness, and emotion that arises and changes in people when they think of and take an interest in the future and follow techniques and activities that can help them lessen the uncertainties ahead and reach their goals. Future-related expectations, beliefs, suppositions, fears, and hopes constitute an integral part of future orientation. Linking this living future with the materializing future-to-be allows a multidimensional and more complex interpretation of the future than does passive forecasting alone. Elaborating this interpretation is worthwhile because it facilitates the deeper understanding of the process of how the future is shaped. Practical futures research based on this facilitates the development of foresight and a sense of responsibility for the future in people, their institutions, and the whole of society much more than the presentation of inevitable future trends independent of us or activities directed at the future in order to master it. This interpretation, however, calls for a thorough reconsideration of the earlier theoretical and methodological assumptions of futures research, and may even require the rejection of some earlier aspects of my own ideas.

I have concentrated on the future and this type of a reformulation of futures research in the last few years. Consequently, my colleagues, Head of Department Erzsébet Nováky, psychologist Istvan Kappeter, and I have elaborated the methods and Hungarian practices of empirical analysis in futures research (Nováky, Hideg, and Kappeter, 1994). Our research has convinced us that society's future orientation is varied, unstable, and changeable, but capable of rapid progress in the years of the transformation itself. There is no better source of change than peoples' positive attitude toward, and active faith and belief in, the future.

We also tested the existence of future orientation on the level of social institutions in order to prove that a society building itself from the grassroots is not alien to Central Eastern Europe as long as social mechanisms allow democracy and self-organization. The World Bank project, "Developing Human Resources," has allowed us to approach the future of professional training in Hungary on the basis of our new hypothesis and methodology. We investigated whether Hungarian society showed any trace of the emergence of new needs, thoughts, expectations, or intentions to act that could carry the seeds of the renewal of professional training. We surveyed the various images of the futures that exist and exert an influence in Hungarian society by analyzing opinions about the present and future of professional training in Hungary on the part of vocational training schools involved in the World Bank program, and different groups of employers and adults involved in child rearing or retraining and further training, all key figures from the point of view of the social function of the system of professional training. Our research has shown that not only politicians, social trendsetters, and futures researchers are able to shape the image of the future and alternative futures, but that all segments of society can also produce such images. These concepts of the future are not just mere ideas, but living and influential motivating forces behind all social activities (Hideg, 1995).

Naturally, futures research can and must propose futures beyond those already found in society. But we must not ignore the future orientation that actually exists in society. Futures research must, furthermore, introduce new and more efficient means of projecting possible futures amid the circumstances of instability. Elaborating future variations of chaos models is one such way. Our departmental research in this subject unequivocally showed that behind the change of regime in the 1980s lay the instability of our social and economic relations, and that bifurcation and qualitatively new courses of development are also possible through the future shaping of these processes (Nováky, Hideg, and Gaspar-Ver, 1997).

With the introduction of my new research results into teaching, the active development of the future orientation of undergraduates has moved to the foreground of teaching futures research. Beside presenting the theory and methodology of futures research, assisting and guiding the activity of the students aimed at shaping independent future alternatives plays an increasingly large role in my teaching. Consequently, I have compiled a series of case studies, each of which acquaints the students not only with the specific problems of studying the future and elaborating forecasts and images of it, but also with the ways and means of forming future alternatives according to their own preparedness, values, and expectations. Through this method we can show, on the one hand, that their attitude to and image of the future can be shaped by their intellectual capacity and that, on the other hand, we can achieve the goal of having futures research taught on an even wider scale.

THE FUTURE FROM THE PERSPECTIVE OF CENTRAL EASTERN EUROPE

The change of regime in Central Eastern Europe has not only given futures research new tasks, but has also shed new light on global problems and the future of the region and the world. The world has opened up. We no longer only contemplate the world, passively wondering how the future will shape up. We are now active players in it. The change of regime has intensified the sense of responsibility we feel for the future, our choices, and our actions. This, in the final analysis, is nothing but our local manifestation of globalization and freedom.

From our perspective on the world from this region, the change of regime has clearly satisfied basic needs and seems to be a determining and fundamentally positive process regarding the future of humanity too. Yet it has also become obvious that globalization and growing freedom do not necessarily go hand in hand. Globalization may make things uniform, and thus the freedom of the people of a given region and the life they choose to lead may significantly be limited. The future of the world also depends on the extent globalization allows local freedoms.

The years since the change of regime have also made it evident that globalization means an obligation to conform, even though this region is already highly motivated to conform. This pressure may be quite forceful but not so unbearable that the region will collapse under its weight and lose its character in the process. We are not one of those regions that propels change and development, and we are highly interested in safeguarding our identity by maintaining our traditions.

The change of regime in Central Eastern Europe means not only that in the wake of communism this region returns to the community of the democratic commodity-producing societies of the developed world, but also that the sudden end to the protective isolation has opened the way to all those global and civilizational crises and problems that other societies have long had to combat. Because these challenges come upon us suddenly and unexpectedly, we stand a chance of finding new solutions to the problems that are far more effective than the existing ones. Yet we can reap the benefit of this only if we manage to make our basically past-oriented identity consciousness future oriented. Thus, the future of the region hinges on a future-oriented identity consciousness and form of existence in a global world. This also gives new meaning to our recently gained freedom.

In the interest of this future, the societies of our region should steadily foment future orientation and foresight primarily by mobilizing learning skills and capacity. Although both the region and Hungary itself have a highly developed educational system, the unsatisfactory nature of the educational system worries me. The educational system does not prepare students for the kind of self-reliance and responsible problem solving required by the changes. In other words, we are not future oriented in the way we teach and train young people. Our societies do not stand a chance of imprinting our own particular face on globalization unless we concentrate on fomenting future-oriented identity consciousness and abilities for social innovation. To do so will undoubtedly enrich the future of all humanity as well.

NEW CHALLENGES NEED NEW ANSWERS

Globalization has challenged futures research not only in Central Eastern Europe, but in all other regions of the world as well. Nowadays, socioeconomic and technological development all over the world can be characterized by transition, in which instability and uncertainty are growing and becoming permanent. As a consequence of globalization, lasting development tendencies have disappeared and the unexpected nature of the future is growing.

Under these conditions, the social role and position of futures research has been shocked as well, because the forecasts prepared by conventional techniques have not come true or the forecast futures are not acceptable to the clients in the society. Failures are characteristic in both lines of futures research. The accuracy of predictive–empirical futures research as a positivistic science has rapidly decreased, because forces not considered or particular decisions have taken the development in another direction. Yet at the same time it is unlikely that the kind of alternative futures undertaken by cultural–interpretative futures studies can solve the great problems facing humanity, or even those of any particular society, and they cannot interpret or explain cross-culturalism (Hideg, 1992).

These facts indicate the strengthening role of randomness in shaping the future, while none of the conventional lines of futures research have been able to control or interpret it. These failures have produced an agenda that requires us to rethink and develop the idea of dynamics, development, social functions, and methodology of futures research in every region in the world.

I believe that futures researchers should also play an important role in the globalization process of the world. We ought not only to call people's attention to the dangers and possibilities inherent in the future, but should also actively participate in developing people's future-oriented identity consciousness and abilities for social innovation. Futures research should renew itself as a science and as a profession through handling this task.

My research experiences in the field of future orientation in society and discovering alternative future prospects arising from the analysis of social change have strengthened my determination to link these two aspects of social movements, and have led me to the realization that the interpretation of the future has become even more complex. Thinking about the theoretical–methodological solution to this dilemma has guided me to general evolution theory and the postmodern currents of scientific theory.

Although general evolutionary theory is very philosophical and has some weaknesses, it can be a useful working hypothesis for every scientific field that deals with the movements of a system, especially with the past and future development of a system. Futures research is clearly such a field. I have come to the conclusion that general evolutionary theory gives the following new and fresh thoughts and approaches to futures research:

- Social systems exist in nonequilibrium states. The relative stability of society is sustained by negative feedback mechanisms, but positive feedbacks cause the transformational renewal of social systems.
- Quantitative growth does not equal "development." Development not only has a qualitative character but it is an irreversible process having uncertain characteristics as well.
- Values, expectations, and new needs are the inner components of social movements. Shifting values, expectations, and human needs trigger social self-developments. Therefore, futures research has to study the future orientation of people, their different groups and institutions, and how they are changing in the period of transformation.
- The scale of possible futures is not endless but is limited by the evolutionary possibilities of systems. On the basis of evolutionary theory, futures research can determine and generate possible evolutionary or developmental paths systematically.
- The holistic approach of this theory can be applied to all fields of futures research. This means that the series of states of a dynamic system as a whole need to be studied and forecast. In this way not only chaotic but also evolutionary modeling can be developed for forecasting. Using this hypothesis, futures research can forecast both the nonevolutionary and the evolutionary possible futures by studying the complex dynamics of systems or societies.

The postmodern theory of science has showed me that futures research is but one of many different ways to interpret the world. The postmodern interpretative meaning of science makes the future alive. These living futures should become the subjects of a renewed futures research. I think that both evolutionary futures research and critical futures studies—two important new lines in futures research—work in these fields of thought. I believe that not only their differences and specific character but also their common perspectives and a possible synthesis of them both should be strengthened in the future. In this way a postmodern futures research could be developed.[1]

I have reached the conclusion that it is general evolution theory that offers the best framework in which my new interpretation of the future can become meaningful, not only vis-à-vis the concept of the future stemming from futures research, but also from a more general and generalized concept of the changes in, and the postmodern meaning of, science itself. Therefore, I think that by studying the modeling of evolution I can reach new methodological means suitable for the practical study of the future. Similarly, it has become clear to me that the research directions and experiments I hold so important have burst my old paradigm of classical futures research and futures studies. There is still a long way to go, however, before reaching the new synthesis and paradigm.[2]

In parallel with the new research lines in futures research, university training programs for would-be specialists in futures research should be reformed. Futures researchers should be trained so as to be able to apply a wide variety of different methods and to help different groups and social institutions to develop their future orientation and to invent their own futures. Futures researchers need to become useful service workers as well. The Internet should also be used both for new research activities and reformed training programs. Through the Internet, living, creative, and multiple connections and cooperations could be built among the different university workshops of futures research throughout the world.

NOTES

1. These topics were studied in the frame of the project, "Renewing Methodology of Futures Research in the Era of Transition," supported by the fund for National Scientific Research from 1995 until 1997. See E. Hideg, *Post-Modern and Evolution in Futures Research* (Budapest: Futures Research Department, Budapest University of Economic Sciences, 1998).

2. This topic will be studied in the project, "Application of Evolutionary Modeling in Forecasting," supported by the fund for National Scientific Research from 1998 until 2000.

REFERENCES

Hideg, E. (1992). Trends in futurology. *Magyar Tudomany, 36* (7), 797–810. (In Hungarian).

Hideg, E. (Ed.). (1995). *Vocational training at the crossroads.* Budapest: Ministry of Labour of Hungary. (In Hungarian).

Nováky, E., Hideg, E., and Gaspar-Ver, K. (1997). Chaotic behaviour of economic and social macro indicators in Hungary. *Journal of Futures Studies, 1* (2), 11–31.

Nováky, E., Hideg, E., and Kappeter, I. (1994). Future orientation in Hungarian society. *Futures, 26,* 759–770.

11

Politics + Science = Futures Studies?

Mika Mannermaa

A long time ago, as a young enthusiast in the field, I wrote the following: "Futures research is basically a normative activity, and the role of values in futures research is more emphasized than in social sciences generally. . . . Futures research should always be related to social development in general, and planning, as well as decision-making activities, in particular. A futures study which does not have any kind of direct or indirect impact on the development of society is totally useless, and cannot really be called a futures study" (Mannermaa, 1986, p. 170).

The Eternal Truth of the Future cannot, of course, be the goal of futures studies. The future is full of surprises, uncertainty, trends and trend breaks, irrationality as well as rationality, and it is changing and escaping from our hands as times go by. It is also the result of actions made by almost innumerable more or less powerful actors.

In this chapter I try to describe the general features of futures studies, especially in its purpose to have impacts on societal development and decision making. The aim is also to show that the change in societal development has brought new challenges to the theoretical and methodological aspects of futures studies. Finally, I'll discuss the problem of linking scenarios of the future to social and political decision making.

FUTURES STUDIES AS A FORM OF SCIENCE AND ART

Futures studies as a research area is understood in this chapter as follows: A futures study has a certain interest of knowledge of the future in the sense that, on the basis of the study of the present and the past, one is presenting well-argued assessments of the future.[1] The purpose of these arguments is to offer a basis for societal planning and decision-making activities as well as for the more general citizen's discussions and activities which are taking place at present.

There is an empirical element of futures studies at present. It is studied from a multidisciplinary viewpoint with the aim of building well-founded development paths on the basis of theoretical and empirical research. It is not justifiable to consider futures studies as a discipline. It is, however, an area of study with some characteristic features and a domain of competence of its own. These features include a clearly future-oriented interest of knowledge, a special way of defining problems in its study, and a research methodology that is partly its own.

The interest of knowledge in futures studies is especially interesting when thinking of societal and political planning and decision making. One way to categorize the interests of knowledge is to use Jurgen Habermas's old categories: *technical, hermeneutic*, and *emancipatory*.

Technical interest of knowledge in futures studies means the attempt to find invariances and to create explanations and forecasts based on regularities in the development. Furthermore, it is to practice rational planning, decision making, and control.

Futures studies characterized by a hermeneutic interest of knowledge aim at better communication and understanding between people in order to make joint activity possible. The prime purpose is not to develop methods and present quantitative forecasts, but to create subjective understanding of social reality.

By emancipatory interest of knowledge in futures studies I mean an attempt to establish a theoretical basis for creating images of the future from alternative subjective and objective premises by using both theoretical and empirical study. Forecasts of objective possibilities are supplemented with studies concerning subjective premises and possibilities to strengthen or weaken them. The "probable" development is only a reference alternative and an object for criticism.

Although all three interests of knowledge in futures studies are needed, the emancipatory interest is to me the most important one. An emancipatory study does not simply study "probable" developments or increase common understanding, but searches for "deviating" alternatives and criticizes even strongly dominant beliefs in order to give space to new ideas.[2]

Futures studies should be seen as a conceptually broader idea than forecasting attempts within one discipline. For example, forecasts made in the fields of technology can be seen as inputs for the large-scale scenarios constructed in futures studies. Futures studies has a methodological domain of competence of its own in its construction of "futuribles" (possible futures), using forecasts made in different disciplines as well as statistics and surveys as its own inputs.

Futures studies has become an ever more important area of study over the last thirty years. This is due, on the one hand, to the inherent future orientedness in all human activities and, on the other, to recent developments in the highly developed societies. Rapid technological, economic, and political changes with unpredictable discontinuities, increased complexity in societal processes, humanity's increasing ability to make decisions with long-range and large-scale impacts on nature, and humanity's own living conditions have all led to an increased need for well-argued assessments of the future based on the systematic study of present and past phenomena; that is, futures studies.

The methodology of futures studies is characterized by the following distinguishing features:

- A well-established tradition of transdisciplinary and multidimensional treatment of problems. Focusing merely on the future development of information technology, on the economic competitiveness of a certain nation-state (e.g., the problems of security–political integration in Europe) gives only partial glimpses of the possible futures.

- Instrumentality and normativity: The results of futures studies hopefully lead to plans, actions, and decisions, directly or indirectly.

- An endeavor to specify and construct evolutionary processes and development cycles as essential methodological tools. In constructing, for example, future developments of Baltic Europe, one has to reckon with the joint impact of processes that follow several distinctive kinds of "inner logics," among them transformation specific to postsocialist societies and economies on the East coast of the Baltic Sea, attempts to modernize welfare states in Scandinavian countries and Finland, development of knowledge-intensive economies in the region's leading countries, the formation of new security and cooperation relations in the postbipolar world period, the development of the European Union along the axes of deepening and broadening, and so on.[3]

- Development in the context of futures studies is not tackled in a deterministic way. Great attention in the framework of its methodology is given to distinguishing between different actors, to charting their activities that aim to modify the reality, and to studying their range of impact and consequences. The relationship between "possibles" and "desirables" is one of the focal points in futures studies. It is not only the accumulation of knowledge about the possibilities in the world surrounding some actor that is dealt with (the actor, besides being composed of the ruling elite or citizenry of some nation-state or their alliance, could also be, for instance, a social group or a movement, a cohort of people as an upholder of some national idea, a cultural community, etc.). The study also concerns dealing with the actor's own desires, fears, values, imagination, will, and the like, and the impact produced by the actions prompted by them. Especially in the evolutionary paradigm in futures studies it is assumed that the development of a society can be described as a process of creative discovery where both stable and chaotic phases play vital roles. Instead of understanding societies in "equilibrium terms" or as "mechanisms," we see a world of incomplete information and changing values, a world where we can meet several different futures: development, turbulence, and even catastrophes.

- Future in the context of futures studies (as the use of the plural form also indicates) is taken as multivariant (futures) and scenaristic. In the scenario approach the development picture is brought into dynamics and, if needed, the branching of alternatives is taken as being multistage.

TURBULENCE CREATES NEW METHODOLOGICAL CHALLENGES

It can be maintained that at the moment humanity lives in a period of transition, a transition from local to global; from monocultural to multicultural; from simple to complex; from fragmented, mechanistic, linear, and sectoral Newtonian understanding to systemic, holistic, self-organizing, nonlinear, and evolutionary "Prigoginean" understanding; from unsustainable to sustainable; from industrial technologies to information and biotechnologies; from industrial societies toward something new. It means that old values, ways of thinking, socioeconomic organizations, institutions, ways to work and act, and power relationships are breaking down, in such a way that new dominating solutions are not yet born, and perhaps never will be either. The future is possibly a mosaiclike combination of different communities and societies, values, ways of living, religions, and cultures. Transition is a creative process, which can produce not only collapses and threats, but also many interesting and challenging solutions to live and act in the society of the future.

I believe that living through a time of societal change is always a subjective experience depending on one's individual, cultural, religious, sexual, and other background. On the other hand, I think that there are good grounds for saying that the increasing complexity, globalization, regionalization, fragmentation, tensions between different cultures and religions and between the rich North and the poor South, the ever-increasing speed of technological and societal change, and the absolute need to create a world of ecologically sustainable development are much more than just "subjective personal feelings."

I find it probable that during the next few decades we will see powerful trends and turbulent phenomena. These will have an impact upon our societal structures and policies, upon the ways we as citizens comprehend the world around us, and, in the deepest sense, upon our values, and also upon the ways we understand the concepts of development and progress. Industrial growth is based on the exploitation of nature in humanity's attempt to create material growth, and this exploitation is approved by industrial economic units (e.g., by the traditional political parties). They have a common value system in respect to the general Western idea of progress; that is, that progress almost always equals growth. In the course of the decline of the old industrial society, the value system of these institutions is falling into problems, as are the institutions themselves. Instead of the old homogeneous idea saying that progress equals growth we may see many different ideas of "progress" in the future.

Today we are increasingly in the midst of a transition of values from the idea of growth and sovereignty of nation-states into something new, having ever-more international, even global, dimensions. Not everyone understands this process, and if they do, they do not like it. The reason is obvious: They will lose something in this process. In an industrial and even a partly agricultural society that considers the sovereignty of nation-states a sacred value, the dominating roles have been played by organizations—smokestack industries and their interest groups, trade unions, and traditional political parties—which are born from the tension between agricultural and industrial society, from the tension between countryside and cities, and from the tension between labor and capital. They all belong to a dying age. So does the whole command center, which so far has been formed by these organizations. For example, in Finland the trade unions, the industrial directors, the government, and the Bank of Finland do not operate effectively in the central command center of Finland anymore. The control of the center has already slipped, and the change process is obviously irreversible. At the moment, other actors, like global market forces, are effectively shaping the essential change processes. Fortunately, people's movements and other grassroots activities also have their moments to act in these turbulent times.

Slow change, gradual improvements, and so on are not the question here. The question is actually about a phase of transition having chaotic features that are not really controlled by anybody. These great changes, or "megaphenomena," that we are witnessing all around us are creating chaos as well as some sort of coherence or sustainability at the same time. Actually, this is my general vision of the world in the future. In an ecological sense, what is needed and what is hopefully happening in the long run is the realization of the principle of sustainability. It has to do with natural laws and that's why the principle is universal.

Sustainability, however, is not a proper concept for dealing with societal and cultural phenomena. Cultures and societal constructions need not sustain. What could be sustainability, for example, in art: sustainable surrealism? Or in science? In technological development? Is not chaos the essential feature of a new scientific theory or technological innovation, breaking the old scientific paradigm or the old technology, and in doing so creating something new and, hopefully, better?

Real development in culture needs this special form of order called "chaos." Chaos is actually like an energy bomb, often necessarily needed to establish something new. The collapse of the socialist bloc is perhaps the best contemporary example of a situation where gradual changes were not fruitful or even possible anymore. The socialist system had to be torn down and driven into chaos in order for a new and better one to be born. Those societies obviously did not have the potential to develop gradually.

Globalization is not only technological or economic process. Its cultural implications can hardly be exaggerated. Cultural coherence, multiculturality, and tolerance of difference will be ever more important issues to be learnt. Multiculturality in its different forms will increase in the future. So far, for example, Finland has been an extremely homogeneous country. The share of foreigners has been less than 1 percent. This figure will surely increase in the future.

At best, the globalization process offers us better possibilities to learn from different cultures, and to live peacefully in a global multicultural community. Conflicts between cultures are naturally possible, too. The more we have physical and immaterial interactions (as in using the Internet) the more we will achieve mutual understanding and respect toward other cultures. A real society of citizenship is possible. This is clearly a learning process for all peoples and cultures.

EVOLUTIONARY PERSPECTIVE IN FUTURES STUDIES

These powerful evolutionary phenomena in the world lead us to reconsider the basic premises of futures studies too. Many of the studies in the futures field have been based on Newtonian ideas that state that the world is nothing but a mechanism, basically a clockwork entity with a constant structure. According to Ilya Prigogine (1985), this way of thinking, however, is not enough in order to help us to comprehend the realities of the world and how they are changing.

During the last ten years or so, several future-oriented researchers (related, for example, to the United Nations University) have been interested in what could be called "complexity" or "evolutionary studies." These involve trying to understand the transformational dynamics of a society in a way which considers chaos as normal phenomena in natural and societal development.[4]

Natural systems—in which we can also include human societies—are essentially systems existing in states of thermodynamic nonequilibrium with nonlinear interactions and a strongly differentiated inner structure. The stationary stable states of systems like these can become unstable due to local fluctuations in the system or fluctuations coming from outside into the system. When these fluctuations are strengthened above a specific threshold value the system can shift to a new dynamic stable state that can be qualitatively totally different from the previous state. Prigogine calls the break between the two states a "bifurcation," and terms the new state "dissipative structures" (Prigogine and Stengers, 1984). Using Kuhn's terminology, a bifurcation is a paradigm shift, whereas the dynamic stable periods in between bifurcations mean living inside one paradigm (Kuhn, 1962).

One should be careful when applying the ideas coming from the studies of complex nonlinear systems, and from what has been generally called chaos theory, to human and social contexts. They are more like hypothetical metaphors than verified facts. On the other hand, it should be remembered that the mainstream social sciences also use metaphors taken from the Newtonian paradigm.

As a preliminary framework, the following hypotheses seem to be interesting when trying to define the contents of the new evolutionary paradigm in social sciences and especially in futures research (Mannermaa, 1991):

- Societies can be seen as dynamic, nonlinear systems, far from a thermodynamic equilibrium. Their components are human beings, communities, and other organizations of people as well as their material and immaterial output, and their environment, other societies and nature. They form their own levels of organization, and they evolve through processes typical to those levels. Although their development is due to the actions of human beings, they cannot be derived from these human activities. Evolutionary processes at a societal level are not always a result of conscious human planning and decision making, even though they may be caused by conscious (and also unconscious or irrational) subprocesses. An inflationary process is an example of this. Both employees who demand higher salaries, and employers who raise prices, act consciously, but the inflationary consequence as such is not consciously planned. Of course, the situation is much more complex, but this simple example is hopefully enough to make my point clear.

- There is asymmetry between the past and the future of a society because the most important societal transformation processes are irreversible. A pendulum in a vacuum is a reversible process: If you make a movie of it, you can watch it forward or backward and it looks the same. But think of such a simple process as writing articles. Many decades ago you used a pen or maybe a mechanical typewriter. Some twenty to thirty years ago the same was done by an electric typewriter. During the last fifteen years or so you have had microcomputers. Do you think that after some twenty or thirty years you will use an electric typewriter again? And later on a mechanical one? And so on? I don't think so, just because of the irreversible nature of this process.

- The self-organizing evolution of societal systems consists of stable evolutionary epochs with some degree of predictability and breaks or chaos phases, the outcomes of which are unpredictable and consist of a variety of possibilities for different future development paths, and even for a collapse of the system. One of the research topics related to this phenomenon has been economists' attempts to find out whether a time series that appears irregular is stochastic (random) or an expression of a deterministic chaos.

- The evolution of societal systems has a tendency toward ever-increasingly complex societies and toward the growth of dynamism in the sense of increased and more rapid flows of information, energy, and material. For example postindustrial society has emergent properties that cannot be found in an agricultural society (increased complexity). It has the functions for satisfying the basic needs, like those in an agricultural society, but also something much more.

- Evolution in societal systems is emergent in the sense that interaction between existing systems has a tendency to create new, higher-level systems with emergent properties typical only to these new levels. At the beginning, a new level is less complex than the levels below it. One illustration is that of the emerging European societal system, which will probably have emergent properties that cannot be deduced from a calculation of the properties of the nation-states in Europe. But still, at its early development phase, it was much simpler than any of its member states.

From these premises the development of a society can be described as a process of creative discovery where both stable (but dynamic) and chaotic phases play vital roles. It is not understood in "equilibrium terms" or through "mechanisms," but rather as a world of incomplete information and changing values, a world in which there are several different futures, as stated before: development, turbulence, and even catastrophes.

Societies that are in a stable state are characterized by governance through established institutions that are highly visible. "Traditional" economic, political, and cultural institutions control the development of a society. In this phase, different local fluctuations—from inside and outside of the system—are moderated by the negative deviation-reducing feedback mechanisms. One of the key issues emphasized, especially by Ervin Laszlo (1987), is that a stable society can, however, shift into a state of instability, bifurcation, in such a way that small social groups and movements ("fluctuations") present on the periphery of the society are strengthened and rise. Consequently, some of them may reach a dominant position in the affected society. This may mean a rapid and unpredictable change into a new type of dominant systemic state.

An example of this type of process is the Silicon Valley phenomenon. Sociologist Bart van Steenbergen (1987), who studied this process, has claimed that it was not so much a technological innovation as it was a social one. Certain young men wanted to create a totally new philosophy of personal information processing instead of going to companies like IBM to have their careers. They started from almost nothing, and now we all know how drastically the personal computers they pioneered have changed our lives, both at work and at home.

Another example is the revolutionary transformation of the socialist bloc in the late 1990s. The sudden collapse of this block is perhaps the best contemporary example of a situation where gradual changes were not fruitful or even possible anymore. The old system had to be torn down and driven into chaos in order that a new and better one could be born. What is fascinating in this kind of a chaos is that you don't really know what will happen in the future. What will happen in Russia in the next decades? Will it become a Mafia-driven primitive market economy, or a welfare state of the Nordic type, having the development level of class C? Or will it become a neocommunist conservative totalitarian dictatorship?

One thing is sure: For futures studies and for the relationships between futures studies and societal development, turbulent phenomena form new, fascinating, but also difficult challenges.

FUTURES STUDIES VERSUS SOCIETAL DECISION MAKING

The World Futures Studies Federation arranged its eleventh world conference on futures studies in 1990 with the theme, "Linking Present Decisions to Long-Range Visions" (see Mannermaa, 1992b). This showed how important the issue of "linking" is in futures studies. It is not only important, but also highly problematic. There are missing links in the chain from general scenarios to concrete political decision making.

One way to categorize futures studies on scientific and societal bases is presented in Figure 11.1. A study can be scientifically credible or not. A scientifically credible futures study presents scenarios that are plausible, consistent, essential, holistic, and multidisciplinary, based on accurate statistical, survey, or another empirical material of the present.[5] Quite independent of its scientific credibility, a study may have a low or high impact on societal discussion, planning, and decision making. In this way we can formulate four different types of futures studies.

High credibility–high impact should be the general goal of most futures studies. Too often this is not the case. As an example of a study like this, Meadows, Meadows, Randers, and Behren's (1972) *The Limits to Growth* should be mentioned. Although heavy criticism based on scientific arguments was raised against *The Limits*, it was a scientific enterprise using mathematical modeling, statistical data, and so on. There was much more "science" in this work than in most scenario studies. At the same time, *The Limits to Growth* really had an impact on societal development. It raised a

Figure 11.1
Credibility Versus Impact of Futures Studies

	Low Credibility	High Credibility
Low Impact	"Not so successful studies"	Most academic enterprises *Beyond the Limits*
High Impact	Brundtland Commission	*Limits to Growth*

global discussion of the ecological threats facing us in the next millennium, assuming that present trends continue to exist in the business-as-usual way in the future too. The report also presented alternatives that could help us to reach the state of sustainable development.[6]

High credibility–low impact is the fate of many academic futures studies. In the case of doctoral dissertations this is quite understandable. The main purpose of these works is to train postgraduate students for competence in futures research, not to influence the world around the researcher. Unfortunately, there are also a lot of examples of futures studies that represent competent research and are meant to have an impact on something but have failed to do so. One of them was the *Global 2000 Report to the President* (Barney, 1980). It was initiated by the president of the United States, Jimmy Carter. The purpose of this comprehensive and good study was to make conclusions about the continuation and consequences of the present trends of population, resources, and environment. The message was alarming, but it was not heard because the next president, Ronald Reagan, and his administration didn't like the results. Meadows, Meadows, and Rander's (1992) follow-up study of the limits, *Beyond the Limits*, is, unfortunately, another example of this kind. Even though the database was better, the computers much more sophisticated, and the message as serious as twenty years earlier, *Beyond the Limits* was left almost unnoticed. It was not a report to the Club of Rome like *The Limits to Growth*, but denigration of the status of the club may still have had an impact on the lack of success of the second report of Meadows and colleagues.

Low credibility–high impact. This situation is when more politics than science is at stake. The report of the World Commission on Environment and Development (1987) (the so-called Brundtland Commission), *Our Common Future*, is an example of a futures "study" that certainly does not represent Big Science (it is lacking theory and methodology), but has had a considerable impact on societal and governmental discussions and decisions. The commission launched the concept of "sustainable development" to the public. Since then, this concept has been a slogan similar to the idea of the "new international economic order" of the 1970s. In principle, programs of political parties are also examples of future statements that may have an impact (or not) on societal development. They are statements of desirable futures without even trying to be scientific studies. Most of them, however, belong to the category of *low credibility–low impact* (in many cases fortunately, one might add).

FUTURES STUDIES AS LEARNING PROCESSES

You need a method. In the earlier sections of this chapter I wrote that the present turbulent situation creates new challenges for futures studies. This should be understood both from the point of view of science and methodology (credibility) and from the point of view of having an impact on the "right" actors.

It was suggested that an evolutionary perspective may serve as one of the new frameworks for futures studies. It helps to create and "test" scientific hypotheses in futures studies. But this should not be understood as the only possibility. During the years of my interest in futures studies I have used several different methods, such as quantitative time-series modeling, soft-systems methodology, expert judgments (Delphi, cross-impact analysis), and different scenario and strategy approaches. I think one should choose one's method according to the topic and the purpose of the study. But, hopefully, one has some method if one intends to do serious futures research. Just writing about feelings may be nice, interesting, and therapeutic, but it is not research.

The most interesting constructions of the future are multidisciplinary and evolutionary scenarios covering a wide range of cultural, economic, technological, and social issues. They can be produced based on forecasts, Delphi estimations, qualitative trend analysis, or the like (from the present to the future), or from a normative starting point ("This is how I'd like the world to be, and the next question is how do I get there"; from the future to the present). In the first case, the empirical material available gives some limitations to the method: The scenarios should be plausible in the light of the material. In the latter case the borderlines are given by the limits of your imagination, not really anything else.

I have tried to stress the previous lessons in my own teaching at various universities as well as in my consulting. The main topics to be covered in the teaching of futures studies are the following:

- The basic theories: ontological and epistemological questions dealing with the concepts of future and futures research, values and ethics in futures studies, and so on.
- Evolutionary perspective, chaos theory, and societal processes.
- Systems thinking and modeling, both quantitative world modeling and qualitative soft-systems methodology.
- Specific methods: time series, scenarios, (mega)trend analysis, strategies, expert methodologies (Delphi, etc.), futures workshops.
- "Exemplars" of significant futures studies (e.g., *The Limits to Growth*).
- Futures studies and societal decision making: popular movements and activism, political processes, and so on.

Especially useful learning processes have been the following practices: I have asked students to write essays on various topics using systems thinking and evolutionary perspectives as their framework. Most of the students have been at the postgraduate level, and they have been experts in their own fields. Applying the evolutionary perspective to their specialty has been rewarding both for them and for me. The irreversible nature of many societal processes; disequilibrium as a natural state of affairs; structural changes (chaos) as well as stable periods in the description of societal development: These and related concepts have all proven to be especially useful metaphors for these students.

High Impact: On What?

I regard it as a kind of a paradox that in the 1990s in my own country, Finland, the official establishment has become more interested in futures studies than ever before. The government, the Parliament, most ministries and other authorities have produced futures and strategy reports. For the first time in Finland's history the government gave a special futures report to the Parliament in 1993, and it seems that this is becoming a regular practice. In 1993 the Parliament established a special futures council, again something that had never happened before. It should be added that these phenomena are not related in any direct way to party politics.

This is highly positive as such. I have been personally involved in many of the activities referred to here (futures work of the government, the Parliament, and the ministries). One can find real interest in futures thinking and studies in these institutions. I think that integrating futures thinking and studies into the traditional parliamentary processes is an important direction and a challenge for futurists in a more general sense in the future too.

One rather good example is the Dutch model. There is a high-level futures studies organization called the Scientific Council for Government Policy in The Netherlands. The council repeatedly raises important societal discussions with its studies on the main themes of the future. The Parliament is even obliged to react to the reports of the council.

But one has to admit that the prevailing political culture in Western countries is almost the opposite to the basic premises of futures studies: short-range instead of long-range, sectoral instead of multisectoral, simple instead of complex, no-change instead of change, and so on. In Finland, for example, the Parliament cannot really discuss the futures reports. It is simply too demanding for most of the members of the Parliament. They have no time and interest in reading heavy reports, and they do not see the importance and meaning of this discussion to their everyday work. They would rather discuss whether the shops are allowed to keep their doors open on Sundays or not. Everyone has an instant opinion on matters like this, and they are the topics through which you either win or lose voters.

The real paradox, however, lies in that it seems the old establishment is not the main innovator and maker of the future. It seems that especially in the highly developed Western countries, which are transforming themselves into the era of information, the main technological, economic, and social innovators are coming from the periphery of the societies. New Internet enterprises, small media and software companies, and new social movements outside the representative institutions will shape the development of the future.[7] The Internet in itself is a marvelous example of how self-organizing processes are streaming all over the world very much independent of what parliamentary decisions and legislation might want to say. The Internet is a "Wild West," for both good and bad.

I very much agree with Alvin Toffler (1994), who says that the decisive struggle today is between those who try to prop up and preserve industrial society (second wavers) and those who are ready to advance beyond it (third wavers). According to him, this is at the same time the superstruggle for tomorrow. Actually, I call this the Number One Battle, the battle between the future and the present. To me its quite clear who will win this battle.

Battle Number Two is the battle between the forces of the future. In the Nordic countries it seems that there are two basic scenarios and their supporting forces. Putting it briefly, Scenario 1 is the transformation of the Nordic welfare society into a globalizing information society. Scenario 2 is a neo- or postliberal (or libertarian) model, where the prime movers of development are market forces. The result of this battle is unclear to me, although scenario 2 is in the lead at the moment.

The history of ideologies, politics, and social movements has not ended. On the contrary, it has very much just started. One of the most interesting and most neglected issues in futures studies is the question of what kind of societal and political forces will shape the future. The political map in the democratic Western countries was born in a primitive industrial society that was quite different from our present societies. The last significant new political movement of the industrial society was, I believe, the Green movement. Now it is one of the old ones. The new ones will be born from the tensions of the information age, like globalization as a societal phenomenon, information as the key strategic resource (e.g., "Should it be socialized or not?"), the information society as a deep class society, and so on.

My point as a futurist here is that these new self-organizing forces are at least as important—probably more important—actors of the future as the traditional institutions. And in this sense they are the key topics, cooperators, and "customers" of futures studies too.

The final truth about the societal context in which we futurists will practice our work in the future can be found on the front cover of the Beatles album, "Sgt. Peppers Lonely Hearts Club Band" from 1967. Take a look.

NOTES

1. In the English literature, "futures studies" is more often used than "futures research." I prefer to use the latter concept when thinking about theoretically and methodologically sound research projects. "Futures studies" is a looser definition covering a wide range of future-oriented projects, and not as research oriented.

2. I have discussed the idea of interest of knowledge in futures studies versus social decision making more thoroughly in Mannermaa (1986).

3. For more of this case, see Terk and Mannermaa (1997).

4. The discussion of complexity initiated by Ilya Prigogine and continued by Peter Allen, Kenneth Boulding, Peter Checkland, Vilmos Csányi, Erich Jantsch, Ervin Laszlo, and many others belongs essentially to Warren Weaver's (1948) well-known domain of organized complexity and what Robert L. Flood (1987) calls the "homo sapiens line" (United Nations University, 1985; Mannermaa, 1991). The concept of complexity is, however, very "complex." Attempts to define it easily go around in circles: "Complexity is studying complex systems" (this problem has been discussed, e.g., in Ploman, 1984; Williams, 1985). It has sometimes been attached to "us" (researchers, people) and sometimes to "reality" (objects, things; Flood, 1987). One way of clarifying it might be to divide it into ontological and semiotic complexity (Csányi, 1989). Ontological complexity means the inherent complexity of "reality" in natural processes (e.g., randomness in thermodynamic processes), in human beings, and in societies, as well as in the relationship between the researcher and the object of research. Semiotic complexity, on the other hand, refers to the complexity of the models we have in our minds or we have made (e.g., the length of a computer program).

5. I am not going into the details of the discussion about the scientific criteria of futures studies here. This discussion has been carried out in Bell (1997), Mannermaa (1991, 1996a), Masini (1993), Simmonds (1988), and Slaughter (1996, 1995).

6. The expression "sustainable development" as such came as a part of the futures vocabulary only in 1987, when the Brundtland Commission presented its report (World Commission on Environment and Development, 1987).

7. I am talking about innovations. The accumulation of capital, a trend toward huge units that is happening around us, is another thing.

BIBLIOGRAPHY

Barney, G. (1980). *The global 2000 report to the president* (3 vols.). Washington, DC: U.S. Government Printing Office.

Bell, W. (1997). *Foundations of futures studies* (2 vols.). New Brunswick, NJ: Transaction.

Csányi, V. (1989). *Evolutionary systems and society: A general theory*. Durham, NC: Duke University Press.

Flood, R. L. (1987). Complexity: A definition by construction of a conceptual framework. *Systems Research, 4*, 177–185.

Kuhn, T. (1962). *The structure of scientific revolutions*. Chicago: University of Chicago Press.

Laszlo, E. (1987). *Evolution: The grand synthesis*. Boston: New Science Library.

Mannermaa, M. (1986). Futures research and social decision making: Alternative futures as a case study. *Futures, 5*, 658–670.

Mannermaa, M. (1991). In search of an evolutionary paradigm for futures research. *Futures, 23*, 349–372.

Mannermaa, M. (1992a). Brundtland Commission and social decision making: The case of Finland. In M. Mannermaa (Ed.), *Linking present decisions to long-range visions* (pp. 122–136) [Selection of papers from the Eleventh World

Conference of the World Futures Studies Federation]. Budapest: Research Institute for Social Studies.

Mannermaa, M. (Ed.). (1992b). *Linking present decisions to long-range visions* (2 vols.). [Selection of papers from the Eleventh World Conference of the World Futures Studies Federation]. Budapest: Research Institute for Social Studies.

Mannermaa, M. (1995). Alternative futures perspectives on sustainability, coherence and chaos. *Journal of Contingencies and Crisis Management, 3* (1), 27–34.

Mannermaa, M. (1996a). New tools and knowledge for a sustainable future. *Futures, 28,* 618–621.

Mannermaa, M. (1996b). On the way to the knowledge-intensive society: Societal and educational development paths in the framework of futures studies. *Scandinavian Journal of Educational Research, 40* (1), 25–41.

Masini, E. (1993). *Why futures studies?* London: Grey Seal.

Meadows, D. H., Meadows, D. L., and Randers, J. (1992). *Beyond the limits.* London: Earthscan.

Meadows, D. H., Meadows, D. L., Randers, J., and Behrens, W. W. (1972). *The limits to growth.* New York: Universe Books.

Ploman, E. (1984). *Reflections of the state of the art and the interest of the United Nations University in the field of complexity.* Paper presented at the Club of Rome Conference, Helsinki.

Prigogine, I. (1985). New perspectives on complexity. In United Nations University (Ed.), *The science and praxis of complexity* (pp. 107–118). Tokyo: GLDB-2/UNUP-560.

Prigogine, I., and Stengers, I. (1984). *Order out of chaos: Man's new dialogue with nature.* New York: Bantam Books.

Simmonds, W.H.C. (1988). Futures research: New starting points. *Technological Forecasting and Social Change, 33,* 377–387.

Slaughter, R. (1995). *The foresight principle. Cultural recovery in the 21st century.* London: Adamantine.

Slaughter, R. (Ed.). (1996). *New thinking for a new millennium.* London: Routledge.

Steenbergen, B. van (1987). *The tension between technology and immaterial culture.* Paper presented at the World Futures Studies Federation conference, "The Technology of the Future and Its Social Implications," September, Budapest.

Terk, E., and Mannermaa, M. (1997). Baltic studies, futures studies. In Antoni Kuklinski (Ed.), *European space, Baltic space, Polish space* (pp. 149–157). Warsaw: ARL/Hannover-EUROREG/Warsaw.

Toffler, A. (1994). *Creating a new civilization.* Atlanta: Turner.

United Nations University (Ed.). (1985). *The science and praxis of complexity.* Tokyo: GLDB-2/UNUP-560.

Weaver, W. (1948). Science and complexity. *American Scientist, 36* (4), 536–544.

Williams, T. (1985). A science of change and complexity. *Futures, 17,* 263–268.

World Commission on Environment and Development. (1987). *Our common future.* Suffolk: Oxford University Press.

12

Maximizing Evolvability: Teaching Futures Studies at the University Level

Jan Huston

MAXIMIZING EVOLVABILITY

My approach to teaching futures studies revolves around what I call the "Theory of Evolving Systems," which creates an "evolving systems map" to elucidate five important insights:

1. Direction of change
2. Sequence of change
3. Parameters of change
4. System migration techniques
5. Emergence and evolution's traps

Direction of Change

In a single evolving universe made up of nested and open coevolving systems, there is a clear direction to the processes of evolutionary change that follows what I call "The Force"—the arrows of time, increasing complexity, sequence of change, and nested forces—toward what can best be described as a cosmic drive to maximize the evolvability of the universe.

Sequence of Change

Qualitatively, an individual system evolves through a five-stage, nonlinear punctuated evolutionary pattern of sequential organizational change—emergence, development, maturity, destabilization, and break—useful in diagnosing the location of a system within its change process. This also means there are two types of evolution: punctuated evolution and classic Darwinian evolution, the latter encompassing stages 2 through 5 but not stage 1, emergence.

Parameters of Change

"The Force" acts as a parameter of possible organizational change by (1) limiting the migratory options available to a destabilized system (stage 4) at its break (stage 5) to three levels—higher, same–lateral, and lower levels—with eight generic possible destinations (i.e., eight alternative futures); (2) regulating the character of the organizational arrangements in the eight destinations; and (3) creating preferred evolutionary roads to travel to these destinations.

System Migration Technique

Prior to its break, a destabilized system (stage 4) experiences phases of criticality and supercriticality, becoming ultrasensitive to any internal or external change. During its supercritical phase, a system develops temporary "paraorganizational" bridge arrangements that simultaneously maintain its existing operations with "shallow learning"—optimizing an existing system—and in parallel explores and assesses its possible fit with available generic destinations in the changing milieu, using a "deep learning process" that challenges existing system assumptions. As a supercritical system closes in on its break, the system comes to favor certain actions or changes over others in a way that reduces the number of available destinations from eight down to two. Eventually, some added change or action overwhelms the system, and in an instant it "bifurcates" and completes its migration into one of the two remaining destinations.

Emergence and Evolution's Traps

Ultimately, the type of exploratory actions employed—optimizing an existing system or amplifying a new system—determines whether a supercritical system migrates to either a different, lateral, or lower-level destination, merely reforming or exploiting its existing structure and thereby devolving, or to a new, higher-level "emergent system" (stage 1), thereby maximizing evolvability and restarting Darwinian evolution. For a supercritical system to emerge at a higher-level system requires it to amplify novel actions reflecting, at a minimum, what I call the "emergent system agenda"—a set of features characterizing the emergence of past evolving systems—so the variety and complexity of its internal organizational structure matches or exceeds the complexity in its changing milieu prior to its break. In contrast, a supercritical system can succumb to one of what I call "evolution's traps," and thus devolve, when it internally attempts to optimize, reform, or exploit the same type of conservative actions that led to its supercriticality. Such optimization results in either continuous internal crisis management for the system or extreme vulnerability to external conditions being imposed at a rate exceeding a system's ability to respond in an adequate, timely manner. In both instances, however, the final outcome is devolution.

MY JOURNEY TO THIS UNDERSTANDING

I came to this evolving systems approach in a rather circuitous way. While my early academic training focused entirely on engineering, I found myself wondering more and more about what our society's technological priorities ought to be and refocused my curiosity toward political science. This shift resulted in the development of an acute disenchantment with the entire political system and its processes. It was only when I learned about what was then the "blue sky" idea of cybernetics that I discovered a nexus for my curiosity, interests, and talents. At that point in time, however, there was no model of what might constitute an appropriate and viable political cybernetic "system."

My curiosity quickly turned toward two areas of interest: computer-mediated communications and biology. For me, computer-mediated communications was a straightforward technological pursuit because on-line networks and groupware offered a clear infrastructure and operational capability necessary for any political cybernetic system. Biology, however, took me in an unforeseen direction. Initially, I expected the structure of DNA to reveal a framework that might somehow be an applicable model for such a cybernetic system. To my surprise, I kept finding myself drawn to the larger issue of evolution. Ultimately, it became clear to me that not only were there multiple forms of evolution, but also all evolving systems shared certain patterned qualitative features, and most important, particular features associated only with the emergence of new evolving systems.

TEACHING AND CONSULTING

While appreciating many of the prevailing methods and techniques employed by those in the field of futures studies, I felt uneasy about the degree of arbitrariness and relativism in these efforts. Consequently, when teaching or consulting futures-related activities, I'm intent on providing a framework for accessing alternative futures that is as firmly grounded in science as possible, so the information conveyed and gained from the exercise is realistic, practical, and reusable over a student or client's entire life.

Philosophically, I start my course or consulting by pointing out that the only constant is change, both gradual and sudden. Taking this one step further, I emphasize that such change comes in three forms of evolution: adaptive Darwinian evolution, emergent nonlinear evolution, and, finally, by appreciating the interrelated nature of these other two forms of evolutionary change, directed evolution (i.e., the ability to design and steer a system's evolution).

Practically speaking, I start my courses by establishing a contextual evolving systems map of a given system's location and direction in space and time (both in terms of Darwinian and nonlinear evolution). This enables students and clients to understand some basic evolutionary ideas: nested systems, stages of system change, and how nested systems create parameters of change that regulate the nature and limit the number of generic alternative futures available for a given evolving system.

In other words, a particular future can be designed and directed providing it first falls within one of the generic alternatives available, as presented by the existing system's nested parameters of change. Thus, it is especially important for students to recognize there are three levels of possible systemic evolutionary change: lower-level migration, resulting in rapid devolution; same- or lateral-level migration, resulting in protracted Darwinian survival of the fittest (meaning slow but eventual devolution); and higher-level emergent migration that restarts a new evolutionary course.

At this point I use both physical and psychological analogies and metaphors easily recognized and applicable to any individual's personal life as an evolving system. Generally, this is reinforced graphically with popular-culture aids, such as movies, music, and science fiction.

Next we discuss the nature of the changing milieu, trying to discern, understand, and sort out the characteristic themes and features within the system's prevailing milieu that might be relevant to the system's generic higher-level alternative futures. In most instances this is easier than it might seem, because more often than not at this point in history both the prevailing and changing milieu can be characterized in terms of global forces, especially technological and economic factors.

Nonetheless, an adequate appreciation of such characteristics is critical to understanding the complex requisite variety an emergent higher-level system will need to incorporate if it is to survive in the new milieu and thereby avoid evolution's traps. In other words, an existing system seeking to direct its evolutionary migration toward a higher-level alternative future must have the requisite diversity of capabilities and complexity internally to equal or exceed the diversity and complexity it must respond to in the new milieu if it is to successfully emerge and thrive.

Here, the Theory of Evolving Systems provides the equivalent of a checklist of necessary characteristics I call the "emergent system agenda"—features present in the emergence of all prior major evolving systems—that any aspiring emergent system must correlate with to "fit" within the new milieu. If there is a high degree of correlation, students or clients can then employ other futures techniques, such as backcasting, to lay out courses of action that should lead toward the preferred higher-level, alternative future. However, if there is only a small degree of correlation among these features, there is little likelihood of a fit, and thus a tendency toward a dystopic or devolving alternative future.

I proceed using recognized psychological analogies and metaphors addressing the nature of various anxiety-reducing strategies employed when an individual is faced with a rapidly changing milieu and the disintegration of one's subconscious cultural framework. The intent is to demonstrate the characteristics and implications of psychotic, neurotic, and transformative behaviors in confronting such change, and how each behavior affects the election of actions leading toward particular levels of generic alternative futures (i.e., lower, lateral, or higher, respectively). Again, I try to reinforce these ideas graphically with the aid of popular culture.

CONCLUSION

To be sure, I have only glossed over an immense landscape here. Still, my experience using this evolving systems approach with both university students and consulting clients has been quite rewarding. The principle reasons, as best I can tell, are (1) I don't try to tell anyone what *the* future will be, (2) I avoid the arbitrary "alternative futures" common with most scenario and visioning approaches to futures studies, and (3) the idea that everything is relative is dissipated quickly, since invariably the vast majority of generic futures are dystopic. Consequently, what students and clients get is a science-based framework in which they themselves can apply their own personal and professional knowledge, both substantive and normative, in identifying and designing their alternative future, thus directing their evolution.

13

Future-Oriented Complexity and Adaptive Studies (FOCAS)

Kaoru Yamaguchi

THE BIRTH OF FOCAS

My first participation in futures studies was during the Tenth World Conference of the World Futures Studies Federation in Beijing, in September 1988.
I then organized an Asian–Pacific regional conference of the WFSF in Nagoya
in the fall of 1989. Through these activities, I gradually began to feel the
necessity of holding future-oriented seminars on a regular basis so that futures
studies would become one of the major fields of interdisciplinary study at
institutions of higher education for the coming complex age of information.

An opportunity for me to propose this idea occurred three years later
when I was invited to attend the UNESCO seminar, "Teaching about the
Future," in Vancouver, June 21–23, 1992. At the seminar I proposed a
series of World Futures-Creating Seminars to be held every summer in
Awaji Island, Japan, with a hope that this seminar series would evolve into a
core program in futures studies for institutions of higher education.

With great enthusiasm and support from the local communities on Awaji
Island, the first World Futures-Creating Seminar was held August 16–19, 1993,
under the main theme of "Renewing Community as Sustainable Global Village." The proceedings were published as *Sustainable Global Communities
in the Information Age—Visions from Futures Studies* (Yamaguchi, 1997).

The second seminar took place August 7–11, 1994, under the main theme
of "Non-Linear & Chaos-Theoretic Thinking—New Scientific–Visionary

Paradigm." Following the seminar, an intensive live-in workshop was held for three days, August 11–13, 1994, to discuss the further development of this seminar series. Participants of this workshop were twelve resource people from the second seminar: Steven R. Bishop (United Kingdom), George Cowan (United States), Nadegda Gaponenko (Russia), Jerome C. Glenn (United States), Jerome Karle (United States, Nobel Laureate for Chemistry in 1985), Pentti Malaska (Finland), Kazuo Mizuta (Japan), Linzheng Qin (China), Tony Stevenson (Australia), Terushi Tomita (Japan), Theodore J. Voneida (United States), and Kaoru Yamaguchi (Japan).

On the last day of the workshop all agreed that the seminar should be renamed so as to reflect the content of what we wanted to pursue in this future-oriented seminar series. In this way, a new research field was born in futures studies: future-oriented complexity and adaptation studies (FOCAS). FOCAS aims to:

1. understand the interrelated wholeness and interdependence of future-oriented complex phenomena (such as natural, environmental, and socioeconomic phenomena) that cannot be linearly predicted.
2. use our brain and technology so that human beings (individuals, communities, and societies) will be able to get better adapted to them.

The FOCAS seminar continues to be held every summer on Awaji Island, thanks to many devoted futurists, scientists, and local volunteers. Simultaneously, a methodology of FOCAS has been steadily developed. The aim of this chapter is to introduce the basic idea of FOCAS.

FIVE INSEPARABLE FIELDS OF STUDY

FOCAS is based on a framework I presented at the first seminar in 1993, in which I posed the following five inseparable fields of study for future-oriented studies:

1. Wisdom and Self-Awareness Studies
   - training for self-awareness and enlightenment through meditation
   - ecological awareness and new holistic philosophies
   - medical training for well-being
2. Future-Oriented Methodological Studies
   - a nonlinear paradigm based on chaos, evolutionary, and complexity theories
   - mathematical programming, statistical inference, and time-series analysis
   - computer programming and simulations for system dynamics
3. Human–Nature Interrelated Studies
   - ecologically sustainable natural and organic farming using effective microorganisms

- creation of new eco-share regions and communities based on natural habitats
- holistic solutions for such environmental problems as global warming, acid rain, depletion of the ozone layer, tropical deforestation, and endangered species
4. Human–Technology Interface Studies
   - renewal of traditional technologies; for example, making tofu and soy sauce
   - use of clean forms of energy, including solar, tidal, and wind energies
   - new ecologically sound orientation for high technologies, such as info-communication, biotechnology, and new materials
5. Interhuman Networking Studies
   - new information and network economics, beyond market economics
   - renewal of traditional and diversified cultures and histories
   - networking of economies, cultures, technologies, and the environment.

BUILDING BLOCKS OF FOCAS

Having identified these five inseparable fields of future-oriented studies, I have to show, as a next step, how they interrelate one another holistically. For this purpose I have renamed these five fields simply as Mind, Model, Nature, Technology, and Economy, as if they constitute the five building blocks of FOCAS. Among these, moreover, I have selected Mind, Nature, and Economy as the most fundamental building blocks of FOCAS, then arranged them in a matrix form as shown in Figure 13.1. Nature is placed in the center and Mind, which observes Nature, is located at the top left, while on the bottom right is placed Economy, which extracts resources from Nature for its reproductive activities.

Whenever Mind comprehends Nature, it presumes some form of Model, and Model, once built that way, begins to influence the way Mind captures Nature in turn. In this way, Model needs to be created as another building block of FOCAS. On the other hand, people need tools to extract resources from Nature and to sustain their economic activities. Eventually the knowledge and skills to make these tools are advanced as Technology. Technology, once obtained this way, begins to regulate the way Economy relates

Figure 13.1
Fundamental Building Blocks

Mind	⟶↓	
↑⟵	Nature	⟶↓
	↑⟵	Economy

with Nature. Hence, Technology becomes another building block of FOCAS. In total, Mind, Model, Nature, Technology, and Economy become five essential and holistic building blocks of FOCAS. Their interrelations are shown in Figure 13.2.

POSITIVE AND NEGATIVE FEEDBACK

A complex whole is formed by the interrelations of these five building blocks. How are they interrelated, then? Their interrelations are set up through positive and negative feedback mechanisms. Positive feedback interrelates building blocks so as to expand and flare up their relations, while negative feedback regulates and stabilizes them.

Example 1

Let us consider Internet technology. When we consider its future development, we usually tend to think of its technological aspect per se. However, if we want to understand it holistically, we have to consider it as an interrelated feedback technology with the remaining four building blocks. For simplicity, let us select Mind and Economy. Questions we have to pose may become as follows:

1. What is an Internet technology per se? (Intrinsic questions to Technology)
2. How does it influence our mind and economy? (Interrelated questions to Mind and Economy)
3. How do our mind and economy, in turn, react with the Internet technology positively or negatively? (Feedback questions to Technology)
4. How does the Internet technology evolve against these feedbacks positively or negatively? (Reversed feedback questions to Technology)

Then, questions 2 through 4 are repeated in an evolving or converging fashion. Figure 13.3 shows these feedback interrelations.

Figure 13.2
Feedback Relations of the Five Building Blocks

Mind	→↓	→↓	→↓	→↓
↑←	Model	→↓	→↓	→↓
↑←	↑←	Nature	→↓	→↓
↑←	↑←	↑←	Technology	→↓
↑←	↑←	↑←	↑←	Economy

Figure 13.3
Feedback Interrelations

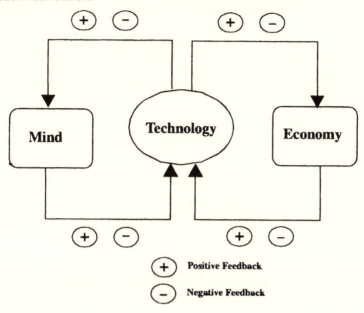

Example 2

Let us now consider chaos theory as a Model, and extend similar kinds of questions to the remaining four building blocks. Questions to be raised may become as follows:

1. How does chaos theory help understand our brain's recognition processes? (Questions to Mind)
2. How does chaos theory explain population dynamics and biodiversity? (Questions to Nature)
3. How can chaos theory help avoid engineering catastrophes? (Questions to Technology)
4. How can chaos theory help explain unpredictable market prices? (Questions to Economy)

Then, for each question, a feedback question like question 3 has to be raised in turn. In this way, the analysis of chaos theory continues holistically.

MISSING FIELDS OF STUDY

Once the building blocks of FOCAS are arranged in a matrix form of five rows and five columns, as in Figure 13.2, we can easily observe twenty blank boxes or elements of the matrix. Since the opposite side of the elements have the same interrelations with the building blocks, only half of these elements constitute the ten missing fields of interdisciplinary studies in FOCAS, which eventually have to be filled in.

To specify such missing fields, consider an interrelation between Mind and Economy as an example. Two opposing attitudes of mind toward the Absolute create two different types of belief systems and religions: one that accepts the existence of the Absolute, such as Christianity, Islam, and so on, and the other that does not accept it or is indifferent to it, such as Buddhism, Taoism, and so on. These different attitudes begin to reflect the universal economic activities with different manners and customs, and these differences begin to cultivate economic activities differently: a birth of culture (Western and Eastern). In this way, Culture emerges as the next stage of the FOCAS matrix to be filled in as a missing element of interrelation between Mind and Economy (Figure 13.4).

Once Culture is augmented in the FOCAS matrix, other interesting feedback questions arise as follows:

- How do different cultures affect economic activities differently: for instance, the workings of the market economy in the West and in Asia?
- How does an economy such as a capitalist market economy or a new information (digital) economy begin to impact cultural differences between the West and Asia?

We are still working along this line of thinking to fill in the remaining nine fields. When they are filled in, the FOCAS matrix of the interrelated wholeness or complexity will be completed, which we like to call the *FOCAS Mandala*. This mandala map becomes very effective for locating where our specific research (a part) is located in the entire world (the whole), and how our worldview based on such research tends to be narrowed down and disciplined.

A complex system is one whose component parts interact with sufficient intricacy that they cannot be predicted by standard linear equations; so many variables are at work in the system that its overall behavior can only be understood as an emergent consequence of the holistic sum of all the myriad behaviors embedded within. Re-

Figure 13.4
Missing Fields of Study Augmented

Mind	$\longrightarrow\downarrow$	$\longrightarrow\downarrow$	$\longrightarrow\downarrow$	Culture
$\uparrow\leftarrow$	Model	$\longrightarrow\downarrow$	$\longrightarrow\downarrow$	$\longrightarrow\downarrow$
$\uparrow\leftarrow$	$\uparrow\leftarrow$	Nature	$\longrightarrow\downarrow$	$\longrightarrow\downarrow$
$\uparrow\leftarrow$	$\uparrow\leftarrow$	$\uparrow\leftarrow$	Technology	$\longrightarrow\downarrow$
Culture	$\uparrow\leftarrow$	$\uparrow\leftarrow$	$\uparrow\leftarrow$	Economy

ductionism does not work with complex systems, and it is now clear that a purely reductionist approach cannot be applied when studying life; in living systems, the whole is more than the sum of its parts. (Steven, 1993, p. 8)

FUTURE-ORIENTED STUDIES

Now analysis of the interrelated whole or complexity has to be extended into the future. When the analysis of the complexity is oriented to the future, the time arrow has to be irreversible and, hence, a concept of evolution becomes effective. Accordingly, it also becomes important to specify a future time for a foreseeable future (though these specifications need not be seriously considered). Without a time specification, futurists' arguments often go astray. This specification of time, however, should not be confused with a linear prediction of the future (Figure 13.5).

Moreover, the specification of time is crucial for the preparation of adaptation against unpredictable natural, environmental, and socioeconomic phenomena. The aim of FOCAS is to enable humanity to become adapted against these unpredictable complex phenomena.

Figure 13.5
Future-Oriented Studies

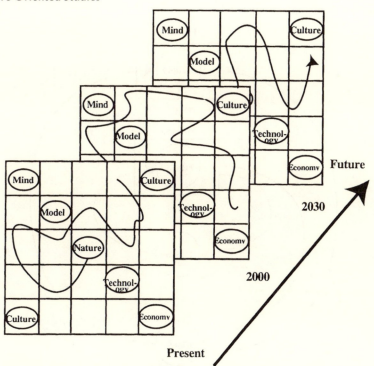

STRUCTURES OF FUTURE-ORIENTED DYNAMISM

Generally speaking, the establishment of a concept itself produces, as its negation, its opposite concept. To see an opposing concept of FOCAS, let us reinterpret it as future-oriented complex and adaptive *systems*, instead of *studies* as defined earlier. Then, the opposite concept of FOCAS would be considered a future-oriented simple and evolving system (FOSES).

When a system becomes complex, three possible states develop in general: it stabilizes, collapses, or evolves. Similarly, FOCAS transforms itself into these three states. Let us consider FOCAS 1 in Figure 13.6. Then, it may

1. Stabilize as a static adaptive state (FOCAS 1)
2. Collapse to the original FOSES (FOSES 1), and reorganize to FOCAS 1 again
3. Evolve to a higher-level FOSES (FOSES 2), and develop to FOCAS 2

Once FOCAS 2 is attained, it will repeat these transformations. As an example, let us consider a business organization like a partnership (FOSES

Figure 13.6
Future-Oriented Complex and Adaptive Systems (FOCAS) and Future-Oriented Simple and Evolving System (FOSES)

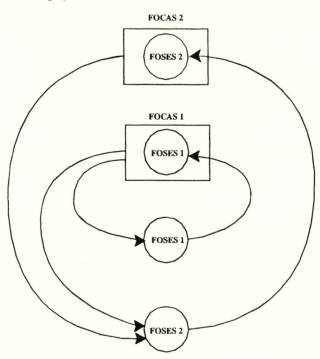

1). As its business activities expand, it is forced to establish branches or divisions to cope with these activities, a process toward complexity (FOCAS 1). It may manage to maintain this complexity as it is. However, it is more probable that the organization may successfully evolve into a higher level of a new simple organization, such as a stock company (FOSES 2), and develop its activities overseas as a complex organization (FOCAS 2). Or it may collapse to a previous small organization, such as a family business (FOSES 1), and try again.

Another example may be our conceptualization process itself. As things get complex, we may try to live with this complexity for a while. However, we may try to overcome it by grouping things into a simpler category, or breaking them down into a more manageable simple scale once again. In this way, complexity evolves into a higher stage of simplicity or collapses into a lower-level simplicity. The highest level of FOCAS we presume as our research objective is the planet Earth itself as Gaia.

HOLISTIC SOLUTIONS TO FOCAS

We are now facing many socioeconomic and environmental problems, such as the population explosion, the polarization of people into the rich and the poor, the breakdown of the capitalist market economy, global warming, water shortage, depletion of the ozone layer, acid rain, and many more. Traditional approaches to solve these problem have been to find solutions within one's own field of academic specialization. These searches for solutions, in turn, have caused other problems.

Recently we have begun to realize that environmental problems are cross-regional, cross-national, and cross-disciplinary, and need international cooperation and interdisciplinary analysis. The methodology of FOCAS we have presented here, though it is still very abstract and at an infant stage of development, will help understand these problems in a holistic fashion. In other words, all we need for better understanding and better solutions is to break down these problems into the FOCAS matrix and analyze (and synthesize) them along the line of thinking presented in this chapter.

REFERENCES

Steven, L. (1993). *Artificial life*. New York: Vintage Books.
Yamaguchi, K. (Ed.). (1997). *Sustainable global communities in the information age: Visions from futures studies*. London: Adamantine.

14

Futures Studies in Pakistan: The PFI

Ikram Azam

Surprisingly, even in my boyhood and youth I was interested in the future as much if not more than in the present and past. This is reflected as much in my fiction and verse as in prose. But the turning point came with the Indo–Pakistan War of 1965. That confronted me with a stark question: Do we have a future as a nation? What is it? What should it be? The question was reinforced with greater ferocity after the dismemberment of the original Pakistan (West and East), on the fall of Phaka (East Pakistan), and the creation of Bangladesh in December 1971. In the mid-1960s I was working at the Pakistan Council for National Integration. By 1971 the country had disintegrated. Why? See my book, *Pakistan's Security and National Integration* (Azam, 1974). It can be generalized that almost all my books and writings are a persistent pursuit of those age-old and ever-new questions and their answers: Pakistan's futures, Third and Muslim World futures, and global human futures (Azam, 1998b, 1998c).

When the Institute of Strategic Studies, Islamabad, was created in 1972 and I became its first secretary soon after, my interest in the future developed into an acute academic–pragmatic interest in futuristics and its real-life applications, largely through self-study and interaction with futuristic individuals and institutions abroad (and some at home).

Thanks to a scholarship generously granted to me by the University of Houston, Clear Lake City, Texas, I did my M.S. in studies of the future

(1987–1988). Simultaneously, Jim Dator of the University of Hawaii welcomed me warmly into the World Futures Studies Federation fold and fraternity. I haven't looked back since then; the going has been good, despite, or because of, all the endless challenges.

Later, I did my Ph.D. (futuristics) at the American University in London in 1989. This university also graciously conferred the D.Litt. (futuristics) degree on me in 1993, in recognition of my services to the field of futures studies, especially as its pioneer in Pakistan.

THE PFI

The Pakistan Futuristics Foundation and Institute (PFI), Islamabad, was created in July 1986 as a registered nonprofit educational welfare trust in the private sector. The institute is an academic and research organization devoted to futures studies at the undergraduate, graduate, and postgraduate certificate, diploma, and degree levels: B.A., M.A., M.Phil., and Ph.D. The PFI started its consciousness-raising, awareness-creating research work right from the start. The academic (teaching) program began in March 1989. The PFI is affiliated with the AUL (American University in London) for its degree programs. It issues its own certificates and diplomas. Though the academic program of the PFI is over a decade old now, it is still experimental, innovative, and learning.

THE ACADEMIC PROGRAM

The PFI academic program is flexibly structured, allowing for built-in adaptability. There is also much innate tenacity and resilience in its motivation.

The first step we took was to examine the University of Houston, Clear Lake, M.S. program in studies of the future for adapting it to Pakistan. Thus, it was made country relevant and user friendly. Initially we decided upon four theoretical core courses and four in the area of real-life applications. After gaining experience over a couple of years, the courses were increased to ten in all. At present we teach the following twelve compulsory core courses of three credits each. These courses are graded and graduated over two semesters (five months each) of an academic year:

Part I. The First Semester: Academic Futuristics

Fl: The *Futures Paradigm* and Readings. Theory, History, Main Schools of Thought, and Applications.

F2: Visionary Futures and Readings. Introductory Philosophy, Psychology, History, Ethics, Comparative Religion, Interculture–Faith Dialogue, Life, Work and Career Counseling, Guidance and Planning, Self-Actualization.

F3: Sociology. General Social Systems Theory, Theories of Social Change, Social

Change, Welfare and Work, Integrated Family Studies, Women in Development, the Futures of Youth and Future Generations.

F4: Research Methodology. Futuristics and Human and Social Sciences, the Scientific Method.

F5: Democracy, Development and Peace Studies. The Global System and *International Political Economy*, Holistic Social Development, Geopolitics, International Relations and Foreign Policy.

F6: Futuristics. Philosophy and History, Vision, Worldview and Values, Theories of History, History as Monitor and Mentor, the Theories, Messages, and Lessons of History, Theories of Time and Space.

Part 2. Second Semester: Applied Futuristics

F7: Pakistan Futures.

F8: The Third World, Muslim World, and Islamic Futures.

F9: Global Human–World Futures.

F10: The Twenty-First Century New Education and Basic Life Skills Paradigm.

F11: Science and Technology as Social Change Agents.

F12: Futuristics, Language, and Literature, Creative Writing, Journalism, Report Writing.

Part 3. Pragmatic Futuristics: Supervised Thesis Research and Writing

B.A. (Futuristics): Minimum one academic year after the required course work at the graduate level.

M.A. (Futuristics): Minimum one academic year after the required course work at the M.A. level.

M.Phil. (Futuristics): Minimum one academic year after the required course work at the M.Phil level (after obtaining the M.A. degree).

Ph.D. (Futuristics): Minimum two to three years after M.A., or one to two years after M.Phil.

Kinds of Courses

Academic

Certificate: Graduate, Postgraduate, and Postmasters. Single Semester: Academic Futuristics.

Diploma: Graduate, Postgraduate, and Postmasters. Two Semesters: Applied Futuristics.

Degrees: B.A., M.A., M.Phil., Ph.D.

Nonacademic: Certificate or Diploma: These are basic or introductory short crash courses of about a working week to one month or even one semester duration. They are in futuristics and related subjects like education, basic life skills, finishing studies, English, and creative writing.

THE MISSION

The PFI mission is to seed and nurture trained futurists in various fields of life. Most of the students are inservice individuals who want to get acquainted with futuristics, if not to specialize in it. Apart from the "traditional" students, they are from professions like education, the civil services, and the armed forces.

THE FOCUS

The focus is on desirable or preferable social change through human resource development by means of education as enlightenment.

THE FACULTY AND SYLLABI

The prime purpose of starting the academic (degree) program was to produce qualified resource persons for the PFI academics. In 1988–1989, I was the only Pakistani with a (foreign) degree in futuristics. Thus, the brunt of the burden in teaching the courses was on me. Fortunately, I had some friends in the local academia and PFI fraternity to help me in teaching related subjects as visiting faculty. It was all voluntary and gratis. After the graduation of the first few PFI–AUL students (M.A.s and Ph.D.s), I could turn to them for help in teaching.

The second issue was of reading material and literature. In 1986 I had donated my personal library to the PFI. While in Houston (1987–1988), I kept on shipping books home. On returning home, I brought back all my books and notes. In fact, books were my main, if not, sole, shopping. Thus, we had enough literature as seeds to sow futuristics for Pakistan at the PFI. Thereafter, we kept on adding to our small stock every year from abroad, especially the World Future Society book shop. Occasionally we were lucky to get some futuristic literature in the local market, also. We also researched, wrote, and produced PFI publications. The theses of our students were of practical interest, and a secure source of knowledge. Unfortunately, because of foreign exchange constraints, we have not been able to order books from our traditional sources abroad since 1997–1998. But luckily, in 1999, the Pakistani bookshops were flooded with some wonderful foreign publications, and almost at throwaway prices.

All these windfalls and breakthroughs have kept us going for a decade academically. We still have no full-time faculty because of financial compulsions, but now we have our own graduates to help us teach, research, and write, as honorary volunteers and as part-time paid or honoraria-receiving devotees of education. Their theses are on real-life practical issues. They have been added to our library as source material.

SOME SPECIFICS

I am now in a position to express my views on some significant specific futuristic issues of interest to the PFI and to me. They are as follows:

1. Social Stability and Change.

2. Methodology.

3. My Vision.

4. Pedagogy, Research, and Publications.

5. Consultancy and Real-Life Applications.

Social Stability and Change

For us at the PFI, while futuristics per se is center stage, sociology is at the core of it, history behind it, and vision ahead of it, beckoning it ever forward on to alternative futures. Methodology and pedagogy make it operative and functional for its real-life applications and consultancy work and services. Research and publications are the means by which futuristics both introspects itself and introduces itself, especially through methodology and pedagogy.

Sociology is at the heart of futuristics. That is because both are innately and intimately interested in the social human being, and therefore in society. Sociology discusses human society as at present (i.e., contemporary society). Futuristics focuses on future societies (and on future generations) and the futures of present societies as they transit to the futures through social change. History is the story of past society turning into present society through historical or social change. Futuristics is also called future history. Thus, the essential rather critical oneness of the past—future continuum in the "history–sociology–futuristics" triad or trinity. This explains the significance for inclusion of F3 (Sociology) and F6 (Futuristics, Philosophy, and History) in the PFI academic program.

A comparative study is made of the main theories of history and of social change, both Western and Islamic. These include the revolutionary, evolutionary, or reformative and transformational theories. The focus is on holistic or integrated–integrative theories, as in Islam, the quintessence of which is peaceful moral transformation. Alternative, preferable, or desirable futures are sought. Education, formal, nonformal, and informal, is stressed as the means of social change through holistic human resource development and self-actualization as enlightenment through self-transcendence. The role of the media, especially the print and electronic media in social change, is highlighted (Kunckik, 1991). The challenges of cultural colonialism and communications imperialism are analyzed (pp. 195–232). The importance of history lies in its messages and lessons. To generalize, it is either a source of inspiration or of shame. In both cases, its lessons are critical for creating the future by reforming the present, both of which are, hopefully, different from—and better than—the past. A paradigm of social change for favorable futures is sought. The role in this of the Islamic concept of the unity of God leading to the unity of all creation and of humanity is integrated into the search for such a paradigm. Since all history—past, present, and future—seeks to size up the significance of time and space in shaping human destiny, the major theories of time and space are also studied, comparatively. Both the materialistic and moral interpretations of time as history, social change, and futuristics are essential for influencing preferable futures. The core concern in social change–stability is to secure a sustainable balance between critical continuity and essential change (i.e., between tradition and modernity or even futurity). According to Arnold Toynbee (1960), cultural tenacity and civilizational resilience along the road to the future via modernization offer some sources of success. Aldous Huxley (1955) found his formula for futuristic survival in *The Perennial Philosophy*, the core values of all the major faiths of humanity, which are its shared heritage. Gai Eaton (1997) (Hasan Abdal-Hakim, a British Christian diplomat and scholar who converted to Islam in 1951), found his answer in Islam, its middle path of moderation and balance in all matters, secular and sacred, especially materialism and moralism. In this he was following Allama Muhammad Iqbal (1980), the founding father visionary poet philosopher of Pakistan.

I believe in a balanced life on the basis of a balance between moralism and materialism. Such a balance is preferential, for it favors prioritizing moralism. I think that the following three driving forces are operative in human life:

1. The universal moral principle (or congenital human conscience) (Azam, 1996b, pp. 137–139).
2. The pleasure principle, or the Freudian "will to pleasure" (Frankl, 1984, p. 104).
3. The power principle, or the Adlerian "will to power" (Frankl, 1984, p. 104).

These three principles or impulses motivate human intention, action, and behavior. They tend to be conflictual, with the second two often ganging up against the first. Life, individual and collective or societal, is relatively peaceful when the first is on the ascent in human affairs and is in control of them. It becomes chaotic and challenging when the pleasure and/or power principles are in the driver's seat. Then we begin to suffer from personal problems and social evils. They could well lead to cut-throat competition, confrontation, conflict, and consequent destabilization, instability, and even anarchy and chaos, or worse still, war, civil or international. The answer is cooperation. It is democratic pluralism and peaceful coexistence. It is for the moral principle to restore harmony. Progress is not possible without peace, hence the presence of F5 in the PFI academics: Democracy, Development, and Peace Studies. Much more research is needed on how to effectively operationalize the moral principle in real life, both individual and collective.

Methodology

The PFI uses the following methods to monitor social change and stability:

1. Scan the media as a persistent pattern for news and views about these issues.
2. Interact with the elite—educated and intellectual, political, policy making and policy influencing—and the leadership, including social and academic.
3. Interact with the average citizen and common man.
4. Attend and participate in public or special functions about or reflective of societal concerns.
5. Organize similar functions.
6. Study such literature.
7. Stay in touch with the women, and youth, and their organizations, especially those involved in the social sector, including education, health, social services, and community care.

Influencing Social Change

Apart from employing the already-mentioned means, the PFI researches and writes about social change subjects in the popular press. This is in addition to its own periodic publications. It now has over thirty books to its credit. The PFI also conducts short and long courses to communicate with its audience. Short crash courses of a general or specific nature are found to be effective. The teaching methodology is eclectic: bilingual (Urdu and English) and even multilingual (using other Pakistani languages) communication about participative and experiential questions is sought and discussion encouraged. The pedagogic methodology is user friendly and audience attractive. It is flexible and adapted to the needs of the students or participants (Joyce and Weil, 1996).

The purpose of PFI education as enlightenment (formal, nonformal, and informal) is learning to live (Azam, 1999a). The focus is on the basic life skills (BLSs), which are

1. Thinking skills.
2. Communicative and language skills, including kinesics.
3. People skills.
4. Self-actualization skills.

5. Life and change coping skills (life change and social change).

6. Lifelong continuing education.

7. Futuristic democracy, development, and peace studies.

8. Islam as a perennial peace paradigm.

9. Integrated family studies (men and women, the child, youth and future generations).

10. Values education.

11. Strategic futurization (planning for the future).

12. Sustainable holistic human futures (Azam, 1996a).

The role of women in education and social change is discussed in detail (Z. Azam, 1994, 1996). History is reinterpreted and Islam explained futuristically for its relevance to the futures (Elahi, 1994; Azam, 1995a, 1995b, 1995c). All this is under the abiding umbrella of, hopefully, perpetual peace (Nawaz, 1996). The real-life applications of futuristics are found to be most interesting for the students and audience in career planning and life planning, and also in problem solving, crisis management, damage repair, and conflict resolution. Likewise they are found in coping with social change and life change, as adequately as possible. Forecasting and planning go together, in that the former is a guide to the latter. It could be used as a planning tool, a means, a device, and an instrument. But exactitude in forecasting is practically more risky and difficult than precision in planning. The way out for both might be alternative forecasting, and certainly, alternative planning. Both are a guide to the futures. But forecasting for the form, formality, or fun of it is a dicey game. Our preference is for planning rather than forecasting per se. Scenarios specifically fascinate students of literature and creative writing, like science fiction.

Whatever we teach, talk about, communicate, or discuss at the PFI or elsewhere has three common denominators knit into it as innocuously as possible. They are futuristics, basic life skills, and values. The PFI courses cover futuristics, English (language), creative writing, education, basic life skills, finishing studies, and journalism. I also teach English to the M.A. students at the National Institute of Modern Languages (NIML), Islamabad. It is the sole state institution of modern languages in Pakistan. At present it is affiliated to the Quaid-e-Azam University, Islamabad. The NIML hopes to soon acquire university or at least degree-awarding status. It may then start an integrated futuristics Ph.D. program in education, culture, language, and literature, with the help of the PFI. Thus, the NIML and the PFI (as its affiliate) look forward to their roles as activist agents of social change by means of education as enlightenment.

Further Research

If it is not possible to start a special, separate, and specialized agency to monitor social change at the societal level, futuristic institutions already in the field (like the PFI) need to be facilitated for the purpose. They can then have a special cell—or at least an expert—devoted to the subject.

My Vision

My vision of a plausible, preferred future is one of global peace, which is, minimally, perpetual, if not perennial (Azam, 1999b). It should be sustainable, and not merely viable. Progress—or holistic human development— is simply impossible without peace. And peace is pawn to disaster if it is not sustainable. Then progress becomes an apology for exploitation. Apart from human nature and its instinct for survival, or the pugnacious instinct, the unchanging challenges to peace are almost eternal. They are

1. The perpetual peace problems. These are the unresolved historical issues (e.g., Kashmir, Kosovo, Bosnia, etc.).
2. The military–industrial complex.
3. Continuing colonialism and impervious imperialism, and consequent exploitation.
4. The national and international exploitative capitalistic systems of political economy.
5. Poverty and the debt trap (local–national, regional, and global).
6. Population explosion.
7. Environmental degradation.

The only hope proffered by the world is democracy. And democracy is a pliant handmaiden to the dictatorship of ever-exploitative capitalism. Likewise, diplomacy divested of moralism and morality is status quo seeking adhocism and expediency redefined or redesignated. The United Nations is too weak to rescue it (peace and democracy) with a conceiveable task force for the purpose, for the United Nations, itself, is prime prisoner to the ongoing and emergent New World Disorder. They are stormtrooped and swarmed by Good Samaritan cliches like the "global village," and slogans like "spaceship Earth." Yes, global village and spaceship Earth, but for whom—the haves or the have-nots?

My vision is one of personal, social, regional, and global sharing and caring as a value system, lifestyle, and behavior pattern—as an instinct, emotion, and habit. Even more, such character traits as are overridingly compulsive and obsessive. The terms for that are altruism, love, and compassion, the champions and companions of peace.

More Research

Is more research needed on how to tackle the aforementioned seven challenges to peace? Or is it a question of initiating, exercising, and asserting the necessary collective political "will to action" to cope with them competently, following it up with persistent real-life action that is sincerely sustained?

They cannot be tackled with the present mind-sets and mentalities, which are conditioned by the Pavlov of history and habit, capitalism. The world needs to search for an alternative paradigm that is humane and holistic, compassionate, caring, and sharing—globally. The seeking needs to be sustained and sincere, and the alternative genuine and authentic. A new conscience and morality are needed to create the new twenty-first century—Third Millennial Man, Woman, and Child—the new humanity, in and of peace. Islam offers one such futuristic alternative paradigm to humankind.

Incorporating the Foregoing in Our Teaching, Research, and Publications

This question has been largely covered in the foregoing pages, but to summarize, it may be stated that the PFI's areas of special interest are the following:

1. Education as enlightenment.
2. Learning to live in order to cope with social change and life change as challenges and opportunities.
3. The basic life skills.
4. Democracy, development, and peace studies.
5. Values education.
6. Islamic studies.
7. Local–national, regional, Third World, Muslim world, and global trends, issues, and problems—and their solutions.

The traditional lecture system is used only as a launching pad. The students and audience are encouraged to think for themselves by asking questions, offering comments, and suggesting possible solutions. Their communicative skills are sponsored. Innate interest, talent, promise, and potential are fostered. Research and writing are patronized by their peers. Above all, role modeling is found to be the most affective and effective method of communication and influence. The PFI tries to be subtle in its suggestions, frank and open in its actions and communication, and sublime in its vision and mission. It is still struggling for survival, and learning from experience.

When I was leaving the University of Houston after my master's in 1988, I suggested to the futures faculty to consider including sociology and social change in their program of studies because of the importance of these subjects to futuristics. In turn, they had cautioned me about futures studies as an idea whose time may not have arrived, like other innovative or revolutionary ideas that come before their time. That is the irony of some precedents and predecessors. Not that they may be or are really precocious or premature, but they are mistakenly considered to be so. Is that true of futuristics in Pakistan, despite all the current lip service to the future? That sometimes seems to be the case for futuristics in Pakistan. Yet we of the PFI remain determined to go ahead. We need all the moral and material assistance possible. There is no dearth of the former (especially advice), but little of the latter. In the meantime, the future has been sloganized in Pakistan. Leave it to the politician and the bureaucrat to profane the sacred. Still, perhaps something is better than nothing?

Consultancy

Consultancy, too, is a globally sloganized buzz word. It belongs to the secret sanctums of connections and kickbacks. The West, it is sometimes suspected, had sought to subvert and bypass the allegedly incompetent and corrupt Third World governments and nation-states by patronizing the self-styled NGOs for so-called social sector development. That is, at least at times if not often, a euphemism for such NGO development. In short, many of these NGOs are monstrously scandalous, to say the least. Such sharks leave little room or scope for the small fry. There is many a mafia in the field, operating behind the scenes. There are several ghosts, also, among the mushrooming NGOs, which exist on paper for the perks involved. It is a corrupt and corrupting system, perhaps deliberately so. Here, again, the well-connected elite are the big beneficiaries, with little trickling down to the poor people on the ground.

So far the PFI has not even done authentic NGO–type professional consultancy work. The only exception is my report *Greening Balochistan*, which I did for the Dutch government through its Andel Associates, in 1996 (Azam, 1997). In it I opined that the future of Pakistan lay in Balochistan, which is 45 percent of the country's landmass and houses only about 5 to 7 percent of its population. I had urged the government of Pakistan to focus its developmental policy thrust on Balochistan. Recently the prime minister stated on a visit to that province that "the future of Pakistan was in Balochistan." The prime minister's program, *Pakistan 2010*, is futuristic.

In 1998 I prepared and published two books for the NIML students and teachers, *Futuristics, Education, Creativity and Creative Writing* (Azam, 1998b) and *Futuristic Creative Report Writing* (Azam, 1998a).

The FF1 researchers, writers, and teachers try to cover our commitment to our futuristic mission as a subterranean movement in all our goods and services: periodic writing for the popular press, publications, teaching, talks, lectures, and seminars. Our consultancy (advice and suggestions) is offered, often gratis, by these means.

REAL-WORLD APPLICATIONS

The real world for us comprises our homes and personal lives, the PFI, our teaching, writing, and research, the related institutional fora, and our social interactions. We try promoting them in our real life and the world. Whenever there is a positive response, we encourage the people's interest in such issues, channeling it into creative discussion. Thus, we think, talk, write, breathe, sleep, dream, and live what we believe in. It is a sacred mission and movement for us: our commitment to the collective global human futures and their future generations. To ensure and secure them, humanity must learn to live in harmony with itself and with Gaia, with Mother Earth and nature. It must rediscover the purpose of creation and the meaning of life. According to Viktor Frankl (1984, p. 108), "Logotherapy regards its assignment as that of assisting the patient to find meaning in his life," a cause, mission, movement, purpose, or person to live for, a vision and guiding image of and for the futures. Humanity today is collectively suffering from what Frankl terms "existential frustration" (p. 106). It needs collective logotherapy for a shared meaning and a common purpose, peace.

This chapter would be incomplete without my expressing my deep debt of eternal gratitude to my life-long conscientious companion and responsible friend, guide, and mentor: my elder sister, Zohra Azam, honorary director of the PFI. She gave me my purpose in life long ago and continues to actively share our collective purpose: futuristics and the PFI. Out of the generosity of her heart, since July 1994 she has loaned us gratis the use of her personal house as the PFI premises and activity center.

Between us, we would like to bequeath the PFI as a loving legacy to future generations. But the PFI has a long way to go for that purpose. It is still struggling for survival even after about thirteen years of existence. The PFI urgently needs to become financially self-reliant. May God help us, for we are determined to struggle on as long as possible.

THE PFI CONTRIBUTION TO FUTURISTICS

To sum up, the PFI's contribution is as follows:

1. It is the sole pioneer of futuristics in Pakistan, both at the educated popular or layman's level and the academic level.

2. It has produced much literature in the area, of special interest to and for Pakistan and the Third or Muslim World.

3. The PFI conceptualized futuristics as a paradigm (e.g., in Ikram Azam's 1996 book, *Strategic Futurization*).

4. It coined the term and research method, "Strategic Futurization."

5. The PFI compiled, edited, and produced two of the earliest books of readings on the subject in recent times: *Futures Studies: Readings* (1992), and *The 21st Century New Economics and Human Sustainability: Readings* (1992).

6. It has done innovative work in education for Pakistan (e.g., *The 21st Century New Education and Basic Life Skills Paradigm* [Azam, 1996a], and *Towards the 21st Century Pakistan: Women, Education and Social Change* [Z. Azam, 1994]).

7. The PFI focus is on social change through human resource development by means of education as enlightenment.

8. It has conceptualized integrated family studies as a viable alternative for, or cocurriculum to, women's studies (e.g., *Woman in the 21st Century* [Z. Azam, 1996]).

9. The PFI stress on basic life skills and enabling education, learning to live, has been widely appreciated (e.g., by UNESCO, Paris).

10. The PFI has been projecting Islam as a perennial peace paradigm, along with democracy, as compatible systems in the Third or Muslim World. It has also been pleading for an ongoing interreligious–faith and interculture dialogue at all relevant levels. As a peace institute, the PFI promotes the ideals of democratic pluralism and peaceful coexistence.

REFERENCES

Azam, I. (1974). *Pakistan's security and national integration.* Islamabad: London Books.

Azam, I. (1995a). *Islami futurism and futuristics.* Islamabad: PFI.

Azam, I. (1995b). *Islami meditation and psychotherapy.* Islamabad: PFI.

Azam, I. (1995c). *Muhammad (SAS!): The sublime futurist.* Islamabad: PFI.

Azam, I. (1996a). *The 21st century new education and basic life skills paradigm.* Islamabad: PFI.

Azam, I. (1996b). *Strategic futurization: Planning for the 21st century futures.* Islamabad: PFI.

Azam, I. (1997). *Greening Balochistan for the 21st century Pakistan.* Islamabad: PFI.

Azam, I. (1998a). *Futuristics creative report writing.* Islamabad: PFI.

Azam, I. (1998b). *Futuristics, education, creativity and creative writing.* Islamabad: PFI.

Azam, I. (1998c). *Thinking aloud futuristically: A book about my books.* Islamabad: PFI.

Azam, I. (1999a). *The PFI prospectus: 1999–2001.* Islamabad: PFI.

Azam, I. (1999b). *Towards the third millennium: The Islami vision, world-view and mind.* Islamabad: PFI.

Azam, Z. (1994). *Towards the 21st century Pakistan: Women, education, and social change.* Islamabad: PFI.

Azam, Z. (1996). *Woman in the 21st century: Roles, responsibilities and rights.* Islamabad: PFI.

Eaton, G. (1997). *Islam and the destiny of man.* Lahore, Pakistan: Suhail Academy.

Elahi, M. (1994). *Ibal as a futurist.* Islamabad: PFI.

Frankl, V. E. (1984). *Man's search for meaning.* New York: Simon and Schuster.

Huxley, A. (1955). *The perennial philosophy.* London: Penguin.

Joyce, B., and Weil, M. (1996). *Teaching methods.* Boston: Allyn and Bacon.

Kunckik, M. (1991). *Communication and social change.* Germany: Friedrich-Ebert-Stiftung.

Iqbal, A. M. (1980). *The reconstruction of religious thought in Islam.* Lahore, Pakistan: Iqbal Academy.

Nawaz, S. (1996). *Pakistan's futuristic peace paradigm.* Islamabad: PFI.

Toynbee, A. (1960). *Civilization on trial.* Oxford: Oxford University Press.

(1999, 25 April). *The Pakistan Observer,* Islamabad.

15

A Generation of Futures Studies in Taiwan

Kuo-Hua Chen

Futures studies in Taiwan holds a unique place in the world. The Division of Futures Studies is housed in the Educational Development Center of Tamkang University, Taiwan. The university has 25,000 students. It enables each student to acquire three perspectives: global understanding, information utilization, and future orientation. Tamkang University is thus the only university in the world I know of whose mission is to "futurize" its students, its society, and itself.

While other universities have futures research centers or professors who teach futures studies, Tamkang University is unique in that the entire focus of the university is on a globalized future-oriented information society. This influence is largely due to the fact that its founder, Clement C. P. Chang, is a futurist himself. A distinguished Chinese scholar, Chang (1998) has an ambitious vision "not only to project future changes but also the ambition to create future changes, and especially the intelligence and courage to make things happen for the tomorrow that we expect to have" (p. 88).

FUTURES STUDIES COURSES

Futurists have the following qualities: They have multidisciplinary interests, the willingness to adopt different ways of knowing, a global orientation, a tolerance for complexity and ambiguity, a long-term perspective, a view of the future as plural and alternative rather than as singular and predictive, and the ability to imagine many different alternative futures as well as to envision preferred futures. However, while futures studies is emphasized in the university curriculum for all students, there is no clear evidence that the students have become futurists. Because futures studies classes are required of students in all majors, the appreciation and cultivation of these qualities may be diluted and even lost altogether as far as students are concerned. Many display no particular creative spirit in taking the class. Since it is "just another required course," few view the subject with any passion. Instead, for some it is considered an easy course that they take in order to avoid other tougher courses. Nonetheless, the instructional style is distinctly innovative, with classes having large video screens, texts, lectures, and meetings with school children. Professors do their best to work directly with each student, even in large classrooms, instead of merely lecturing to them.

Even with creative pedagogy, Tamkang is a useful case study of what happens when futures studies is mandatory. However, we should not focus exclusively on educational factors in order to explain the limitations of futures studies in Tamkang. There are other influences as well, such as the larger issue of Taiwan's role in the world economy.

Because of Taiwan's having gone from poverty to riches in a short period of time, many of the values of futures studies are in conflict with the values of modern Taiwanese, whose most immediate concerns are (1) short-term strategic issues, (2) continued economic growth, (3) one future and not many alternative futures for Taiwan, (4) geopolitical dangers associated with China, and (5) by and large, a pragmatic, traditionally Confucianist approach to the world.

The idealism of futures studies, its concern for both social and technological innovation, and its overriding quest for a better world does not appear to have any immediate value to these sensible, modern Taiwanese students. Instead, they worry about getting good jobs in Taiwan's growing economy and not drifting off into the next century. Likewise, Taiwan's corporations themselves do not engage in long-range planning. They prefer to wait for new technologies to be created and produced by others and then purchase them. Once purchased, they find immediate applications for these technologies. They are thus content with a secondary role in the world economy.

However, it can be argued that if Taiwan desires to go the route of Singapore and increase its per capita income from $16,000 to $26,000 it will have to become a stronger player in the world information economy. Doing so means innovation, forecasting emerging technologies, and escaping from the confines of thinking only in an economistic–strategic fashion and beginning to make serious use of the many tools and perspectives futures studies has to offer.

Thus, while Tamkang University has pioneered in clearing the path for the adoption and use of futures studies in Taiwan, Taiwan itself has yet to enable people to walk down that path. This could change dramatically, however, as the imperatives of the world knowledge economy impact Taiwan and Taiwan finds itself being chased by the new economic tigers, India and others.

Futures Studies in Taiwan has largely been linked to economic development and wealth creation. It has not entered Taiwan in its more alternative, environmental or cultural–spiritual, future-generations form. However, just as the world knowledge economy will force it to become more foresight oriented, changes in the age cohort will also take the field of futures studies in Taiwan in different directions.

TRANSFORMING FUTURES

Tamkang University has been promoting futures studies—or advancing futures, to echo the title of this book—for three decades. The long journey of futures at Tamkang has been advanced through many phases (see Chang, 1998, for a detailed retrospective). The achievements are, without a doubt, enormous and their influences are very extensive in Taiwan. Looking further ahead, a number of scenarios are worth noting in bringing out a deeper enthusiasm and passion for the future.

Integrating the ways our various futures studies courses are taught is the most vital process. The courses are designed to introduce major themes and forcing factors of the future from the perspective of each academic discipline. Hence, there are courses on "Futures Studies in Sociology," "Futures Studies in Economics," "Futures Studies in Politics," "Futures Studies in Technology," and "Futures Studies in Environment," each offered by the faculties of the corresponding academic areas. Despite a unified emphasis, a missing ingredient among these courses is a shared objective and an orientation toward the cultivation of futurists who are passionate about the future.

In 1998, Yu-Ying Teng and myself did some small-scale research to survey expert opinion. A three-round Delphi technique was utilized to obtain opinions from a group of faculty members teaching futures studies courses. A consensus was reached that in order to develop coherence among all the courses, the following "underlying principles" need to be emphasized:

- Recognizing, adjusting, and creating the future.
- Cultivating visions and senses of the future.
- Establishing a worldview with an attitude of caring and participating.
- Developing an acute sense of observation.
- Questioning authority and being a critical thinker questioning "known facts."
- Giving insight into long-term trends.

- Adapting to team-based and interdependent working relations.
- Becoming familiar with knowledge of advanced technological products.
- Being concerned with the potentials and impacts of future technologies.
- Caring for the future welfare of minority groups.
- Respecting diverse viewpoints on alternative futures.
- Advocating the essentiality of transdisciplinary and multicultural approaches.

Recently the futures studies program has begun to articulate what a "local" version of futures studies would look like; that is, there is a serious concern to develop a futures studies that, while global, is rooted in the soil of Taiwan. A large number of our faculty members are Western-trained scholars; hence, we rely largely upon information from the Western world for teaching as well as conducting research. Shaw (1999) vividly puts it this way: "Taiwan is a democracy more informed by classical Greek philosophers than by Chinese. . . . And everybody loves an Ivy League degree" (p. 23).

Nevertheless, among Asian society even he envisions that Taiwan is the best bet to nurture and avoid any kind of "brain drain" among its future generation and notes his belief that Taiwan possesses the right combination of institutions that will allow talent to blossom. The desire and excitement of exploring intellectual property could be quite an influence on the academe of Taiwan.

It would be inexcusable for us to accept or duplicate ways of thinking from the West without question. We aim not to "catch up" with the quantity and innovation of research methodology, but to encourage creative thinking and respect for opposing viewpoints. The field of futures studies, among many others, provides an opportunity for satisfying the enthusiasm of any non-Western scholar. While intellectuals have experienced greater pressure from Western scientific knowledge, we are also faced with the challenge of higher standards in both behavior and values. All in all, it takes only a few powerful ideas to change the world.

RESEARCH ENDEAVORS

It is often considered bliss in academia to do research that is teachable, and to teach so as to inspire further research. While life has yet to treat me that well, I do find research a wonderful challenge. As a Western-trained sociologist, previously most of my research was primarily confined to conventional sociological topics. Thus, futures studies was considered alien to me before I joined the Division of Futures Studies at Tamkang University. As time passed and I gained more experience and exposure to the area, I have found myself profoundly inspired by the writings of many futurists, such as Wendell Bell, Sohail Inayatullah, Eleonora Masini, Richard A. Slaughter, W. Warren Wagar, and others.

In reviewing the "Sociology of the Future," I ardently agreed with Bell (1996) that sociologists should return to moral discussions on how to improve the well-being of societies. Moreover, I could also sense the commitment of many nineteenth-century social analysts, such as Marx, Weber, Marshall, Spencer, and Durkheim, all of whom carried out their comparative and historical studies with normative intent (Bell, 1997). "They were concerned with where their own societies were going and with what might be done to facilitate or block these tendencies" (Hopkins and Wallerstein, 1967, p. 35).

Most of my research (K.-H. Chen, 1996, 1997) has been done with an intense focus on macrolevel analyses. In addition, large-scale secondary data and sophisticated statistical analyses outweighed the concerns for quality of social development. Given the influence I have had from the futures field, I have made a significant modification in my recent research projects. The research that I am conducting now reflects some of the theoretical and methodological bases of my teaching. Luckily, all of the research projects have won the recognition of the National Science Council of Taiwan.

The first is a three-year project, entitled "Biotechnology and 'Biodemocracy'—Cloning and Its Socio-Psychological Impacts on the Public." This research aims at exploring the level of societal awareness of genetics and cloning. Public interest, value orientation, and associated attitudes are among the foci of issues.

Another research project that is currently being undertaken has to do with Taiwanese attitudes toward migrant workers, since the degree of acceptance toward immigrants within a society has been considered as a prominent indicator of the quality of societal development. It becomes even more significant as the individual society attempts to reconstruct its cultural and value identity in order to deal with increasing that society's demographic diversity.

The third project under way has as its research topic, "The Social Construction of Death." The conception of death plays a major part in affecting changes in an individual's ideas and opinions as well as the transformations of social values and norms from meaningful interactions of every human group. In other words, the function of death serves not only as communicating belief and symbol systems between man and society reciprocally, but reestablishing an altered self-conception and social order.

Many of my colleagues in futures studies at Tamkang University share the same research ideology: to examine and improve the well-being of societies from a global and holistic perspective (C.-F. Chen, 1998; Tung, 1997; Wang, 1999). While many of us rely heavily upon research methods from other social science disciplines such as sociology and economics, study of the future helps to generate more genuinely important ideas. Furthermore, research in our division has also been greatly enriched through the use of a transdisciplinary and collaborative team that aids in integrating visions as well as ideas of specific topics or problems through a more holistic view, in contrast to the tendency toward fragmentation with the narrow focus obtained through a single discipline.

ENVISIONING THE FUTURES OF TAIWAN

At a recent visioning workshop in Taiwan led by 1999 Tamkang Chair in Futures Studies Sohail Inayatullah, Jyh-Horng Lin, and myself on May 6, participants were split into two groups. One group imagined a globalized Taiwan, with each citizen being super-rich, with their own airplane. Another group imagined a softer, slower, organic future, where farming was crucial. Technology linked them globally but there was no "e-mail imperative." Quality-of-life issues were as important as wealth issues. Thus far, when these issues have been raised, the economic imperative has been dominant. Wealthy Taiwanese make money in Taiwan but send their children and families abroad to other nations for quality of life (and to escape the spectre of China). However, an emerging age cohort that does not remember the poverty of fifty years ago desires a better quality of life and, like their Western counterparts, is concerned with one particular alternative future, that of a Green, more spiritual society.

Other young Taiwanese, while less Green, are concerned about a neo-Confucian future. This came out in one recent scenario workshops also conducted in May 1999. Four scenarios were developed for Taiwan. The first was the "Road Runner" (rapid continued growth), the second was "Neo-Confucianism" (virtue, slower growth, future generations orientation), the third was "Paradise Lost" (China invades or the economy crashes), and the last was "Taiwan.com," globally linked to the Net and to a world government system that provides Taiwan with the security it needs. These visions and workshops show that while traditionally Taiwan had one future, alternatives are springing up.

To help continue this "futurizing" process, the Division of Futures Studies has begun an international futures journal, simply titled *The Journal of Futures Studies* (http://www.ed.tku.edu.tw/develop/JFS). Its focus is on Asia, globalism, and economic futures, as well as on methodology. It hopes to not only raise an Asian voice for futures studies but also to continue exploring the long waves of world economic development. Correspondingly, we hope that Tamkang will play its role not only as the birthplace of futures studies in Taiwan, but also as the center of futures studies in Asia. We also look forward to a future in which Tamkang fully joins the world futures community.

With these ambitions, futures studies is already developing at the youth as well as university levels. A recent series of workshops focused on how young Taiwanese children imagine the future. Imaginary future schools were drawn by quite young children and illustrated in a variety of ways. During group image-sharing sessions, most simply said they wanted to avoid going to school and to sleep in. But what was nonetheless crucial is that young people are for the first time being asked about their future and are beginning to explore the possibilities.

In this sense, while futures studies in Taiwan has traditionally been narrowly defined, it has developed quite an extensive base of support. Thus, as the next stage of futures studies takes hold—more global in scope, more alternatives based, more visionary, as well as more empirically based, with hard data for preferred scenarios—the transition will be quite easy, even effortless. And this is, naturally, what has been behind the efforts of Professor Chang all along. As a good Confucian, he clearly understands that education, above all, is ultimately the key to all of our futures.

REFERENCES

Bell, W. (1996). The sociology of the future and the future of sociology. *Sociological Perspectives, 39* (1), 39–57.

Bell, W. (1997). *Foundations of futures studies.* Vol. 1: *Human science for a new era.* New Brunswick, NJ: Transaction.

Chang, C.C.P. (1998). Three decades of futures studies at Tamkang University. *Futures Research Quarterly, 14* (3), 88–96.

Chen, Chien-Fu. (1998). *New life style of leisure in Taiwan.* Paper presented at the annual meeting of the World Future Society, Chicago.

Chen, Kuo-Hua. (1996). An institutional approach to world-systems analysis. *Journal of Futures Studies, 1* (1), 67–86.

Chen, Kuo-Hua. (1997). *Global transactional networks and economic growth.* Paper presented at the annual meeting of the World Future Society, San Francisco.

Hopkins, T. K., and Wallerstein, I. (1967). The comparative study of national societies. *Social Science Information sur les Sciences Sociales, 6* (5), 25–58.

Shaw, Sin-Ming. (1999, May 31). "It's true. Asians can't think." *Time*, p. 23.

Tung, Chuan-Chuan. (1997). Taiwan's labor movement in the new international division of labor. *Journal of Futures Studies, 2* (1), 33–49.

Wang, Yumin R. (1999). Political change and public security: The prospect of Taiwan. *Futures, 31*, 57–72.

16

Teaching Futures-Seeking Policy Process

Markku Sotarauta

Our way of thinking and our way of perceiving the world and its processess are clearly but frequently furtively rooted in strategic thinking, planning, and activity. Our worldview guides our way of perceiving the course of development, and the overall forces and actors having influence on it. It leads to the perceiving of some things and the nonperception of others. Behind administrative and planning systems and procedures there is generally some sort of either conscious or unconscious mental model of the nature of development and the factors having influence over it. It does not directly refer to the nature of development as an absolute phenomenon. It arises from experience, education, and expectations.

In this chapter I examine how teaching regional planning in the Department of Regional Studies and Environmental Policy of the Finnish University of Tampere provides students with views of development and modes of thinking about planning that bind together futures-oriented strategic thinking and interactive communicative policy processes. To ensure that the practical presentation of the teaching has a firm foundation, I first survey the ongoing change in policy-making procedures with the help of the concepts "the government of uncertainty" and "the governance of ambiguity." Attention is next focused on futures-seeking communicative strategy, which is one form of the governance of ambiguity. Finally, the practical course in regional planning is presented as an example of both innovative teaching methods and the combining of policy processes and futures-seeking strategic planning.

SETTING THE CONTEXT:
TOWARD THE GOVERNANCE OF AMBIGUITY

The Government of Uncertainty

When Finland became a welfare society according to the Nordic ideal, the systems of public administration depended on an approach that can be called "the government of uncertainty." Its roots are to be found in the Enlightenment, which left behind three phenomena that had a profound effect on Western societies: democracy, a belief in reason, and a linear conception of time. Simultaneously, thoughts arose of the possibility of planning social life, of exerting influence over the future and controlling it. Alongside this developed one of the most highly refined arts of the modern West: the art of breaking things down. So skilled are we at this that we frequently forget to put the pieces back together again. Breaking things down relies on the conviction that social problems are "tame," that they can be delineated, with cause and effect identified and explained.

For the government of uncertainty, the system became centrally coordinated and sectorized. It was assumed that goals could be clear, or that they could be defined and clarified in the preparatory work preceding decision making. In planning, attention was paid to the process by which the best possible means were selected by decision makers using consultation, mathematical models, reports, and surveys so that a precisely defined problem could be solved by the best possible means. It was believed that resources would be forthcoming in ever-increasing abundance. Thus, political attention centered on their allocation. Existing structures and functions were not called into question. In Finland, the creation of the welfare society was governed by a rather strong shared vision of a desired future.

In the 1960s and 1970s, the creation of the welfare state was perceived in practice not so much as being the government of uncertainty as being the administration of the channelling of ever-growing resources for the needs of the welfare state. However, examination of the basic theoretical assumptions in the background shows that planning was a means of eliminating uncertainty from activity, and uncertainty was ultimately seen as merely lack of knowledge and information. It was believed that development could be kept under control by goals and means derived from scientific deduction.

However, as Dryzeck (1993, p. 218) states, planning based on scientific objectivity is virtually impossible, because (1) the general laws of society—on which it is believed the strategies of public actors can be based—are difficult to define in a watertight way, and thus are unattainable; (2) social goals are rarely pure and simple, and values are usually open to question, vacillating and many sided; (3) the intention of actors may override the causal generalizations of the planner—people may simply decide to do things differently; and (4) interventions aimed at the course of development cannot be empirically verified without the intervention being realized.

The basic assumptions of the government of uncertainty began to crumble in the 1970s and 1980s, but this process has gone even further in the 1990s. The 1990s have seen increased emphasis placed on self-guidance, learning, interaction, and communication. Although Finnish public administration has been taken closer to the new ideals through decentralized power and by emphasizing self-guidance on the one hand and cooperation on the other, the procedures of the government of uncertainty continue to have their effect on structures, processes, and attitudes. The rigid attitudes and structures of the government of uncertainty persist and cause problems because contemporary problems are the result of several inseparable factors, and their root causes cannot be traced back to individual factors. Many problems are common in one way or another, and no organization has the sole power and means to carry through programs to solve them. In order to really grasp problems in the new century it will be necessary to be able to transcend various institutional, sectoral, territorial, and mental borders as barriers.

It has been increasingly emphasized that there are various networks in society (i.e., entities composed of parts that are interdependent). The problem of the programs of the centralized and sectoral government of uncertainty lies in the fact that the networks and contemporary issues refuse to be bound by administrative limits. Decisions concerning one network or issue are made in several different organizations, both public and private. Different programs and decisions may be contradictory because they split various networks without perceiving the whole.

The Governance of Ambiguity

In the governance of ambiguity, the point of departure is not necessarily the search for right answers, as it is in the government of uncertainty, but rather how people contending against issues from different sides and perspectives can join forces in the search for new questions and new answers. This entails the admission and recognition that power is shared. Bryson and Crosby (1992) describe a world of shared power and define it as "shared capabilities exercised in interaction between or among actors to further achievements of their separate and joint aims" (p. 13). Actors may in this case be individuals, groups, organizations, or institutions. Governance presupposes a striving on the part of those involved to a common understanding in a situation characterized by differences of opinion, different objectives, ignorance, different views of the future, and lack of information. The ability for governance implies a tension between conflict and order, and that this tension be put to good use.

Despite this, Western policy making is still commonly perceived as a planning procedure in which an effort is made to produce programs guiding the development of various areas of society. The main tools for bringing influence to bear here are guidance, control, and regulation (Stenvall, 1993, p. 64). In the governance of ambiguity it is typical that faith in exerting influence on societal development by direct means has diminished, and thus the governance of ambiguity depends on the interaction of several actors and on a selection of combined indirect and direct means that are not planned in advance by any unit. As Royall (1993, p. 51) states, modern governance stresses supporting the emergent models. The forces constantly seeking for equilibrium are, most of the time, self-sustaining without any need for special attention from public administration, or, as Dunsire (1994, p. 170) states, the total amount of governance is far greater than the total amount of administration. Thus the governance of ambiguity should not be seen as mere processes of public administration and planning. Leadership, management, and planning through increasing interdependence and plurality presuppose the ability to act as part of a cooperative network in the midst of a pluralistic and overlapping field of actors that is no more private than public.

The governance of ambiguity can thus be seen as emerging from sociopolitical processes on the basis of interaction of relevant actors. Kickert (1993, p. 195) states that in governance it is essential to see that the "ruler" of the complex systems is not some external third party—an actor bringing to bear influence from above and outside—but the effect of different actors on each other and on themselves. Interaction not only reflects complexity but also is in itself complex, dynamic, and pluralistic. Thus, in the old sense, models of governance cannot be set up: They live and change with the situation. At the same time, the challenge to futures research opens up to understand better than before both the policy processes of the present and their relation to possible futures.

As the government of uncertainty crumbles, it would appear that we are moving from centralized, highly coordinated practices toward more self-guiding, decentralized, and pluralistic systems. It may be that we are witnessing the emergence of a system of governance that leads to a multiple overlapping negotiation system between various actors (both in the public and private sectors) at different levels. It seems that the only way to cope with the current pace of change is to accept and benefit from an increasing interplay between various actors at different levels. In this case there is no monolithic center that exerts extensive governance over factors determining development, and thus formal and hierarchical policy making no longer has such an important role in the formation of development as it once had (see Table 16.1).

What is interesting in Table 16.1 is not the new forms and contents of public policy making themselves, but the fact that the development view is

Table 16.1
Characteristics of Government of Uncertainty and Governance of Ambiguity

	Government of Uncertainty	*Governance of Ambiguity*
Development view	Linearity, predictability, and continuity	Evolutionary view of development; complexity, discontinuity, and unpredictability
	Shared worldviews and conceptions of future	Different worldviews and diverging conceptions of future
	Cause-effect relations	Cause-effect relations blurred over time
Structure	One dimensional	Multidimensional
	Centralized integration	Decentralized integration
	Hierarchies	Networks
	Division into units	Entities and parts
Governance processes	Top-down	Top-down and bottom-up
	Unilateral dependence	Multidimensional
	Strong, do-it-alone dependence principle	Do-it-together principle emphasized
	State dependent	Dependent internationally, nationally, regionally, and locally
Planning	Formal and hierarchical	Network management, communicative planning
	Separation of planning and implementation	Planning, decision making, and implementation differences blurred
	Approaches and analyses based on averages, from rules to exceptions	Approaches and analyses for each situation, from exceptions to rules

changing, that entirely new qualitative relations are in the making between policy making and communities. Moreover, the nature of linkages within administration is in a state of change.

As the new century dawns, we are faced with several social problems requiring fresh solutions. At the same time we are faced with the question, What blocks intended strategies and visions from being realized; what blocks the desired future from emerging? It may be that the solutions to many of the contemporary social and environmental problems on the one hand, and success in economic competition on the other hand, may not be found as directly as earlier believed in the design of creative intended strategies or appealing visions, but in the quality of the processes of decision making, policy making, cooperation, knowledge creation, and so on. The core questions are how human beings are able to agree on what the issue is and how to redefine it in order to work together; how to approach the redefined issue, from what direction to approach, and with what framework approach is possible; and how to be able to create an approach that empowers relevant actors having some kind of interest in the issue in question to participate in the policy process from their own standpoints.

COMMUNICATIVE PLANNING AS A FORM OF
GOVERNANCE OF AMBIGUITY

Governance of ambiguity emphasizes interaction and thus communication. This results in seeking means of understanding and accepting different perspectives and seeking together for meaningful aspects of various issues. Achieving a common understanding may be more fruitful than directly implementing compiled visions. Healey (1992) states that in communicative planning, knowledge of circumstances, causes, effects, and moral values is not only a calculation based on a predefined scientific approach, but knowledge that is constantly created in the discussion of views, opinions, and facts. As Healey holds, communicative planning places great emphasis on the interaction of different actors, and thus it is not, like its predecessors, planning that defines the future; rather, it constantly seeks futures. Its images and metaphors are dependent on the experience of those participating, abstract knowledge and understanding, and technical analysis. The pervading theme of solving problems is pursued through conflicting contentions and the juxtaposing of their reasons.

This then highlights the notion that while the claims of planners and analysts should not be accepted as received truths, neither is it the case that every claim is as valid as the next one. Various arguments may be rhetorical and intended as a defense of someone's own power and position (Fischer and Forester, 1993, p. 3). Likewise various arguments about possible futures may be more part of the political game than of objective analyses. It is no longer only a matter of asking what is said, but also of when it is said, to whom, in what manner, and how. Throgmorton (1993) actually goes so far as to claim that all planning is rhetorical activity. Various scenarios, analytic methods, questionnaire surveys, computer modeling, and so on are not methods of producing objective knowledge, but rather of rhetorical imagery. They wield the power of persuasion. They are always aimed at some actors. Likewise, all arguments connected with planning are responses to some other arguments.

Communicative planning at its best creates a lasting basis to understand the field of pluralistic values and objectives in which social problems are to be solved. At its worst it is a continuously revolving merry-go-round of talk and does not lead to action. However, in communicative planning, at all events, attention is also paid to discussions, quarrels, confusions, uncertainty, surprises, the real meaning of plans, and so on, and hence the skillful planner is the one who can identify the points of intersection of the various interest groups' and organizations' visions, goals, and strategies and also the links between the problem at hand and the strategies of the various organizations. The skillful planner is further the one who can extract the crucial issue from this network and so arrive at achieving something. The main issue is thus not sought only in shared ideals but also among ideals, actors' own interests and solutions, as well as what might be called the "common good."

Simultaneously, the basic questions for strategic planning and essentially related futures research come full circle. Frequently the question behind strategic planning has been how to govern and reduce multidimensionality, ambiguity, and short-term thinking with the help of strategic planning. In the governance of ambiguity, the question is how multidimensionality, ambiguity, and short-term thinking can be harnessed to further the futures-seeking strategy process.

CHANGING FACES OF STRATEGIC PLANNING

Once the basic question behind strategic planning has come full circle, strategy processes as a part of futures research are seen in a new light. Simultaneously the challenging question appears as to how communicative processes and futures research can be linked together in teaching. This question is important because many studies have shown that in both companies and public administration, strategic management does not control decision making according to the ideals of the rationalistic model. Strategic decision making is rather described as a political free-for-all, with all its negotiations and wrangling of different interest groups (see Mintzberg, 1994).

In Finnish policy making in the 1990s, the emphasis was on partnership, cooperation, and coordination. The new thinking carried the activities of Finnish public administration in the direction of the governance of ambiguity. There is still some way to go. Despite the emphasis on interaction behind the new modes of action, the view of the role and task of strategic planning is still "classical" (see, e.g., Bryson, 1988). This culminates in stressing the forming of a vision, setting goals, seeking focal points, analyzing threats and opportunities, evaluating the environment, formal planning processes, and program documents. However, it can be said that classical strategic planning is a contemporary version of instrumental rationalism-rooted planning (see Sager, 1994). In practice in public policy making, the issue is always also that of cooperation, discussion, quarreling, confusions, uncertainty, ambiguity, surprises, plans left on the shelf, and so on. If the classical view is overemphasized, the danger exists that a great planning machine will come into being whose main products are development programs but not action. Plans formerly relegated to the shelf were full of details. Now there is a danger that they will be full of visions, SWOT analyses, and strategies (SWOT is a strategic planning analysis method widely used in Finland and elsewhere. The initials stand for Strengths, Weaknesses, Opportunities, and Threats).

In the 1990s Finland was in any case becoming inundated with strategic development programs. Modes of thinking and acting originally developed in the U.S. corporate sector have been arriving in Finnish policy making. In the 1980s it was the words and concepts that came, but modes of action did not actually change as much as vocabulary. Only in the 1990s did real strategic thinking and planning have the necessary conditions to take root in activity.

Strategic planning, however, has not turned out to be such an efficient producer of success as the handbooks and consultants indicated. At times it has been difficult to shape a unique comparative advantage because scenarios have remained at too general a level, divorced from action, while SWOT analyses have been augmented by many important matters without an awareness of what was to be done with them. Strategic programs have frequently not progressed beyond the general level. Simplicistically put, it has been decided in these "to support all that is nice and beautiful and to avoid all that is nasty." Thus, almost every activity can be interpreted as supporting the strategy, depending on the perspective and goals of whoever is making the interpretation. This means that intended strategies are everybody's and nobody's. For this reason they do not embed themselves in the actions of organizations. Strategies easily remain floating; they continue to be paper among more paper. The credibility of the main tenets of classic strategic planning is also undermined by the fact that very frequently in strategic planning existing and incipient patterns are recognized, to be legitimized with the help of strategic planning (see Sotarauta, 1996; Sotarauta and Linnamaa, 1997).

Sometimes all unfinished business is compiled into strategy papers and futures-oriented strategies have been implemented in a year. Then, when the time to make decisions comes, the strategy papers are forgotten, the world has changed, and "now is not the time to make strategies; now is the time to balance next year's budget."

The brief introduction to fallacies of strategic planning given here is pessimistic, even cynical, but above all it is one-sided, narrow, and partly wrong. Strategic planning has not produced only failure. It has caused actors to take a broader view of things from different perspectives, greater and more profound consideration than before has been given to futures, actors have recognized their own strengths and weaknesses and learned to understand them better, excessive preoccupation with detail has been avoided, sectoral boundaries have been transcended, activities have been pursued consistently and persistently, and so on. Strategic planning as a part of policy making is like human life itself—some good, some bad—and always plenty to learn.

Attempts to eliminate the problems of strategic planning have generally been made through developing new methods that take better account of the future, by making better analyses, by being more creative, by refining reports, and by committing better to the program development. The root of the trouble, however, is that policy makers and politicians ways of under-standing themselves and their operations seem not to have changed as much as the general policy environment. Their view of policy making is still dominated by rational planning models, models that draw on product, ac-complishment, and goal-oriented approaches that operate within means–end structured problems (i.e., within instrumental rationalism). In addition, the thinking as well as the strategic planning models developed for the private sector are not directly applicable to public purposes.

As such, classical strategic planning does not suit the world of shared power: the political game going on within policy making in which there are no turns for making moves, in which teams and combinations change in the course of the game, and in which the difference between opponent and teammate is fine indeed. The game requires the understanding of the logic of a pluralistic and multiobjective dynamic network. It requires the adop-tion of the governance of ambiguity and an understanding of the nature of interactive strategy processes.

The classical strategic planning in general use in Finnish public adminis-tration, with its visions, scenarios, strategic analyses, and strategic goals, is a shade too clear-cut and bound as an approach. The problem is that strate-gic planning has been too narrowly understood. The focus has too often been on only a few core issues. All too often the focus is on what is the desired future, what is to be done, and in what situations. Thus questions like who will do it, how will it be done, and what is the quality of the process like are neglected. The new focus presupposes good quality pro-cesses; it presupposes soft strategy.

Soft strategy recognizes that we are always managing interorganizational and communicative processes, and flux rather than stability defining the order of things. Therefore strategy cannot be merely a classical planning procedure. Strategy formulation, an artful design, is only a minor part of the overall strategy process, intended strategies are always only abstrac-tions in our minds, and in most cases they are focused on some other actor in the field. At the same time it is acknowledged that the visions, aims, and strategies of other organizations do not necessarily resemble those of one's own organization, and thus policy-making process is an art of reconciling and balancing a variety of goals and interests both within and across organi-zations. The stand taken behind soft strategies is communicative, open, and flexible. In this view, soft strategies are not plans to rewrite, not plans to implement as such, but overall processes that provide decision makers with strategic consciousness and a way to mirror single decisions and actions in proportion to both present situations and the future environment (see Sotarauta, 1995, 1996, 1997).

Even if the communicative process and its quality is stressed, intended strategies are still needed. They provide the framework to continuously seek consistency in action, not only in classical tradition, but in an argu-mentative carousel.

TRANSFORMING THEORY INTO TEACHING

Point of Departure for Teaching and Overall Objectives

As stated initially, our ways of thinking, our ways of perceiving the world and its processes, are frequently but furtively guided by a background of strategic thinking, planning, and action. Organizations drawing on too-rigid perceptions easily develop a surface tension below which the talk is only of matters within the dominant strategy. Nothing new arises, nothing is questioned. Silence reigns in the organization.

One of the purposes of communicative planning is to break the silence, to make the surface tension tremble and break so as to create chances for new issues to break through. In the training of leaders, planners, and so on already active in practical working life, the instructor's primary task is to provide such impulses, which will bring about a rupture of the inculcated modes of thinking so that new modes of thought can be transformed into actions. With "new" students the situation is different. They have not yet had time to evolve their own strong thinking models and their own views of planning, and the surface tensions that maintain these has not yet been developed. The development is underway, and the task of education is to help students to evolve supple modes of thinking that leave room for continuous learning and for the recognition and acceptance of other, different modes of thinking.

Since the 1990s the great challenge for teaching has become the linking together of the sometimes very rough communicative processes and sometimes rather idealistic strategic planning "in search of a better world." The following shows how this was attempted in teaching in futures-seeking regional development policy process in the University of Tampere, Department of Regional Studies and Environmental Policy.

On a general level, the university's courses in regional studies can be divided into those that disseminate knowledge and those that teach skills. The former type includes courses on regional development and theory and practice of planning. Research skills are taught in the particularly extensive course on research methods, but planning skills have formerly been included in courses with a bias toward disseminating knowledge. In 1995 a new course was introduced (planned by Torsti Hyyryläinen and Markku Sotarauta) by which it was possible to extend teaching skills to cover strategic planning and regional development. When the course was planned the objective was to achieve a new kind of pedagogical entity through which it would be possible to on the one hand combine better than before theoretical and practical aspects and on the other hand focus better on learning by doing. In a nutshell, the course is as follows:

Focus of course content
- Strategic planning in promotion of regional development, the overall frame of reference being EU regional policy and its Finnish application. Special attention to be paid to regional and local strategy processes.

Guiding idea of the course

- to practice those skills needed in communicative strategic planning and to enhance knowledge of practical strategic planning on the principle of "learning by doing."

Course objectives

- to enhance student's conception of contemporary futures-oriented strategic planning by combining theory and practice through activity.
- to familiarize students with practical planning situations.
- to familiarize students with methodology in strategic planning and futures research and communicative planning.

Skills to be practiced

- evaluating and analyzing foreign and Finnish strategic development programs.
- compiling different types of strategic planning approaches, working methods, and techniques of strategic planning.
- oral and written presentation, working and discussing in groups, presenting multidimensionally and illustratively.
- survival in communicative processes.

One core idea of the course is to familiarize students with the working rhythm of the contemporary planner. For this reason several fast-moving practical tasks are accomplished. Practical assignments are done both individually and in groups. However, individual assignments are always done as part of a group and they are included as part of a group effort. Although the course is by nature biased toward learning by doing, there are also lectures. However, these are brief and only raise various themes; thus, the lectures are intended to be thought provoking to support and direct the accomplishing of practical assignments and to offer an exposition of the theme to be addressed rather than to "teach" it in its entirety.

PROGRESS OF THE COURSE

The practical course in regional planning falls into three phases. In the first of these, students are introduced to the "shop front" promotion of regional development (i.e., the formal aspects of it and of strategic planning related to it). In addition to the institutional structure, the part of planning that is visible on the outside—development programs—is examined. The objective of the second phase it to get behind the scenes: to learn to understand how plans live, change, and develop in communicative policy processes; what goes on in the field. Thus, the general objective of the second phase is to identify the nature of games. In the third phase students enhance their knowledge and skills in groups on separately chosen themes. The objective of the third phase is to collect the observations made in the earlier phases and to enhance skills in a separately selected theme related to futures-seeking strategy processes.

CONCLUSIONS

From the mid-1990s the meaning of strategic planning and futures research in Finnish public administration in general and in regional and local development has been characterized by many changes. It may be stated as a generalization that all the municipalities of Finland and the regions have made their own strategies. In addition, more and more of them have been using scenario planning to support their strategy work. Simultaneously, great differences can be discerned between different regions and municipalities in both the quality of output and above all in significance to activity. As a further generalization it may be stated that if the preparation of strategies and scenarios has been a narrow performance led by holders of official posts, then the meaning of these is likewise narrow. However, if sufficient time has been devoted to the process and if sufficiently extensive and open discussions have been held, then contemplation of the future has at least had an indirect bearing on policy making and decision making. The process has had direct effects and the output itself has generally had an indirect effect.

On the basis of my research on strategic planning at regional and local levels, the logic of combining futures-seeking development and policy processes can be summarized as follows:

1. Discuss at sufficient length (i.e., discuss the basic issues of development with various parties, taking different perspectives into account). This is not a "one-off" part of planning; rather, in order to ensure a really effective discussion it should be constantly ongoing in one form or another.

2. Only after sufficient communication can a realization come to light in a wide range of actors as to which themes are current from the point of view of regional development and futures.

3. Only personal realization can lead to a matter being truly grasped. This is essential if strategies are to become part of the actors' "spinal cords" and not merely flourish on paper and in ceremonial speeches.

4. Real commitment can only follow after sufficient communication, personal realization, and grasping of the issues.

Such a process is no linear planning process progressing from planning to decision making, from decision making to implementation, from implementation to evaluation, and so on to a new round of planning. Rather, it is a continuous communicative process in which different elements dovetail into one another in many different ways.

In a network society the need for a communicative approach is constantly increasing, and as Forester (1993) states, we need a "critical pragmatism," pragmatics with vision. Planning can no longer be seen as technical problem solving, but, as he states, planning can be seen as a questioning and shaping of attention, and organizing it. One of the key problems of today is that key actors are not trained or experienced in dealing with such soft questions. There is a need to redirect the focus because current policy thinking is dominated by the classical strategic planning models that are not adequate in collaborative forms of policy making. Policy makers do not know how to handle communicative processes and their sometimes elusive quality. Thus, our aim has been to reduce this gap between contemporary needs and education by bringing sometimes confusing policy processes into teaching too.

Student feedback on these efforts has been very positive. Students are interested in the new modes of working. They believe that things are retained better in memory if they do them hands on instead of just listening to a lecturer. The hands-on approach has long been a core issue in teaching regional studies at the University of Tampere, and the course outlined in this chapter has introduced new modes of working and a view that connects future and processes more firmly.

Despite the positive student feedback, the early stages of the course are not easy. Students are accustomed to being confronted with ready-made facts and models, after which comes practice. In this course, students are only introduced to issues and then they practice hands on. A typical student comment at the beginning of the course is, "How can we do this task when the matter has not yet been properly taught to us?" Only at the end of the course do the pieces begin to fall into place for the students.

The way of teaching the course and its relation to conventional teaching can be illustrated through an analogy to teaching people to swim. If one were to set about teaching people to swim using conventional university teaching methods there would first be lectures on the history of swimming, the different schools of thought, and the basics of the principle swimming techniques. Next there might be videos of swimming to show the students what swimming looks like. Given sufficient financial resources, there might even be a study trip to the beach to see swimmers, and the students could try for themselves what the water feels like. At the end of the course, the students would be given a certificate stating that they have successfully completed the basic course in swimming. But would they be able to swim? I doubt it.

If we were to set about teaching the students to swim according to the principles of the courses introduced here, there would first be a few lectures to arouse student's interest in swimming, its importance would be discussed, and so on. Students would further be advised that to stay at the surface, the arms and legs should be moved in a certain way. Next, the class would be thrown in at the deep end. The teachers would go in after them, give advice and show by example, support and encourage, but the swimming would be the result of the students' own perceptions and realizations. The teachers' task is to pilot them in the direction of that realization and give them something to build on. What is essential in this type of teaching is that theory is brought as near as possible to practice through the support of the teacher in the closest possible student–teacher and student–student interaction. Would the students be able to swim after such a course? Perhaps. At least they would stand a better chance.

REFERENCES

Bryson, J. M. (1988). *Strategic planning for non-profit organizations*. San Francisco: Jossey-Bass.

Bryson, J. M., and Crosby, B. C. (1992). *Leadership for the common good: Tackling public problems in a shared-power world*. San Francisco: Jossey-Bass.

Dryzeck, J. S. (1993). Policy analysis and planning: From science to argument. In F. Fischer and J. Forester (Eds.), *The argumentative turn in policy analysis and planning* (pp. 213–232). Albany, NY: UCL Press.

Dunsire, A. (1994). Rigging the arena: New light on old practices. *Hallinnon tutkimus, 13* (3), 170–176.

Fischer, F., and Forester, J. (1993). Editors' introduction. In F. Fischer and J. Forester (Eds.), *The argumentative turn in policy analysis and planning* (pp. 1–20). Albany, NY: UCL Press.

Forester, J. (1993). *Critical theory, public policy and planning practice: Towards a critical pragmatism*. Albany: State University of New York Press.

Healey, P. (1992). Planning through debate: The communicative turn in planning theory. *Town Planning Review, 63* (2), 143–162.

Kickert, W. (1993). Complexity, governance and dynamics: Conceptual explorations of public network management. In J. Kooiman (Ed.), *Modern governance: New government–society interactions* (pp. 191–204). London: Sage.

Mintzberg, H. (1994). *The rise and fall of strategic planning: Reconceiving roles for planning, plans, planners*. New York: Free Press.

Royall, F. (1993). Lost opportunities: The case of labour market management in the Republic of Ireland. In J. Kooiman (Ed.), *Modern governance: New government–society interactions* (pp. 51–62). London: Sage.

Sager, T. (1994). *Communicative planning theory*. Newcastle-upon-Tyne: Avebury Ashgate.

Sotarauta, M. (1995). Argumentative mirroring: Local governance as the art of fine-tuning dilemmas of strategy. In M. Sotarauta and J. Vehmas (Eds.), *Regions and environment in transition: In search of new solutions* (pp. 67–84). Tampere: University of Tampere, Department of Regional Studies. [Research Reports Series A16].

Sotarauta, M. (1996). Kohti epäselvyyden hallintaa: Pehmeä strategia 2000-luvun alun suunnittelun lähtökohtana [Towards governance of ambiguity: Soft strategy as a starting point for planning in the beginning of 21st century]. *Acta Futura Fennica, 6* (entire issue).

Sotarauta, M. (1997). Escaping the strategic policy-making traps by soft strategies: Redirecting the focus. *Nordisk Samhällsgeografisk Tidskrift, 24*, 48–62.

Sotarauta, M., and Linnamaa, R. (1997). *Kaupunkiseudun elinkeinopolitiikka ja prosessien laatu: Tampere, Turku, Oulu, Seinäjoki, Vammala and Parkano benchmarking-vertailussa* [Local development policy and the quality of the policy process: Tampere, Turku, Oulu, Seinäjoki, Vammala and Parkano as cases in point]. Tampere: Tampereen yliopisto. Aluetieteen laitos, sarja A19.

Stenvall, K. (1993). Public policy planning and the problem of governance: The question of education in Finland. In J. Kooiman (Ed.), *Modern governance: New government–society interactions* (pp. 63–73). London: Sage.

Throgmorton, J. (1993). Planning as a rhetorical activity: Survey research as a trope in arguments about electric power planning in Chicago. *Journal of the American Planning Association, 59* (3), 117–144.

17

A Journey to the Future in the United Kingdom

Graham H. May

A PERSONAL ODYSSEY

During my first degree in geography, one of the favorite questions asked was, "What is geography?" At the time in the 1960s there seemed to be something of a crisis in the subject, as the traditional descriptive accounts of different regions and landforms were challenged by both the natural sciences and the positivist approaches then popular in the social sciences. Geography was seen by some as rather old fashioned, with little to contribute to the new technological age. Part of the problem was probably due to the position that geography held in the curriculum being at the same time an art, a science, and a social science. Unlike most other disciplines it did not belong exclusively to one academic tradition but straddled the boundaries, resulting in internal disputes about its area of concern and its methods. It still does, and though the same question is still being asked, geography appears to have overcome its identity crisis to become one of the most popular courses in U.K. universities. In the interim many strands have been developed, ranging from the highly quantitative (Haggett, 1965) to the social critiques of writers like David Harvey (1973), which have led to the emergence of a more critical and theoretical base (Herbert and Thomas, 1990). It also increasingly overlaps with other disciplines, particularly in science and social science. What once appeared to be a weakness has emerged as a strength.

From this geographical background I moved into a career and a master's degree in town planning and encountered another profession and discipline that was continually asking, "What is planning?" and, perhaps due to its active intent, "What should planning be?" If geography had a split personality, planning, particularly in the United Kingdom in the late 1960s, was eclectic in the extreme. Having started out from a grounding in environmental determinism based on the experiences of the nineteenth-century public health and housing legislation, from which planning law in the United Kingdom developed, the 1960s were a period of reassessment. For the first time it was becoming apparent that many of the policies planning had espoused as bringing about the good society through the control of land use were not producing the expected results. Not only were existing problems not being solved as they should have been, but new problems were emerging in the very areas built to solve the old problems. Rather than influencing behavior in a deterministic way, it was becoming apparent that land use was interrelated with economic, social, and political issues in a much more complex manner.

One of the most significant developments of the time was the importation of the ideas of systems theory from the biological sciences. Not only did this influence the academic approach to planning (McLoughlin, 1969; Chadwick, 1971), it was also incorporated into new planning legislation. Land-use transportation models using the new computing capability then available became the accepted approach, replacing the Geddesian survey–analysis–plan methodology of earlier years. If the urban system could be accurately described in a model and calibrated to fit the past, it was assumed that it could be cranked forward to forecast the future that was to be planned for. Complex though some of the models became, the future they forecast frequently failed to materialize, at least in part because as the economy globalized and society changed, the model of any individual urban region did not incorporate sufficient variables to accurately reflect the emerging reality. Eventually, partly as a result of increasing challenges from its own shortcomings, the growing questioning of planning by the environmental movement, and political changes, the systems approach retreated into specialist areas such as population forecasting, retail impact studies, and traffic planning.

An even greater influence on planning in Britain broke like a tidal wave in 1979. The postwar consensus, of which planning was part, was blown apart by the Thatcher revolution intent on rolling back the frontiers of the state. The very notion of planning was challenged at every level; only the market could allocate resources efficiently and effectively, and any attempt to intervene in the economy or with the development process was politically suspect. Thousands of jobs were said to be locked up in the filing cabinets of local authority planning departments, and taste in urban design should not be dictated by a professional clique. That planning survived the onslaught is something of a surprise, but it did so by adapting and focusing on the growing concern for urban regeneration as the full force of international competition, released by the government's policies, destroyed the traditional industries of much of Britain. Ironically, another force also appears to have played a role in preventing the demise of planning, Nimbyism. The very voters who supported Thatcherism were themselves vehemently opposed to the development pressures it released onto their rural shires. Their main protection was planning control, to which all development in the United Kingdom is subject. Political pressure was exerted and the controls were kept, but as a consequence planning effectively became the local administration of central government policy. Only relatively recently, in the 1990s, has there been a growing awareness of the need for strategy and vision, which was lost during the previous decade.

During this time two developments were particularly influential in my own thinking as I moved from local government to higher education to lecture in the politics of the environment. First, at the start of the 1970s two books were published that have had a significant influence on the development of my approach to futures. *Future Shock* (Toffler, 1970) and *The Limits to Growth* (Meadows, Meadows, Randers, and Behrens, 1972) have rather different perspectives on the likely future. The first is essentially upbeat, seeing humanity on a developing trajectory based on advances in scientific knowledge and related changes in technology. The second regarded that historical development as unsustainable in the future and humanity damned unless lessons were learned and changes made quickly. These very different perspectives, both derived from an examination of trends then evident and equally valid in their own terms, when added to my experience with planning confirmed the conviction that the future has to be approached critically and cautiously. Predictions that are based on only one perspective of the future, be it technological optimism or environmental pessimism, are unlikely to be accurate. What is important is open debate about the future that acknowledges the inherent uncertainty of our relationship with it and the dynamic nature of the human condition.

Second, the opportunity to lead a number of student study visits to Germany reinforced my own view that U.K. planning had taken a wrong turn and that a strategic approach was a vital component of any decision system. Although the German planning system tends, in its fullest application, to be overbureaucratic and inflexible, it, and the similar systems in most other Western European countries, has retained both large-scale and long-term perspectives of the kind that were abandoned in the United Kingdom in the 1980s. Indeed, a study for the Swedish government noted, "Nowhere in society are people's futures mortgaged so far ahead as when the municipalities plan housing projects, earmark uses of land and build highways" (Ingelstam, 1974). In casting doubt on the ability of the planning system to effectively forecast and plan for the future, the realization that development necessarily has a long-term impact was also lost.

Planning is concerned, like it or not, with the future, but in the United Kingdom at least its approach to the future seemed naïve. Early British planning took a deterministic view, believing that environmental action would solve problems across a wide social range. From the perspective of the systems models in vogue in the 1970s the future would be like the present, only more so. It also appeared, in both of these approaches, that if planning could solve the problems of the present the future would be problem free and planners would effectively put themselves out of a job. The difficulties of prediction, including the future impact of policy decisions and the dynamic nature of the future, were not understood. Consequently, planning contributed to its own difficulties by making claims it was unable to substantiate. From the perspective of the Thatcherite New Right, on the other hand, planning was bound to fail because it was neither able to predict the future nor to provide the circumstances for economic success. It had, in their view, been no small contributor to the failure of the British economy in the postwar period and as a result was part of the problem rather than part of the solution.

From the early 1970s on, my interest in futures developed, initially from an environmental planning base. A number of teaching opportunities, first in planning courses (May, 1984) opened up, until in the 1990s it was possible to develop the first master's degree in foresight and futures studies in the United Kingdom and write a book exploring my own approach to futures (May, 1996).

RELEVANT THEORIES

Throughout this experience many theories have influenced my thinking, but none has become the central theme of my approach to the future and to futures studies. Rather, several make partial contributions to an eclectic mix. From planning has come a belief in the ability of the human race to influence the future in a positive direction, what Polak (1973) termed "influence optimism" and an appreciation of the value of systems theory in exploring the importance of interrelationships in understanding reality. Concern for the environment, again related to a background in geography and planning, reinforces the use of systems in a ecological context, but not to the extent that the environment dominates to the exclusion of other concerns. Indeed, some years ago, when it was suggested that futures studies might find its rationale in environmentalism, my own experiences with the failures as well as successes of planning led me to conclude that such an approach would be an unwise restriction. The environment is an important and ultimately critical factor in human survival, but deterministic approaches such as those on which early British planning was based, and the more extreme writings of some environmentalists (Goldsmith, Allen, Allaby, Davoll, and Lawrence, 1972), seem clearly inadequate. Such extreme statements, which purport to know the future, do more harm than good to futures studies.

Planning, policy making, and problem solving all tend to a belief in rationality. Rational decision making, in its purest form, relies on assumptions of perfect understanding of the issue of concern; an ability to imagine all possible solutions, make an effective choice between them, and implement the solution with the expected results. These conditions are seldom present, as limitations in knowledge or budgetary or time constraints force a less than complete decision-making environment upon us. Rationality is consequently nearly always bounded. Where decisions with future consequences are involved, the limitations are further extended by the difficulties of prediction and the nature of many of the issues involved, for as Mendell (1978) noted, "The future is an ill-structured problem" (p. 149).

Some light on the nature of futures problems is thrown by theories of catastrophe, chaotics, and complexity. Catastrophe theory provides insight into the occurrence of break points that may develop from the continuation of existing trends beyond a certain level. Situations that appear reasonably stable may suddenly flip into a different state without any major shift in the forces bearing on them. Chaos theory may at first sight appear to undermine the idea of futures studies and our ability to influence the future, but in increasing our understanding of the reality of our world it provides a better basis from which to work. Paradoxically, it suggests that a degree of predictability may lie within unpredictability and that we should free ourselves from the positivist and rationalist pursuit of perfection in favor of improvement. As such, they may not herald the end of the Enlightenment, as some have suggested, but rather its enlightenment, much as adolescent certainty in tempered by adult experience. Anderla, Dunning, and Forge (1997) note that chaos is closely linked to complexity theory, and complex systems, according to Casti (1994), are

- unpredictable and often lead to counterintuitive results.
- full of feedback–feedforward loops that enable them to respond and absorb shocks.
- decentralized, with many decision points.
- irreducible, in that slicing them up in to subsystems destroys their very nature.

The resulting mix of theoretical approaches has resulted in two central themes in my approach to the study of the future: paradox (May, 1996) and learning (May, 1997). Paradox is defined as "a seemingly absurd or contradictory statement, even if actually well founded" (Tulloch, 1993, p. 1102). The definition points to some of the difficulties we experience with such situations when we are looking, as we have traditionally done, for clear causes and effects and simple single solutions. Paradoxical situations are complex, often counterintuitive, and not susceptible to simple one-club solutions. Just as the future is continually advancing ahead of us as we journey through time in the dynamic present, so our understanding of the world and our situation is developing. New ideas about the way the world works are continually being developed and challenging current wisdom. A classic example from my own experience as a geographer is the theory of platetectonics, which made the previously ridiculous notion that the continents could be fitted together like a jigsaw respectable. At some stage even this theory may give way to another that fits the future state of knowledge more accurately. Such is the nature of our knowledge and of life. Change, which is omnipresent, necessitates a learning approach. Bertrand de Jouvenel (1967) prescribed a valuable approach in the form of his concept of a "surmising forum . . . where Advanced or forward looking opinions about what may be and about what can be done will be put forward. And since the passage of time brings new situations and sows new seeds, clearly this forum must be in continuous operation. It is not a matter of foreseeing the future once and for all, but of discussing the future continuously" (p. 277). This can be a difficult argument to substantiate in an environment used to identifying problems that it is assumed can be solved before passing on to the next one, because it undermines that belief and may appear to be a claim that futurists should have a job for life. It is, however, based on an understanding of the dynamic nature of the human condition, where knowledge is always less than complete and changing.

FUTURES METHODS

There are a wide range of methods available to futurists, from the predictive to the creative. Predictive methods that aim to foresee the future before it occurs seem to assume a fixed future that may be revealed to those with the necessary skills to uncover it. At the other end of the spectrum are those creative approaches that regard the future as open to human influence and the realization of imagined states that have not existed before. In-between are methods that accept the limitations of prediction and concentrate on managing the present with the future in mind. Different circumstances are best served by methods drawn from across this broad spectrum, but if the future is open to the influence of choice then methods that allow for alternative outcomes are more appropriate. The scenario process, based around the concept of alternative futures rather than accurate forecasting of one inevitable future, is central to this approach. A wide-ranging scan of significant factors is necessary to overcome the tendency of many forecasts to be too narrow and miss critical but apparently external influences. In exploring the implications of alternative futures the capability of computer models to examine the consequences of different assumptions is particularly useful, as can be the more creative techniques in developing images of previously unknown situations.

An inherent difficulty in the use of scenarios to explore alternative futures is the apparent distinction they make between our customary use of the singular when talking of *the* past and *the* present. Plural futures is immediately distinct and foreign to our normal pattern of thinking. It is only when we begin to examine how we know the past and the present that uncertainty and consequently the opportunity for alternative explanations arise. The most obvious examples of this occur where attempts are made to find the cause or apportion blame following an accident. There are always likely to be perspectives that lead to different conclusions. The further back into the past we look the more difficult it becomes to know for certain what happened. Why did the dinosaurs die out?

From this emerges an area for further examination: What is our relationship to the future? Do we really have an impact on it or, as Einstein suggested, does all time exist but is only gradually revealed to us as we experience the present? Equally, will we ever be able to close the forecasting gap? At present forecasts in many areas turn out to be inaccurate, in that the forecast differs from the actuality when the period forecast becomes the present. But there are areas in which accuracy has improved as increased understanding of the systems involved and the techniques available for making the forecasts have developed. Examples include weather forecasting, which has become more accurate as knowledge of the weather system has grown and the ability of high-powered computers has enabled the system to be simulated more exactly, and urban models, which it is claimed can predict to within plus or minus 5 percent where people will live, work, and shop and what they will buy (Utley, 1997). Are these examples of patterns that can be predicted over the relatively short term but will gradually break down as circumstances change; where human decision is involved, self-fulfilling prophecies; an inevitable future determined by our genes, our upbringing, or our socioeconomic status; or some of those few examples where we have been able to break through the time barrier into an already existing future? There is room to further explore our relationship with the future and our ability to direct developments toward alternative outcomes.

A PREFERABLE FUTURE

It is relatively easy to envisage possible, probable, and preferable futures, but each is influenced by the perspective from which we view the world. Allen Tough (1994) has produced a useful list of general characteristics that future generations might be expected to prefer us to leave them, which he derived from a role-playing exercise in a range of locations. Peace, security, a healthy environment, avoidance of catastrophe, improved systems of governance, increased knowledge, the well-being of children, and continuing learning would be accepted by most as worthy aims and likely to characterize a future preferable to the present, where several do not exist in many places. The problems arise in the details. A peaceful future is probably the preference of both sides in Northern Ireland, but one sees only a united Ireland as acceptable while the other is implacably opposed to the idea and regards the continuation of union with the United Kingdom as nonnegotiable. Whether a successful peace is obtainable from the current compromise, which each side interprets differently, remains doubtful. To some in the United Kingdom, improved governance would be achieved through closer integration with the European Union, including membership in the single currency, but others are vehemently opposed to what they regard as a loss of sovereignty. The examples could be extended, but even these indicate the problems of agreeing on what a preferable future would be, and even where there is agreement on that, how it might be most reliably achieved.

That does not undermine the idea of envisaging preferable futures, but it does indicate the care with which our own preferences may need to be considered from the perspectives of others. A future of the kind outlined by Tough (1994) is difficult to disagree with as an ultimate aim, but perhaps the critical need at this stage is a future in which the means to achieve such a future through debate rather than open conflict are established. Even that is not an easy matter.

REFLECTION OF THIS APPROACH IN THE M.A. FORESIGHT AND FUTURES STUDIES

To date the experience gained in my journey to the future is best expressed in writing (May, 1996, 1997) and in the philosophy of the master's degree offered by Leeds Metropolitan University, which was developed by a team of staff from across the university. The philosophy of the course is set out in the document that was prepared for validation by the university.

It has become increasingly clear that human decisions and actions play an important part in determining the future of both humanity and the world in which we live. At the close of the 20th century we are faced with a range of questions in economic, social, political and technological fields which could have major significance for the future. Many of these questions raise important ethical issues but they are also frequently surrounded by uncertainty as to the impact of alternative courses of action that could be taken. To make effective decisions we would need knowledge about the future that we cannot possess, yet we are often forced to make decisions which have long term implications in conditions of considerable uncertainty. Foresight and Futures Studies aims to critically examine the difficulties associated with making decisions with long term future consequences in conditions of uncertainty and to provide methods through which these difficulties can be minimised.

By focusing attention on the future Foresight and Futures Studies is concerned with the direction that society is taking, rather than where it has come from. In doing so it offers a unique perspective and affords opportunities for the development of the understanding and skills necessary for dealing effectively with the future. (Leeds Metropolitan University, 1996; a fuller version is available at http://www.ac.uk/hen/benv/fore/fore-in.htm)

CONCLUSION

It was H. G. Wells (1932/1989) in the 1930s who asked why there were many professors and students of history but none of foresight. Sixty years later there are a few, but academe remains wedded to empiricism and critical analysis despite the clear need for greater consideration of the issues with major consequences for the future that now faces us. Within several disciplines there are those devoting their efforts to the study of particular concerns, such as global warming, but there remains a vast difference between the numbers of those who would call themselves historians and those who would call themselves futurists. Those who do use the label are more often found in the commercial sector, where past success is less relevant than future performance to the survival of companies. Governments too are beginning to recognize the value of foresight, as the U.K. Foresight Programme and the European Union's Futures Studies Unit, attached to the Office of the President of the Commission, among others, indicate. Education is increasingly seen as crucial to the development of both the economy and society, but it needs to be an education that is relevant to the future and assists us to deal with the decisions we need to make, often in circumstances of considerable uncertainty, that have important implications for our future. The constructive study of the future is needed now more than ever before. It will not solve all the problems or find all the right answers, but it has an important part to play in human affairs as we enter the third millennium.

REFERENCES

Anderla, G., Dunning, A., and Forge, S. (1997). *Chaotics: An agenda for business and society in the 21st century*. London: Adamantine.

Casti, J. L. (1994). *Complexification: Explaining a paradoxical world though the science of surprise*. New York: HarperCollins.

Chadwick, G. (1971). *A systems view of planning: Towards a theory of the urban and regional planning process*. Oxford: Pergamon.

de Jouvenel, B. (1967). *The art of conjecture*. London: Weidenfeld and Nicolson.

Goldsmith, E., Allen, R., Allaby, M., Davoll, J., and Lawrence, S. (1972). A blueprint for survival. *The Ecologist, 2* (1), 1–42.

Haggett, P. (1965). *Locational analysis in human geography*. London: Edward Arnold.

Harvey, D. (1973). *Social justice and the city*. London: Edward Arnold.

Herbert, D. T., and Thomas, C. J. (1990). *Cities in space: City as place*. London: David Fulton.

Ingelstam, L. E. (Ed.). (1974). *To choose a future*. Stockholm: Swedish Ministry of Foreign Affairs, Secretariat for Future Studies.

Leeds Metropolitan University. (1996). *MA foresight and futures studies course document*. Leeds, UK: Author.

May, G. H. (1984). Futures studies in higher education. *Futures, 16*, 86–93.

May, G. H. (1996). *The future is ours: Foreseeing, managing and creating the future*. London: Adamantine.

May, G. H. (1997). The Sisyphus factor or a learning approach to the future. *Futures, 29*, 229–241.

McLoughlin, J. B. (1969). *Urban and regional planning: A systems approach*. London: Faber and Faber.

Meadows, D. H., Meadows, D. L., Randers, J., and Behrens, W. W. (1972). *The limits to growth*. London: Earth Island.

Mendell, J. S. (1978). The practice of intuition. In J. B. Fowles (Ed)., *Handbook of futures research* (pp. 149–161). Westport, CT: Greenwood Press.

Polak, F. (1973). *The image of the future*. Oxford: Elsevier.

Toffler, A. (1970). *Future shock*. London: Bodley Head.

Tough, A. (1994). What future generations need from us. In Institute for the Integrated Study of Future Generations (Ed.), *Why futures now?* Kyoto: Future Generations Alliance Foundation.

Tulloch, S. (Ed.). (1993). *Complete wordfinder*. London: Readers Digest.

Utley, A. (1997, November 28). Leeds v-c makes a million. *The Times Higher*, p. 52.

Wells, H. G. (1989). Wanted—Professors of foresight. In R. Slaughter (Ed.), *Studying the future*. Melbourne, Australia: Commission for the Future and Australian Bicentennial Authority. (Original work published 1932).

18

Global Issues and Futures for Planners: The Heuristic Model

Sam Cole

FUTURES AND PLANNING PEDAGOGY

Professional planners are often institutionally caged in cautious and conservative roles and obliged to pay attention to present realities: They cannot appear too off-the-wall, and they need to demonstrate some empirical justification for their proposals. In contrast, futurists often pride themselves on their creativity, thinking outside the box, and so on, and have developed forums that allow some license in this respect. Almost by definition, futures studies should envision possibilities beyond the time horizon of extrapolation and forecasting. These differences accepted, most futurists and planners would agree that futures studies can be a useful adjunct to many planning exercises, especially if together they combine imaginative thinking with sound empirical analysis. A shared challenge for futures studies and strategic planning, therefore, is how best to synthesize information in a systematic manner in order to be better able to assess trends and alternatives. The heuristic method described here represents one attempt to address this problem. Although it is not restricted to student exercises or global futures, I shall emphasize these applications in this chapter.

In futures studies, scenarios are ideally developed from a mix of verbal, empirical, theoretical, philosophical, and anecdotal information; fantasy, fact, and fiction. In general, a scenario consists of a selection of variables, their past trends and the interactions between them, and some assumptions about future changes. This information may be expressed in a combination of structured visual, verbal, and quantitative ways (such as cross-impact, future histories, and simulation). The heuristic method embodies elements of each of the widely used methods shown in the following list:

- Trend Extrapolation: Projects past trends into the future for some given period of time. Assumes that the future will in some way be an extension of past trends.
- Dynamic Systems Analysis and Computer Modeling: Shows how various variables in different areas interact with each other, within a whole systems context, over time.
- Cross-Impact Analysis: Shows how choices concerning one variable interact with choices concerning another variable, providing a table of all possible combinations of choices for each variable and showing which combinations are viable and which not.
- Delphi: Poll experts in some area on what events they think are most probable (or preferable) and when they are most likely to occur; also the reasons for their answers. Summarize results to experts; ask them to take poll again and maintain or revise their position, as desired.
- Scenarios: A possible sequence of events that "could" happen in the future, based on certain initial conditions or assumptions and their consequences. Typically futurists construct several scenarios to demonstrate best case, worst case, most probable case, and so on.

In practice, the links between the qualitative and empirical components of futures scenarios are usually quite vague. Implementation tends to polarize between quantitative modeling methods that focus on a restricted number of empirically measured variables and qualitative methods that rehearse a wide range of sometimes elusive variables but make little use of empirical data. This also reflects two kinds of futurist: practical forecasters who focus on "probable" futures tied to the extrapolation of present trends, and visionaries who seek "desirable" futures that are likely to be achieved only beyond the trends. The heuristic method attempts to combine these approaches by providing a fairly simple and "open" system that can be used to make projections for an arbitrary selection of interacting variables.

Briefly, a set of key variables are selected and their growth rates and interactions are quantified on the basis of a variety of empirical and impressionistic evidence. Students fill a cross-impact table with measures that represent the key variables and relationships. Although the modeling exercise ultimately involves quantification, the aim is not to produce more "accurate" forecasts. Rather, it is to encourage students to appreciate the importance of taking a systemic approach to forecasting, and to show just how unpredictable and contested the future is. Students are invited to develop their own ideas, challenge others, and represent conventional worldviews or frameworks of many-faceted negotiations.

As with most methods, a primary benefit of the heuristic method is that it obliges us to organize information. Typically, a group of students selects a set of issues and then each member becomes the "expert" with respect to a given topic, such as conflict, culture, education, or technology. In this case students share specialist knowledge and learn to work as a multidisciplinary group, Alternatively, students may develop their own data or projections. This then becomes an exercise to confront opinions and analysis. In either case, students learn to formalize connections between complex issues and to deal with many variables simultaneously.

One element of the seminar, so far only partially implemented, has been to develop an interactive Web site whereby students can develop an impact analysis by answering an on-line questionnaire and view the resulting projections and policy scenarios. The intention is to link this to similar efforts by public agencies and futurists to create information networks and dialogues with communities.

Much has to be covered during the semester. Since the modeling can only be one small part of this, as far as possible we must build on students' technical skills in statistics and use of spreadsheets. These considerations more or less dictate the approach, but I would be remiss not to mention several excellent alternatives (see, especially, Hughes, 1996).

A CLASSROOM EXAMPLE: THE GIFS MODEL

The Global Issues and Futures (GIFS) course comprises seminars, guest lectures, films, readings, and exploration of issues on the Web, culminating in group activities and presentations.[1] The final product is typically a "scenario" devised by the group, with individual students being responsible for specific topics and activities. For example, a given student might research the historic relationship between technical change and economic growth, how different futurists and forecasters view trends in the next century, and what the possibilities are for change. Often the topic will be tied to the student's master's degree thesis topic. The tasks and activities in sequence over the semester can be summarized as follows:

Task	Purpose
Selecting issues and becoming an "expert"	Identify sources (Internet and readings)
Discuss seminars on controversial topics	Recognize and challenge viewpoints
Group work, papers, and summary charts	Organize a communications network
Research the history of the issue	Understand the background and perspectives
Creating a resounding cliché for the scenario	Provide an imaginative and appealing storyline
Developing structured verbal scenarios	Provide an itemized temporal description
Representing the scenario and outcome in a "quantitative" model	Bring specialist know-how into the collective exercise

Evaluating outcomes and exploring policies Confronting and recognizing tradeoffs
                                             between competing goals

Revising the process   Check consistency across the scenario

ALTERNATIVES FOR SCENARIO BUILDING

Scenario building is central to each group's final project. Whilst the primary aim of a scenario is to tell a convincing story about the future, this can be initiated in several ways. For sake of pedagogy, three approaches are distinguished: forecasting, envisioning, and polling. Each approach tends to draw on different methodologies and data, provides different kinds of forecasts, and treats uncertainty differently. Forecasting draws on formal models and estimation techniques. Envisioning draws on science fiction imagery and metaphors and historical analogy and incidents. Polling draws on media culling and surveys of experts, including Web-based questionnaires. Directly or indirectly, most futures studies involves a mix of these, even though they emphasize one approach. Each appeals to a different kind of audience, or lends itself to particular topics. Each approach demands a different appreciation of how the impact matrix is constructed and used. These three approaches and their differences can be summarized as follows:

APPROACH	forecasting	envisioning	polling
BASIS	empirical	theory or issues	representative
VARIABLES	limited	selective	diverse
PAST	estimation	process	experience
FUTURE	projection and variants	stylized futures	survey or Delphi
OUTCOMES	narrow band of probabilities	a map of possibilities	a soup of future events
UNCERTAINTY	statistical	plausibility	representative–consensus
AUDIENCE	public policy makers	general audience	business and community

The differences reflect a host of issues: the topics considered; timescale; the orientation–perspective, philosophy–skills, and so on of the futurist(s); and the anticipated audience. Forecasters typically concentrate on a restricted range of issues for which there are "hard" data, such as that found in government statistics, and account only implicitly for soft variables, such as political convictions. In contrast, these same "soft" issues may be the driving variables in scenarios or polling methods.

By "worldview" here we mean an overarching view of the world such as liberalism, conservatism, Marxism, and latter-day revisionisms. Even where not quantified, each can be thought of as fairly consistent and coherent bundles of ideas about issues, history, and desirable futures (see, for example, Freeman and Jahoda, 1978). They provide a kind of intellectual algebra that allows us to deduce interpretations of situations based on the accepted wisdom and values made explicit in the worldview. The advantage of using worldviews as the basis for scenario construction is that they are all associated with a fairly wide body of literature. Each tends to be focused on selected areas of interest and to have evolved its own terminology and code. By "perspective," we mean a more particular interpretation, such as environmentalism, feminism, or Third Worldism. By "topics," we mean central issues such as population growth or nuclear war, or core issues such as information technology resource constraints or events in scenarios such as "cybertopia," "limits to growth," or "after the apocalypse." The payoff from taking an issue-oriented approach is that it confronts topical issues directly and has a populist appeal.

Scenarios may be also be built around contrasting degrees of involvement or severity of an event or trend, such as high or low economic growth, degrees of global warming, levels of political conflict, or variants of cultural diversity. Nonetheless, the method is designed to be fairly "open" in terms of issues, perspectives, and futures, and to provide an instrument for forming views as much as propagating them.

A good scenario tells a convincing story. This story is refined and modified during the course of a futures study by the interaction of the people, methods, and issues involved. Each element should contribute something to the outcome. Often the scenario will be contrasted with other, less desirable alternatives. At the very least, therefore, a model has to be able to deal with these several scenarios and counterscenarios to bring information from several sources into the negotiation.

SETTING UP THE SCENARIO TABLES

The scenario-building exercise requires students to quantify perceptions of past, present, and future. First we try to confirm the historical trend, establish the base scenario forecast, and critique the prevailing situation. From this we can argue for alternative futures and demonstrate policies and explore strategies that culminate in preferred futures. In the context of the seminar, constructing a scenario typically involves identifying and assessing a range of issues, variables, and outcomes. The overall task typically includes a number of activities, each of which may involves a sequence of steps:

Activity	Steps
selecting scenarios	providing a verbal description
selecting key variables	ranking importance
evaluating trends	assess historic and present growth
identifying interactions	reviewing empirical data
understanding outcomes	assess severity of forecast crises
recognizing uncertainties	checking competing analysis
exploring policies	review credibility and feasibility

Obviously, a major question is what items should be included? Why is a given topic important? What is the issue? Different worldviews highlight or play down the importance of particular variables. In the example, given students identified a number of issues that they considered to be important. The selected items were conflict, culture, education, poverty, technology, economy, population, and environment. For many futurists, these variables may seem rather unimaginative or overly Occidental. These are variables of interest to planners, although in principle there is no restriction on the choice. Each of these items and their mutual interrelationships was then examined in more detail by the class. Some discussion concerned what to do about missing but implicitly important items, and how or whether to subdivide the world. In the example, the world is considered as a whole *The Limits to Growth* (Meadows, Meadows, Randers, and Behrens, 1972) style. The trade-offs between clarity and complexity, simplicity and oversimplification, and so on, as in real-world policy making, are resolved by pressure of time.

On the other hand, "heuristic" should not mean "anything goes." While we could make an arbitrary selection of variables and a plausible set of relationships between them, the idea is rather to help us to represent our ideas about important variables in a consistent and poignant fashion, to address the relationships between them systematically, and so to refine our ideas.

SYSTEMS AND CONCEPTS

Ideally a rich debate ensues in class over how to conceptualize and define such cornerstone variables as culture, environment, or conflict. Even with agreement on their importance, there is considerable diversity on what they are and what they mean. For example, conflict could be defined as the number of deaths from wars, institutional violence, crime, and so on, but could also include psychological stress or a propensity to violence, including the size of the military or arms races. Similarly, environment may be conceptualized as an abundance of ecological diversity depleted by demographic and economic advance, but with an intrinsic capacity for regeneration, or simply as a remaining level of mineral resources. Again, with levels of human exploitation of environment, is nature ours for the taking, are we the caretakers of nature, or what?

The more variables that are included, the more careful one has to be in identifying causal sequences. For example, a simple demographic economy model might assume that net population growth declines as the economy expands, but if an education sector is included there may be several direct and indirect interactions. Education and economy are mutually reinforcing but have opposite effects on population growth (via reduced birth and infant mortality rates and increased life expectancy). Beyond this, it is evident that issues are mutually defined. For example, making technology an explicit variable means that its effect must be discounted from the internal workings of the economy.

Although there may be considerable overlap, potentially each item makes a more or less distinctive contribution to every other. Conflict contributes directly to economy growth through destruction of production capacity during warfare and through manufacture of armaments, culture contributes through the way it affects the organization of production, education provides production skills, technology provides innovations, environment provides considerable externalities such as air and water, and population provides the labor force. Students are encouraged to seek justification for each of these contributions in economic and social theory and the corresponding empirical studies.

Other effects might be treated as indirect: for example, the spin-off innovations from conflict and conflict preparedness are a contribution of conflict to technology growth, which in turn contributes to economy growth. Similarly, culture and environment historically have been major sources of innovation. Since economic growth might also stimulate education and technology, these too may be strongly reinforcing. Such mechanisms between groups of variables may be considered as separate subsystems. For example, culture, education, and technology together provide a "knowledge subsystem," with formal and informal, traditional and modern components.

By this stage of the class, the point is made that somewhere in his or her head everyone has an opinion about everything through expertise, appreciation, extension, prejudice, or dogma, and that there are a great deal of conflicting theory, data, and bias on most issues. Nonetheless we have also created a class structure for identifying, explicating, and even negotiating alternatives. Thus, there is a need to consider what to do about uncertainty or disagreements within a group: whether to include this as a measured uncertainty in the model, or for students to construct separate versions representing their disparate observations and resulting projections.

ISSUES AND INTERACTIONS

To construct the model, data are entered in a spreadsheet table: basically a cross-impact matrix. In order to do this, students must answer questions: Are the levels, as defined, increasing or decreasing, fast or slow? What evidence is impressionistic, anecdotal, or assertive, and what is empirical? Is the situation with respect to each issue worsening or improving? How do we decide whether a particular change is to be considered "favorable"?

In order to make projections, information must be translated into current rates of change (i.e., percent per year), the strength of mutual interactions, an so on, which forces the further question of how big is "big," or how much is a "major contribution." While for some variables (such as economy and demography) there may be reliable quantitative estimates on current and historic growth rates, for many others we must make informed guesses. For this students make extensive use of Web sites, research documents, and other source materials. With eight variables there are sixty-four possible interactions, which would be the entries in Table 18.1.

Table 18.1
Self-Impacts and Cross-Impacts

ISSUES	Conflict	Culture	Education	Poverty	Technology	Environment	Economy	Population
Conflict								
Culture								
Education								
Poverty								
Technology								
Environment								
Economy								
Population								

The net growth rate of each variable is the sum of positive and negative contributions. Some are internal to the issue subsystem (e.g., births and deaths in the population, economic growth via investment, etc.). This is what the relevant discipline, such as demography or economics, might focus on.

Even though futures scenarios cover a wide range of topics, formal global models tend to concentrate on economy–population models and, more recently, on so-called integrated economy–population–environment models (for a review, see Cole, 1997). Essentially, these items are covered by the nine bottom-right entries in the matrix. In forecasting-type studies it is usual to consider these entries first, since for them there are some data, at least for the growth rates of populations and economies. On the other hand, there is less consensus on the cross-interactions between these variables, begging certain questions: Does increased abundance of environment affect population growth? Does economic activity deplete environment? How does increased economic activity increase population growth?

Setting up the remainder of the table requires that all other relationships are hypothesized using the knowledge of cross-disciplines such as economic anthropology, policy institutes, as well as inspired intuition based on anecdotal and partial information. The diagonal entries in the matrix are the internal changes within the subsystem (as defined). This includes all processes that are not to be made explicit. Discussion of these raises questions such as the following:

Conflict: How important are arms races, domino effects, peace movements? Does this lead to positive or negative reinforcement of conflict?

Culture: Do cultures reinforce each other? Does increasing diversity lead to more diversity?

Education: To what extent does education involve a self-reinforcing cycle of reproduction?

Poverty: Does poverty reinforce itself? To what extent is this a direct effect rather than an indirect effect via demography, education, economy, etc.?

Technology: Does a high level of technology increase the rate of innovation and diffusion?

Environment: Does the environment have a restorative Gaia-like regenerative capability?

Economy: How important are the residual effect of investment, trade, etc. on growth?

Population: What is the contribution to population growth from births and deaths?

The other entries represent the cross-impacts between the selected variables (e.g., how abundance of environment or the level of conflict affect population or economy). This morphological analysis poses a good many tricky questions (e.g., can we separate the investment, trade, etc. effects from environment, technology, and human resource endowments?). The following lists show typical questions to be addressed in relation to conflict to the other variables. Even seemingly banal questions such as the impact of conflict on population have extremely complex answers.

Cross-Impact of Conflict (top-row entries)

Culture   Polarizes culture or destroys marginal cultures?
Education   Does conflict change the level of education or only its content?
Poverty   Does conflict create poverty?
Technology   Does conflict stimulate technological change?
Environment   Does conflict destroy environment?
Economy   Does conflict destroy productive capacity?
Population   Does conflict deplete population?

Cross-Impacts on Conflict (first-column entries)

Culture   Does diversity of culture lead to conflict or help mediate it?
Education   Does diversity of education lead to conflict or help mediate it?
Poverty   Does poverty promote conflict?
Technology   Does technology exacerbate conflict?
Environment   Does an abundance of environment reduce the level of conflict?
Economy   Does a rising economy reduce conflict, or vice versa?
Population   Do population pressures increase conflict?

The readiness with which students (or anyone) moves from the tentative answers to such questions to empirical values to insert in the table varies considerably, just as with any cross-section of futurists. Nonetheless, with due encouragement and varying degrees of skepticism, it is possible to agree

Table 18.2
Growth and Cross-Impact Estimates for the Year 2000

ITEMS	Conflict	Culture	Education	Poverty	Technology	Environment	Economy	Population
Conflict	2.5%	-1.5%	0.0%	1.0%	1.0%	-0.5%	-1.0%	-0.5%
Culture	1.1%	1.0%		0.0%	1.0%	0.5%	-0.4%	
Education	-1.0%		1.0%	-1.0%	1.0%	0.0%	0.0%	-1.5%
Poverty	1.0%		-1.0%	0.8%	-0.2%	-0.5%	-1.0%	-0.5%
Technology		-0.5%	1.0%	0.5%	2.0%		1.0%	
Environment	-3.0%	0.5%	0.0%	-1.0%	-2.0%	0.5%	1.1%	0.6%
Economy	-1.0%	0.0%	1.0%	-1.0%	1.0%	-0.5%	2.0%	0.2%
Population	1.0%	0.0%	0.0%	1.0%	-0.5%	-0.5%	1.0%	3.5%
Net Growth	0.6%	-0.5%	2.0%	0.3%	3.3%	-1.0%	2.7%	1.8%
Uncertainty	15.0%	10.0%	5.0%	5.0%	5.0%	10.0%	3.0%	2.0%

on the results shown in Table 18.2. One important catalyst in negotiating this "agreement" was to allow a fairly wide range of disagreement, as measured by the extent of uncertainty in growth rates in any given year.

Two technical issues of paramount importance for quantitative students have been relegated to the appendix: the actual equations used in the model, and the process whereby opinions and quasi-data are translated into the numbers used in these equations.

BACKCASTS AND FORECASTS

Backcasting—running the model backward in time—allows us to check whether the assumptions that we make about present trends provide an explanation of the past.[2] The backcast shows levels of population, economy, technology, and education unambiguously increasing through time, and the level of environmental resources falling, as perhaps most historians would accept. The past trends in conflict, culture, and poverty are more contentious (Figure 18.1).

Item	Past Fifty Years	Last Century
Conflict	variable	similar to present
Culture	declining diversity	more than present
Education	increasing	less than present
Poverty	increasing	more than present
Technology	increasingly rapid growth	much less than present
Environment	increasingly depleted	more than present
Economy	rapid growth	much less than present
Population	declining growth	much more than present

Figure 18.1
Backcasting History

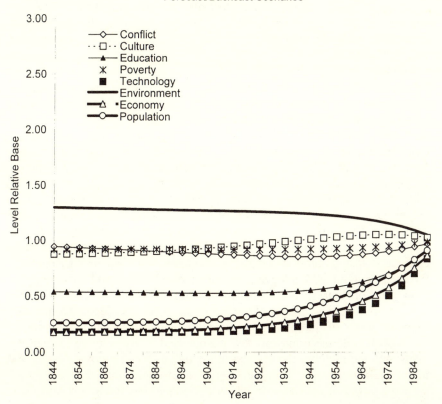

Forecast/Backcast Scenarios

Backcasting provides a way of filtering explanations—several worldviews may provide plausible visions of the future—but they can provide nonsensical backcasts. This was one element of the Sussex critique of *The Limits to Growth* (Cole, Freeman, Jahoda, and Pavitt, 1973). For example, in the seminar, when students introduced their agreed understandings of the "conservative" and "environmentalist" worldviews into the GIFS model, it was evident that the former offered a far better fit with their perceptions of the past. In contrast, the perceived environmentalist view, which better matched the sentiment of the class, would not project back plausibly more than a few decades.

How might we interpret this affront? Reject the findings, use them to reassess our presumptions, or try to address the trends on their own terms and try to find an explanation? For example, the model shows that in the past—up to the turn of the twentieth century—there was a systemic relationship between variables: The interactions between variables provided a set of positive and negative feedbacks that constrained them to a mutually balanced path. Approaching the mid-twentieth century, this scheme appears to break down, as fewer variables, especially the economy and technology, begin to dominate the behavior of all others, undermining the former balance. This tendency becomes even more established as we project into the future (Figure 18.2).

Into the future, levels of culture and environment are forecast to decline increasingly rapidly to zero. Population, poverty, and conflict increase, and then decline as culture and environment are depleted. Despite this, economy, technology, and education continue to rise steadily. Projecting further into the future, population and conflict also disappear, yet economy and technology continue to grow exponentially. The environmental and demographic forecasts fit with a *The Limits to Growth* (Meadows et al., 1972) scenario. However, the economic trends are quite contrary.

At this point some students argued that the assumptions should be revoked. Others sought explanations of such results in terms of our explicit assumptions (one of the supposed benefits of formal modeling). For example, they determined that a principal reason for the forecast decline in conflict is that cultural diversity has declined, and this in turn declined through the assumed homogenizing effects of education and technology.

In terms of futures studies, it is equally important that we use the projections to provoke new images of the future or, at the very least, interpret the trends in terms of the images and paradigms created by other futurists. A world with little environment, few people, and overwhelming technology maps onto the nightmare portrayed in the political satire movie *Brazil*. We might even use a more positive filter. For example, the projections may outline a world of the future in which technology has finally totally substituted nature, a continuation of long-standing trends, or technology has replaced human biology, an emerging trend. A world with no people but massive technology and economic activity also invokes a Datoresque future of robot civilizations, with the few remaining humans exhibited in zoos. Nor need the visions be earthbound. Obviously, we cannot take the projections too literally: What do we mean by no more nature, or no more culture? After all, robots and humanoids will develop a rich diversity of cultures, and bioengineering and terraforming will provide us with a new nature. Not all students were happy with this optimistic spin, remarking on cherished elements of our existent world (see Figure 18.3).

Item	Next Fifty Years	Next Century
Conflict	rising	declining
Culture	all diversity lost	no more culture
Education	increasing	increasing
Poverty	steadily increasing	slowly decreasing

Figure 18.2
Mutual Feedbacks between Variables

Past

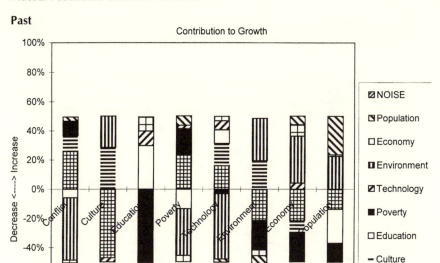

Future

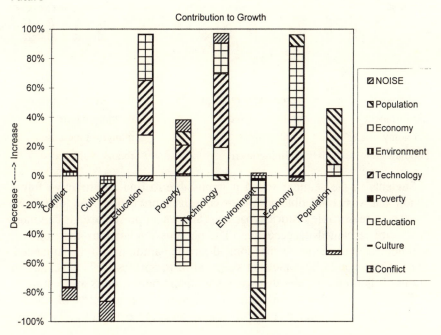

Figure 18.3
Projections into the Future

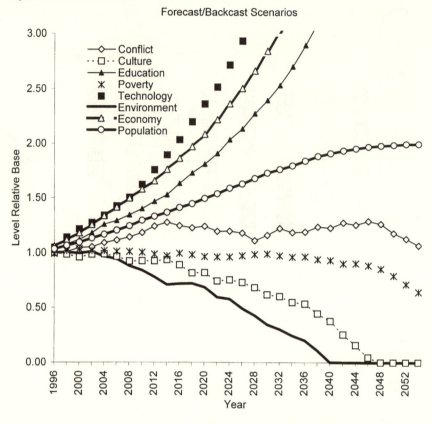

Forecast/Backcast Scenarios

Technology	increasingly rapid growth	much less than present
Environment	totally depleted	no more nature
Economy	rapid growth	manyfold increase
Population	declining level	totally collapsed

Students in the seminar found it impossible to find an attractive future vision that was compatible with their consensus projections. As long as we insist on a reasonable historical backcast and we let present trends continue, the future remained unacceptable. The obvious implication—that futurists will not find surprising—is that some dramatic paradigm shift is demanded. Even if one should be somewhat skeptical of the profession's penchant for drama, it is pretty evident that some significant policy shifts are required.

The greatest challenge for students, therefore—as prospective planners—is to find plausible policies that will deliver an acceptable future. To do this we adjust the data in the model to change the projections. Again, some rules have to be established: The art of planning is to use resources wisely, if not optimally. Policies have to be realistic: Strategies that obviously demand great resources must be traded off against others, and some strategies are likely to be politically and functionally incompatible with others. Students sought a strategy that would reduce the level of poverty and loss of culture and environmental resources by reallocating economic and educational resources (Table 18.3 and Figure 18.4). This meant that the rate of growth of the economy and technology declined but the loss of culture and environment was reversed. A skeptic might argue that such a "solution" and outcome are obvious. But again what matters here is the process and also the relative magnitudes of the required changes. They are neither marginal (i.e., likely to come about through the normal adjustment processes of a liberal society), nor do they appear so dramatic as to require a wholesale shift in human values and lifestyles.

Item	Policy	Outcome for Item
Conflict	no direct policy	steady then declining
Culture	education for diversity	steady
Education	changed emphasis	increasing
Poverty	steadily increasing	steady then decreasing
Technology	changed emphasis	reduced rate of increase
Environment	less damaging technology	decline then recovering
Economy	less growth oriented	reduced rate of increase
Population	education of women	slowed rate of increase

Arguably one of the most important results of any futures study is an awareness of the extent and implications of uncertainty. For planners this

Table 18.3
A Strategy for a Preferred Future

ITEM	Conflict	Culture	Education	Poverty	Technology	Environment	Economy	Population
Conflict								
Culture								
Education		0.5%			-1.0%			-0.5%
Poverty								
Technology				-0.5%		0.5%	-1.0%	
Environment								
Economy								
Population								

Figure 18.4
Revised Projections into the Future

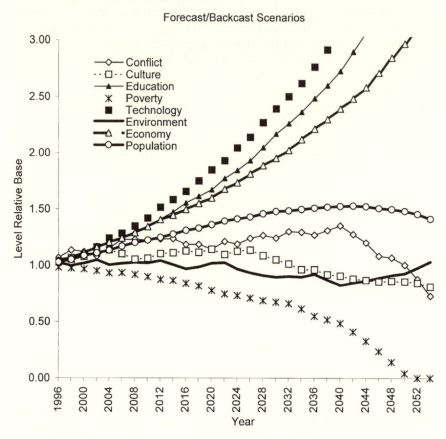

Forecast/Backcast Scenarios

translates into the need to devise strategies that are robust to unforeseen events. By running the model many times with random fluctuations determined by the agreed uncertainties, we can calculate high and low projections or a statistical distribution of projections for each variable. Figure 18.5 shows typical results for the population variable. The wide uncertainty arises indirectly from fluctuations in other items, primarily conflict, suggesting the need to revisit the selected strategy.

Students complete the semester by presenting a collaborative scenario as well as individual future-oriented papers on one of the key topics of their scenario, integrating their favored forecast from the GIFS model. Overall, the approaches lead to a very rich discussion, forcing students to be more rigorous about their assumptions and to focus keenly on the logical implications of their assumptions. Do they get closer to a better understanding of

Figure 18.5
Uncertainty and Probability

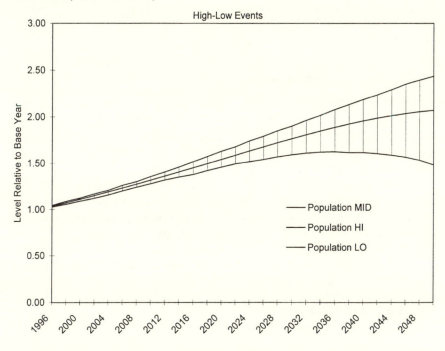

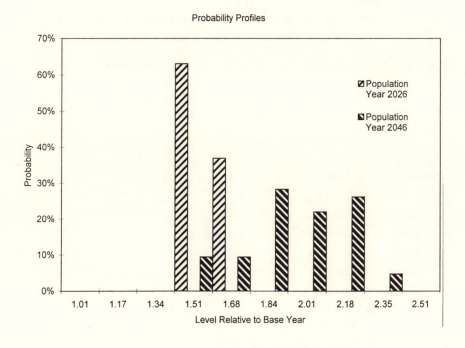

the possibilities for the future? I would like to think so, even though that is not the main purpose of the experience.

APPENDIX

The Equations of the Heuristic Model

Planning students usually have some experience in the use of spreadsheets, so this is the medium of choice for the computer implementation of the heuristic model. It is important also to have relatively simple user interface. A key component of the interface is a table showing the selected variables (or items) and the self- and cross-interactions between them (Figure 18.6).

The net change in each item is measured as its annual rate of change and the interactions are measured in terms of contributions to annual growth (or decline) in the level of each item. The direction of change is positive if increasing the contributor (the row variable) is expected to increase the level of the column variable.

The second key component are the time-step equations, which are based on the assertion that, for example, if there are four variables then

Growth of 1 = Contribution from 1 to its own growth
+ Contribution from 2 + Contribution from 3 + Contribution from 4

Each contribution is assumed to be equal to some parameter x, the current level of the item. To calculate the trends in each item we update from year to year, so for each variable,

Next year level = this year level + this year growth + uncertainty

The last term recognizes that, depending on how the data are generated, there are several sources of uncertainty: systematic, statistical, empirical,

Figure 18.6
Sample Interface Table

	Item 1	Item 2	Item 3	Item 4
Item 1	self-interaction 1.1	cross-interaction 2.3	etc.	
Item 2	cross-interaction 2.1	self-interaction 2.2		
Item 3	etc.			
Item 4				
Net Change	total for item 1			
Uncertainty	range in item 1			

theoretical, disagreements between respondents, and so on. Formally, the full model is

$$L_1 \text{ (next year)} = L_1 + (I_{11} \times L_1) + (I_{21} \times L_2) + (I_{31} \times L_3) + (I_{41} \times L_4) + E(L_1)$$
$$L_2 \text{ (next year)} = L_2 + (I_{12} \times L_1) + (I_{22} \times L_2) + (I_{32} \times L_3) + (I_{42} \times L_4) + E(L_2)$$
$$L_3 \text{ (next year)} = L_3 + (I_{13} \times L_1) + (I_{23} \times L_2) + (I_{33} \times L_3) + (I_{43} \times L_4) + E(L_3)$$
$$L_4 \text{ (next year)} = L_4 + (I_{14} \times L_1) + (I_{24} \times L_2) + (I_{34} \times L_3) + (I_{44} \times L_4) + E(L_4)$$

where Ls are the current levels, Is are the entries to the table, and $E(L$s$)$ are the uncertainties in the levels. The model may be set up as a spreadsheet with tables and figures such as those shown in this chapter to highlight key data and results. To simplify setting up the cross-impact matrix, the levels are all set to 1 (unity) for the base year (say, 2000).

Typically, one or two students in each class with a science or engineering background are able to program a model from its core underlying ideas. Other students are able to enter data, make modifications, devise new charts, and so on. This capability adds credibility to the exercise and instills a collective sense of empowerment throughout the class. On balance, a basic simple model that can be comprehended at all levels is preferable to a more "realistic," but impenetrable black-box approach.

From Qualitative Responses to Quantitative Inputs

The boundaries between "hard" and "soft" data are much fuzzier than most planning students and planners acknowledge. For example, most social and economic data rely on "expert judgments." This makes it less unreasonable, perhaps, to integrate these in a quantitative model. There are, nonetheless, many problems in the translation of verbal scales (e.g., "small" through "big") into quantitative measures. Nonetheless, implicitly or explicitly, we do this all the time (e.g., analysis of attitude surveys using ranked ordinal categories). Several approaches have been explored. For example, we can begin with purely verbal assessments of the growth rate of each variable, as in Table 18.4.

Table 18.4
Verbal Description of Changes

ISSUES	Conflict	Culture	Education	Poverty	Technology	Environment	Economy	Population
Verbal	escalating	reducing	specializing	worsening	accelerating	depleting	dynamic	slowing

As an intermediate step, verbal measures may be translated into a ranked symbolic scale (e.g., P = positive, NN = strongly negative) or a number scale (e.g., award points from minus five to plus five), as in Table 18.5.

To begin with, select base growth rates that are within the bounds of credibility for a sustained period (i.e., decades), such as a few percent positive or negative each year. For example, world economic and population growth are currently about 2.8 and 1.6 percent annually, respectively. Other growth rates are less well-known, but their doubling time can be hypothesized (Table 18.6).

Overall, mechanical translation of ordinal scales into cardinal scales (via a look-up table) appears to be sufficient for most forecasts, but typically will not give satisfactory long-run backcasts. The cross-impact variables may be measured in a similar fashion.

The uncertainty in growth rates also may be assessed by asking how certain we are about our agreed values. Alternatively, the growth rates may be the statistical average of a large number of responses (e.g., from a questionnaire survey) and the uncertainty based on the standard deviation of the mean response (Table 18.7).

Table 18.5
Qualitative Description (Intermediate Step)

ISSUES	Conflict	Culture	Education	Poverty	Technology	Environment	Economy	Population
Ranked	P	NN	P	NP	PP	N	PP	P

Table 18.6
Quantified Description

ISSUES	Conflict	Culture	Education	Poverty	Technology	Environment	Economy	Population
Rate%	1%	-2%	1%	0%	2%	-2%	3%	2%

Table 18.7
Uncertainty

ISSUES	Conflict	Culture	Education	Poverty	Technology	Environment	Economy	Population
Rate%	15%	10	5%	5%	5%	10%	3%	1%

NOTES

1. The example from the Global Issues and Futures Class can be found on the Web at http://www.ap.buffalo.edu/~samcole/heuristic.htm. Visual Basic and Excel versions of the model may be downloaded from the site.

2. There has been much misunderstanding about backcasting as a technical exercise. It has been argued, for example, that it contravenes the laws of thermodynamics, or that time does not run backward. In the real world this may be true. In a time-step model the real issue is simply how well our assumed algebraic relationships and data fit with our understanding of the past. The only requirement is that the model can retrace the backcast. With a bit of fine tuning of the inputs, the model will run backward to before the first millennium.

REFERENCES

Cole, H., Freeman, C., Jahoda, M., and Pavitt, K. (Eds.). (1973) *Models of doom: A critique of the limits to growth*. New York: Universe Books.

Cole, S. (1997). Futures in global space//WWW.MODELS.GIS.MEDIA. *Futures, 29*, 393–417.

Freeman, C., and Jahoda, M. (1977). *World futures: The great debate*. London: Martin Robertson.

Hughes, B. (1996). *International futures: Choices in the creation of a new world order*. Boulder: Westview.

Meadows, D. H., Meadows, D. L., Randers, J., and Behrens, W. W. (1972). *The limits to growth*. New York: Universe Books.

19

Planet Eaters or Star Makers?

Christopher Burr Jones

FUTURES AS AUTOBIOGRAPHY

Engaging in the study of the future and teaching futures studies is my avocation. Most of the time I am a professor of political science, but my scholarship and writing are almost exclusively in futures studies. In a way, being a political scientist and a futurist makes perfect sense, given that the future has become so politicized. In this chapter I hope to relate to you what I do and what I think it means to be an academic futurist. Since many readers may be new to the field, I also hope to give you a sense of what futures studies is—from my perspective. Along the way, I will ask you to consider whether we humans are planet eaters or star makers.

Growing up in the suburbs of the San Francisco Bay area (first decade), in Latin America in the 1960s (second decade), and then in California and Hawaii in the 1970s set the stage for my entanglement with futures studies. As I think back on all the influences that led me in this direction, I have to seriously consider the massive quantities of science fiction that I have read, and those "worldly" experiences that came from living abroad, such as living near an active volcano, on two tropical islands, in the Southern Hemisphere, through a revolution, and the other turmoil of the 1960s. I think that it was probably Sputnik, Telstar, monorails, and Japanese transistor radios that "turned me on" to the future, because my first decade of life was a cornucopia of technological wonders that suggested a future limited only by my own imagination. Dancing Disney visions of cavorting in space and touring on the moon. Why not?

But I did not live in total thrall with technology, either. There was the Frankenstein story, nuclear weapons testing (the Cold War), and also those lingering questions about what had happened to the *Titanic*. Maybe the *Titanic* story was such a big deal in the 1950s and early 1960s precisely because it was a metaphor for our (mostly) unbridled enthusiasm for nuclear power, for faster cars and rockets, for technological fixes of all sorts. And after all these years, the *Titanic* is still a metaphor for the age: a symbol of our hubris, a symbol of the fragility of our science and technology in the face of the awesome powers of Mother Nature—which we ignore at our peril. Yet we have continued to press ahead, to conquer nature, to control our very nature. We still fast and furiously push the envelope of possibility, constantly opening new doors to the future. How could one not be interested in the future, in the consequences of these enormous forces humans are unleashing on the world and on the very cosmos? Futures studies is "where it's at," the intellectual arena where researchers, scholars, and activists of all races, colors, creeds, and protoplasm preferences congregate to study change at a species and planetary level.

Futures studies—my attraction to it, involvement in it, and profession of it—is necessarily autobiographical. My impression of most if not all FS practitioners is that they have a vision or a passion for FS because of some deep-seated driving force in their lives. Thus, to understand best the teaching of futures studies and the gist of the field is to understand that there is a deeply personal level to its practice. That does not make it any less valid or valuable, but it does mean that there is a profound contextual dimension to consideration of the field. There are methods and techniques that "stand alone," but one should not lose sight of their origins and uses within a wide array of moral, ethical, and political contexts. There is no "objective" study of the future, but rather a very personal window on change and intimate images of the future.

STUDIES AT MANOA

A brief synopsis of my journey in the field begins with taking a class from futurist Jim Dator at the University of Hawaii in 1979. A prospective law student, I found the attraction of studying futures studies for a few years (to get a master's degree) more appealing. During those three years of master's work, I took advantage of an opportunity for an internship with Clem Bezold at the Institute for Alternative Futures (Washington, DC), attended my first World Futures Studies Federation world conference (in Stockholm), developed a thesis on space development, helped organize the informal Futures Group meetings at the University of Hawaii, and in general geared up for work as a futures researcher. Then a teaching assistantship forced me to shift gears from a law degree entirely.

I caught the teaching bug and decided to stay in Hawaii and tackle doctoral work, to pursue my growing interest in the then-emerging "Gaia Hypothesis." Over the next decade I was a researcher for the Center for Development Studies and the Hawaii Research Center for Futures Studies, taught intermittent courses in futures studies and political science, and became more active in the WFSF (conferences and workshops in the former Yugoslavia, Hungary, Spain, and Costa Rica). After completing my doctorate in 1989, I continued working as a researcher and part-time lecturer in Honolulu. In 1992 I was offered a generalist position teaching political science at Eastern Oregon University, and relocated after nearly fifteen years in the islands.

As a one-person department in Eastern Oregon, I have been blessed with the flexibility to teach and research in my area of interest, which has remained futures studies. I have continued to remain active in futures professional organizations, to publish in the area, to attend international conferences, and to expand my experiences in conducting workshops in alternative futures. In addition to the standard political science and government courses I am expected to teach, I also teach "Introduction to Futures Studies," "Simulation Politics," and "Alternative Futures and Political Design," all as standalone FS courses. Other courses, such as "Women and Politics" and "Environmental Politics," have strong futures components, and all of my courses are "tainted" to some extent by my interest in looking toward the long-term future of those subjects (e.g., the presidency and state and local government).

My work—that which I feel is most significant—is directed at saving the world. It is certainly a cliché, and yet it honestly is the motivation that sets the best futurists apart from the mere speculators. I do not claim to be among the best, but I have many role models. This is one reason why I have gravitated toward the WFSF, an organization that has been a magnet for many of the world's best futurists.

For many of these people, the impetus for inquiries into the future has been the *global problematique* as presented in *The Limits to Growth* and other work of the Club of Rome (see Moll, 1991). At the same time, there has been strong opposition to this aspect of future studies, especially in the work of the late Herman Kahn and Julian Simon. To some extent these "technological optimists" have their points, such as continued technological fixes to natural limits to human expansion and resource substitution. My own view is that humans are pushing the limits of ecological systems and the elasticity of Gaian homeostasis (the global dynamic equilibrium). I have written elsewhere about the conundrum of human development at this stage of our evolution and basically believe that our current economic and political systems are unsustainable (Jones, 1994, 1996).

The question for me has been, How do you make the connection between the planetary-level vitality and people's daily decision making? The answer to a great extent has been to question student's assumptions, problematize their futures, and help them look for their own preferred futures. The bottom line: Get them to see that their decisions, their patterns of action, contribute to the future in both subtle and overt ways. From consuming patterns to career choices, they have some responsibility for what they "get" for a future in twenty or fifty years.

ON THE ROAD TO FIJI

One of the most eye-opening periods of my own life was a research project I did with Dator and anthropologist Barbara Moir early in my graduate studies. This was a project, funded by GTE Laboratories, designed to look at the state of telecommunications technologies and futures images of individuals in six Pacific island states in 1984–1985 (Western Samoa, Fiji, Papua New Guinea, Tuvalu, the Northern Marianas, and Palau) (Dator, Moir, and Jones, 1987). It was a pathfinding ethnographic futures research project that used an open-ended interview methodology to probe individual's hopes and fears for the future. In addition to the ethnographic approach (pioneered by Textor, 1980), the research probed the role and impact of telecommunications and computers on these island societies. The interviewees were managers or technicians in the telecommunications and computer fields.

There were a number of revelations. It perhaps should not have been a surprise, but a typical comment was, "No one ever asked me before what I want for the future." Many of the participants seemed actually empowered by the interview process. Over the years I have reflected on this and wondered what, if any, long-term impact the research had on any of those individual's lives.

The revelations about the role of technology in social change in these small island countries, and their unexpectedly high level of awareness about global change, particularly environmental change, were most eye-opening. Seeing firsthand the enormity of social and cultural dislocation, the mind-blowing transition of societies from subsistence to cash economies, from oral communication to digital satellites in one generation, all made a big impression on me. More sobering was the lesson that technology innovation—at least in these societies—was a destructive force. It underscored the realization that technology is not neutral, that it has political and economic realities imbedded in it. Going into this project, I think we all hoped to see the potential of these small Pacific microstates to "leap frog" from agricultural to postindustrial stages of development (thus avoiding the destructiveness of industrial society). The reality was (at least in the mid-1980s) that all of these societies were locked into cycles of dependency and technological reaction and repercussion. The external driving forces were profound and palpable.

The most unexpected result for me was the common concern among South Pacific islanders for the health of rainforests, not in their region only, but also in Amazonia, Africa, and Southeast Asia. I had assumed that their fears for the future would be parochial or regional, not global. I gained a great deal of respect for the concept of the global village.

Subsequent research projects in the late 1980s shifted my personal focus from technology to climate change, global warming, and sea-level rise in the Pacific Islands. This work was a natural political progression, because it involved linking global change to local decision making. We had the task of getting policy makers to understand that they had to make sometimes difficult decisions in the context of uncertainty. For example, in one project in the Marshall Islands (where the average height of the atolls is at present only a few feet above sea level) it was clear that the consequences of global warming–induced sea-level rise would be catastrophic. But given the uncertainties about the state of the scientific forecasts a decade ago, decision makers were generally loath to stick out their necks. In our project, we worked with students, community groups, and government leaders to consider the consequences of possible sea-level rise and actions that could be taken to mitigate or adapt to the potential changes. We used techniques such as audiovisual presentations, brainstorming, and alternative futures exercises. The Marshallese took the problem seriously. In the meantime, the growing evidence for climate change, particularly increased frequency and severity of hurricanes, abnormally high tides, and actual sea-level rise, has alarmed island leaders across the world enough to become very vocal in international meetings and take the high moral ground in urging curbs on First World greenhouse gas emissions.

For the most part, however, political leaders are still ill-equipped to tackle issues where uncertainty is high, and "muddling through" has continued to be the safest route for them to take. But time may be running out for short-term thinking. That is why the *Titanic* seems an apt metaphor for why one should engage in futures studies, because we seldom consider enough of the contingencies and possible consequences of new technologies. At a more fundamental level we also need to consider the underlying assumptions embedded in those technologies, social organizations, and infrastructures we are in such a hurry to build.

THERE GOES THE *TITANIC*

At the most fundamental level, we have a technological society that has outgrown its socioeconomic system. We have powerful new technological systems (hardware and software) but woefully inadequate management and ethical "orgware" to deal with them. As a metaphor, the *Titanic* works at a number of levels. First, it models the centrality of technology innovation as the dominant force of social change for our species. It acknowledges the forces of nature as critical factors in our planning and species-level adaptation. And it obliquely reflects one other important driving force of change: social mobility and culture shifts (global migration patterns, for example). Think of the *Titanic*'s state-of-the-art control systems, propulsion, and airtight compartments: She was the spaceship of the last century; a towering symbol of wealth and progress. Moreover, in its contemporary resting place, it is revealing its secrets to us, in part thanks to robotic state-of-the-art control systems, propulsion, and air-tight compartments of our times.

Thus, the story of the *Titanic* and her icy grave are illustrations of the central role science and technology play in social change. While it seems clear that technology has not always been the dominant source of change in humanity's million-odd years of experience, it clearly is today. Other sources include environmental forces, social movements and demographics, and spiritual influences. In my FS courses, emphasis has been on the technological theories of social change. Alvin Toffler's (1981) explication of the "three waves" of technological change, for example, remains a compelling description of the role of technology's driving force over the last 20,000 years. Marshall McLuhan's ideas have also impacted my teaching. His recently reissued *The Medium is the Massage* (1996) is as insightful and "on target" as it was thirty years ago. My predispositions to see this technological dynamic as intrinsic to social change has been time-and-again reinforced by my teacher, Jim Dator. The question is, Can we steer the ship away from the icebergs ahead? Are our feedback mechanisms, values, and decision making up to the task of making our way across seas of change?

Other maritime metaphors include Jim Dator's (1993) "tsunamis" of global change: demographics, economics, technological innovation, environmental change, and globalization of culture. Central among his tsunamis is the transformational role of technology. Dator also warns of the tsunami of global environmental change, and this is another driving force I give great attention to in the classroom. Environmental change was unquestionably the central factor driving human social change for thousands of generations until the end of the last Ice Age. Evidence points to the Ice Ages as a force in technological change (clothing, tool refinements) during the last glacial period, not the other way around. Toward the end of the last glaciation, however, the tables were turned and technology has now increasingly dominated the landscape of human change. Yet a runaway greenhouse effect or new glacial cycle precipitated by human development may once again bring environmental change to the forefront. As recently as the "Little Ice Age," this force played a dramatic role in human behavior. Ferdinand Braudel (1981) has written persuasively about the role of climate change in Europe during the late Middle Ages. James Lovelock's (1979, 1988) work on the Gaia hypothesis also posits that climate change is an often dramatic force with which humanity needs to contend. The Gaian message is intriguing: The planetary system is a cybernetic system that attempts to sustain "optimal conditions" for life on the planet. It is a dynamic system set in a cosmic context: Humans are perhaps an evolutionary luxury the planet can ill afford. It's back to the drawing board to work on those state-of-the-art control systems, propulsion, and air-tight compartments once again.

In addition to technology and environment, students need to understand some of the dynamics of social change within society itself. A communications theory holds that social change is fostered by opinion leaders, those individuals two and three standard deviations out from the middle of the bell curve. Another theory holds that it is the artists and nonconformists rather than representatives of the status quo who are the agents of change. Broader social movements also play significant roles in social change: In the United States the progressive movement brought about political reforms, the socialist movement forced changes in child labor laws and factory working conditions, and the women's movement continues to press for improvements in women's social and political status. It is critical for students to understand these forces of change as well, because the forces of technological and environmental change can seem so monolithic by comparison.

In addition to the broadest forces of change and change theories, I also spend time in some classes exploring other forces of change, including spiritual transformation, economic long waves, cosmology, and macrohistory.

The spiritual dimensions of change come into play in the discussion of influential social movements, particularly in my "Environmental Politics" and "Women and Politics" courses. This is still a relatively small component of the general topic of social change and stability, but a provocative one. Given the growing influence of Eastern philosophy and religion in the West and the importance of the spiritual visionaries in the futures movement, I also explore a spiritual transformation society in my "Alternative Futures" course.

Economic driving forces have been the subject of so-called long cycles of social and cultural change (such as the Kondratieff theory), which argue that economic and technological changes intertwine to produce economic boom-and-bust cycles that span decades (Rosser and Rosser, 1994; Boswell and Sweat, 1991).

Physical cosmology is related to environmental change theory, but looks at the role of astronomical phenomenon on geological-scale time frames. Examples include the influence of Earth's multiple planetary motions and orbital variations (e.g., the Milankovich glaciation theory; Imbrie and Imbrie, 1979), the theory of cyclical cometary impacts due to a distant companion star called Nemesis (Vandervoort and Sather, 1993; Thomsen, 1987; Fisher, 1985), and near-Earth asteroid and comet collisions. While such low-probability phenomenon may seem remote to human concerns, increasingly they have captured popular attention. Scientifically speaking, these exogenous forces may play a larger role in evolution and planetary health than has been generally accepted.

Macrohistory is a related long-term concept (Galtung and Inayatullah, 1997). While some macrohistorians mostly consider one or two driving forces (such as technology or spiritual values) others look at the broader civilizational patterns through which cultures evolve. If nothing else, exposing students to these ideas is a way of expanding their consciousness or broadening their minds. Exposure to theories of social change is a good introduction to the "Big Picture"—expanded their frames of reference—valuable not only toward training good social scientists, but also giving students tools by which they can contextualize their experiences in a time of rapid social change.

I learned growing up about the power of culture after experiencing different cultures in Latin America and the Caribbean, and the shock sometimes of transiting them. It made perfect sense to me after reading Toffler's (1970) *Future Shock* that change within cultures could be at least, if not more, emotionally disconcerting and even dis-easing. Despite the popularity of Toffler's book, it seems to me that people mostly still behave as though they live in a static world.

TEACHING THE FUTURE

Before I turn to how I integrate futures studies into the classroom, I should lay out some of my assumptions about what higher education means to me. A few excerpts from the statement of my teaching philosophy:

A primary role for any educator is to convey a body of knowledge over which she or he has command. Increasingly, however, in many subfields of political science and generally in futures studies, that body of knowledge is growing and changing—often dramatically. This has large implications for the purveyor and recipients of that knowledge: it means the "expert" must work ever harder to stay in command of that knowledge and it may mean acknowledging the limits of the expert's knowledge. For the student it means being more responsible for her or his own knowledge and drawing from more sources than previously necessary.

Thus, my role as an educator is also to empower my students to find the motivation and competence within themselves to be responsible for their own learning. That means helping them find and develop the skills necessary to engage in that process. For me that means trying to break out of the traditional dependence relationship—to foster student independence and ultimately, hopefully, interdependence. Another important role is that of facilitator in drawing in and utilizing the collective knowledge of my students who bring their own experiences and contributions to offer. It is my firm belief that the student–teacher learning experience is not a "one-way" process, but rather a mutual collaborative experience. . . .

One of the most fundamentally important sets of skills which students should take with them is critical thinking skills. Especially in a world of rapid change, students need to be able to question underlying assumptions and values embedded in the technologies they use and the institutions to which they belong. Critical thinking skills become not only important in adapting to change, but to survival in a world increasingly uncertain and unpredictable.

As a generalist, I am also committed to making cross disciplinary and inter-disciplinary connections for students. I endeavor to get students to see the details of their learning experience within broader contexts—to see the Big Picture—and to better understand the interconnections which exist between apparently discrete bodies of knowledge and processes surrounding them in the world. One of the more difficult tasks is to instill the need for and advantages of cooperative learning, and not just the individualistic approaches to learning which seem to be so pervasive in the American educational system.

In practical terms, there have been a limited number of futures techniques and methods I have adapted to my own classes. Foremost has been the idea of futures—that there is not a single future "out there," but plural futures—many alternative paths that are possible beyond the present. Specific methodologies are actually a complex of techniques loosely called "alternative futures." One of the basic assumptions is the idea that there are "images" in our minds that influence our actions. This is drawn primarily from the work of Fred Polak (1961) and Elise Boulding (1971, 1995). Polak's work is compelling and exists in a world that is largely underexplored (at least from a Western perspective). His research argues that each civilization has a guiding image of the future, those ideas that people carry around with them about their futures. Furthermore, he classified the images as either transcendent and escatological (or not). These visions inside one's brain bear on one's hopes and fears and become "self-fulfilling" prophesies. Moreover, from a political standpoint, manipulating "images of the future" becomes a powerful controlling force. This is a lesson not lost on Madison Avenue, political campaign consultants, and transnational corporations.

Jim Dator (1979, 1983) expanded Polak's idea, and in the late 1970s and early 1980s collected images of the future taken from political statements and strategic plans as well as movies, television, literature, and popular culture. His efforts to understand alternative futures and then explore their implications has spawned a whole school of thought in futures studies, the "Manoa School" (Jones, 1992). Thus, the study of alternative futures has had a large impact on several generations of futurists. The techniques and methods include visioning, scenario building, alternative futures images matrices, and narrative and contextual exercises such as "backcasting," "incasting," and similar types of futures brainstorming exercises.

Dator developed a matrix of four "generic" alternative futures that he designated "Continued Growth," "Collapse," "Conserver Society," and "(High Tech) Transformational Society." He then arrayed them by different "aspects of society," such as education, family, health, and economics. This key development has expanded into the "incasting" techniques pioneered by Dator, Wendy Schultz, and others involved with the Hawaii Research Center for Futures Studies (HRCFS) (Schultz, 1991; Schultz, Rodgers, Jones, and Inayatullah, 1991). The central idea is that you can take any one of the four (or similar) coherent and cohesive images of the future and use its basic assumptions to deduce and characterize that society's "basic aspects": government, education, environment, and so on. As a teaching exercise, it has been useful to demonstrate some of the choices available to us if we are able to act upon our visions of the future.

Backcasting is a technique also adapted by Schultz and HRCFS researchers from the work of Elise Boulding from her "World without War" visioning workshops. The basic idea here is to have participants take a given future (for example, a high-technology society) in A.D. 2050 and then to describe how that future evolved from the present, a type of backward "scenario writing from the future." In other words, what plausible events, developments, and forces of change brought about the future society in question? What Boulding developed as a "future history" exercise, HRCFS and colleagues, with backcasting, have allowed workshop participants to engage themselves in with futures images. Used in concert, incasting and backcasting appear to expand people's awareness about the consequences of individual actions, the broader implications of collective decision making, and the power of imagery itself (examples from teaching space development and a workshop on global governance follow at the end of this section).

Backcasting is a fairly easy technique to help achieve a more specific "scenario" for any organization. In addition, the scenario can be fleshed out with other creative techniques such as creating "futures headlines" or news stories, a common device in contemporary science fiction literature and movies. Individual narratives ("stories") and visioning exercises are other related techniques used to flesh out alternative futures created in visioning or brainstorming exercises.

This is clearly an area that deserves greater attention and more social science scrutiny. Polak's work is largely ignored and underappreciated, if it is known at all, by other social scientists. For example, many people have considerable interest in the effect of media violence on children. I believe we should have a similar concern about the prevalence of apocalyptic images in the media of people's visions of the future. Much more research needs to be done on the relationship between the media's images of the future (commercials as well as movies) and preferences and values regarding the future. There is also a lack of follow-up data on the extent to which futures visioning and alternative futures exercises influences people's decision making in the long term.

Environmental scanning is near the top of my list of methods to struggle with the challenges of technological, environmental, and social change. The term "environmental scanning" in futures studies is associated with the complex of activities surrounding trend identification and analysis, emerging issues analysis, and some kind of organizational structure or output (such as cross-impact analysis or narrative and scenario building). Each of those can work as separate techniques in their own right, but collectively comprise a kind of "futures radar" or early warning system to identify opportunities, challenges, and dangers on the horizon. These techniques were among the first I was exposed to in my FS training. For me, emerging issues analysis is the "cutting edge" of the field, the cutting edge of the future itself, where the possibilities of fundamental change first show on the radar screen. Not surprising, it is trend and emerging issues work that has been the most popular with the lay public. Faith Popcorn (1992) and John Naisbitt (1984) are good examples.

Environmental scanning, trend analysis, and the alternative futures methods outlined here are my preferred means for monitoring and adapting to the future. They are not just some "techniques" used to train people in "futures" skills; they are iterative devices that affect the trainer as well as they trainee. It is hard to be a neutral, outside observer of these exercises once you get involved with their use.

The courses in which I have most extensively used alternative futures methods have been "Simulation Politics," "Political Design," "Alternative Futures," and "Introduction to Futures Studies." Essential to these courses is an introduction to the ideas of scientific and cultural paradigms (the fundamental assumptions of society), basic theories of social change, and identification of the driving forces of global change. Of critical importance, whether it be teaching political science or futures studies, is that students begin to question their paradigm and reality—an epistemological agenda. It becomes a Socratic process to question the structures of power and reality. Only by uncovering the assumptions of (in my case) Western industrial society can we free ourselves and be open to other possibilities: other realities and alternative futures. In concert, many of the techniques addressed here do the trick. By forcing students out of their epoch and into the next, they can begin to see that those aspects of the present we take for granted (e.g., fossil fuels, male dominance) are not immutable constants, but simply variables.

Some facets of environmental scanning and emerging issues analysis are integral to each of these classes; for example, in my "Simulation Politics" course, students are obligated to scan the science literature (increasingly Web resources) for developments and innovations in space transportation, habitation, and general development. Students are asked to explore the possible consequences of a range of technological and social developments (examples include molecular and genetic engineering, human longevity, artificial intelligence, advanced robotics, and virtual reality).

"Simulation Politics" revolves around the annual Solar System Simulation run by anthropologist Reed Riner at Northern Arizona University. In this course, students are thrust into the world of (circa) A.D. 2073 in one of a number of settlements in various parts of the solar system, and engage in an electronic "pedagogical environment" where they interact with other college classes through the Internet. While the role-playing simulation deserves a lengthy discussion itself (see Riner, Chapter 3 in this volume), one of the dramatic outcomes of the exercise is the extent to which individual attitudes about space development change. Students who begin the course with negative attitudes toward the space program, or who have a low opinion about space exploration (usually the cost argument), find that they not only understand better the reasons for space development but appreciate it as more probable (even inevitable) by the end of the course. This has been a common experience in the use of backcasting exercises (a component of "Simulation Politics"), where the process of stepping back through a logical causal chain of events appears to support plausible alternative futures.

A workshop during a conference in Novosibirsk, Russia, illustrates the latter point (Jones, 1995). The culmination of an afternoon workshop had participants backcast a "World Government in 2050 A.D." The premise of the last phase of the workshop was that around 2050 a world government is established. Small breakout groups each worked out future histories for specific aspects of society (e.g., health, education) and integrated them into a master timeline. Despite participants from a dozen different countries and some difficulties with language, there was remarkable convergence. Many of the group admitted in the debriefing afterward that the exercise had left them (myself included) much more optimistic that a global government might happen in "only" fifty-five more years. It did not necessarily make anyone believe that such a future was more probable per se, but it did indicate how certain forces of change and specific developments could work toward realizing a scenario.

WILL TREES HAVE STANDING?

One thing I do profess to my students is that the possibility for social and political change over the next century could be nothing short of transformational. That is, the scope of change could be many orders of magnitudes greater than over the last century. Thus, what is plausible or imaginable today could easily be defied by actual changes. Is utopia plausible? Perhaps not, but my preferable future would certainly be many orders of magnitudes better than today. That optimism is informed by many of the "advances" of the present age: better nutrition and health care, hygiene, sanitation, greater longevity, education, and communication systems. It is tempered by the "problematique" of environmental degradation, resource depletion, starvation and disease, warfare and violence, and greed. The nexus or conundrum is, Can we survive as a species following our stunning success in the natural world?

Anthropologist Jim Funaro (1999, 2000) has labeled our species a "planet eater," which can be juxtaposed with Olaf Stapledon's (1968) science fiction where humans evolve into god-like beings with fantastic powers.

Most descriptive for me is James Robertson's (1978) "sane, humane, and ecological" future articulated in his *The Sane Alternative*. The popular images that appeal to me are the ecological futures described in Marge Piercy's (1976) *Woman on the Edge of Time*, Ernest Callenbach's (1975) *Ecotopia*, and Starhawk's (1993) *The Fifth Sacred Thing*. These are all stories that depict plausible, compelling visions of a future, combining postindustrial technology. Their values are environmentally friendly and stress collective collaboration rather than competitive capitalism. What is useful from a teaching standpoint is that these are not utopian in the sense that they are "out of reach." They are really eutopian—not perfect—still "working out the kinks." To most students these are plausible if rather low-probability futures.

But what if we are star makers and not simply planet eaters? Dator and HRCFS's transformational images of futures are also persuasive. Two variants are the Spiritual and High-Tech scenarios. They posit changes that are so profound, their societies would hardly be recognizable from today's perspective. While they may also seem like low-probability futures, they are premised on the idea that quantum leaps can take place in human civilization. The incredible pace of technology innovation certainly offers such revolutionary possibilities (nanotechnology and biocomputers are just two examples).

There is also a good case being made for growing global spiritual–ecological consciousness (Elgin, 1997). A substantial dimension of the contemporary futures movement is, if not prophetic, at least *visionary*. A long list of "visionary futurists" would include thinkers inside the futures movement, on its fringes, and those whose ideas have been influential on two generations of futurists: Pierre Teilhard de Chardin (1965), William Irwin Thompson (1978), Marilyn Ferguson (1980), Ken Wilber (1980), Willis Harman (1988), and Duane Elgin (1993). Barbara Marx Hubbard (1998) and Oliver Markley (1998) have made important contributions to this spiritual dimension of the FS literature and have both been active in the futures research community.

Perhaps not as preferable but in many other ways compelling and increasingly plausible, is a High-Tech Transformation. Envisioned by Dator, it is a turbulent but liberating future mediated increasingly by technology, computers, robots, artificial intelligence, and ultimately molecular and genetic engineering. Ironically, both futures could converge at the point where "mind over matter" becomes the reality paradigm: the Spiritual more ordered and calm; the High-Tech chaotic and exciting.

"Sane, humane, and ecological" makes the most sense, conservatively speaking. Our collective behavior as a species is very destructive to the nonhuman environment, and our interspecies behavior continues to be violent and destructive. From a Gaian perspective, we are not simply spoiling our nest, but threatening the regulatory dynamics of the whole planet. We may not like the consequences of our actions. From a global perspective, we simply have to pull together. My vision is of a world in better balance: ecosystem, gender, and individual and community mental health. A garden planet, with heavy industry exported off-planet. A spacefaring people too.

Ultimately, it seems probable that environmental movements will have greater influence in the years to come, even in a "business as usual" future. Christopher Stone's (1974) classic law review article, "Should Trees Have Standing?" poses a perfect pun for the times. Aside from the very interesting questions surrounding the legal standing of trees or species or ecosystems, it also suggests a more fundamental futures question: As an increasingly urban species, are we losing touch with nature in a fundamental way?

ELECTROGENS AND MOSH POTATOES

Teaching does not exist in a vacuum, yet many in the academic community seem oblivious to the changes swirling around us. Times are changing and students are changing. As I write this, the latest annual UCLA Higher Education Research Institute poll of American college students has been released, which documents the continuing decline in respect for government service, apathy toward politics, laziness, and boredom with formal education (Gose, 1998). My own experience is that students do get "turned on" when they are empowered and challenged to come up with strategies to cope with and adapt to the forces of social and technological change ahead. Because so much of their formal education is reactionary rather than anticipatory, they are discouraged from thinking about the future. What future? many of them ask. Given that much of what students are interested in comes from their cultural education (movies, MTV, comic books, spectator sports, music, etc.), it is no wonder their visions of the future are bleak.

That is why it is important to try to "blow their minds" whenever possible—and FS does this extremely well—in order to jog their thinking and break them out of their mental ruts. Even in my more sedate government classes, I challenge them to imagine the improbable (e.g., voting by computer, choosing Congress by lot, the breakup of the United States). What are the implications for society of global changes that students may well experience within their lifetimes?

Futures pedagogy does have to face both the promise and the perils of the tsunamis of change with respect to university students today. Students are more lazy and bored than ever and demonstrate a postmaterialist bent quite different from their baby-boomer parents. While laziness and boredom are perhaps perilous, the promise of the future is among the many compelling aspects of teaching alternative futures. And while younger students are often clueless, there is a richer mix of nontraditional students in the student body than ever. These students are often the only visible energy in classroom discussions of traditional political science issues, but cloning, solar energy, maglev, virtual reality, and Internet politics always spark general interest. I mention these things because I think the context of futures pedagogy is in many ways the material and the audience with which we have to work.

My experience with college students coming up is that they are less connected to the same reality that I am. By that I mean that their knowledge of the world is different. While there are some exceptions, students today have an ever-more tenuous grip on history and traditional values. Their knowledge of the world seems more fragmented, segmented, and shallow than the last generation of students. This appears to be consistent with Dator's predictions about the coming social upheavals driven by the emerging cyber culture (Dator, 1997; Jones, 1997). His recently revisited 1967 article, reprinted from the dawn of the futures field, argues presciently about the consequences of the "plastic personality" (situational ethics) and the breakdown of the family. I have met the plastic person and he is us. At least us and our kids.

As articulated in the Manoa School of futures studies, futures studies should be a critical (in the best sense of the word) project, reflecting the analysis of neo-Marxism, feminism, and poststructuralism. This means that my teaching is informed by (but does not necessarily promote) these ideologies. For example, the tension, especially between poststructuralism and modernism, is an essential contribution to an understanding of the central paradoxes and conundrums of the third millennium. But I personally look for a balance between modernism and "the rest." If students are morally wandering toward poststructuralist nihilism, they need to consider moral questions. Futures studies also contains these elements of moral authority (Masini, 1996; Bell, 1997). Just because we can clone humans, should we? I think that students, when they are forced to confront these questions, may begin reluctantly, but inevitably become excited about their involvement in their own futures.

Members of the newest adult generation have been called "mouse potatoes" for their affinity with the new technologies, but my sense is that they are more often mosh potatoes: alienated, apathetic and french fried. *Wired* magazine is a good example of how some twenty-somethings have latched on to high-tech, wild desert rituals, and cyber libertarianism. But I think that fundamentally they are a more mature species of electrogens. McLuhan's children are beginning to emerge. It is somewhat ironic that the debates today in academia continue on the mechanization and corporatization of higher education, but one unanticipated driving force that may change these institutions dramatically is the raw material, the students themselves.

The flip side of the global problematique is the inestimable ability of humans to dominate their environment and to make it work for them. There is a transcendental quality to human efforts that makes all things seem possible. While there is a great deal of hubris in that statement, the record so far would seem to indicate that we have acquired godlike powers to manipulate the world. While we cannot be oblivious to the forces at work in the universe that are beyond our control, we are in the driver's seat of our own destiny. As futurists and teachers, it is our responsibility to make the world (nay, the universe) a better place, to charge our students and clients with imagining preferred futures and making them happen. And to watch out for icebergs.

REFERENCES

Bell, W. (1997). *Foundations of futures studies. Vol. 2: Values, objectivity, and the good society*. New Brunswick, NJ: Transaction.

Boswell, T., and Sweat, M. (1991). Hegemony, long waves, and major wars: A time series analysis of systemic dynamics, 1496–1967. *International Studies Quarterly, 35* (2), 123–150.

Boulding, E. (1971). Futuristics and the imaging capacity of the west. In M. Maruyama and J. Dator (Eds.), *Human futuristics* (pp. 29–53). Honolulu: Social Science Research Institute, University of Hawaii Press.

Boulding, E. (1995). Image and action in peace building. In E. Boulding and K. Boulding (Eds.), *The future* (pp. 93–116). Thousand Oaks, CA: Sage.

Braudel, F. (1981). *The structures of everyday life: The limits of the possible*. New York: Harper and Row.

Callenbach, E. (1975). *Ecotopia*. Berkeley, CA: Banyan Tree.

Dator, J. (1979). The futures of culture or cultures of the future. In A. Marsella, R. Tharp, and T. Ciborowski (Eds.), *Perspectives on cross-cultural psychology* (pp. 369–388). New York: Academic Press.

Dator, J. (1983). Loose connections: A vision of a transformational society. In E. Masini (Ed.), *Visions of desirable societies* (pp. 38–45). Oxford: Pergamon.

Dator, J. (1993). American state courts, five tsunamis, and four alternative futures. *Futures Research Quarterly, 9* (4), 3–90.

Dator, J. (1997). Valuelessness and the plastic personality. *Futures, 29*, 667–669.

Dator, J., Moir, B., and Jones, C. B. (1987). *A study of preferred futures for telecommunications in six Pacific Island societies*. Honolulu: Social Science Research Institute and the Pacific International Center for High Technology Research.

Elgin, D. (1993). *Awakening Earth: Exploring the evolution of human culture and consciousness*. New York: William Morrow.

Elgin, D. (1997). *Global consciousness change: Indicators of an emerging paradigm*. San Anselmo, CA: Millennium Project.

Ferguson, M. (1980). *The aquarian conspiracy: Personal and social transformation in the 1980s*. Los Angeles: J. P. Tarcher.

Fisher, A. (1985, June). Death star. *Popular Science, 226*, 72–77.

Funaro, J. (1999, March 4). Are societies and culture and inevitable result of intelligence? Panel presentation, CONTACT XVI/99 conference, Santa Clara, CA.

Funaro, J. (2000, March 3). The human partnership: Machines R Us. Panel presentation, CONTACT 2000, 17th annual conference, Santa Clara, CA.

Galtung, J., and Inayatullah, S. (1997). *Macrohistory and macrohistorians: Perspectives on individual, social, and civilizational change*. Westport, CT: Praeger.

Gose, B. (1998, January 16). More freshmen than ever appear disengaged from their studies, survey finds. *The Chronicle of Higher Education*, p. A37.

Harman, W. (1988). *Global mind change*. Indianapolis, IN: Knowledge Systems.

Hubbard, B. M. (1998). *Conscious evolution: Awakening the power of our social potential*. Novato, CA: New World Library.

Imbrie, J., and Imbrie, K. (1979). *Ice ages: Solving the mystery*. Short Hills, NJ: Enslow.

Jones, C. B. (1992). The Manoa School of Futures Studies. *Futures Research Quarterly, 8* (2), 19–25.

Jones, C. B. (1994). Cosmic Gaia and future generations. In T.-C. Kim and J. Dator (Eds.), *Creating a new history for future generations* (pp. 43–59). Kyoto: Institute for the Integrated Study of Future Generations.

Jones, C. B. (1995, October). Interweek '95: The futures of world governance. *World Futures Studies Federation Futures Bulletin*, pp. 15–16.

Jones, C. B. (1996). Conundrum and vision: Professing on the hinge of history. *Futures, 28*, 600–603.

Jones, C. B. (1997). Plastic fantastic future? *Futures, 29*, 672–673.

Lovelock, J. (1979). *Gaia: A new look at life on Earth*. Oxford: Oxford University Press.

Lovelock, J. (1988). *The ages of Gaia: A biography of our living Earth*. New York: W. W. Norton.

Markley, O. W. (1998). Visionary futures: Guided cognitive imagery in teaching and learning about the future. *American Behavioral Scientist, 42* (3), 522–530.

Masini, E. (1996). A future with dignity. *Futures, 28*, 626–629.

McLuhan, M. (1996). *The medium is the massage: An inventory of effects*. San Franscisco: HardWired.

Moll, P. (1991). *From scarcity to sustainability*. Frankfurt am Main: Peter Lang.

Naisbitt, J. (1984). *Megatrends: Ten new directions transforming our lives*. New York: Warner Books.

Piercy, M. (1976) *Woman on the edge of time*. New York: Fawcett Crest.

Polak, F. (1961). *The image of the future* (2 vols.). New York: Oceana.

Popcorn, F. (1992). *The Popcorn report: Faith Popcorn on the future of your company, your world, your life*. New York: HarperBusiness.

Robertson, J. (1978). *The sane alternative*. St. Paul, MN: River Basin.

Rosser, J. B., Jr., and Rosser, M. V. (1994). Long wave chaos and systemic economic transformation. *World Futures, 39*, 197–208.

Schultz, W. (1991). Words, dreams, and actions: Sharing the futures experience. In B. Van Steenbergen, R. Nakarada, F. Marti, and J. Dato (Eds.), *Advancing democracy and participation* (pp. 201–206). Barcelona: Centre Catala de Prospectiva and Centre UNESCO de Catalunya.

Schultz, W., Rodgers, S., Jones, C., and Inayatullah, S. (1991). *Office of state planning scenario building/vision project*. Honolulu: Research Center for Futures Studies.

Stapledon, O. (1968). *Last and first men & Star maker*. New York: Dover.

Starhawk. (1993). *The fifth sacred thing*. New York: Bantam Books.

Stone, C. D. (1974). *Should trees have standing? Toward legal rights for natural objects*. Los Altos, CA: William Kaufmann.

Teilhard de Chardin, P. (1965). *The phenomenon of man*. New York: Harper and Row.

Textor, R. (1980). *A handbook on ethnographic futures research* (3d ed.). Stanford, CA: Cultural and Educational Futures Research Project, School of Education and Department of Anthropology, Stanford University.

Thompson, W. I. (1978). *Darkness and scattered light*. New York: Anchor/ Doubleday.

Thomsen, D. E. (1987, February 14). Signs of nemesis: Meteors, magnetism. *Science News, 131*, 100.

Toffler, A. (1970). *Future shock*. New York: Random House.

Toffler, A. (1981). *The third wave*. New York: Bantam.

Vandervoort, P. O., and Sather, E. A. (1993). On the resonant orbit of a solar companion star in the gravitational field of the galaxy. *Icarus, 105* (1), 26–48.

Wilber, K. (1980). *The Atman project*. Wheaton, IL: Theosophical Publishing House.

20

The Challenge of
Teaching Futures Studies

Jordi Serra del Pino

PRIOR QUESTIONS

Teaching futures studies poses many challenges. Some of them are of a psychological nature, others are epistemological, while others still are strictly methodological and pedagogical concerns. On top of this, the future is one of those subjects about which most of us know very little, but about which all of us are quite eager to opine.

"The future" is a familiar concept in Western cultures. The notion of past, present, and future is deeply rooted in our collective mind. We live in a linear conception of time. This understanding of time and its unfolding is one of our main cultural foundations. It permeates our languages (which are structured around tenses) and, therefore, our minds. We seldom give conscious thought to any of this; we simply use these concepts unwittingly. As a matter of fact the same is usually the case when doing futures studies. However, futurists cannot accept blindly just any conception of time. We must be fully aware of the nature and unfolding of what it is we are working with. Thus, any endeavor related to the teaching of futures studies will have to consider this matter of time.

Psychological challenges are connected to this matter as well. Most futurists, including myself, seem unconsciously to rely on our own experience when forecasting the future. We tend to trust methods or forecasts that accord with our intuition. This relying on intuition is both an advantage and a disadvantage in futures studies. In many instances ideas about the futures rest on the causal link—implicit in the linear conception—that *A* provokes *B*. Therefore, acting on *A* gives us information and/or control over the future of *B*.

But at the same time futures studies has a very counterintuitive side. Those of us who have been working in the field for some time know that the future has a way of ending up quite different from what we expected. Thus, we soon learn to leave our own experience and intuition aside. Still, the intuitive perspective is an advantage when teaching futures, because everybody, or at least everybody with a linear sense of time, feels pretty much the same. The counterintuitive side is more of a challenge and provokes all sort of reactions: denial, suspicion, laughter, disinterest.

The epistemological challenge lies in the specific character of futures studies as a discipline. That is, what is futures studies? Is it a science? A body of knowledge? Or is it just a professional activity? Each of the answers take us to new problems.

A SCIENCE, A JOB, OR WHAT?

If we define futures studies as a science or a specific body of knowledge, then we have to deal with the issue of the future as an object, an entelechy or a conscious creation. But the future does not really exist, or at least it cannot exist, because once it does, it immediately turns into the present. This is true, but it is not an unsolvable obstacle in itself; after all, many other sciences deal with entelechies: justice, circles, numbers, power, values, beauty—you name it. However, we should not diminish the specificity of the future as an object, even though this specificity is not the result of its nature, but of its content or, if you wish, of how we give meaning to the notion of the future. Such an enterprise—and we have to keep in mind that we are considering these questions from a teaching perspective—takes us to a new obstacle: The future does not delimit an area of knowledge, but rather a temporal context. This also is not a problem in and of itself. We have spent centuries studying the past (with exactly the same difficulties) and we have somehow managed. No, the real difficulty lies in two aspects. The first is that this temporal context is always moving and it is extraordinarily fluid. True, we do revisit the past from time to time, but the past is far more stable than the future. What seems to be so very much the future at one moment will be seen as far too present in the next moment, and then deep into the past in no time. The second aspect is, precisely, how to give content to this temporal context. That is, what should we cover when studying the future? I have two answers, the easy one and the complex one. The easy one is "everything." The complex one is "almost everything."

One way to avoid all of these concerns is to characterize futures studies simply as a professional activity. If we concentrate on the methodological aspects—on the mechanisms and procedures to forecast, design, and control the future—we can skip all of the previous theoretical concerns. Even more, we can produce good work as futurists. But then, I always wonder, if you want to be an architect, is it enough to master the technical skills, or do you need to incorporate some esthetic sensibility and some social—even philosophical—knowledge? If you want to be a physician, it is enough to learn medicine, or it is also important to include some human sensibility, psychology, and tact? I could go on with more examples. For me, mastering just the methodological aspects is like looking with only one eye: It lacks depth, and can result in wrong perceptions.

At this point the kind of procedural challenges that teaching futures studies poses is beginning to be clear, particularly if you try to cover all these aspects, or even just some of them, in your discourse. Finding the adequate proportion in all these questions, how to present them, and more important how to make them interesting and relevant, is the ultimate challenge.

Whenever I teach futures studies, I always follow the same approach, based on three components: concepts, theoretical underpinnings, and methods, and in that order.

CONCEPTS

The reason to start with concepts is very simple. Most of the time, if not all of the time, I face an audience with no knowledge whatsoever of what futures studies really is, but with many opinions of what it could or should be (particularly in my country, where knowledge has never been a requisite to forming and expressing an opinion). So it is very important to start defining and delimiting what futures studies is, and also what it is not. The concepts part serves this purpose. It provides the students an early introduction into the basic elements of the discipline. I am always very keen on being clear from the beginning. I want to be sure that if later on I use the term "forecast" instead of "prediction," for example, my listeners will understand the implications of each term.

In my geographical context this concept stage is even more important. "Futures studies" is the accepted term in the Anglo-Saxon environment, but in Europe, "prospective" is the more common term. Thus, for instance, in my country I am a "prospectivist" not a "futurist." The distinction is important, because "prospective" is not a literal translation of "futures studies." While the latter is driven by a quest to improve our knowledge of the future, for prospective this is merely the first stage, as we will always try to find how we can influence the future to better our expectations. Thus, futures studies seems to be knowledge driven, while prospective is—ultimately— action driven. For me it is very important to introduce this distinction from the beginning, because it implies different attitudes toward the study and work related to the future.

The length of this first part is directly tied to the scope of the course as a whole. In any case, it should ideally include, at the least, an introductory definition of "prospective" and its main traits—transdisciplinarity, globality, plurality—and the peculiarities of prospective in relation to other, connected disciplines, such as planning, foresight, futurology, strategic management, future generations studies, and so on. The two basic approaches—the exploratory and the normative—are then discussed. Afterward, the distinction between prospective and futures studies is introduced, which permits the inclusion of futures studies corollaries: futures research and futures movements. Next, the difference between a forecast and a prediction is presented, which lets us introduce nicely the important notion of "alternative futures." When that is done, I find it useful to bring in Jim Dator's fundamental paradigm of futures studies, which allows me to explain the components or materials of futures studies—images of the future, and trends and events—and introduces the two following parts of the course dealing with theory and methods:

$$
\begin{array}{c}
\text{Theory} \\
| \\
\text{Trends—Images—Events} \\
| \\
\text{Methods}
\end{array}
$$

THEORY

Getting into theory is mostly dependent on the way you approach futures studies. If the focus is that of technical skills, it is easier to skip theory; not that you do not need it, but you can pretend you don't. If your focus is that of science or a body of knowledge, you cannot avoid theory. After all, how can we do science without a theory?

In the theoretical stage I cover two areas: the theoretical underpinnings of futures studies in the fields of philosophy, anthropology, sociology, politics, and psychology; and the various theories of social change. The joining of the two parts is somehow forced, but it gives me plenty of opportunities to enrich the presentation if the audience is receptive.

Usually I start by showing how different disciplines have approached the subject of time. I review what philosophy and the natural and social sciences (especially anthropology) have said about it. It is not a very exhaustive recollection; just enough to let the students realize the richness behind the concept. I begin with science, according to which time exists and has a direction—from the Big Band to the Big Crunch—but I also remind them that science is unable to tell us what time is like before the bang or after the crunch. I also explain that different cultures have distinctive perspectives of time; that some of them have no clear concept of the future, while others have a totally subjective conception of time. At this stage I introduce the difference between linear and cyclic conceptions of time, with the spiral as a combination of both. This last point gives me a chance to move onto philosophy. After that, I tackle some of the theories that characterize time as a creation of our language, with some support from psychology and brain science. All together, this allows me to offer a quite comprehensive description of time. During this part I try very hard not to offer definitive statements, but just to suggest alternative views. At this point someone will be sure to ask how all of this relates to futures studies. My answer is that we can only produce meaningful forecasts and scenarios if they are consistent with the receiver or client's perception of time, not to mention that a futurist oblivious to these aspects could end up unwittingly colonizing other people's futures.

Before entering into the theories of social change (and stability), I like to bring in what I consider their antecedent: macrohistory. This is the direct result of my exposure to the work of Sohail Inayatullah. The thought of people like Giambattista Vico, Shu Ma Chien, and Ibn Khaldun are good examples of some of the early attempts to find patterns and laws in the evolution of cultures and societies. In addition, each author reflects the idiosyncrasy of his culture and times, just as each of us does now, and reinforces the previous part about different cultural conceptions of time (Galtung and Inayatullah, 1997).

The importance of founding futures research on theory cannot be emphasized enough. As I said already, there is a great tendency to characterize futures studies as a mere professional activity without any regard for theoretical concerns. This is a great mistake, because it deprives our work of its necessary underpinnings. Without a theory to back up our conclusions we will have to rely entirely on our "expertise" and "prestige." If we fail or make mistakes, we will probably lose our credibility, as we should. However, we have to acknowledge that there is a vast range of theories for us to choose—which is a nice way to say that no theory covers all the requirements—and that every futurist has to decide which theory seems to provide the most powerful or satisfying explanation. As an example, I explain my own recipe, which is a mixture of technology studies and sociology. Basically, I focus on technological development as a catalyst of social change, and then I introduce elements of age-cohort analysis to refine my conclusions. In any instance, I insist that there is no a such a thing as the "right" or "best" theory: A Marxist will focus on class conflict and the economy, another person will follow the theory of Kondratiev long-waves, others prefer some other theory of cycles, and so on. The choice of a theory per se does not predetermine the quality of the futures research, though some things will be illuminated by one theory and other things will be hidden from view. In any case, some flexibility cannot hurt and may offer useful alternative insights into the subject under study.

The last thing I do before getting into the methods part is to review the evolution of futures studies as a discipline and the main approaches it has followed in recent decades. I start with the predictive focus that futures studies had in the beginning. This approach was deeply embedded in linear temporality and faith in progress, growth, and the future's promise of better times. Later on, I introduce how this approach was criticized as too Western centered and too insensitive to cultural particularities, leading to the development of cultural or interpretative futures studies, which introduced a relativism regarding what is true and what is real or best. Unfortunately, this kind of futures studies was also used by some to prove the superiority of Western futures studies over others, which resulted in greater harm than that caused by the predictive mode. Finally I explain the approach that emerged as a reaction to all this: critical futures studies. This approach was deeply influenced by poststructuralism. Its strength lies in the systematic questioning of how things should be in any determinate way in the future, particularly why we should assume that the future should be like the present. This mode is a very powerful way to problematize the present and the powers that be. I also add that the three approaches are still functioning, that the predictive mode is probably the most used even now, as it is the one that is best suited to offer what is most in demand; namely, forecasts and scenarios. I am also very clear about the fact that, despite its power, critical futures studies is not very well suited for elaborating and designing scenarios, and that one should be extremely careful if working from the cultural approach.

METHODS

When all this is done, we arrive at the methods stage, usually the part most people are really waiting for. The decision to put methods at the end is tough. Some people cannot wait to learn about the "hocus pocus" futurists use. But there is no other way to do it. I compare it to the process of building a house. First you need to know the materials you are going to use—the concepts. Then you need to know something about structures, foundations, pressures, and the function of the house—the theory. Then you are ready to learn how actually to build the house—the methods. My question is always the same: Would you trust an architect without knowledge of the materials, structures, foundations, pressures, and the future use of what it is he is proposing on the blueprints? Probably not. Why would you trust a futurist who only knows methods?

Given that there are a great variety of methods, and even more kinds of classifications, it is complicated to decide how to approach this stage. What I do is to start by making a list of the methods available, as comprehensive as possible, and the different criteria to sort them out: Rick Slaughter's (1984) classification along the hard–soft axis; Eleonora Masini's (1993) categories of objective, subjective, and systemic methods; the French method "la demarche prospective" (de Jouvenel, 1993); and finally I add the last contributions from poststructuralism (Elmandjra, 1984; Inayatullah, 1990; Sardar, 1999) and participatory approaches (Bezold, 1996; Dator, 1996b). The idea is that after this, every time I introduce a method, the students will be able to understand it according to the different criteria, and hence know more about it.

I usually start with trend analysis and extrapolation, and I do so for several reasons. In the first place, it shows that futures studies is based on data and empirical research to some extent. Second, it is a method that helps to make a connection between the past, the present, and then the projection into the future, which ties in nicely with people's intuitions about the future. Finally, it shows that futures studies is based on common sense. Trend analysis and extrapolation offers a comfortable introduction to futures methods. In addition, it allows me also to introduce further elements when talking about its assumptions and limitations as a method: linearity from the present, lack of alternative perspectives, and the impossibility of dealing with complex issues—handling just one variable at a time.

This last point gives me a good cue to introduce the next method: cross-impact analysis. This method is either despised or loved by most futurists. For me it is just a good way to bring in another concept about the future; namely, the future is going to be at least as complex as the present. Therefore we need methods that accept and deal with complexity. In my approach, cross-impact analysis is the initial procedure and operates with several variables at the same time and works on their interrelations. Incidentally, this gives an opportunity to introduce systems theory and models, which are central elements of other methods. Specifically, it is a good entrance for what is the main futures method in Europe: structural analysis.

But before getting into formalized methods, I like to present the Delphi approach. Delphi is in high disrepute by a major sector of the profession. Years of abuse have placed Delphi in a uncomfortable situation. But following my discourse, it makes sense to talk about Delphi at this point, since it also ties to another extended (and up to a point, intuitive) opinion: that experts know best. Delphi has been terribly misused, and many times it has been used to label exercises that could hardly have passed as a survey, at best, much less as a true Delphi. But it is a very frequently used method, so any futurist should at least know it. Besides, if its original focus (to convene a group of experts to produce information about the future in a structured way) is in decline, it still can be used as a test step in a research program. Given the present systems for sending, receiving, processing, and storing massive quantities of information, a Delphi can be used as a refining stage inside a futures research. I believe that Delphi can still have a useful function, but I'm aware that right now it is a little burnt out and will need some time to recover usefulness again.

After that, I move on to the French futures method, *la démarche prospective*. One thing has to be noted at this point. In the Anglo–American context, the different methods are seen as relatively independent, as complementary or alternative, depending on the case. But in the French situation the different methods are conceived as steps in a continuum toward the completion of the futures research process; namely, futures scenarios. The two essential parts of the French technique are the structural analysis and the set of actors. Both are highly formalized methods, with a great emphasis on quantification and modeling. The assumption is that the more the method formalizes the process, the more chances there are for refining the subjective inputs.

Structural analysis is a substantial advancement over cross-impact analysis, with which it shares its foundation in systems theory, but it goes beyond it in two aspects. Structural analysis is specifically designed to deal with many variables—an analysis with sixty or more variables is common—and it studies not only direct relations among the variables but especially the indirect relations. The rationale is that indirect relationships take longer to occur, therefore the more you search for indirect relations the further you go in the future. It has to be said that structural analysis is probably the king method in Europe. It has been used intensively and has gained a good reputation. Surely the rigor of its development, the amount of data it can produce, and the fact that it provides very good descriptions of the subject under research are decisive factors in its popularity. Yet its shortcomings have to be acknowledged too. Structural analysis is very costly in terms of time, effort, and—usually—money. It has a tendency to reduce alternatives and eliminate novelties, as it is overly dependent on the diagnosis of the present situation. Finally, and more important, it is incapable of accounting for the objectives, projects, strategies, fears, wishes, and so on of the agents involved.

Precisely to solve this last point, the set of actors was designed. We must remember that the two methods are considered as steps in a continued process toward the completion of futures scenarios. The set of actors is the method that analyzes the objectives and strategies of all the agents involved in the subject under study. It also weighs the different influence and dependence of each actor, and therefore evaluates its capacity to achieve its objectives. The set of actors is the perfect complement for structural analysis, and is a very good tool to measure what is often very difficult to valorize: the project, intentions, means of action, and influence of every actor, provided, of course, that you can have access to this kind of information, which is not always easy to achieve.

Following the French perspective, the logical end of any futures research is the production of futures scenarios; hence, it makes sense to introduce the concept of a futures scenario at this point. The scenario is a tricky concept, since it can be both the final result of a futures research—the product—and a method in itself. As a product, a scenario must accomplish three basic requirements. It must be coherent, consistent, and plausible. As a method, it does not define any specific procedure, just a particular approach to the research more based on the description or narration than on the analysis. To this end, when doing a scenario it is legitimate to borrow elements from other methods and information from any source.

After I've covered the French methods I move on to a group of methods that approach futures research from other angles. The first is backcasting, also called "Apollo forecasting," the technique "par excellence" for normative studies and the cornerstone to making it believable that it is possible to shape the future. Despite the fact that some people find it hard to accept that we can build the future (for me it is more difficult to understand how we cannot affect the future in one way or another), the advantage of backcasting is that it is tied to a principle of traditional wisdom: You will harvest what you have sown. Incidentally, it also gives a good ground to elaborate Rick Slaughter's (1995) foresight principle.

The second method of this group is one of which I am particularly fond, since it is a specific contribution of the "Manoa School," my school: incasting. Incasting is the only deductive method, to my knowledge, in futures studies. Beginning from a set of four or five predetermined images of the future, it allows the futurist to deduce several alternative futures scenarios for the object of the research. Some people may object that it does not seem a very useful method. My reply is always the same: The benefit you get from incasting is the ease by which you can introduce alternative futures situations, which—in my experience—is often in great need in many futures researches. Not only that, incasting offers an easy way to start a study and map the options worthy of being developed. Finally, it is a great method to introduce people without previous experience in futures studies, due to its simplicity and its potential for fun.

The last method I present are futures workshops. The main reason I do so is because futures workshops are not strictly a method but more a way to conduct futures research in a participative and structured manner, with emphasis on the participative. Futures workshops were first designed by Robert Jungk, and then developed and refined by Elise Boulding, both of whom I had the luck of meeting and learning from. In this area I am also very indebted to Wendy Schultz for her teachings.

Futures workshops can be very diverse, depending on their objectives and the circumstances. Ideally they should at least contain an analysis block, where the main futures challenges are listed; a projection block, where we try to surpass the challenges through futures visioning; and a constructing or refining block. Depending on whether we intend to just formulate objectives or to create futures scenarios, we will use this part to consider the alternatives listed, their implications, and the possible effects, in order to build coherent and structured images of the future. Finally, we may have an implementation or follow-up block. If the participants decide to follow the activity of the workshop in any sense, or to carry out its objectives or conclusions, this part will help to plan the next steps.

Futures workshops are an excellent method to get people involved. They are specifically designed to allow people without previous knowledge or experience in futures studies to participate in research in a relevant and meaningful way. Of course, there is limited control over their development and results, which is the reason why some futurist do not like to use them in the professional arena. Also, workshops problematize the notion of futures experts: In a workshop, everybody is an expert of the future, at least potentially. The attitude toward workshops is highly dependent on the futurist's vision of futures studies and the future in general: The more you move in the predictive approach, the less you will like workshops; the more you are in the critical approach, the more you will appreciate them.

Futures workshops can have other collateral benefits. For instance, in situations where an issue has created some opposing factions, thus making it difficult to find a way out, futures workshops can have a healing potential by helping the factions to concentrate on shared future objectives rather than on present conflicts. Also, in cases where a collective, an enterprise, or an association is stagnant or going through a crisis and has no projects for its future, a futures workshop can be a good way to define a goal that can mobilize the members of the collective and revitalize the organization. On other occasions, a futures workshop is just a way to generate consensus and support around a futures project.

The good news is that futures workshops are becoming more and more accepted in the business world. After years of demanding facts, figures, percentages, and certainties, more and more enterprises are beginning to appreciate the potential of futures workshops as a tool for envisioning futures and carrying them out collectively. The real cause of the recent popularity of futures workshops lies in the fact that people are tired of being mere spectators in futures research, particularly in matters that affect them directly. In this sense, we will see an increase in the number and uses of futures workshops and, hopefully, improvements in their methodological design and operation.

WRAPPING UP

The one thing I always do before finishing, no matter what the exact content of my class, is to tell the students that, at the bottom, futures studies involves a lot of common sense, plus some techniques and rules, with indispensable megadoses of creativity, imagination, novelty, and, why not admit it, some drops of absurdity. After all, in the unforgettable words of Jim Dator (1996a), "Any useful statement about the future should appear to be ridiculous." I am tempted to say that, so far, I have had my full share of well-deserved derision.

REFERENCES

Bezold, C. (1996). The visioning method. In R. Slaughter (Ed.), *Knowledge base of futures studies* (vol. 2, pp. 167–175). Hawthorn, Australia: DDM Media Group.

Dator, J. (1996a). Foreword. In R. Slaughter (Ed.), *Knowledge base of futures studies* (vol. 1, pp. xix–xx). Hawthorn, Australia: DDM Media Group.

Dator, J. (1996b). From futures workshops to envisioning alternative futures. In R. Slaughter (Ed.), *Knowledge base of futures studies* (vol. 2, pp. 161–165). Hawthorn, Australia: DDM Media Group.

de Jouvenel, H. (1993). Sur la demarche prospective: Un bref guide methodologique. *Futuribles, 179.*

Elmandjra, M. (1984). Reclaiming the future: Futures studies in Africa. *Futures, 16*, 374–378.

Galtung, J., and Inayatullah, S. (Eds.). (1997). *Macrohistory and macrohistorians: Perspectives on individual, social, and civilizational change.* Westport, CT: Praeger.

Inayatullah, S. (1990). Deconstructing and reconstructing the future: Predictive, cultural and critical epistemologies. *Futures, 22*, 115–141.

Masini, E. (1993). *Why futures studies?* London: Gray Seal.

Sardar, Z. (Ed.). (1999). *Rescuing all our futures: The future of futures studies.* London: Adamantine.

Slaughter, R. (1984).Towards critical futurism. *World Future Society Bulletin, 18* (4), 19–25.

Slaughter, R. (1995). *The foresight principle: Cultural recovery in the 21st century.* London: Adamantine.

21

Giving Images a Chance:
Images of the Future
as a Tool for Sociology

Anita Rubin

I still have not made up my mind whether I should see myself as a sociologist with a futures orientation or as a futurist with a sociological emphasis. Be it this way or that, there are some very interesting aspects that can be seen as the possible contacting surfaces of the two fields of knowledge: sociology and futures research. My basic conviction is that social sciences inevitably both trigger and enforce social change. However, I feel that this understanding has become somewhat obscured in current sociology. Current sociology has the nature of being more analysis oriented than action oriented. Sociologists would rather observe, discuss scientifically, and conceptualize and lay emphasis on meaning structures than expose themselves by taking risks, taking stands, participating, and giving emphasis to responsibility. Somehow sociology has become distant, theoretical, clean, and—perhaps for that very reason—even a little hypocritical. Very few sociologists seem to want to get the dirt of "social reality" in their hands anymore; for example, by getting involved with socioeconomic processes or public policy issues. They would rather choose to discuss qualities, significance, cultural representations, and structures. Wendell Bell (1997), Eleonora Masini (1993, in this volume), Anthony Giddens (1996), and Erik Allardt (1995) have all made the same kind of critique of current sociology.

Perhaps the cause for this state of current sociology can be traced from the past, from the more participatory attitudes, approaches, and practices that didn't seem to lead to anything lasting at the time. Or perhaps it is just the normal movement of a pendulum reaching the opposite side. Who knows?

However, I am also aware that there can be dangers in a sociology that is too strongly action oriented. There are examples in the immediate past of what kind of failures, tragedies, and unexpected consequences social experiments can cause in culture and politics when people have tried to change things before fully understanding the processes that bring them about.

Popper (1963) took a very skeptical attitude toward the idea that the main task of social sciences is to predict the future. He warned from the vantage point of historicism, and made a clear distinction between scientific predictions and unconditional predictions. However, Popper also said that the responsibility of a philosopher—and in this case, a social researcher—is to give rational critiques both to the social problems and to the proposed solutions different groups or persons offer to solve them, and not blindly to accept or follow any of them. However, we should not be satisfied with interpreting the world, but should also be willing to get involved in trying to change it.

Giddens (1996, p. 5) urges sociologists not to remain detached from the matters of practical policy but to participate with courage in the debates their work might arouse. This attitude prevents both choices made too rapidly and the settling of terms with inadequate knowledge. Instead, it gives way to the exploration of alternatives. I understand this not only as the kind of scholarly discussions that have been criticized already but also as taking bold stands and accepting the responsibilities that arise when different alternatives are considered.

By its general cross-scientific approach and nature, which encourages discussion of differing values, futures studies can be seen as a tool for sociological thinking also in this respect. The main point is not to gain exact foreknowledge of the future—it is impossible—but to explore the alternatives and then initiate, participate, and encourage discussion of the qualities of these alternatives (Boulding and Boulding, 1995, p. 8).

I want to explore whether futures studies in general, and the study of people's images of the future in particular, can reveal something specific and new concerning what the future will be like. From a more normative point of view, it is also interesting to explore, by promoting more thorough value discussions, what the future should be like. What meaning do people give to these images, and how do they direct human decision making, both on the individual and social levels? Should prediction, or forecasting, as I rather see it, be considered in favor or against social change? What is the role and meaning of people who have some thoughts about the future in the process that produces the future?

The theory of change that I have used as the framework for my thinking is based on the application of evolutionary models in social sciences, and more specifically, the idea of evolutionary transition as progressive differentiation toward increasing complexity that explains social change. In my research I explore the ideas, visions, and images of the future that people have, and I explain them as the interpretations of the present possibilities and preconditions. The contents of how the future is seen, what is anticipated, hoped for, or feared, tells us something essential about the present. These interpretations reveal the tone of the time and of the reality that people are living through. While the reality of today can be seen as a production of yesterday's choices and decisions, so also the images of the future are the projections of today.

These displays of anticipated reality can be incommensurable, inconsistent, and contradictory by nature, but they still exist simultaneously and affect our present choices. The concepts of the future and the images that arise from them are factors that direct human behavior and the choice of attitudes in the present situations of decision making. Each individual's idea of the future, together with the prevailing social facts and commonly shared ideas and expectations, have a contributory influence on the general direction of human decision making and actions in the present day. Thus, the image of future can be seen as a tool for coping in the present (Rubin, 1995, 1996).

WHEN CHANGE ITSELF IS CHANGING

At present, we who live in the Western societies are experiencing a time of media, globalization, and networking. We speak of late modernity as the age of plurality, individualism, creativity, and ambivalence, characterized also as the age of uncertainty, unpredictability, unexpectedness, confusion. The range of possibilities seems to have grown into unparalleled measures, while the size and complexity of the problems on the global level appear impossible to solve with the means we have available.

Individual identity is supposed to be built from the flows of shattered information that are real-time and simultaneous, while our human way of treating information is still consecutive and logical by nature and strives to construct clear and coherent wholes. All this produces cultural flatulence in these late-modern frames: We suffer from both spiritual constipation and the diarrhea of consumerism at the same time.

It is my basic assumption that transitional phases form an inevitable and unavoidable part of social and societal development processes, typical to all societies at all times. The course of development molds the society from less complexity to a more complex social reality. According to the writers who have applied evolutionary models to social sciences from the point of view of futures studies (e.g., Allen, 1994; Laszlo, 1991, 1996; Malaska, 1991; Mannermaa, 1991; Pantzar, 1991; see also Mannermaa, Inayatullah, and Slaughter, 1993), transition can be described as a period of critical shift between two states of steady development. During the steady phase, change is more quantitative by nature and thus easier to predict, while the transitionary periods add more a qualitative and dialectic character to it.

The length of this shift period is not predictable, and the features of the steadier period that follows it cannot be anticipated or determined from the features of the time of transition. The transition is characterized by discontinuities. Thus forecasting is not possible if one tries to describe the future only by exploring the features of the present. The task of knowing about the future also calls for visionary abilities, "vistas of the future" (Malaska, 1993). Moreover, the transitional development appears to be irreversible by its empirical nature. The phenomena characteristic of the time prior to the transition, and the ways and theories used for explaining and especially predicting these phenomena, are unreliable during the transition.

The once reliable master narratives lose their explanatory capability in describing the ongoing reality. Some of the objective features of a social situation in transition are viewlessness, confusion, unpredictability, uncertainty, and unexpectedness. Transition augurs great changes in social infrastructure, culture, economic practices, politics, and policy making (e.g., Giddens, 1991, pp. 32–34, 53; Covey, 1992, pp. 70–72).

Like many other social scientists, Giddens (1996, pp. 101–103) also criticizes the use of evolutionary models in a theory of social change. His critique is based on the idea of human intentionality versus the idea of adaptation. He says that in the evolutionary models, the stimulus to social change is understood as exogenous, and questions this by referring to certain consequences that can clearly be seen as internally and intentionally generated. He does not accept the idea of mere "blind" mutation causing change in social reality, and says that this kind of change, transferred to human society, cannot cope with the distinctive characteristic of intentionality and purposeful intervention in the attempt to control and direct social development.

However, when we think of the role of the human actor in inducing change, we see that Giddens forgets one of the very basic ideas in futures-oriented thinking about social change. Even though human activity is intentional, some of the actual results and consequences of decisions and functions reach far beyond what was originally intended. These unexpected and unintentional consequences are exactly the essence that brings about turbulence and transition.

The period of socioeconomic and cultural transition means that many such things that used to be stable and permanent do not seem to be so anymore. Many long-prevailing beliefs and models of explanation are no longer valid or able to explain the world and its quickening change which leads to still greater unpredictability and chaos in many areas. The character of change itself has changed. "Development" is no longer the same as "growth"—a steadily rising curve—but unpredictable and confusing instead.

People feel that since the world has changed, coping and adjustment require different actions, capabilities, and readinesses from what worked before. Because of this instability, life is not as easily understandable and manageable as it used to be: The feeling of uncertainty grows. It is as if the string has broken and the beads of events that formed the necklace of our everyday life, the continuity and logic of the reality, have all rolled here and there. It takes a lot of extra effort and time to find the beads and thread them back onto their string and see the necklace instead of a pile of loose beads.

HOW TO RECYCLE WISDOM AND VALUES

One way to strive to overcome the negative aspects of transition has been the growing emphasis on individualism, the individual's right to make choices. This tendency on the personal level, however, brings about other kinds of problems that affect culture and social life. There are features in our current culture that accentuate the realization of our wishes and hopes and the attainment of occasional goals at the cost of wisdom and values (von Wright, 1988). Bauman (1996, p. 186) says that nothing in our current culture is really irreplaceable anymore. Accordingly, instead of only one history, there is a variety of alternative images of the past deriving from different interests and worldviews. Late modernity is described as the world of individuals: It keenly accepts and supports the differences between people. Instead of putting pressure on generalizations, homogeneity, and similarities, as is done in the concept of modernity, late modernity emphasizes the importance of originality and individual creativity.

This basic right, however, brings about confusions and new ethical problems (e.g., the withdrawal of a collective ethos). Collective ethos, or generally shared moral perspectives, values, and traditions, do not support the individual in the situation of decision making or choice anymore. While social structures are being replaced by information structures and the old, traditional collectivity is disappearing, individual people feel more and more insecure and confused, powerless in facing social and political phenomena, especially at the global level.

The strengthening emphasis on self-fulfillment and the freedom of choice tends to turn people's eyes away from the contents of "being" and values. It is so much easier and safer to write scholarly essays on how we should discuss more about ethics and values than to start to publicly analyze their contents. It is the very essence of late modernity, or postmodernity, if you like, to evade total explanations. Accordingly, people seem to have lost interest in moral issues and avoid ethical considerations that could deal with things greater than the wishes and expectations of an individual. Morals become a private matter and norms are more and more labile, growing lighter and lighter. In the end, this might result in the loosening of social ties and the weakening of all social integration. (Taylor, 1991, pp. 37–41, 45).

However, at the same time some other events or features that are typical of late modernity press us to deeper moral considerations to which we have to respond more and more from the individual point of view. First, the present is decisively different from previous times in human history: The meaning of information as the prime mover of economy and technology is constantly growing. As a result, we are facing completely new ethical challenges, not only in respect to information technology, but also nanotechnology, biotechnology, artificial intelligence, and so on.

Second, this time also offers us something completely new in the sense that people's possibilities have grown into nearly incomprehensible measures, in relation to both the dimension of global resources and the dimension of time. The impacts of communication and media are immense: News can be received from all over the world in real time. It is often said that people can get in touch with almost anybody by the new means of communication at any time and place they wish. Contrarily, people are able to make local decisions that can affect on a global level and/or whose consequences become visible or have impacts that may last for hundreds or even thousands of generations (Milbrath, 1989). We are constantly reminded that the time-related distance between our contemporary decisions and actions and their future consequences heightens our responsibility to future generations.

Third, as a result of the growth of economic activity and technology, the size and interwovedness of the global "problematique" has grown too. For example, environmental problems cannot be solved without dealing with issues like poverty, equality, hunger, wars, climate, and so on. This intertwinement of phenomena claims completely new paths in our logical thinking to understand them, let alone to find the means to solve them.

Fourth, the change in attitudes and awareness on a global level is also a new phenomena caused by the growth of information: People are still more aware of these possibilities, as well as of the big responsibilities these possibilities lay on their shoulders. It is said that ever since people saw the first photographs of the Earth taken from space satellites—the Earth as a green and blue ball, so beautiful and yet so vulnerable—it has not been possible to think of the world the same way as before. The world needs to be protected. That has been one of the most effective elements in the process of globalization.

This change in our knowledge structures on the "metalevel," however, does not match with the ideas of late modernity that emphasize individuality and pluralistic values. A moral dilemma arises when the growing level of knowledge inevitably brings about the need for value discussions and increases people's morality and awareness of global issues (e.g., of the environmental problems).

The process of individualization can be connected to the process of industrial society, which requires us to undress its ways of living from their frames and reframe them again according to the new challenges of late modernity. That way, individuals have to plan, write, arrange, darn, and patch their own biographies; act, stage, show, and direct their own stories, identities, social networks, commitments, and ideologies (Beck, 1996, pp. 27–28).

The process of individualization can also be seen as fragmentation of life into separate circles: People have ceased understanding the big social systems and the collective ways of thinking that derived from them (Allardt, 1995). This structure that imposed the guidelines or boundaries for their everyday decision making and activities for so long has become useless. Instead, people rather adapt their actions and decisions to the variety of social situations. That is why there is a growing paradox of what is required from a person in order to be successful or even happy.

There is a clear inner inconsistency and illogicality in present-day thinking about individualism: The more individualized the society in which we live is, the less moral will or political interest and influence there seems to be among private citizens. Liberal individualism seems to give promises of more freedom and rights and private happiness, but when this freedom and these rights are not connected directly to social responsibility they tend to separate "rightfully" from the care of common responsibilities and concentrate on gaining personal welfare (Hellsten, 1997).

IMAGES OF THE FUTURE AS TOOLS FOR COPING

I am preparing my dissertation on the images of future of young people. According to several previous studies (e.g., in Australia, England, the United States; researchers like Masini, etc.), there is a gap between the images of personal futures (a mixture of hopes and positive expectations) and those of the environment, homeland, and the world (mainly negative, impending global threats). I have found the same result in my research, and now I'm concentrating on how this discontinuity can be explained.

My basic idea for understanding this is that the contradictory images arise from different interpretations of the present (Western) transition from modernity through late modernity to something new, and similarly, from industriality through late industriality to something new. The images reflect this simultaneous existence of different and partly contradictory interpretations of reality (seen as the concept of the world, concept of the human, institutions, etc.), which on their part reflect socioeconomic and cultural change. The basic model of change is based on the application of evolutionary theories in social sciences, and the social interpretation of modernity (e.g., Giddens, 1991; Bauman, 1993; Taylor, 1991; and others).

The ways in which people construct their images of the future are not always very rational, even though some people might believe they are (see, e.g., Etzioni, 1988). The human idea of the future is not only based on a sharp analysis of a single moment or action and its varying factors, it is also affected by emotions, fears, hopes, personal history, and experiences, as well as the general views, values, and opinions shared by society and the environment. The orientation toward the future is based on how these images become parts of a person's reality and thus also how they become determinants of his or her behavior and decision making.

Many factors behind a person's everyday decision making and activities derive from these images of the future. According to Whaley and Whaley (1986, p. 4), several of the current and future choices and actions of a person are based on estimates of the probability that these images will actually come true. Some probabilities are seen as positive and desirable, some neutral in tone, while some others are seen as negative and undesirable. These images influence a person's actions: He or she tries to avoid those actions and functions that would make the negative image more likely to come true than the positive one. Likewise, he or she tries to behave so that the future situation, shown by his or her positive image, will result. If the image is powerful enough, a person can spend a great deal of time in these decisional processes.

An image per se is a mental tool, flexible and changeable, and very personal in nature. It is born when a perceived event reaches consciousness and the target of perception is given significance and an emotional charge. It is used in the processes of analyzing and organizing one's conceptions of reality into a useful, sensible, and controllable order. The use of images in one's personal way of coping with the world has thus to do with the qualitative development of thinking. The images are important, especially in the processes of perceiving large and complex wholes. A person's orientation toward the future is based on making these mental images a part of reality and then directing his or her actions and decision making along the lines drawn by these images.

The term "image of future" was first defined by Fred Polak and Kenneth Boulding in the 1950s (Boulding and Boulding, 1995, p. 96; see also Bell, 1997, this volume). A person's images of the future derive from different time-bound and value-related conceptions of the world, which, in the times of transition, can coexist simultaneously and still include components and features that are contradictory to each other. They affect the individual who, when making decisions and choosing ways of action, utilizes this knowledge with the experiences and knowledge he or she has gained from the past, and connects them with the available information of the present. Knowledge is attained by exploring the past, considering one's own experiences, as well as one's future aims and expectations, and by setting them into the structures and realities of the present moment.

These images affect a person's behavior and selection of choices in the present, which, for their part, influence how the future will actualize (e.g., Inayatullah, 1993). Images of the future are largely formed and affected by the social environment, especially the media. Education, tradition, values, attitudes, and media-related things like newspapers, television, radio, movies, and literature, especially science fiction, determine the general images of what the future is supposed to look like (Hirsjärvi and Remes, 1986, p. 66).

Without a clearly futures-oriented point of view in, for example, education, the images of the future can be seen as reactive in nature and based on the issues, trends, and especially threats of the present moment. Also, concentration on present problems and issues that are understood as negative trends toward the future causes a clear reactive strategy focusing on adopting ways to cope instead of exploring and using proactive and creative strategies. Some studies indicate that people see the future as a threat that is closely linked to their special field of expertise and interest. Thus, the basic nature of the strategies they adopted for coping with the future were mere reflections of these threatening phenomena: They were reactions to their own dystopic images (e.g., Bjerstedt, 1992; Remes, 1993).

Bjerstedt (1992) also researched what people think of their own possibilities of influencing their future. A person who feels that he or she can affect the future is willing to use foresight so as to try to anticipate and influence it. His or her actions are goal directed and purposeful; he or she strives to create strategies that will make the best possible future (Nurmi, 1995).

On the other hand, a person who does not feel that he or she can have a say on what the future will be like finds the future impossible to be outlined, confusing, and often also preordained and inflexible. When facing this kind of a future, he or she has to return continuously to his or her original aims and strategies and thus has to reinterpret the situation over and over again (Nurmi, 1995). He or she finds himself or herself as only a pawn in a game with almost no possibility of influencing the outcome. These forces are too big and too mighty, making his or her degrees of freedom very few.

This dilemma becomes especially visible in the division between one's own personal future versus the future of one's environment (Nurmi, 1995). The more often a future-oriented issue deals with one's own future, the more often the resulting image of the future is formed of dreams and hopes, and the more important it is for the person in question. When attention is diverted from one's personal future toward the wider world, the future looks bleaker and more hopeless. Overwhelming, uncontrollable global problems are brought up, such as poverty, hunger, environmental and ecological disasters, and so on (Nurmi, 1995).

Images of the future are thus involved in a dialectic process that has a lot to do with coping in the present: While our present situation gives the tone to our general image and understanding of the future, our ideas and visions of the future actually more or less determine our present state of mind. They also then determine our present decision making and actions. In this way, images of the future can be linked to the concept of life management.

TEACHING FUTURES

Teaching futures orientation and futures studies is a very challenging task. A few years ago the Finland Futures Research Centre ran a school project together with the Board of Education of Finland. The idea of this project was to find out how to introduce futures-oriented thinking to education on all school levels. The project produced information on what methods and themes are best used with different age groups and school levels and how to include this kind of material in school curricula.

The main findings were that, first, it is possible for futures-oriented education to be integrated in many different study subjects, but the most effective way, especially for the high school and vocational levels, would be to build a separate entity on futures studies. The results also showed that students' futures awareness can be developed, especially by concentrating on phenomenal experiments and by using learning environments that support this "do it yourself" attitude.

However, it also became clear that teachers need to be educated first in futures orientation. Even the conceptual focus of future-related issues and themes was unfamiliar to most of the participating teachers, while there were not enough educational materials available at the time to assist them.

That is why I became involved in teaching the teachers. First I wrote a guidebook for educators in futures-oriented thinking (Rubin, 1995). The book introduces four main themes—the features of transition, values and value conflicts, the concept of being human, and what "time" is all about—and then explores various futures-related topics, such as sustainable development, the environment, population growth, power issues, economy, and work. Finally, the book introduces some methods in futures studies that can be used practically in school environments; for example, how to organize and run futures workshops, make scenarios, or arrange projects with futures themes.

I also run scenario workshops for teachers. The method I use has been developed during the last few years and the aims are, first, to make the participants familiar with futures-oriented concepts and modes of thinking; second, to teach them a method to be applied in classroom situations, and third, to introduce a way of making proactive future strategies instead of mere reactive strategies. The intention is to make the participants aware of the fact that being prepared for tomorrow means that we recognize what is probable, what is possible, what is conditionally possible, what is preferable, and what is to be avoided. All our decision making—be it on the personal or the social level—is based on these options. The levels of probability and possibility are not uniform. As an example, it is probable that tomorrow is a cold winter day in Finland. It is possible that it snows tomorrow. The level of conditionality comes into the picture by making a plan: If it doesn't snow, we will go skiing. I hope it won't snow, but after seeing the weather forecast, I am afraid that it will. Or Auntie Mary will come and make a surprise visit, or I'll catch the flu. In order to be prepared for all these different possibilities, we have to make alternative plans. Value discussion and the consideration of preferences are included when we think of the preferable futures and make these alternative plans.

To learn all this, we usually make four scenarios: (1) continued growth, (2) catastrophe, (3) reversion to the past, and (3) transformation (Dator,

1979). These scenarios are then used as a tool for value discussion and the formation of a futures model, a realistic, positive, logical, and possible-to-reach model for a preferable future state. Then, finally, it is time to consider the means to make it all happen.

I also give lectures in which I concentrate on the images of the future, and I especially want to emphasize the importance of the formation of positive images of the future. My research results show that the images of young people are unrealistic and (as to the future of the environment, the country, the world) very pessimistic. Young people also feel that they cannot affect the future. The general attitude does not support the building of logical wholes: Young people often lack information about the past as well as the consequences of things and happenings. That is why I think that it is very important to teach young people that the future is a result of today's decisions and activities, how to build logical wholes, and how to affect what the future will be like.

CONCLUDING REMARKS

Sociology and social and educational policies can gain from information about what people think of their future possibilities and fears. This information is useful in the study of possible socioeconomic or political processes, positions, expectations, attitudes, and possibilities in light of transition and individualization. It can also shed light on discussions of the future development of the welfare state, globalization, trends toward marginalization, isolation, the spread of extreme movements, racism, and so on.

That is why I'm convinced that knowledge about people's ideas about the future—their images of future—is so important, both on the level of personal decision making and growth and on the social level: how to make better decisions for a better society. My preferred future is one where this human digestion of late modernity is in balance, successfully coping from cultural, spiritual, social, and economic points of view.

The big problem of present times is that people lack inspiring visions of the future that can be shared collectively. The integrating forces that keep culture and society together and coherent—positive expectations and hopes for a better future—have been lost in the abyss of the late-modern transition. For instance, all education—that is, what is taught, how it is taught, and why it is taught—originates from some image of the future prevailing in society (Toffler, 1974, p. 3). So if the prevailing social image of the future is unclear, confusing, and/or negative, and there is no publicly shared positive vision of the future toward which to strive, there is a tendency for marginalization and alienation to grow in society.

I think that one of the big problems in the near future is the growing impact of different extreme movements that characteristically tend to bind this general confusion into one all-covering explanation. In times of confusion, some person has typically arisen who says he or she can tell right from wrong, good from bad, and in general smooth out the too-complex features of social reality. Extreme social disorder permits some authority (be it a guru, guide, leader, or priest, or a new religion, ideology, or social movement) to offer clear and coherent wholes instead of, or rather formed out of, the shattered pieces of information we all live in. But, of course, this can also be a opportunity at the same time it is a threat.

REFERENCES

Allardt, E. (1995). Tiede ja olennaiset kysymykset. *Tiedepolitiikka, 20* (4), 5–12.

Allen, P. (1994). Coherence, chaos and evolution in the social context. In M. Mannermaa, S. Inayatullah, and R. Slaughter (Eds.), *Coherence and chaos in our uncommon futures* (pp. 11–22). Turku: Finland Futures Research Centre.

Bauman, Z. (1993). *Postmodern ethics*. Oxford: Blackwell.

Bauman, Z. (1996). *Postmodern lumo* [The enchantment of postmodernism] (P.-L. Ahponen and T. Cantell, Eds.). Tampere, Finland: Vastapaino.

Beck, U. (1996). Politiikan uudelleen keksiminen: Kohti refleksiivisen modernisaation teoriaa [Reinventing politics: Toward the theory of reflexive modernization]. In U. Beck, A. Giddens, and S. Lash (Eds.), *Nykyajan jälijillä*. Jyväskylä: Vastapaino. (Finnish translation by L. Lehto from *Reflexive Modernization, Politics, Tradition and Aesthetics in the Modern Social Order*, Polity Press, 1994).

Bell, W. (1997). *Foundations of futures studies. Vol. 1: History, purposes, knowledge*. New Brunswick, NJ: Transaction.

Bjerstedt, Åke. (1992). Conceptions of future threats and developments: Psychological starting points and educational possibilities. In U. Svedin and B. Aniasson (Eds.), *Society and the environment* (pp. 229–255). Amsterdam: Kluwer Academic.

Boulding, E., and Boulding, K. (Eds.). (1995). *The future*. Thousand Oaks, CA: Sage.

Covey, S. (1992). *The seven habits of highly effective people: Powerful lessons in personal change*. London: Simon and Schuster.

Dator, J. (1979). The futures of culture/cultures of the future. In A. Marsella, R. G. Harp, and T. J. Ciborski (Eds.). *Perspectives in cross-cultural psychology* (pp. 369–388). New York: Academic Press.

Etzioni, A. (1988). Normative–affective factors: Toward a new decision-making model. *Journal of Economic Psychology, 9* (2), 125–150.

Giddens, A. (1991). *Modernity and self-identity: Self and society in the late modern age*. Cambridge: Polity Press.

Giddens, A. (1996). *In defence of sociology: Essays, interpretations & rejoinders*. Cambridge: Polity Press.

Hellsten, S. (1997). Markkinarationalismista moraaliseen individualismiin [From market rationalism to moral individualism]. *Kanava, 25* (9), 499–503.

Hirsjärvi, S., and Remes, P. (1986). *Voidaanko tulevaisuuteen vaikuttaa? Koulutus ja tietoyhteiskunta-tutkimuksen osaraportti* [Can the future be affected? Partial report on the project of education and the information society]. Jyväskylä: University of Jyväskylä, Institute for Educational Research.

Inayatullah, S. (1993). From "who am I?" to "when am I?" *Futures, 25* (3), 235–253.

Laszlo, E. (Ed.). (1991). *The new evolutionary paradigm.* New York: Gordon and Breach.

Laszlo, E. (1996). *Evolution: The general theory.* Cresskill, NJ: Hampton Press.

Malaska, P. (1991). Economic and social evolution: Transformational dynamic approach. In E. Laszlo (Ed.), *The new evolutionary paradigm.* New York: Gordon and Breach.

Malaska, P. (1993). Tulevaisuustietoisuus ja tulevaisuuteen tunkeutuminen [Futures awareness and piercing into the future]. In M. Vapaavuori (Ed.), Miten tutkimme tulevaisuutta. *Acta Futura Fennica, 5*, 6–12.

Mannermaa, M. (1991). Evolutionaarinen tulevaisuudentutkimus [Evolutionary futures research]. *Acta Futura Fennica, 2.*

Mannermaa, M., Inayatullah, S., and Slaughter, R. (Eds.). (1994). *Coherence and chaos in our uncommon futures.* Turku: Finland Futures Research Centre/ Turku School of Economics.

Masini, E. (1993). *Why futures studies?* London: Grey Seal.

Milbrath, L. (1989). *Envisioning a sustainable society.* Albany: State University of New York Press.

Nurmi, J.-E. (1995). Tavoitteet, keinot ja illuusiot—ihminen tulevaisuutensa tekijänä [Aims, means and illusions—Human as the maker of his/her future]. *Tiedepolitiikka, 1*, 5–12.

Pantzar, M. (1991). *A replicative perspective on evolutionary dynamics: The organizing process of the US economy elaborated through a biological metaphor* (Research report 37). Helsinki: Labour Institute for Economic Research.

Popper, K. (1963). *Conjectures and refutations.* New York: Basic Books.

Remes, P. (1993). *Future readiness in vocational adult education* (Institute for educational research, publication series A, research report 52). Jyväskylä: University of Jyväskylä.

Rubin, A. (1995). Ote huomiseen. Tulevaisuustietoisuus opetuksessa [Grasping tomorrow. Futures awareness in education]. *Tulevaisuussarja 5*, 117.

Rubin, A. (1996). Alas apatia. Tulevaisuus omiin käsiin [Down with apathy. Taking future into one's own hands]. In P. Remes and A. Rubin (Eds.), *Tulevaisuutta etsimässä. Tulevaisuusteema opetuksessa* (pp. 41–86). Helsinki: Board of Education.

Taylor, C. (1991). *The ethics of authenticity.* Cambridge: Harvard University Press.

Toffler, A. (1974). *Learning for tomorrow: The role of the future in education.* New York: Vintage Books.

von Wright, G.-H. (1988). Arvot ja tarpeet [Values and needs] (Opening lecture in von Wright colloquium series). *Futura, 1*, 88.

Whaley, C., and Whaley, H. F. (1986). *Future images: Futures studies for grades 4 to 12.* New York: Trillium Press.

22

Futures Praxis: Consulting and Teaching Futures Studies through the World Wide Web

Paul Wildman

Consulting in and teaching futures studies through networked learning was a new experience for me. It requires a team process in its design, operation, and evaluation. This chapter will explore a network approach to cogenerative, future-oriented learning. Conclusions will then be drawn about future developments in teaching and consulting in future studies through the World Wide Web (WWW). The focus will be as much on the learning process and content as it is on the technology.

CONSULTING FUTURES

My futures consulting over the past several years has included the following diverse activities:

- Community futures via the social impact assessment component of an environmental impact statement for a land developer trying to develop an "off-grid" sustainable community for 2,000 people on 200 hectares of land in a rural setting.

- Political futures by working with an Australian political party to develop a futures policy and to "futurize" their existing policies.

- Learning futures as part of a team setting up an "off-grid" "multiversity" in a rural setting.
- Science futures as a corporate futures consultant to a "new science" research institute in Australia, the Science–Art Research Centre.

In all instances, the "Web dimension" of the consultancy has been established drawing on lessons learnt from my teaching futures studies on the Web. What seems to be emerging clearly is that in Australia we have realized that our future is no longer riding on a sheep's back or coming out of the ground from a coal mine. At first we believed in the British Empire, then the United States, then Asia. Now none of these seem to be able to hold together in this century, let alone the next. Consequently, the organizations listed here are finding a huge chasm in their strategic planning processes and recognize this as a "futures gap."

Clearly also, existing organizations—especially government ones—no longer have the ability to change rapidly and seem to be reacting like dinosaurs in tried and true ways without extending their adaptive capability. They try to control more and more via bureaucracies. These responses to the future still are just that—responses. Little "big-picture" stuff seems to come in, and responses seem to be more acts of desperation than considered, historically anchored strategies.

Nevertheless they are a start. These reactions can be used as NIMBYs (Not In My Back Yard) by the environmental movement as a starting point that can lead toward a clearer understanding of, and linkings to, bigger-picture contexts. Important also is that these reactions provoke questions that encourage students to begin more future-oriented thinking.

Consultancy provides a great opportunity to use directly the strength of the WWW, which allows "consultant" and "consultantee" to coauthor the text, the substance of the consultancy. In all my consultancies I try to interface through both informal and formal learning processes.

The informal—and more powerful—is seen as "study clubs" in "learning organizations," while the formal is sought in terms of credit toward an M.S. in futures studies within a private university, in this instance the International Management Centres. Further, the WWW provides praxis opportunities to network "netergy." This came home to me with feedback from one student, who said, "I've been a distance ed. student for three years and before the Futures course with its e-mail contact I had never spoken to another student, and a lecturer rang me once when I was late for an assignment."

STRATEGIC AREAS IN DESIGNING AND TEACHING USING WEB-BASED COURSEWARE

This section identifies and reviews areas that proved to be strategically significant in the design of the course.

Authoring the Curriculum

The content author (Sohail Inayatullah) was chosen as an expert in the futures studies field, linked to the World Futures Studies Federation. Dr. Inayatullah chose to design the unit within the standard three-by-fifty-hour modules, thus creating, in effect, a tour of the futures field with Sohail as tour guide. His task was to provide a context for the articles, e-mail discussions, and assessments through inclusion of the cultural and intellectual history of each writer who contributed material to the unit. In this instance, the first step in course development was to acknowledge the epistemic biases of each author, thus framing the future and the course, while allowing it to be open.

The unit structure has three modules:

- The first gives an overview of the methods and theories of futures studies.
- The second module offers specific emerging issues that promise to transform society: robotics, telecommunications, microvita, globalism, genetics, gender cooperation, metaphor, and governance.
- The third module looks at unconventional visions of the future. This section is more culturally diverse than previous sections, having, for example, essays on African, Buddhist, Islamic, Tantric, and world systems futures, certainly not worldviews that one would get in most neighborhood grocery shops or bookstores in Australia.

Each module is designed for a particular type of approach: the first philosophical, the second content focused, and the third that of the idealist dreamer and actor. Authors were selected for their leadership in their field and the thoroughness of their essays, as well as the level to which they could relate personal stories, since the text is constantly enlivened by storytelling. Each section includes textbook-type questions that then feed into learner interaction using e-mail-based feedback sections after each reading, and Web-mounted student assignments with the lecturer's critique. Rather than asking for feedback, which tends to elicit loyal responses, the goal of the unit is to give students a framework to investigate their own personal and institutional futures.

Web Design

An innovative Web-based unit such as the futures course requires a well-designed Web presence. It is not enough just to convert paper-based documents to an electronic medium and expect it to be effective. While not being entirely divorced from the underlying paper structure, this unit experimented with several methods of presenting information to a digital audience, which are described throughout this chapter.

Feedback is an important aspect of this unit, and so each article has an option that allows the reader to tell others what they thought of the article. Because users must authorize themselves via username and password to the

Web browser before entering the unit (using the WWW security mechanisms), it is possible to prevent students from viewing other students' feedback before providing their own. Once a student has given feedback on an article, he or she is then free to read all other students' feedback on that article. Each of the three modules also has an associated coffee shop–bulletin board, electronic mailing lists through which students and teachers can communicate with each other. These mailing lists are archived on the Web and can be viewed by date, thread, author, or subject.

Finally, in order to facilitate the input of students who are using this material, a simple Web interface to the .htpasswd file was developed that allows authorized users to add, modify, or remove usernames or passwords within this file. Authorized users can also add or remove other users, thereby making the system self-contained and maintainable by people with minimal Unix knowledge or experience.

Instructional Design

Instructional design in the development of the futures unit was a matter of considering how best to utilize Web technologies for teaching and learning. Initial discussions regarding the strengths and weaknesses of electronic course delivery focused on the scope for asynchronous interactivity offered by computer-mediated communication (Rice, 1995). It was agreed that the potential was there for an innovative and unique course, not only because of the avant-garde nature of the subject area, but also due to the delivery methods being considered.

Thus, the facilitation of learning through electronic dialogue, on-line data gathering, and collaboration between teachers and student peers provided exciting goals for the teaching of this futures studies unit. Additional use of technologies such as full-length audio tapes (thirty minutes), telephone tutorials, and teleconferencing were also considered and could be incorporated in future reviews of teaching strategies. In particular, the work of Mason and Kaye (1989) provided a great deal of encouragement for the use of computer-mediated communication. This helped to inform the team not only of the distinct benefits of this kind of delivery, but also gave us ideas about what has worked for others and the pitfalls to be avoided (such as the intensive demands on computer memory required to download large graphic, audio and video components of the materials, and e-assignments, which look like long e-mails (Ng, 1994; Rowntree, 1977).

Since the flexibility of Web delivery is not only a result of the level of dialogue possible between lecturer and student but also of the level of interconnections possible between students, effective use of hypertext links and hyperarchiving is an important feature of the final course product (Cheek, Cook, and Rudge, 1995). The possibility of bringing together electronically the living and breathing experts of the World Futures Studies Federation for dialogue and critical reflection with the enrolled student body is also a uniquely vital component of Web-based study.

The e-mail and hypertext archive facilities built into the course design also serve to promote both interaction (between people) and interactivity (between individuals and electronic resources). By its nature, the Web is a democratic environment with the extent and pace of interaction and interactivity being determined by each individual learner (Rice, 1995). To some degree the development of students' writing skills (whether on line or off line) can be enhanced by providing a structured format that necessitates student contributions to electronic discussion throughout the course. Practice in writing is thus gained by measured steps in a collaborative and inspirational context.

The major weaknesses identified in the use of the Web for course delivery centered around the technical difficulties and equity issues for students establishing connectivity. A further concern was the question of whether the university server would be reliable enough to handle increasing volumes of traffic as a result of its developing international presence on the Web.

Learning Design and Delivery

The key issue in this area involved assessment and what can be called "elsewhere learning."

Assessment

Assessment had to be developed with an emphasis on interactivity in order to reflect the more collegial nature of networked learning. There are three assessments, each of about 2,500 words. The first is a more-or-less standard theory piece and the second is an attempt at interactive peer assessment, with each student distilling his or her e-mail contributions into a 2,500-word paper. No outside referencing is required or sought, and the lecturer's opinion is given only after the students have collectively come to a grade. The third assessment allows the student to focus directly on his or her work environment by applying the lessons learned from the previous two modules. This assignment is where the student professionally focuses his or her work into a vocationally relevant area.

The unit also offers students access to an editorial panel to review their papers (one of the three assessments) and help them to prepare them to a conference-presentation standard. These can also be published in the Futures Studies Monograph series. One mature student who took advantage of this opportunity had her externally critiqued and rewritten assignment accepted (her first ever) for a WFSF conference held in Brisbane. For her presentation, she drew strongly from the work of Dr. Wendy Schultz, only to find Dr. Schultz in the audience. Such is futures synchronicity.

Elsewhere Learning

The multimedia "elsewhere learning" format of WWW was chosen because it is technologically mediated. As such, it can handle many interactive users simultaneously—many-to-many. It is time- and place-independent, and interactive. This may be compared with conventional distance education, which is hard-copy mediated—one-to-many, and time- and place-independent. Finally, the traditional "classroom teaching" approach of face-to-face lecturers is unmediated, with medium interactivity—one-to-many, and time- and place-dependent.

PEDAGOGICAL INSIGHTS AND REFLECTIONS

We need to remember that the traditional "chalk 'n talk" classroom educational environment was developed centuries before the technologies of today (including print) were even considered possible. Many of us are familiar with the concept of replicating existing educational environments through the use of alternate technologies. It is not uncommon when discussing the use of technology to hear people say that we need to make it as much like the "real" situation as possible. Some firmly believe this is essential for success, others take a different point of view.

The use of technology may extend interaction, provide a variety of delivery options, improve student access, and encourage learning, but it is imperative that it be transparent, easy to use, and well managed. The Internet, for example, offers an opportunity to deliver courses globally. It also raises quality-assurance issues. How is quality maintained if there is little content-validation process or instructional design input (Wildman and Inayatullah, 1996)? How can institutions undertake their copyright responsibilities if staff can release materials directly to the Net without a vetting process? What of the instructional quality of the material? Technology, while a powerful tool, if poorly managed has the propensity to erode the standards being achieved in education and, in particular, distance education today.

The following are some key pedagogical issues that arose during the development and running of the course.

Orality Versus Literacy

Over 90 percent of the world's cultures are oral, typically using symbolic systems of meaning-making, such as myth, song, and dance (Ong, 1982). Early versions of the Internet that were entirely text- and ASCII-based offered little opportunity to embrace, celebrate, and maintain this cultural diversity. Thus, nontextual cultures faced, and still face, an uncertain future. Inclusion of multimedia capacity in Web platforms such as Internet Explorer and Netscape do offer an opportunity, albeit a small and technologically complex one, to include symbolic logic and not only linear logic. This is an example of the tension between noetic and poetic realms of meaning (Campbell, 1988; Phenix, 1964).

In today's society, with its predominant Western positivist scientific and technological imperatives, there is an enormous danger that culturally diverse discourses will be lost to the dominant rational textuality of Western English. This also calls to mind the postmodern critique that today power is manifest as the language the world. One may well ask, whose language? Whose world? How is this languaging occurring?

Maintaining Content Authenticity in a Turbulent Medium of Media

Multimedia-based interactive learning changes certain things forever:

- the style of education from "classroom teaching" to "elsewhere learning."
- the mode of teaching from "sage on the stage" to "guide by the side."
- the roles of student and lecturer into coauthors as they use interactive communication modes.
- the power relationship between lecturer and student as assessments and feedback are made available to all participants.

In the midst of these challenges, and with new ones being presented every day, course content, veracity, and authenticity can be overlooked in the multitude of details and potentials of the medium of media. The role of the lecturer, now as learning coach, can easily get lost in all the arcaneia of academia, on the one hand, and "html" on the other—getting the latest blink on a variable colored screen. The course has to actually say something beyond the on-screen flashing buttons.

In many ways the traditional roles of lecturer, student, and class have become institutionalized as "sacred," as if learning is only allowed in a fixed way in order to maintain stability in a changing society. In this regard, academics have a special responsibility to represent text fairly in context and critically to direct it, through interaction with the learners, toward an ethical outcome. This requires earnest endeavor, diligent application to the task, strategic questioning, provocation, critical thinking, professional praxis, and personal attention to the needs and capacities of each student. Clearly not every student is the same and thus the course overall needs to respond affirmatively to the fact of different student learning styles.

Reflections on Maintaining Student Presence in an "Ever Opening" Text

In producing a hypertext, we, as first authors—for in hypertext, readers are also overtly authors—found ourselves confronting a number of dilemmas. The main dilemma for us initially was to grapple with the fact that in producing what we hoped would be "open," flexible, and relatively unstructured learning and teaching materials we, in fact, had to be extremely structured in our approach to the development of the actual hypertext. We confronted, for instance, the need to provide for management of individualized reading pathways, vertically, horizontally, or diagonally through the text, by writing screen-sized paragraphs, individually titled. However, the very act of creating a title for a specific piece of text meant that in some ways we were creating closure with that title and the associated "hot links" that direct the reader to other sources.

Similarly, to cater to intratextual leaps in the hypertext (reader selected), the author-optioned jumps across topics need to be located where ideas intersect. This technique may prevent total "free floating" inside hypertext. Thus, in the very desire to open text for reader self-direction, we found ourselves creating more and more techniques for both closure and the concealment of that closure. We were in danger of reestablishing and renaturalizing authorial control, with the presence of the reader again reduced to the position we had constructed within the hypertext.

Changing the Locus of Authenticity

As the technology available through the WWW becomes more multimedia oriented, the student may well be challenged by seeing the point of credibility as the screen and the technology to mark up, do Web searches, load graphics, and so on. In this sense, the "locus of authenticity" moves from the text to the technology for accessing the text, from the message to the medium.

From Information Highway to Songlines in the Morphogenic Web

Some concern has been expressed at the internet metaphor of the information highway (IH). This suggests it may be "memed" with the same inherent problems of physical highways; for example, simply going from two to four to six lanes as demand requires without considering alternatives. Here, information is seen as many still see highways, as an unqualified social "good" (Judge, 1998). This overly positive view of information comes from the way the IH links to science, where information becomes deified as "objective." If information is so good, more information must be even better. As H. G. Wells (1994) said in the mid-1930's, how will all this help prevent the continuing fragmentation in meaning? How will this contribute to the emergence of a global consciousness, a world mind that is collective and diverse rather than centralized and conformist? How will we maintain criticality and resist the textual and multimedia pull of education toward infotainment, edutainment, and concept tourism?

For us, the issue is not one of highway travel, with its better and bigger cars and wider and wider highways. Rather, it is the ability to ask, "Travel for what?" Possibly a more relevant myth or metaphor may be "songlines of meaning" in our morphogenic fields (Judge, 1998).

FROM "SAGE ON STAGE" TO "MUTUAL MAGIC"

If used in the sense discussed here, the Web offers great opportunity for networked and cogenerative learning. As one moves to cogenerative learning, where students and lecturer cogenerate the pedagogical materials, the traditional "power over" of the lecturer dissolves and becomes more "power with" the students. For instance, students in the futures studies course contribute personal details to the geographic roll, the on-line discussion with authors and others interested in futures issues via a hyperarchiving bulletin board, adding their comments on readings and agreeing to have their assignment marked-up, including the lecturer's comments thereon, and peer assessment (note that actual marks remain private, between the lecturer and student). In these ways, we move from the sage-type expert "teaching" the students to a learning coach facilitating mutual learning, a sort of "mutual magic." The "footprints" of the students emerge clearly in the learning processes and materials.

Evaluation: Course and Peer Review

Evaluation feedback questionnaires were developed for the following:

- Course content.
- Learning facilitation (a modification of an existing form).
- Webbing (designed to assess the use students made of the Web, its usability, and technical backup).

Evaluations have generally been positive, with key recommendations emerging for on-line technical assistance in setup and easier assignment submission processes. These recommendations have been put in place.

NEXT STEPS

Unit development based on student feedback and Web-browser developments for the units next offering include the following:

- Networking between universities and organizations internationally to provide an international master's in futures studies.
- Interlinking between my consultancies so that credit for a futures study course and university learning will be strengthened.

- Student contributions to the course to date will remain available to succeeding generations of students in order to enhance the unit's cogenerative learning context.
- Matching of the futures studies course with two independent study units and a two-unit thesis gives five units out of an eight-unit master's so that futures studies has now been developed into a master's specialization option within the existing master's program.

CONCLUSIONS

We live in an age when educational and information technologies are afforded so much status that the knowledge they convey can be seen as secondary to the technical feats used to convey that knowledge. In such an age, it is easy for educators to become seduced by technical wizardry without ever pausing to consider whether such magic is necessarily "good," "innovative," "desirable," or for the equitable betterment of the learning process and the promotion of each student's active participation in learning. Yet learning innovations must also be more than merely packaging old material in new and visually exciting electronic ways. There must be sound pedagogical reasons for the innovation.

This chapter has provided a review of the development of a World Wide Web–based futures studies course and its links to my consultancy processes. Such learning processes can feed forward into my consultancies and also allow master's students to take the benefits of such interaction to their workplaces, where they may become the "mentors" of future-oriented networked learning in their organizations. Over the two years of the course so far, the number of students has doubled. Simultaneously, an increasing number of organizations are becoming interested in adding a "futures dimension" to their operations. Consequently, in Australia I would argue that it is possible to teach and consult in futures creatively. Indeed, an increasing number of students are interested in doing just that. I hope that publications such as this book will also enhance this trend.

ACKNOWLEGMENTS

This chapter was developed with the input of Sohail Inayaullah and extends an article I developed in 1996 for David Hicks.

REFERENCES

Campbell, J. (1988). *The power of myth*. New York: Doubleday.

Cheek, J., Cook, J., and Rudge, T. (Eds.). (1995). *Hypertext: Issues in blending tradition and technology to optimise the "present" reader*. Canberra, Act: Higher Education and Research Development Society of Australia.

Dator, J. (1990). It's only a paper moon. *Futures, 22*, 1084–1101.

Judge, A. (1998). From information highways to songlines of the noosphere. *Futures, 30*, 181–188.

Mason, R., and Kaye, A. (Eds.). (1989). *Mindweave*. Oxford: Pergamon Press.

Ng, J. (1994). *Distance learning using a multimedia network system*. Unpublished honours thesis, Curtin University of Technology, Perth, Australia.

Ong, W. (1982). *Orality and literacy: The technologisation of the world*. London: Methuen.

Phenix, P. (1964). *Realms of meaning: A philosophy of the curriculum for general education*. New York: McGraw-Hill.

Rice, M. (1995). Constraints on the use of computer mediated communication to facilitate learning. In *Proceedings of 1995 Access through Open Learning Conference (ATOL)*. Lismore, Australia: Norsearch.

Rowntree, D. (1977). *Assessing students: How shall we know them?* London: Harper and Row.

Wells, H. G. (1994). *World brain: H. G. Wells on the future of world education*. London: Adamantine. (Original work published in 1938).

Wildman, P., and Inayatullah, S. (1996). Ways of knowing and the pedagogies of the future. *Futures, 28*, 723–740.

23

Postmodern Education:
A Futures Perspective

David Hicks

My interest in futures is a long-standing one arising out of my work, which is mainly, but not entirely, with practicing teachers and students training to be teachers. This focus on education in schools puts a particular slant on my futures work. In essence, I am interested in how to help busy teachers and their pupils think more critically and creatively about the future and the appropriate research needed to support this (Hicks, 1998b).

THEORIZING EDUCATION

In her account of contemporary political ideas, Goodwin (1987) highlights the notion of competing ideologies; that is, "a doctrine about the right way, or ideal way, of organizing society and conducting politics, based on wider considerations about the nature of human life and knowledge" (p. 27). This notion of ideology lies at the heart of the human endeavor, which can, of course, never be "value-free." Education is therefore contested territory and philosophers and educators have long debated the various purposes of education. Kemmis, Cole, and Suggett (1983) have accordingly identified three differing metaorientations within education: the vocational–neoclassical, the liberal–progressive, and the socially critical. Each perspective or ideology makes fundamentally different assumptions about the nature of

knowledge, the purposes of education, the role of the school, and the organization of teaching and learning itself.

Those educators who are concerned about the turbulent nature of national
and global change today will often take a socially critical perspective. They
believe that education has a crucial role to play in challenging rather than
reproducing existing societal inequalities by preparing students to participate in social, political, economic, and environmental activities as active
and responsible citizens. Richardson (1990) suggests that this involves the
weaving together of two educational traditions:

> The one tradition is concerned with learner-centred education and the development
> and fulfillment of individuals. This tradition is humanistic and optimistic, and has a
> basic trust in the capacity and will of human beings to create healthy and empower-
> ing systems and structures. . . . The second tradition is concerned with building
> equality, and with resisting the trend for education to reflect and replicate inequalities in
> wider society of race, gender and class. . . . Both traditions are concerned with whole-
> ness and holistic thinking, but neither, arguably, is complete without the other. There
> cannot be wholeness in individuals independently of strenuous attempts to heal rifts
> and contradictions in wider society and in the education system. (pp. 6–7)

Socially critical education is thus about changing both self and society.
Such a perspective is taken by many educators today, including environmental educators (e.g., Fien, 1993; Huckle and Sterling, 1996), global educators (Selby and Pike, 1996), and futures educators (Tough and Rogers,
1996; Hicks, 1994).

More broadly, such educators have also commented on the differing roles
that education plays under modernity and in postmodern society. Writers
such as Bowers (1993) have highlighted the ways in which modern education has helped reify Enlightenment beliefs and values, which, together
with scientism and capitalist economics, have resulted in widespread ecologically unsustainable practices. On this, Orr (1992) writes, "Education in
the modern world was designed to further the conquest of nature and the
industrialisation of the planet. It tended to produce unbalanced, under-
dimensioned people tailored to fit the modern economy. Postmodern education must have a different agenda, one designed to heal, connect, liberate,
empower, create, and celebrate" (p. x).

The scope of futures studies has been well mapped out by Bell (1997),
Slaughter (1996), and others while Inayatullah (1993) has argued that the field
"largely straddles two dominant modes of knowledge—the technical concerned
with predicting the future and the humanist concerned with developing a
good society." For futures educators working with a socially critical perspective, it is the latter mode that is of the most interest. Dator (1996) thus
argues that helping people clarify the nature of their preferable futures and ways
of working toward these is at the heart of futures studies. Teachers have periodically been interested in such matters for at least the last twenty-five years.

Toffler's (1974) *Learning for Tomorrow* was one of the early texts that alerted educators to the exciting range of possibilities in the classroom. Fitch and Svengalis (1979) provided an historic resource in *Futures Unlimited: Teaching about Worlds to Come*, which drew extensively on the insights of futurists but interpreted them in a way that was accessible to classroom teachers. Riley's (1989) more recent *Toward Tomorrow* and Beare and Slaughter's (1993) *Education for the Twenty-First Century* have shown what good writing by futures educators should look like. The increasing recognition that a futures perspective is vital at all levels of education is born witness to by the 1998 *World Yearbook of Education*, which has as its focus futures education (Hicks and Slaughter, 1998). Futures education today then is an international concern manifesting differently in different national contexts. Sometimes this is as a specific subject within the school curriculum, as in Queensland (Hicks and Holden, 1995), but more often it is seen as a dimension within the curriculum itself (Hicks and Slaughter, 1998).

THEORIZING SOCIAL CHANGE

In dealing with a range of global and futures-related issues, educators have clearly had to theorize about social change, but in a way that is accessible to busy teachers. It is this latter concern, I think, that makes such theorizing a fundamentally different proposition to the work of social scientists per se. In my own work I draw on three different but overlapping notions.

One model that has been used by socially critical educators is that proposed by Milbrath (1989) on changing worldviews or belief paradigms. This grew out of previous cross-national attitude surveys that he had been involved with during the 1980s. These seemed to show that people's attitudes and values over a wide range of issues could be related to two quite different sociocultural paradigms: "[The] study provided solid evidence that a new paradigm is emerging which differs significantly from the dominant social paradigm. This emerging paradigm is being developed by environmentally oriented thinkers who constitute a kind of vanguard. They advocate a new set of beliefs and values that people have begun referring to as a new environmental paradigm" (p. 118).

The dominant social paradigm (DSP) typifies the Western worldview of the last 300 years, with its emphasis on economic growth over environmental protection, a belief that there are no limits to growth and that basically present society is working reasonably well. The emerging new environmental paradigm (NEP), on the other hand, puts a higher value on environmental protection and appreciates that there must be limits to growth and that this requires transformation to a more ecologically sustainable society.

The hazards of modernity are now well recognized (Giddens, 1990) and Milbrath (1989) quotes Berry (1988) to support his notion of competing paradigms: "It's all a question of story. We are in trouble just now because we do not have a good story. We are between stories. The old story—the account of how the world came to be and how we fit into it—is not functioning properly, and we have not learned the New Story" (p. 123).

While running the risk of oversimplifying the nature of social change, the idea of shifting worldviews or belief paradigms is a useful one. Busy teachers, who are primarily concerned with their daily classroom practice, do find this a useful device for beginning to look at values debates in society today.

This brings us to more complex theories of social change, which hinge around the notions of modernity and postmodernity (e.g., Harvey, 1990; Kumar, 1995). Since, by definition, socially critical educators have much to say about both social and educational change, it is not surprising that those working in higher education—but much less so those in schools—have a keen interest in debates about the nature of postmodern society (Usher and Edwards, 1994).

Such debates are complex, but, in essence, as Walker (1996) argues, they relate to three interrelated dimensions of the modern world: postmodernity as a temporal epoch, as a cultural style, and as a method of analysis. Most commonly the latter takes the form of deconstructive postmodernism; that is, distrust of the great metanarratives of modernity, such as science, Marxism, or Christianity, seen no longer as repositories of any final truth about the human condition. Whilst it is surely necessary to deconstruct the myths-story of modernity, since it has led to enormous global progress and enormous suffering, this leaves us, as Thomas Berry (1988) commented, "between stories." It is little wonder that we approached the year 2000 full of doubts and uncertainties, if not fears, about the future (Jacobs, 1996).

Anxiety is neither a good basis for learning nor for leading a fulfilling life. Whilst it may be analytically helpful, my undergraduates and teachers find deconstructive postmodernism of little practical help to them in their personal and professional lives. However, several commentators (Rosenau, 1992; Walker, 1996) also recognize a variant known as constructive or revisionary postmodernism. This, by contrast, attempts to extract us from the relativism of much postmodern thinking by arguing that positive sociocultural initiatives do exist that must now be built on to create a new and more equitable "story." "Going beyond the modern world will involve transcending its individualism, anthropocentrism, patriarchy, mechanisation, economism, consumerism, nationalism and militarism. Constructive postmodern thought provides support for the ecology, peace, feminist, and other emancipatory movements of our time, while stressing that the inclusive emancipation must be from modernity itself" (Griffin, 1988, p. xi).

Finally, that there is some evidence of social change in the direction that revisionary postmodernists would welcome, is indicated by the work of Inglehart (1990) described in his *Culture Shift in Advanced Industrial Society*. This reports on longer-term social surveys that show a shift from what

Inglehart calls materialist to postmaterialist values during the 1970s and 1980s; that is, a growing emphasis on the quality of life and self-expression accompanied by a decline in traditional political, religious, moral, and social norms. This is further supported by his more recent work (Inglehart, 1997).

ENVISIONING PREFERABLE FUTURES

Having taught about global and futures-related issues to pupils, under-graduates, and teachers for many years, I am very aware of how dispiriting this endeavor can be unless handled carefully. To learn only about the prob-lems of environment and development, for example, is to invite despair. Clearly we need to know about the nature of the problems we face and their possible causes and interrelationships, but this on its own can lead to feel-ings of hopelessness and "psychic numbing" (Staub and Green, 1992). These pedagogical complexities have been well illustrated by Tough and Rogers (1996), who show that an effective learning process in this context involves cognitive, affective, existential, and action elements. Above all else, it is clear that humans need some vision of wider goals to provide hope and a sense of purpose in difficult times.

My own recent research has therefore focused on three related areas: young people's hopes and fears for the future, how undergraduates and educators envision their preferable futures, and the sources of hope that educators draw on in postmodern times. The literature on young people's views of the future is scattered, but increasingly a focus of attention for futures educators. My own work with seven- to eighteen-year-olds in the United Kingdom, using questionnaires and interviews, looked in particular at what their hopes and fears were in relation to personal, local, and global futures (Hicks and Holden, 1995; Hicks, 1996a). We were also interested as educators in how this differed depending on age and gender.

We found that hopes and fears were often mirror images of each other. Their fear was that something bad would occur, their hope was that it wouldn't. What they wanted overall in their personal lives, in order of importance, was a good job, a good life, a good relationship, and to do well at school. In their local communities they wanted less pollution of the envi-ronment, better amenities and services for young people, no crime, and greater prosperity. Globally they wanted no more wars, no pollution, no poverty or starvation, and better relationships between countries. While this list is a little terse, it nevertheless indicates how aware young people are of local and global issues, and what their preferences for the future are. Sadly, most commented that they had learned very little about these matters in school, although they would very much like to.

Some of the sharpest insights about young people's preferred futures has come from the work of Hutchinson (1996) with secondary school pupils in Australia. Whilst their probable futures were often pessimistic and despairing, most of their preferable futures show a great sense of vision. Hutchinson was thus able to identify the following broad categories:

- Technocratic dreaming: an uncritical acceptance of techno-fix solutions for all problems (especially popular with boys).
- Demilitarization and greening of science and technology to meet genuine human needs.
- Intergenerational equity: accepting responsibility for the needs of future generations.
- Making peace with people and planet via a reconceptualization of both ethics and lifestyles.

Variations on these four preferred futures were often described in great detail, although again pupils had not necessarily learned anything about such matters at school.

My own work on preferred futures was prompted by Elise Boulding's (1994) long experience of running futures workshops in the 1970s and 1980s. In these she used a process of individual visualization to help participants access images of their desirable futures. In describing the outcomes of innumerable workshops, she noted the existence of what she called a "baseline" societal future; that is, common features that turned up in nearly every envisioning experience, whatever the type of group. These were men and women working together, no age segregation, racially mixed communities, learning taking place "on the job," nonhierarchical, local growing of food, low-profile technology, and people operating out of a different sense of social awareness.

My own findings from running similar workshops with both undergraduates (Hicks, 1996b) and educators (Hicks, 1998a) broadly endorse this notion of a baseline future. The undergraduates that I worked with, many of whom had made no special study of global issues and who were given no guidance on possible workshop outcomes, identified the following as key components of their individual preferred futures:

- Green: clean air and water, trees, wildlife, flowers.
- Convivial: cooperative, happy, relaxed, caring, laughter.
- Transport: no cars or pollution, public transport, bikes.
- Peaceful: no violent conflict, security, global harmony.
- Equality: fair shares for all, no poverty, no hunger.
- Community: sense of, local, small, simple, friendly.
- Justice: equal rights for people and planet, no discrimination.

To cynics and the disillusioned, such visions are seen as "unrealistic" and fanciful. However, all the preferred futures identified in the research mentioned here seem to support and reinforce each other. What they may represent is a wider and deeper—but often unconscious—need for a more just, sustainable, and human-scale society than most of us experience in the industrialized world today. In that respect these preferred futures may be seen as the submerged dreams of revisionary postmodernism and part of the driving force leading toward the postmaterialist values noted by Inglehart (1990, 1997).

PRINCIPLES INTO PRACTICE

My own work at Bath Spa University College has three main components: initial teacher education, contributing to a global futures B.S. degree, and research and publications. Most of my writing over the years has been directed at teachers and student teachers, showing, first and foremost, how global and futures issues can be taught in primary and secondary classrooms. This is where teachers most need advice and, if they are given practical support here, they will then also take on wider issues about curriculum and educational change.

All students training to be teachers at the college take three compulsory half-modules on futures education, environmental education, and intercultural education. Since the first two are my responsibility, I am able to share my interests and enthusiasm with them in both visionary and practical ways. They often comment that these modules provide an important foil to the traditional subjects that they spend most of their time studying. Outside college I have contributed to the current debate among geographical educators about what their subject can contribute to education for the twenty-first century (Hicks, 1998c). There are few self-professed futures educators in the United Kingdom, so there are always opportunities for in-service and consultancy work.

The Faculty of Applied Sciences also offers a B.S. in global futures. This focuses on a range of global issues, particularly those to do with environment and development, and explores debates about the nature of sustainable development. I contribute the futures element to this course, drawing very much on the work of the futurists and others cited in this chapter. Each year the second-year students stay for a week at the Centre for Alternative Technology in mid-Wales, where they participate in workshops on renewable energy sources, organic horticulture, reed-bed sewage systems, and sustainable living. Most find this a fascinating and thought-provoking experience (Hicks and Bord, 1994).

As described, much of my research has been oriented toward exploration of people's preferred futures. Most recently, however, I have become interested in the sources of hope that socially committed educators draw on in their work. To teach regularly about global and futures issues, whether the environment, human rights, or peace and conflict, can potentially be a depressive business. Since education in the United Kingdom has also been in

Conservative-induced turmoil for some time, many educators often feel harassed and under stress. The research process, which combined interviews, autobiographical writing, and a focus group, was itself identified as a source of inspiration by participants (Hicks, 1998a). They commented on the need to build "communities of hope" in troubled times and the crucial role that education can play in this endeavor (Freire, 1994; Richardson, 1996). Among the sources of hope that they identified in their lives were the following:

- Human creativity: individual and communal; music, song, and dance; painting and sculpture; utopias; books, stories, and poetry.
- The natural world: constancy in nature; rebirth in the land; continuity and timelessness; the season; animals; regeneration.
- Collective struggles: for justice; solidarity; people who suffered or died for a cause; networking and activism; people working together.
- Other people's lives: amazing people; those who do their own thing; children, now and in the future; heroes.
- Relationships: families, friends, and loved ones; gifts given by them; all those who support us.
- Faith and belief: religious and spiritual traditions; the politics of daily life; new ideas.

Postmodern education from a futures perspective requires that we teach in a spirit of hope and optimism. There is crucial work to be done in our schools, and the futures field provides a rich reservoir of innovative ideas for all educators. Richardson (1996) comments, "A map without utopia on it, it has been said, is not worth consulting. Yes, but it matters what sort of place the utopia is, and what sort of linkages it has with reality, and the kinds of path and route back to reality which it emboldens and clears. A utopian vision should help us to grapple with the realities we know, and try to change them and improve them" (p. 51). If all education is for the future, then surely exploration of the future needs to play a more central role in education.

REFERENCES

Beare, H., and Slaughter, R. (1993). *Education for the twenty-first century*. London: Routledge.

Bell, W. (1997). *Foundations of futures studies* (2 vols.). New Brunswick, NJ: Transaction.

Berry, T. (1988). *The dream of the Earth*. San Francisco: Sierra Club Books.

Boulding, E. (1994). Image and action in peace building. In D. Hicks (Ed.), *Preparing for the future: Notes & queries for concerned educators* (pp. 61–84). London: Adamantine.

Bowers, C. A. (1993). *Education, cultural myths and the ecological crisis*. Albany: State University of New York Press.

Dator, J. (1996). Futures studies as applied knowledge. In R. Slaughter (Ed.), *New thinking for a new millennium* (pp. 105–115). London: Routledge.

Fien, J. (1993). *Education for the environment: Critical curriculum theorising and environmental education*. Geelong, Australia: Deakin University Press.

Fitch, R., and Svengalis, C. (1979). *Futures unlimited: Teaching about worlds to come* (Bulletin 59). Washington, DC: National Council for the Social Studies.

Freire, P. (1994). *Pedagogy of hope*. New York: Continuum.

Giddens, A. (1990). *The consequences of modernity*. Cambridge: Polity Press

Goodwin, B. (1987). *Using political ideas*. Chichester: John Wiley.

Griffin, D. (1988). *The reenchantment of science*. Albany: State University of New York Press.

Harvey, D. (1990). *The condition of postmodernity*. Oxford: Blackwell.

Hicks, D. (1994). *Educating for the future: A practical classroom guide*. Godalming, UK: World Wide Fund for Nature.

Hicks, D. (1996a). A lesson for the future: Young people's hopes and fears for tomorrow. *Futures, 28*, 1–13.

Hicks, D. (1996b). Retrieving the dream: How students envision their preferable futures. *Futures, 28*, 741–749.

Hicks, D. (1998a). Always coming home: Towards an archaeology of the future. *Futures, 30*, 463–474.

Hicks, D. (1998b). Educating for sustainable futures. In S. Inayatullah (Ed.), *The knowledge base of futures studies* (vol. 4). Hawthorn, Australia: DDM Media Group.

Hicks, D. (1998c). Geography and the future. In R. Carter (Ed.), *The primary handbook*. Sheffield, UK: Geographical Association.

Hicks, D., and Bord, A. (1994). Visions of the future: Student responses to ecological living. *Westminster Studies in Education, 17*, 63–69.

Hicks, D., and Holden, C. (1995). *Visions of the future: Why we need to teach for tomorrow*. Stoke-on-Trent, UK: Trentham Books.

Hicks, D., and Slaughter, R. (Eds.). (1998). *Futures education: World yearbook of education 1998*. London: Kogan Page.

Huckle, J., and Sterling, S. (Eds.). (1996). *Education for sustainability*. London: Earthscan.

Hutchinson, F. (1996). *Educating beyond violent futures*. London: Routledge.

Inayatullah, S. (1993). From "who am I?" to "when am I?" *Futures, 25*, 235–253.

Inglehart, R. (1990). *Culture shift in advanced industrial society*. Princeton, NJ: Princeton University Press.

Inglehart, R. (1997). *Modernization and postmodernization: Cultural, economic and political change in 43 societies*. Princeton, NJ: Princeton University Press.

Jacobs, M. (1996). *Politics of the real world*. London: Earthscan.

Kemmis, S., Cole, P., and Suggett, D. (1983). *Orientations to curriculum and transition*. Melbourne: Victorian Institute for Secondary Education.

Kumar, K. (1995). *From post-industrial to post-modern society*. Oxford: Blackwell.

Milbrath, L. (1989). *Envisioning a sustainable society*. Albany: State University of New York Press.

Orr, D. (1992). *Ecological literacy: Education and the transition to a postmodern world*. Albany: State University of New York Press.

Richardson, R. (1990). *Daring to be a teacher*. Stoke-on-Trent, UK: Trentham Books.

Richardson, R. (1996). *Fortunes and fables: Education for hope in troubled times.* Stoke-on-Trent, UK: Trentham Books.

Riley, K. (1989). *Toward tomorrow.* New York: Scholastic.

Rosenau, P. M. (1992). *Post-modernism and the social sciences.* Princeton, NJ: Princeton University Press.

Selby, D., and Pike, G. (1996). *Reconnections: From national to global curriculum.* Godalming, UK: World Wide Fund for Nature.

Slaughter, R. (Ed.). (1996). *The knowledge base of futures studies* (3 vols.). Hawthorne, Australia: DDM Media Group.

Staub, S., and Green, P. (1992). *Psychology and social responsibility.* New York: New York University Press.

Toffler, A. (1974). *Learning for tomorrow: The role of the future in education.* New York: Vintage Books.

Tough, A., and Rogers, M. (1996). Facing the future is not for wimps. *Futures, 28,* 491–496.

Usher, R., and Edwards, R. (1994). *Postmodernism and education.* London: Routledge.

Walker, J. T. (1996). Postmodernism and the study of the future. *Futures Research Quarterly, 12* (20), 51–70.

24

Visionary Futures: Guided Cognitive Imagery in Teaching and Learning about the Future

Oliver W. Markley

The overall thrust of my teaching and professional writing has been about equally focused on (1) general futures research methodology (i.e., how to discern formative trends, issues, and alternative futures, and how to use them for various types of clients), and (2) normative forecasting (i.e., the visualization of futures that are highly preferable, even if not highly probable). A position paper summarizing the first focus is "Explaining and Implementing Futures Research" (Markley, 1989). One summarizing the second is "Global Consciousness: An Alternative Future of Choice" (Markley, 1996).

But probably my most important contribution as an educator has been in the use of creativity, visualization, and guided cognitive imagery. This came about due to a pivotal event early in my career as a futurist, when as a fresh postdoc hired by Willis Harman to lead methodology development at the new futures research think tank we were creating at the Stanford Research Institute (SRI, now SRI International), I got my first taste of professional paradigm change.

The pivotal event was this: In 1970, after about eighteen months of intensive research to generate as many internally and sequentially plausible alternative future "histories" as we could derive from the existing literature of utopias, dystopias, science fiction scenarios, and so on, and from our own unique qualitative modeling method (Harman, Markley, and Rhyne, 1973), our first major results indicated that of some fifty of the most highly plausible alternative future histories for society, only a handful were by any stretch of the imagination desirable, and most of them involved deep-seated transformation of underlying attitudes, images, and policies in response to problems involving overpopulation, resource depletion, pollution, dangerous weapons buildups, and so on. Harman (1969, 1979) dubbed all of these "The World Macroproblem."

With my methodological responsibilities in mind, I, in turn, reasoned that research methods based on rational or analytic modes of thinking are, in principle, not suitable for creative exploration of transformational alternative futures because such thinking modes are more or less simply mechanistic extrapolations of what has gone on before. Instead, we needed to develop methods that would rely on *intuition*, both as a way to discern how various alternative futures might "work" even though based on a different cultural paradigm than the one now dominant, and as a way to guide exploration of preferable future possibilities.

A search of the literature and professional practices of cognitive, humanistic, and transpersonal psychologists and workshop leaders, as well as those of other practitioners using tools and processes for accessing intuition, led to the conclusion that the most appropriate technology for this purpose was that of "visual thinking" and "guided cognitive imagery." Early research studies at SRI actually using this approach as a formal technique include the pioneering SRI studies "Contemporary Societal Problems" (Markley, Curry, and Link, 1971), and "Societal Consequences of Changing Images of Man" (Markley and Harman, 1982), the first known study to formally attempt the use of Kuhnian "paradigm" concepts in connection with the whole human society, not just scientific communities.[1]

TWO SETS OF GUIDED COGNITIVE IMAGERY PROCESSES

Over the past twenty-five years I have used many different visioning and guided cognitive imagery exercises with audiences of all ages and sectors of society, but particularly with corporate managers and professionals and in a graduate-level course at the University of Houston, Clear Lake called "Visionary Futures." However, I have thus far published only two approaches to the use of guided imagery methods, choosing to put forward only those that have proven to be the most robust for practical purposes and ethically appropriate in that they are relatively unsusceptible to misuse either due to incompetence or manipulative intent. Each of the approaches and methods described here are based on well-tested scripts that can be read "as is" or adapted by reasonably skilled facilitators who wish to use them.

A Virtual Time-Travel Method for Visionary Futures Exploration

One approach is especially useful with audiences that have little or no background with either futures studies or visualization exercises. It involves an imaginary "time-travel" journey in which the participant envisions living in a number of scenes involving different culturally specific locations, both past and future. After being guided to experience the sensory inputs appropriate to each scene (as if actually living there), the participant considers one or more questions that trigger intuitive knowledge relating to a specific theme of interest. For example, in the published versions of this exercise (Markley, 1994; Markley and Burchsted, 1997), the theme is "experiencing the needs of future generations," and the sequence of scenes and illustrative questions is as follows.

The Nomadic Era

The exercise begins with an imaginary journey back to the nomadic era, in which a tribe is facing climate changes that are diminishing their food supply. The participants are asked to imagine what it would feel like to be a member of the tribe faced with these types of changes. They are asked to explore such questions as "How do people in your tribe deal with problems that threaten your future? What do they do to find the answers they need?"

Transition to Industrialism and Urbanization

In scene two of the exercise the participants travel forward to a different historical era, when the impacts of colonialism are being felt in many parts of the world and traditional indigenous village life is giving way to industrialized society. They are to imagine themselves as village elders and from the perspective of what they as elders most deeply value to search for answers to questions such as, "What needs to happen in order that future generations will be able to live by the traditional values of our people, should they choose to do so?"

The Short-Range Future

The "daydream" then shifts one generation, or twenty to thirty years into the future. Participants are asked to imagine having tuned into a "virtual reality" TV show that summarized the big events of the year (twenty-five years in the future) and to consider questions such as, "What progress has been made in dealing with problems such as growth in population, pollution, and so forth? What is now possible due to new technologies? What do people find important when they consider these types of problems?"

The Long-Range Future and Very Long-Range Future

The virtual time traveler next journeys 200 years, or about eight generations; and then very far ahead, to some 2,500 years or 100 generations into the future. In each, participants are asked to consider some important questions. For example, "How would you describe what the quality of life is like here? What actions by previous generations caused things to turn out this way? How do people in this time and place go about guiding the society?"

Scanning our History for Patterns

The imagistic daydream concludes with a quick review of all the historical time periods—past and future—that were visited during the journey. As the participants scan across them, they are asked to get a sense of what was common and what was different in each; to answer questions such as, "What things stood out for you as most important?" Finally, given what they had seen about human history, both past and future, participants are asked, "If you could send a message from the future back to the present, so as to communicate what future generations most urgently need from us, what would that message be?"

Discussion

Depending on the purpose and nature of the audience, the filling out of a brief questionnaire and/or a period of loosely structured discussion follows the exercise, and this, of course, is where major learnings get crystallized. Because the exercise is such a gripping experience for many, however, it is sometimes difficult to focus discussion on the learnings to be derived from the simulation rather than on the "gee whiz" phenomena that were experienced. Nevertheless, the approach is a profound way to increase one's appreciation for the dynamics of history—past and future—and it is a particularly "appropriate technology" for visionary exploration of transformational futures by "newbies" to futures studies.

As evidence of this, graduate students in business administration and environmental management whose only exposure to futures thinking was this exercise have frequently reported it as being a professionally life-changing event due to the way it waked them up to the importance of reflecting on very long-range ecological concerns in their professional lives. Graduate students in studies of the future, on the other hand, tend to take their participation in the exercise much more in stride; it simply didn't show them that much that was new. For more on this, especially regarding results with adults and school children, please see Markley and Burchsted (1997, p. 717ff). The complete script and accompanying questionnaire for participants is available on the Internet at http://www.cl.uh.edu/futureweb/expfutgen.html, as well as in Markley (1994).

Four "Depth Intuition" Methods for Visionary Futures Exploration

A second approach to visionary futures exploration, learning, and teaching I have found quite useful is one that takes up where the first approach leaves off in terms of familiarity and skill required, both of the leader and of the participants. This "depth intuition" approach involves four discrete methods, each with detailed scripts for leaders, first published in the *Journal of Creative Behavior* (Markley, 1988) and subsequently reprinted as a chapter in *Source Book for Creative Problem-Solving: A Fifty Year Digest of Proven Innovation Processes* (Parnes, 1992). Depending on how they are adapted, these methods can be used separately or as a set, and are particular suitable for three broad classes of future-oriented applications: problem solving, policy analysis, and strategic planning, both personal and corporate.

Method One. Focusing on Current Concerns: A Procedure for Need Finding

This process is based on the "focusing" approach developed by psychologist Eugene Gendlin (1981). It employs a step-by-step approach for getting in touch with "What needs concern me right now?" or "What stands between me and feeling o.k. about . . . ?" The method, when successful, leads to a psychophysical "felt shift" (as in the "a-ha" moment, so emphasized in creativity work), involving bodily based feelings that precisely identify any focus of concern needing to be realized. Depending on how the method is used, it can help ascertain intrinsic values and motivations (i.e., "What I most deeply believe and care about") as against extrinsic ones ("What I think I should care about"); or it can be used to identify obstacles needing to be handled that stand in the way of attaining a desired objective (including those that are held "unconsciously"). It is important to note that much precision by way of results may not be possible until the method has been practiced sufficiently, because the psychophysical focusing skills it requires take practice to develop.

To illustrate how the method can be used, if a behavioral scientist desiring to begin a personal–experiential inquiry into futures studies were to use this method of "need finding," let us suppose that the thing that comes into focus is a "sense of challenge" rooted in the unknown requirements for successfully investigating a new professional and intellectual territory, particularly one that is fundamentally interdisciplinary and may even involve a new paradigm, as that term has come to be used.

One way of using the results of this approach is to go immediately into action. A preferred response is to use the results of Method One as input to Method Two.

Method Two. Revisioning Current Concerns:
A Procedure for Transforming Perceived Problems into Opportunities

This process is adapted from suggestions in the provocative book, *The Inner Guide Meditation*, by Edwin Steinbrecher (1978). In a way that reflects the insight, often attributed to Einstein, that "you cannot solve a problem at the level in which the problem is held," this procedure involves intuiting and exploring the essential meaning of a given problem situation as expressed in an appropriate symbolic form (which may be an image, a phrase, a metaphor, etc.). The "energy of higher consciousness" is then used to transform the symbolic representation from what feels like a problem into that which feels more like an opportunity. It is a most amazing process to experience, and one that not infrequently leads to creative solutions that were beyond reach to conceive beforehand.

To continue our example, our behavioral scientist might begin this method with the problem focus obtained in Method One, a sense of the challenge involved in learning to use new interdisciplinary concepts and tools of futures research. The symbolic representation he or she initially gets might be the image of a skull and crossbones, which upon investigation (using the exploratory questions asked by the guide that are part of the script) turns out to symbolize the fear of death of familiar, old discipline-based ways of working, which may have to give way if one is to expand and embrace new ways involving a different and unfamiliar paradigm. The transformation process of the method leads to a second image, that of a phoenix bird rising from flames, a traditional symbol of rebirth.[2] The exploratory questions asked by the guide about the new image lead to an experience of an invigorating sense of challenge at the thought of taking on something new and exciting, rather than feelings of dread at having to give up something old and dear. This is an illustration of "turning a problem into an opportunity."

As with Method One, one way of using the results of this approach is to go immediately into action. A preferred response is to use the results of both Methods One and Two as input to Method Three.

Method Three. Experiencing Alternative Futures I:
A Virtual Time-Travel Procedure for Assessment of Strategies

This process is based on a body of theory that, although highly relevant to the philosophy and practice of alternative futures research, is beyond the pale of what most futures researchers are willing to embrace because of its source: "channeled" material in the book *Seth Speaks*, by Jane Roberts

(1972). Although rather more complex than the simplistic summary given here, this process involves conceptually nothing more than first choosing two or more alternative policy options regarding some problem or opportunity of concern (e.g., the problem-oriented output from Method One and the opportunity-oriented output from Method Two), then holding the intention in consciousness (as in a simulation exercise) to implement one option rather than the other while in a guided imagery process not unlike the virtual time-travel procedure described earlier to observe experientially the short- and long-range impacts of choosing this particular policy option. One then imagines "zeroing out" the simulated intention to pursue the first option and instead holds the imagined intention to implement the second policy option and experientially travels through the future that stems from it, and so forth. The results are usually very clear-cut as to which specific future feels more desirable and why. Thus, this is a most practical tool for strategically assessing various policy options of concern, whether they be personal or planetary in scope.

To continue our hypothetical behavioral scientist example, Method Three might be based on two policy options: (1) making the personal–professional choice of doing nothing further about futures research, on the one hand, or (2) on the other hand, "taking the plunge" and beginning to use futures-oriented concepts and tools in one's professional work in order to make it more personally satisfying and useful to society.

As to what the results might look like, consider the case of a clinical psychology student who protested that a "left-brain, rational–analytic" final exam was not appropriate in the author's graduate course, "Visionary Futures." The author, in turn, challenged the student to use Method Three, and to let the results speak for themselves in making the choice whether or not to require the final exam. The results? In the version of the script used, the participant was to choose a vehicle through which to travel through the future. Our student, always wanting to experience being a pilot, chose a T-33 jet trainer. In the alternative future involving no final exam, the jet had a real hard time taking off the runway, was relatively unstable in flight, and seemed always on the edge of lapsing into uncontrolled flight conditions. In the alternative future in which there was a final exam, the jet took off strongly and was soon doing aerial acrobatics, which were seen and admired from the ground by the student's parents, family, and friends. Needless to say, the experience quickened the student's willingness to take the rational–analytic final exam, which the instructor, from the beginning, had recommended as a way to integrate better the cognitive concepts of the course with the behavioral skills that had, by that time, been well learned.

It is important to note that when appropriately facilitated this method works quite well in business as well as academic settings, and with "newbies" as well as to those more experienced with guided cognitive imagery methods for strategic visioning. For example, the author recently led a team from a Fortune-50 corporation investigating planetary marketing strategies, using this approach to investigate the long-range implications of Western corporate strategies to embrace marketing to Third World nations versus Third World isolationist strategies for "corporate America." The results were, in the words of the corporate team leader, "breathtakingly clear" that the more inclusive policy option (for American corporations to seek Third World markets rather than avoid them) is better for corporations as well being better for the Third World. "After all, we *do* all live in the same planetary 'spaceship,' and increasingly, what ruins a whole region threatens to ruin the whole world."

Method Four. Experiencing Alternative Futures II: A Transcendental Procedure for Exploration of Possible–Probable–Preferable Alternative Realities

This procedure differs in that its value tends to be intrinsic and idealistic, rather than extrinsic and practical. But for some readers it will be the most valuable of the set, for it offers a fast, safe, and efficient way directly to experience the transcendental source of one's being, and from there to explore one or more alternative probable and/or preferable realities that could emerge in the future (including the future that is intuited as one's "ideal expression").

Based on ideas communicated to me by Dr. Caroline Myss, this guided cognitive imagery procedure more or less simply involves the climbing of a very long, circular staircase in which, as you climb, you experientially unburden yourself (i.e., be aware, imagistically, of having; then "let go") of the following sequence: possessions, relationships, emotional reactions, judgmental evaluations, compulsive awareness of the physical body, the level or zone of probabilities, of possibilities, and of creative emergence, and into the experiential awareness of source. By reversing the direction and skillfully navigating in consciousness into alternative possible–probable–preferable realities of interest (i.e., domains that match the explorational concerns of the student, client, or participant), much of great value can be intuitively experienced and learned.

Obviously, a rather high degree of art is involved in guiding and following this type of process with efficacy, and this type of procedure perhaps stretches to the limit what can be accomplished by using visionary approaches to teaching and learning about the future in the setting of a university classroom. But the procedure is a most powerful way to "draw forth that which is latent within" (the core meaning of *educare,* the Latin origin of the word "education"), and one that not infrequently leads to a fundamental change in outlook and/or career direction for the participant, much like Willis Harman's seminar in consciousness and human potential at Stanford, which altered the career direction and subsequent future of so many graduate students, including the author.

To conclude our behavioral science example, it is not unreasonable to hypothesize that if the participant had enough skill and interest to get this far in the sequence of methods, that he or she would, in this exercise, find that his or her vocational vision for the future includes an expansion of personal–professional paradigm to be more interdisciplinary, more futures oriented, and more open to exploring new concepts and hypotheses, such as "global consciousness," that offer new paradigm possibilities for attaining the transition to a global society that is both sustainable and humane.[3] But, on the other hand, the participant could discover that he or she has been a workaholic for too long, and that now is the time to relax and enjoy family and friends, hobbies, and the like to a greater extent than before.

CONCLUSION:
ON THE NEED TO COUPLE SOCIAL ACTION RESEARCH WITH FUTURES RESEARCH AND POLITICAL ACTIVISM

Rather obviously, some of the premises underlying the methods presented in this exposition are not in keeping with key foundational assumptions about the nature of reality held by many behavioral scientists. Nevertheless, these "noetic" technologies for visioning are based on trainable skills, can be replicated, and are consistent with the canons of science, even though they would systemically extend the conventional paradigm of the behavioral sciences in certain key ways (Dunne and Jahn, 1987; Harman, 1988).[4]

But should behavioral scientists take the time and trouble to expand their paradigm in the directions indicated by this chapter? As the final example of how I teach futures research, consider the following.

In the opening anecdote about alternative futures research at SRI in 1970, a key piece of the story was left out: The work was done under contract to the U.S. Office of Education, which, as part of the "War on Poverty" had commissioned two research centers to study alternative future possiblities for the year 2000 and to derive policy implications for educating the youth in ways more relevant to the future in which they would be actually living. The bottom-line policy implication we put forth was this: Develop an ecology-oriented curriculum for grades K–12 as soon as possible, to prepare the citizenry more wisely to deal with the long-range ecological problems we saw ahead. Our education clients returned a year later saying essentially, "Stop doing your very long-range research and focus on shorter-term policy topics (emerging education technologies, education for the disadvantaged, etc.), because in trying to implement your policy suggestions we find that the planning horizon of the Office of Education is the four-year reelection cycle bringing in a new commissioner, and not having a Congressional mandate to develop a whole new ecology curriculum, we are unable to proceed with this important initiative." In fact, it was only after the famous Earth Day demonstration in 1972 that the U.S. Congress enacted enabling legislation for ecology-oriented educational policy, which taught me a great deal about the necessity of coupling alternative futures research with political activism in order to make headway in society with ideas whose time has not yet come.

The action research tradition so honored by *American Behavioral Scientist* is an ideal way to bridge the gap between visionary futures research and the realpolitik of society. As Walsh (1984) makes clear in his consciousness-raising monograph, *Staying Alive: The Psychology of Human Survival*, this line of development for the behavioral sciences is not only desirable, it is essential, both to planetary ecology and to the well-being of our children, our children's children, and their children's children.

NOTES

1. As a professional side note, it is perhaps now appropriate to point out that we chose not to include an explicit mention of the more visionary methods in our statement of methodology because we considered them too far from the dominant paradigm of the social and behavioral sciences at that time to be credible as a formal research technique. Whether this omission was ethically appropriate is now posed as a question for both students and professionals in relevant disciplines. For more on this, see Kleiner (1996).

2. The image of the skull and crossbones and the phoenix were not just "thought up." They were actually experienced by the author as he simulated being a typical reader doing the methods described here when writing this chapter.

3. "Global consciousness" is a phrase meaning at least two kinds of things: (1) expansion of consciousness beyond the confines of an egocentric sense of self, thereby including transpersonal experiences and self-identity that is transcendent in time and space; and (2) functionally adequate awareness of ecology as a whole system of physical and nonphysical interactions across time. As shown by the emerging discipline of deep ecology, neither of these two requirements is really independent of the other. Rather, they are as two sides of the same coin. For more on this, see Markley (1996) or http://www.cl.uh.edu/futureweb.spaceship.html.

4. The word "noetic," as used by the Institute of Noetic Sciences, derives from the Greek *nous* (mind, consciousness, or transcendental ways of knowing). It has become a preferred term for the author when speaking of the domains of consciousness traditionally referred to as "spiritual" when teaching in an open-enrollment, public university setting. But the word "spiritual" also proves serviceable in this context as long as it is made clear that "spiritual" does not equate to "religious." "Spiritual," used this way, is a technical term, as distinct from "physical," and "noetic" is a term that inclusively integrates both.

REFERENCES

Dunne, B., and Jahn, R. (1987). *Margins of reality: The role of consciousness in the physical world.* New York: Harcourt Brace Jovanovich.

Gendlin, E. (1981). *Focusing* (2d ed.). New York: Bantam Books.

Harman, W. (1969). *Alternative futures and educational policy.* Stanford: Stanford Research Institute, Educational Policy Research Center. (Policy memorandum no. 6).

Harman, W. (1979). *An incomplete guide to the future.* New York: W. W. Norton.

Harman, W. (1988). *Global mind change: The new age revolution in the way we think.* New York: Warner.

Harman, W., Markley, O., and Rhyne, R. (1973). The forecasting of plausible alternative future histories: Methods, results and educational policy implications. In *Long range policy planning in education* (pp. 299–385). Paris: Organization for Economic Cooperation and Development.

Kleiner, A. (1996). *The age of heretics: Heroes, outlaws, and the forerunners of corporate change.* New York: Doubleday.

Markley, O. (1988). Using depth intuition in creative problem-solving and strategic innovation. *Journal of Creative Behavior, 22* (2), 330–340.

Markley, O. (1989). Explaining and implementing futures research. In H. Didsbury (Ed.), *The future: Opportunity not destiny* (a book of readings for the World Future Society's sixth general assembly). Bethesda, MD: World Future Society.

Markley, O. (1994). Experiencing the needs of future generations: A step toward global consciousness. In *Thinking about future generations* (pp. 206–221). Kyoto: Institute for the Integrated Study of Future Generations.

Markley, O. (1996). Global consciousness: An alternative future of choice. *Futures, 28,* 622–625.

Markley, O., and Burchsted, S. (1997). Experiencing the needs of future generations with adults and children. *Futures, 29,* 715–722.

Markley, O., Curry, D., and Link, D. (1971). *Contemporary societal problems* (Report no. EPRC-6747-2). Menlo Park, CA: Stanford Research Institute, Educational Policy Reseach Center.

Markley, O., and Harman, W. (1982). *Changing images of man.* New York: Pergamon Press. (Based on the 1974 SRI International, Center for Study of Social Policy, report no. 4, *Societal cosequences of changing images of man* by Joseph Campbell, Duane Elgin, Willis Harman, Arthur Hastings, O. W. Markley, Brendan O'Regan, and Leslie Schneider).

Parnes, S. (1992). *Source book for creative problem-solving: A fifty year digest of proven innovation processes.* Buffalo, NY: Creative Education Foundation Press.

Roberts, J. (1972). *Seth speaks.* Englewood Cliffs, NJ: Prentice Hall.

Steinbrecher, E. (1978). *The inner guide meditation.* Santa Fe: Blue Feather Press.

Walsh, R. (1984). *Staying alive: The psychology of human survival.* Bounder, CO: New Science Library.

25

Producing a Better World: Theory, Education, and Consulting

Ian Lowe

THEORETICAL BACKGROUND

Social choice theory attempts to analyze the course of human events in terms of collective choices. It is distinct from naïve determinism, based on the assumption that the course of events is essentially determined by technical innovations or market forces. It is almost trivial to show that these views are unrealistic. The theory of technical determinism is based on the idea that any given technology has a momentum of its own, with consequent inevitable social effects (Dickson, 1977). Television has distinct characteristics that make communication using that technology qualitatively different to print, radio, or face-to-face meetings, a truism summed up memorably in McLuhan's famous (and often misquoted) observation that the medium is the massage. But television in countries such as China or Nigeria is controlled by the governing regime and is basically an organ of state propaganda; at the other extreme, in the United States of America it is controlled by private corporations and is basically a marketing machine. In most other countries the role of television is somewhere between these two extremes. Thus, the social impact of television is not an inevitable consequence of its technical features, but partly a result of political choices about the level and location of political control of the technology, as well as being influenced by cultural and linguistic factors.

Many economists believe that the course of human events is determined by economic choices made in some form of market, but it is impossible to justify the extreme form of this belief. No modern industrialized society has anything like a free market. Even in such extreme cases as Thatcher's United Kingdom or Reagan's United States, the government accounted for about one-third of all economic activity. Overtly political choices determined the level of use of nuclear power, the standard of medical care, the transport choices available, and the safety of the streets. Only an extreme economic romanticist would want the distribution of nuclear missiles to be determined by market forces.

Economic theory holds that a market is the most economically efficient way of allocating limited resources, but serious problems can arise if the distribution of resources that are genuinely limited is left to market forces. Markets make no pretense of equity, and most economists ignore the problem that the free operation of markets will usually lead to inequitable results, as Adam Smith (1776/1976) recognized. Those who can pay a high-enough price will usually get what they want at the expense of those with more limited means. There are more fundamental problems. Future generations cannot, even in principle, express their preferences in today's market, so their interests are ignored when the allocation of resources is left to market forces. The same argument applies to other species. So allowing the allocation of limited resources to be determined by the market is effectively a political decision to put the wishes of the present generation of humans before the needs of all future generations and all other species. Laissez-faire may be laissez, but it will never be fair. The market-oriented approach could only lead to sustainable solutions by happy accident; I believe it is our responsibility to our own descendants to try to do better than that.

Some proponents of social choice theory could be accused of an equally naïve view that the political process leads to decisions that reflect the overall view of society. Most voting systems allow, at best, the election of the party or coalition which reflects the best compromise for a majority of voters, while many systems do not even achieve that. A voter might want to support the broad economic strategy of Party A, the social agenda of Party B, and the foreign policy proposed by Party C, but that choice is not available. The famous "paradox of voting" shows that it is almost impossible to determine a collective choice of the community, even if a government wanted to do that (Walker, 1994). Many electoral systems make no attempt to provide a democratic choice; in one famous instance of creative electoral arrangements, a state government in Australia was returned with 25 percent of the popular vote (Coaldrake, 1989). In any real political system, voters in marginal seats have more influence than voters in safe seats, pressure groups have more influence than individual voters, and individuals or corporations that are sufficiently wealthy can exercise disproportionate influence.

That being said, it can be argued that a typical political system is usually in a state of dynamic equilibrium, with various individuals and groups trying to shift the balance in one direction or another. One U.S. analyst has argued that what we call public policy is actually the temporary equilibrium in the power struggle between competing interest groups, with each of those groups continually seeking to shift the balance in their favor (Latham, 1965). Various interest groups have used this principle to shift public policy in nations with some form of democratic government: environmental organizations, the gun lobby, groups seeking to widen or narrow access to abortion, and so on.

My work in the futures area is based on the idea that there is always a range of futures available, depending on social choices. Making available information about the various consequences of different choices should, in a rational world, lead to the adoption of better choices. The obvious problem with this approach is that no society is homogeneous, so there may not be an obvious "best" choice. There may be agreement on the ends to be sought but disagreement about the means to be employed. At a national level, a strategy that would, for example, lead to greater equity by raising the living standards of the poorest citizens will probably be opposed by those who believe, or profess to believe for the sake of political argument, that the poor are more likely to benefit from a strategy of promoting higher rates of economic growth and hoping for a "trickle-down" effect. There are many occasions in which a policy that would improve the situation of some people may lead to negative impacts on others. Strategies to reduce emissions of greenhouse gases are opposed in many countries by fossil-fuel interests. Improved public health systems are often opposed by private providers of medical services. At local levels, proposals for new roads or bridges are usually contentious because the benefits for some, in terms of better access, cause additional pollution, noise, or social dislocation for others. My approach has been to try to spell out the costs and benefits of, or the winners and losers from, each alternative course of action (Gale and Lowe, 1991). This improves the chance that these factors will at least be considered in the debate. As a social activist who seeks to make the public aware of choices that would move societies in directions that are more likely to be sustainable, I often find myself in direct conflict with interest groups seeking to promote alternatives that are clearly unsustainable but financially attractive in the short term (Lowe, 1989; Beasley, 1996).

Conventional social survey techniques make it possible to ascertain the current state of public opinion, but these have two fundamental problems. They are usually based on choices between known alternatives; for example, surveys regularly ask voters which of two endorsed candidates they would prefer, rather than asking whether there might be another choice they would prefer to either. The second problem is more fundamental. Surveys rarely force people to set priorities or make difficult choices; thus, it is possible for those surveyed to support both lower taxes and a wider range of government services, or to want cleaner air without any restrictions on private cars. Some psychologists have devised more sophisticated methods of measuring public attitudes to avoid this problem (S. Brown, 1980; Stainton Rogers, 1991). This approach shows that society is much more complex than is often suggested by simple binary choices such as left versus right, market oriented versus interventionist, or environmentalist versus techno-crat. In such areas as health care and environmental protection, several distinct bundles of attitudes can be identified, each internally coherent and rationally derived from a particular set of values. Since a free society admits a range of values, there will always be a consequent heterogeneity of atti-tudes to social choices.

A PLAUSIBLE, PREFERRED FUTURE

It has been clear for at least twenty-five years that the growth trajectory of industrial society cannot be sustained (Meadows, Meadows, Randers, and Behrens, 1972; Birch, 1976; Milbrath, 1989). The urgent task is to develop a strategy to redirect social and economic development along a path that would be genuinely sustainable. That is a very ambitious undertaking, as it requires an understanding of physical, chemical, biological, social, political, and economic factors. It is not surprising that most people decide that the task is far too difficult and concentrate on something less demand-ing. For example, economists often act as if producing a vibrant economy would solve all other problems. A significant step forward was the publica-tion of the Brundtland report, *Our Common Future*, which documented the interdependence between economic and ecological futures with the telling observation that we will be unable to maintain living standards unless our future economic decisions are ecologically rational (WCED, 1987). Sus-tainable development was defined in the same report as a pattern of activity that meets present needs without reducing the opportunities available to future generations. Thus, an activity cannot be regarded as sustainable if the scale of resource depletion or environmental damage would reduce oppor-tunities for future generations. These are important criteria. Proposals for resource development rarely consider what economists call the opportunity cost, or the value to future generations of still having those resources avail-able. Practices that dissipate resources to render them useless, such as blend-ing lead into automotive fuel, are still tolerated or even encouraged. In most countries the burden of proof in disputes about the environmental impact of proposed developments still rests with the objectors; it is assumed that the development should be allowed unless it can be indisputably proven that serious damage would be caused. A responsible approach to sustainability would consider all natural resources, both biological and geological, as a capital stock to be used wisely for the long-term good. It would also con-sider the social impact of proposed developments, locally and internation-ally. Activities designed to conserve resources and maintain the natural environment could cause social upheaval, while it is increasingly likely for conflict to result from different regions or nations basing their developmental plans on the same physical resource, whether it is fish, petroleum, or potable water (L. R. Brown et al., 1996; Fleay, 1995; Ophuls, 1977).

A rational evaluation of economic performance demands a more sophisticated measure than the gross domestic product (GDP). Using as a measure of progress the sum of all economic activity is grossly misleading, suggesting that community welfare is enhanced by such events as road accidents, robberies and natural disasters. It has been wisely said that the GDP measures all things except those that make life worthwhile. We need to develop better measures of community well-being, such as the various indicators of welfare or progress that have been suggested (Daly and Cobb, 1989; Hamilton, 1997). Rather than operating as if we were a business in liquidation, getting rid of our stock of assets at bargain prices to any passerby to produce cash flow, we need to behave as if we intend to be long-term inhabitants of this planet. We share it with millions of other species, so many that we still have only a vague idea of how many there actually are, but our destiny is inextricably intertwined with those other species in the complex ecological system of Earth. Shaping a sustainable future depends critically on recognizing those ecological realities and developing the knowledge base that would allow us to make rational choices (SoEAC, 1996; UNEP, 1997).

Another significant impediment to sustainability is inequity. Injustice, real or imagined, has always been a source of tension. Those of us who live in the industrialized nations account for about 20 percent of the human population, yet we consume over 80 percent of the natural resources now being used. At the recent Kyoto conference of parties to the Framework Convention on Climate Change, the reluctance of some Organization for Economic Cooperation and Development (OECD) nations to reduce their emissions was a crucial barrier to any meaningful involvement of the large developing countries such as China. The Australian government, as an extreme example, was essentially saying that China and India should not aim to have sewerage, hot water, and refrigeration available to all their people so Australians can expand their usage of motorboats, helicopters, and electric toothbrushes. The global arms budget is a truly obscene waste of resources—and human ingenuity—if we are serious about sustainable development.

So my vision of a preferred future is one in which we will have learned that we share a common ecological destiny with other people, other nations, and other species. That recognition will have produced an awareness that we need to use resources wisely and minimize the impact on natural systems of meeting our needs for food, shelter, clothing, health care, and transport. Much of our current technology is so primitive that it is entirely conceivable for changes that would allow the entire human population to have the basic requisites of a civilized life (von Weizacker, Lovins, and Lovins, 1997). That transition is likely to require a value change so that profligate consumption is recognized as irresponsible. It is credible for such a fundamental value shift to happen relatively rapidly, as shown by the recent changes in attitudes toward smoking in shared space or using aerosol sprays. Global climate change may yet be the great educator that will stimulate the value shift away from seeing consumption as an end in itself to recognizing it as a means to achieve the desired end of a civilized lifestyle (Milbrath, 1989).

INCORPORATING FUTURES VISIONS INTO TEACHING

All science students at Griffith University undertake a compulsory first-year unit on science, technology, and society (STS), as part of which I present a group of lectures on the role of science and technology in determining our future. Rather than presenting a fixed view of the future, the lectures develop the general idea that our individual and collective choices will determine which of the various possible futures we develop from our present starting point. The Griffith teaching team has also produced a book covering the material in the STS course, and a study guide is in preparation to allow it to be used as a resource for distance learning (Bridgstock, Burch, Forge, Laurent, and Lowe, 1998).

I also convene two second-year undergraduate units, which both have a strong futures emphasis. "Science, Technology, and the Modern Industrial State" traces the development of industrial society and its evolution to the present day, then explores the factors shaping the future of our society. "Bio-sciences, Medicine, and Society" concentrates on the social impacts of recent developments and likely future trends in the biological sciences and medicine. In both courses students are encouraged to present their own thoughts by allocating 40 percent of the assessment to presentation and defense by students of seminar papers. We stress that there are no predetermined correct answers to the questions posed; the students are judged by the quality of the research and arguments presented.

Higher-degree candidates whose work I have supervised have tackled a range of projects examining various aspects of futures, ranging from integrated pest management to space programs.

RESEARCH AND CONSULTING

A variety of research projects have used futures thinking to explore options for Australia. A major project, Australia's energy futures 1980–2030, funded by the National Energy Research, Development, and Demonstration Council, consisted of an extended exploration of the economic, environmental, and resource implications of a range of alternative approaches. It showed that all the high-energy futures that would result from a business-as-usual approach lead to serious problems (Lowe, 1986). A project funded by the government of the state of Tasmania developed what became known as a "greenprint"—an alternative development blueprint for the state—by extended consultation with community leaders. It showed that an approach to future economic development based on sustainable use of natural resources would be better in economic terms than the traditional approach of hoping for new mineral projects (Lowe, 1990b). A range of studies have explored the possible policy responses to environmental problems arising from use of fossil fuels, including promotion of conservation measures and solar energy. These show that a wide range of conservation measures provide economic benefits as well as reducing carbon dioxide emissions (Lowe, 1990a). That work was then used by the Australian government's Working Group on Energy Use, part of its Ecologically Sustainable Development project (ESDWG, 1991).

Two current research projects, funded by the Australian Research Council, make use of futures methodologies. A study of the electricity industry is exploring the effects on prospects for energy conservation and alternative generation technologies of different possible regulatory structures. An ambitious study of sustainable urban development is exploring public responses to a range of measures that would redirect the future pattern of urban life in Australia along directions that could be maintained for the foreseeable future. The approach is to determine specific aspects of development that are not sustainable, then develop a range of alternative responses and test public attitudes toward those options.

In 1988 I directed the Australian government's Commission for the Future. With ten established staff and several others working on specific contracts, this small agency was charged with increasing public awareness of developments in science and technology likely to have significant social or economic impacts. Among its important achievements during that year were dramatically increased public awareness of global environmental issues, new educational resources with a futures emphasis, and public discussion of ethical questions posed by developments in human genetics. In the 1990s the political fashion changed toward market-oriented approaches and the commission's public funding was eventually discontinued. Among recent consultancies, one for Queensland Rail estimated the energy needs for using different mixes of transport technologies to meet estimated future demand for passenger and freight movements (Lowe, 1997), while another for the Department of Natural Resources explored different possible environmental taxes or levies. As I finalized this chapter, I had on my desk a request from an international mining company to assist their senior managers to explore various possible future patterns of government policy, especially in the area of environmental regulation or incentives for better performance. This represents a growing awareness in the business community that the most successful corporations are those that expect the unexpected, because they have already explored sensible responses to a wide variety of unlikely events.

In all these cases, a clear benefit arises from the use of futures techniques. The outcome is not just an addition to the stock of human knowledge, desirable as that is. In each case the research has provided a possible program of political action by exploring the various consequences of different possible responses to contemporary problems. This scenario approach can, at least in principle, lead to more informed decision making by allowing politicians and bureaucrats to understand the likely consequences of their policy choices. So the futures researcher is able to fulfil a key role of the public intellectual in these times: to assist the making of decisions that would redirect the trajectory of human development onto a path that could be sustainable. This program of work led to the Australian Broadcasting Corporation inviting me to copresent the 1989 Boyer Lectures on the topic, "Changing Australia" (Gale and Lowe, 1991).

CONCLUSION

A recognition that the future is significantly shaped by the choices of individuals and groups informs my teaching, research, and consulting. In each case, the approach allows me to fulfill a basic responsibility of intellectuals: to explore options for the future of human society. At a time when it is increasingly apparent that the current pattern of social and economic development cannot be sustained into the distant future, that is both an important task and a powerful tool for producing useful change.

REFERENCES

Beasley, W. (Ed.). (1996). *Proceedings of the international conference on chemical education*. St. Lucia: University of Queensland.

Birch, C. (1976). *Confronting the future*. Ringwood: Penguin.

Bridgstock, M., Burch, D., Forge, J., Laurent, J., and Lowe, I. (1998). *Science, technology and society: An introduction*. Cambridge: Cambridge University Press.

Brown, L. R., Abramowitz, J., Bright, C., Flavin, C., Gardner, G., Kane, H., Platt, A., Postel, S., Roadman, D., Sachs, A., and Starke, L. (1996). *State of the world 1996*. Washington: Worldwatch Institute.

Brown, S. (1980). *Political subjectivity: Applications of Q methodology political science*. New Haven, CT: Yale University Press.

Coaldrake, P. (1989). *Working the system: Government in Queensland*. St. Lucia: University of Queensland Press.

Daly, H. E., and Cobb, J. B. (1989). *For the common good*. Boston: Beacon Press.

Dickson, D. (1977). *Alternative technology and the politics of technical change*. Harmdonsworth, U.K.: Penguin.

Ecologically Sustainable Development Working Groups (ESDWG). (1991). *Final report energy use*. Canberra: Australian Government Publishing Service.

Fleay, B. (1995). *The decline of the age of oil*. Annandale, Australia: Pluto Press.

Gale, F., and Lowe, I. (1991). *Changing Australia*. Sydney: ABC Books.

Hamilton, C. (1997). *Towards a genuine progress indicator*. Canberra: Australia Institute.

Latham, E. (1965). *The group basis of politics*. New York: Octagon Press.

Lowe, I. (1986). *Australian energy demand 1980–2030: Report to National Energy Research and Demonstration Council*. Nathan, Australia: Griffith University.

Lowe, I. (1989). *Living in the greenhouse*. Newham, Australia: Scribe Books.

Lowe, I. (1990a). The potential contribution of reducing domestic energy usage to slowing climate change. In D. J. Swaine (Ed.), *Greenhouse and energy* (pp. 90–96). East Melbourne, Australia: CSIRO Publications.

Lowe, I. (1990b). *A sustainable development strategy for Queensland: Report to the Department of Premier and Cabinet*. Nathan, Australia: Griffith University.

Lowe, I. (1997). *Energy and emissions for different transport modes: Report to Queensland Rail*. Nathan, Australia: Griffith University.

Meadows, D. H., Meadows, D. L., Randers, J., and Behrens, W. W. (1972). *The limits to growth*. New York: Universe Books.

Milbrath, L. W. (1989). *Envisioning a sustainable society*. Albany: State University of New York Press.

Ophuls, W. (1977). *Ecology and the politics of scarcity*. San Francisco: W. H. Freeman.

Smith, A. (1976). *The wealth of nations*. Oxford: Clarendon Press. (Original work published 1776).

Stainton Rogers, W. (1991). *Explaining health and illness*. London: Harvester Wheatsheaf.

State of the Environment Advisory Council (SoEAC). (1996). *State of the Australian environment 1996*. Collingwood, Australia: CSIRO.

United Nations Environment Programme (UNEP). (1997). *Global environmental outlook*. Nairobi, Kenya: UNEP.

von Weizacker, E., Lovins, A. B., and Lovins, H. L. (1997). *Factor four: Doubling wealth, halving resource use, a new report to the Club of Rome*. St. Leonards, Australia: Allen and Unwin.

Walker, K. J. (1994). *The political economy of environmental policy: An Australian introduction*. Kensington, Australia: University of New South Wales Press.

World Commission on Environment and Development (WCED). (1987). *Our common future*. Oxford, UK: Oxford University Press.

26

Cocreating a Futures Studies Course with Unionists

Arthur B. Shostak

Negative stereotypes about working-class Americans abound, thanks in large part to colorful and irascible TV figures like Archie Bunker, Ralph Cramden, and Kramer on *Seinfeld*. When you add the media's preoccupation with the inexcusable missteps of certain notorious blue-collar union leaders (the Teamsters' Jackie Presser and Jimmy Hoffa come immediately to mind), it would seem that working-class unionists would not be a very promising group for a college-credit course in futuristics (or much else, for that matter).

Determined to put the lie to that costly image, the AFL–CIO in 1974 opened the nation's only union-directed residential college-degree program. Housed at the George Meany Center for Labor Studies on a 240-bed campus in Silver Spring, Maryland, the National Labor College offers a degree from Antioch College or from the college itself. Unionists are resident on campus for two weeks a year, at a six-month interval, and do an impressive amount of earnest course work on a correspondence basis in the interim.

Despite carrying a full workload back home all year long with their unions and trying to maintain a decent family life, the vast majority of matriculates (average age, thirty-five) successfully complete the program in three or so years, an accomplishment many previously thought not a likely part of their lives this time around. To the great pride of their immediate families and their union employers (and sponsors), some 300 or so Meany Center alumni now boast a bachelor's degree in labor studies.

One year after the center college-degree program began I was invited to teach a basic sociology course and another in industrial sociology, an honor I have enjoyed for over a quarter century ever since. Quickly impressed with the eagerness in class of my working-class colearners, I sought and received permission in 1988 to introduce a third elective, a college-credit course in futuristics.

Having first introduced the subject to college students at Drexel University back in 1980, I thought I could merely tweak it a bit and adapt the syllabus and readings with little or no problem. How wrong I was! The challenge here proved formidable.

To begin with, unlike my Drexel undergraduates, my union adult colearners had little or no formal background: Few had read or even knew about Alvin Toffler's (1970) best-seller, *Future Shock*. Few had any familiarity with classic dystopian works like Aldous Huxley's (1932) *Brave New World* or George Orwell's (1949) *Nineteen Eighty-Four*. Even fewer knew any of the utopian literature, even that of the church, albeit most dimly sensed that much of the ideological conflict that had animated the 1960s and 1970s entailed profound disagreements about the preferable future(s) and how to get there from here.

To compound this problem, my union colearners—unlike my Drexel undergraduates (who were fifteen to twenty years younger on average)—were initially very resistant to the sort of venturesome thinking required in a futures course. Accustomed to a world of harsh realities, frequent disappointments, daily heartache, and defensive cynicism, many were initially reluctant to engage in the "willing suspension of disbelief" that William James identified as a requisite for fresh learning.

Every year since 1988 I have learned from course evaluations and frank feedback from the best of my twenty-five students a little bit more about how to do the course better. I now approach the challenge with seven major tools, all of which in combination win over nearly every colearner.

First, I encourage hope by highlighting historical matters of which they have little or no prior knowledge. To counter the bleak view with which many begin the course, I review the extraordinary progress we have made as a species in extending our lifespan, raising the level of well-being, and strengthening the infrastructure of governance and civility.

Taking care not to ignore painful gaps in equity and the atrocities that mar the front page daily, I help my colearners process their many grievances with runaway capitalism and other mortal threats to the world's well-being. I go on, however, to emphasize my belief that more has been gained than lost in recent centuries, a trendline that I think we have it in our power to extend for time indefinite, provided we find the willpower, creativity, and capacity to care enough about one another.

Second, I review recent well-known successes of major unions in this or that organizing drive or political campaign. I emphasize the long-range planning entailed in such campaigns, and identify such planning as a key component of futuristics. I also discuss how Fortune-500 companies and all major branches of federal, state, and local government make extensive use of futuristics.

I highlight corporate and labor union successes in introducing new products and services they are familiar with, and in this way underline the powerful potential of forecasting applied to payoff matters. This establishes the many significant rewards possible from our academic subject, and whets their appetite for bringing this new tool—long-range planning—back to their union sponsor. (I mention here my success over the years in bringing top union leaders in as panelists at the annual meeting of the World Future Society. These power holders generally earn strong applause from initially skeptical if not hostile attendees once the unionists make plain their respect for forecasting as a serious component in running the labor movement. I also talk about my occasional consulting with this union or that eager to explore ideas with a professional forecaster.)

Third, I refer over and again to the democratic dimension in futuristics, emphasizing thereby their responsibility for becoming major players in helping to decide our future(s). I reject the notion that there is any one future to be predicted, as in the absurdity of the paper's daily horoscope column. Instead, I work closely with them in explicating probable, possible, preferable, and preventable futures. We assess the strengths and weaknesses of each, but only after first uncovering and weighing the major values underlying each. I rail against nonvoters and other demonstrations of apathy. I explore the sources in class consciousness, class rivalry, and power monopolies that undermine participation. I get them to tell of their own voter-registration efforts, their local union meetings to debate policy issues, and many such labor efforts to make a difference, and I link all of this to futuristics. We make the future in the present, I maintain, either through acts of commission or omission, but the responsibility—especially in one of the most advanced democracies the world has ever known—is fundamentally ours.

Fourth, I put special emphasis on mind-boggling matters, the better to get unionists to reassess their unexamined assumptions and struggle to take an open-minded approach. Futurists, I explain, are not optimists or pessimists so much as they are possibilists. Giving Isaac Asimov credit for this thought, I use it to segue to science-fiction notions that challenge much conventional thinking (e.g., cyborgs, terraforming Mars, interplanetary travel, etc.).

Lest my colearners privately dismiss this as dreamy fiction, I also highlight science-fact developments that are almost as fantastic as those dreamt up by Asimov and his creative fellows. We explore biotech "miracles," the prospects where nanotechnology is concerned, the possible impact of wearable computers and personal intelligent agents on our lives, and so forth and so on.

Fifth, I explain the tools we have in futuristics for gathering data (Delphi polls, expert-genius interviews, large-scale polling projects, computer processing of massive data banks, etc.). I also discuss the tools we have for assessing impacts of developments (e.g., technology assessment techniques, social indicators research, computer simulations, etc.). Special attention is paid to tools we have for evaluating forecasts and learning from their fate. Above all, however, I focus on the values inherent in reliance on this tool or than one, and on the transferability of any of the tools to the special forecasting needs of organized labor.

Sixth, I take great care in my choice of literature. Trial and error has taught me that the books must be engaging, clear, short, and relevant. It helps as well if they are available in an inexpensive paperback edition.

From the outset I have used a great utopian novel, *Ecotopia*, by Ernest Callenbach (1975). While written in the mid-1970s, it remains creative and prescient. Better still, it offers a plausible upbeat scenario for America's thoroughgoing overhaul, a blueprint my colearners find fresh. I also use a more recent book, *Creating a New Civilization*, by Alvin and Heidi Toffler (1994). Unlike much of Toffler's writing, this thin volume is cogent and compelling. An introductory essay by Newt Gingrich lends something special, given labor's steadfast opposition to what many think he is about.

I have decided to experiment with using *Beyond Humanity*, a 1997 paperback by Gregory S. Paul and Earl D. Cox, easily the most mind-stretching book in futuristics I have come across in years. Their forecast of what they call an Extraordinary Future, one predicated on the securement soon of artificial life (far beyond artificial intelligence), very advanced robotics, and nanotechnology impacts, truly takes forecasting where it has seldom if ever gone.

I prepare my own chapter-by-chapter true–false open-book take-home quizzes to accompany my texts. Colearners thank me for this in course evaluations, as it helps me highlight what I want them to focus on, and they take pleasure in getting high scores week after week. Each quiz features two write-in questions that ask what surprised, pleased, dismayed, or puzzled them the most in the assigned reading.

Finally, I make a point in closing the course of connecting it to one overarching possibility that could just make labor's renewal a better-than-ever prospect. I call this scenario the CyberUnion Prospect, and use it to pull together many strands of the semester's work. A CyberUnion stands out in its employment of futuristics (a perspective), infotech (cutting-edge tools), and tradition (a commitment).

Employing futuristics, a CyberUnion will replace the narrow "putting-out-fires" orientation of most unions with a longer perspective, one that encompasses the here-and-now but extends five and ten years beyond it. It will replace a narrow tolerance for shopworn communication tools (newsletters, mailings, etc.) with a high-tech perspective, one that upgrades familiar tools (as in adding color to the newsletter) even as it moves to the cutting edge (e-mail for all, listserves for many, etc.). It will replace hollow observances of union traditions with wholehearted celebration, the better to ensure that labor's high-tech gains are always accompanied by comparable high-touch advances (e.g., a local's history and traditions could be "captured" in a memorable CD-ROM provided to all).

These attributes should help put labor unions on a par with the CyberCorps rapidly coming their way. They should be able to get Americans to think of unions, and not just of corporations, when they think about successful cutting-edge twenty-first century organizations. They should send the message that labor is finally and actually "with it!," a message of import for the union's potential and actual membership, the media, the public, and the business community alike. And they should empower the rank-and-file as never before. This model could invigorate adapters, inspire the membership, favorably impress prospective members, intimidate labor's opponents, intrigue vote seekers, and in other valuable ways significantly bolster labor's chances.

Naturally, I have each class do an anonymous evaluation of every aspect of the course, especially the books and the essay assignments that guide their learning over the six-month interval between the week-long start of the course and the one wrap-up session with which we close it out. I take their assessments quite seriously, so much so that I have no hesitation about considering my adult enrollees as colearners with me in a joint intellectual (and spiritual) adventure.

An elective course, "Futuristics" generally gets a full enrollment, and in the hallway scuttlebutt apparently ranks very highly. The danger to it comes from other quarters: For example, two old straightlaced faculty recommended to the dean two years ago that the course be cancelled and squeezed instead into an hour of my "Intro to Sociology" course (so as to free up elective time for other course offerings). With no involvement on my part, both alumni and current students circulated a "keep-the-course!" petition, and a delegation went into the dean's office to rail against its elimination. The course continues as since 1988, and I might even someday begin to speak to these two "colleagues" again.

Overall, I believe trade unionists are organic "futurists," devoted as they are to grievance resolution, collective bargaining, and political influence, each a profound exercise in making the future in the present. All the more important is their matriculation in a college-level course that surfaces much that they need to know if they are to strengthen their record as future shapers. I am very pleased to pioneer here, and hope to soon learn of many more such efforts wherever free-trade unionism is struggling to help create a world closer to our heart's desire.

REFERENCES

Callenbach, E. (1975). *Ecotopia: The notebooks and reports of William Weston.* Berkeley, CA: Banyan Tree Books.

Huxley, A. (1932). *Brave new world.* Garden City, NY: Doubleday, Doran.

Orwell, G. (1949). *Nineteen eighty-four.* New York: Harcourt, Brace.

Paul, G., and Cox, E. (1997). *Beyond humanity: Cyberevolution and future minds*. Rockland, MA: Charles River Media.
Toffler, A. (1970). *Future shock*. New York: Random House.
Toffler, A., and Toffler, H. (1994). *Creating a new civilization: The politics of the third wave*. Washington: Progress and Freedom Foundation.

27

Diagnosing Global Change: Educating the Economic Strategist

Ernest Sternberg

At a time when economic sectors rise and decline in a decade, when innovation is so rapid that products become obsolete in two or three years, and when cyber-driven globalization penetrates every enterprise, communities and regions around the world must be prepared to respond to the forces of economic change. Among the multiple forces affecting my city and region, which combination of them will drive the local economy? How can we adapt to, and perhaps even try to influence, these forces for the community's protection? How might we turn these changes to our region's advantage, creating economically successful, stable, and sustainable communities?

What I find most appealing in futures studies is that it gives me intellectual frameworks and bodies of literature through which to begin, if not to answer at least to better formulate, these questions: to begin diagnosing the forces that overwhelm local economies. Teaching in a graduate professional program in city and regional planning, my colleagues and I have had the opportunity to bring such ideas to our graduate students.[1] In particular, I have tried to inform them about topics I will summarize here: the forces of capitalist transformation, technological revolution, paradigm shift, and sectoral dissolution that are reshaping local economies. These students are not likely to become futurists or futures consultants. Rather, as eventual practitioners in planning, a more-or-less well-established profession, they have to learn about futures from courses and readings that are incorporated into a larger professional curriculum.

I will focus in these pages on how we have tried to bring futures literacy to one particular professional subfield usually known as "economic development planning." In North America it consists of a loosely aligned group of several thousand practitioners who work for cities, regions, states, and provinces to retain business and boost prosperity. This group's obscurity, despite its fair size and influence, may reflect the uncomfortable paradox that underlies it: that in societies committed to free-market ideology, professionals have been at work to oil the workings of the market for the community's benefit.

As the modern, mechanized, hierarchical, industrial economy has waned, the field of economic development, too, is being reinvented. Practitioners who may have formerly focused on acting as publicists and deal makers to attract business—activities that used to be called "smokestack chasing"—must now take on a larger and more challenging role. They must learn how to help their communities adapt to global economic forces. They must, in the coming decade, transform themselves into a new breed of professionals, whom I will call "economic strategists." The strategist's job is to inquire into the confluence of competitive, technological, and industrial forces that drive the local economy. They must learn to diagnose their locality's prospects amid the interacting forces of global change.

Some of the skills needed to do so have long been taught in urban and regional planning programs, including the one I teach in. These include the capabilities to "survey" (take an overview) of local conditions, understand local culture and history, get to know members of local firms and business groups, and operate astutely in a freewheeling, politicized setting. They also include capabilities in analyzing economic data, said to identify local firms that trade with the rest of the world, as opposed to those that depend on sales within the region.

The planning curriculum may even teach practitioners how to understand economic change. Old forecasting methods have a continuing role here. They help us project incremental changes in population, traffic congestion, land availability, and the composition (age, gender, job skills) of the labor force. With good grounding in conventional economics, the students may even be taught how to recognize cyclical changes, those due to short-term economic fluctuations, like trade shifts and recessions.

But these skills are mere rudiments. The bigger challenge is to inquire not just into incremental adjustment or cyclic variations but into fundamental change. Since my own work has focused on this topic, I can now summarize (with apologies in advance for the heavy-handed reference to my own writings) four types of fundamental economic change.

The most profound changes are thoroughgoing capitalist transformations. We are by now all conversant in the idea that we have entered, and perhaps already surpassed, the postindustrial economy, in which information and rational calculation underlie wealth. Simultaneously, we have entered a global economy, in which every producer must respond to global alliances, multinational competitors, multiethnic workforces, and international financial flows. But the transformations do not stop there.

Ours is a time of widespread fundamentalisms and ultraparochialism, in which religions, sects, and ethnicities rediscover ancient verities and exert ecclesiastical control over commerce. It is, furthermore, a time in which global holding companies and multinational corporations consolidate an ever more pervasive dominance over local business. Yet it is also a time when entrepreneurship is rampant, and the most economically vibrant regions have generated innovative accumulations of small, new enterprises.

In short, regions are buffeted by multiple economic transformations, some reinforcing each other while others press in diverging directions (Sternberg, 1999b). States and cities must increasingly formulate strategies through which they can make their way in this new economy. They need futures-literate economic advisors to help them do so.

Though it is often believed that these capitalist transformations are pushed along by new technologies, I have come to think that it's best to see technological revolutions as being analytically separable. Take the rise of the information economy as an example. On the one hand, we can view it as one capitalist transformation among others, driven by internal strains in the market system, the strains caused by the increasing complexity of business enterprise and the economic environment. These complexities constitute an intracapitalist force spurring demand for information and giving rise to the information industries.

On the other hand, new technologies enable and reinforce the pervasive spread of information. It is through microelectronics, satellites, fiber optics, and switching and networking technologies that the information economy has amassed its extraordinary, dynamic power. The internal capitalist dynamic combines recursively with technological innovation, generating massive industrial change.

Such technology-led revolution has periodically overtaken capitalism ever since the nineteenth-century industrial era, generating successive, overlapping waves of change. At various times the technological drivers were railways, internal combustion, electricity, and synthetic chemistry. What distinguishes our time is that we are being overtaken by multiple, multiply interacting, technological revolutions. As photonics (advanced optics and optoelectronics) and recombinant DNA technology take off, we are already confronted with new hyphens, like pharmacogenomics, biomaterials, and neural networks as we continue to undergo the cyber-whelming of everything.[2]

In this technological deluge, new industries bob up while old ones are engulfed, and all must tread in ever more turbulent economic waters. Since each region has a unique complement of industries, each must respond differently to these technological forces. Each region must create innovative competencies selectively and invest in research institutions strategically, decisions dependent on futures-literate economic leadership.

In every region, local firms must also respond to business paradigm shifts: changes in the organizational procedures and intellectual protocols through which firms interact in the market economy. Though they may be short lived, these paradigms are much more than the fads they are sometimes taken for. They are, rather, shared assumptions about how to navigate the market. In times of overwhelming uncertainty, firms adopt them for fear of being left behind, thereby influencing other firms to follow suit.

What is more, firms must make their way among multiple paradigms undergoing multiple shifts. Firms focus on core competencies in which they seek to attain global excellence, but also to manage a diversified portfolio of activities—requiring varied competencies—to reduce exposure and increase security. Firms coordinate ever more complex operations on a global scale, enlarging the corporate scope of control, but reduce complexity through decentralization, outsourcing, and contracting. They hope to develop stricter procedures and more reliable internal regulations, but also to foster creativity, nurture personal development, and create good work environments.

Acquisitions and mergers compete with divestments and vertical disintegration. All engage in ever more exotic forms of interfirm linkages. New arrangements for warehousing and shipping, new contingent work arrangements, new demands for lifelong learning, new marketing media, new methods of inventory keeping, new multinational workforces, and new pressures from global financial markets—not to mention the most obvious, the cyber-upheaval in business practice—all add up to an economic environment that has become preposterously complex.[3]

In a time of worldwide internetworking, no firm is likely to have better or worse "information" (understood in the narrow sense of data or facts) than another. Competitive advantage arises not from fleeting data, but from longer-term capacities to adapt, cooperate (with some, while competing with others), and learn. Contrary to expectation that telecommunications with make distance meaningless, it is turning out that locality does make a difference, if the locality's leaders have the strategic capability to create environments conducive to innovation and collaboration.

What may be least well appreciated is that we live in the midst of still another force for change, the force of sectoral dissolution, which undermines the institutional and intellectual boundaries that have for so long been taken for granted. Hoary divisions between public and private dissolve to be reconstituted as new hybrid "public–private" partnerships, collaborative arrangements, clusters, and networks. This is more than "civic society," since it does not operate simply as a third sector alongside the more traditional ones, but as new relationships that breach the traditional boundaries (Sternberg, 1993).

What has especially interested me recently is the breakdown of another boundary, that between culture and economy, though each has long been seen as self-contained with respect to the other. With the increasing surfeit of material goods and information (for those in the world who can afford them), corporate capitalism increasingly generates the most desirable product of all, personal meaning. Now foods appeal through their sensuality and nostalgia, retail establishments draw customers through their reconstruction of exotic worlds, people sell their labor through the deliberate performance of the self, and tourist destinations operate as sellable experiences designed for popular consumption.

Relying on content generated by the media, especially the movies, the world's corporations increasingly sell products (clothes, cars, foods, toys, services) enhanced through evocative characters, scenes, situations, images, and narratives, components of meaning that are now trademarked, privatized, and disseminated under corporate control. Whereas farms, factories, and information processors once stood at the core of the economy, now the culture producers do: the museums, news-gathering organizations, music firms, and, above all, movie studios. Whether they distribute content through television, theaters, the Web, or new hybrid appliances, these core-culture producers are the makers of the meaningful content through which ordinary products acquire the fantastic capacity to assuage desire. The result is a new capitalism in which art and commerce collapse into each other, turning commodities into icons and workers into performers (Sternberg, 1999a).

In the midst of this cultural–economic dissolution, the regions that succeed are those that foster creativity, generate pop stars, resemble movie sets, turn city streets into tourist artifacts, and subject all communications to one overpowering requisite: the projection of a desirable image. The states and regions that will prosper will find the strategic advice by which to guide themselves through this new landscape of images and similitudes.

In the face of such overwhelming change, the economic strategist's job might seem impossible. Three factors make it manageable, however. First, he or she does not seek what evades the rest of us: to comprehend the global economy, as it were, anatomically, as if it consisted of empirically discoverable frameworks and sinews. Rather, he or she recognizes the new economy as a set of emergent constructs, to be grasped through acts of willful interpretation. Second, he or she does not, or should not, work as a disconnected expert, advising from above, as if he or she had some overarching perspective unavailable to others. He or she should, rather work as a participant and facilitator, bringing together groups of others in the region to foster multiple perspectives, enable insight, and reduce confusion. Third, he or she has the advantage of interpreting from the perspective of the region. In the midst of global transformation, the well-prepared planner gains leverage through intimate knowledge of the locality.

After all, the local effects of global change depend on each city's or region's unique combinations of economic assets. Regions vary in industrial mix, workforce skills, research institutions, transportation and communication infrastructures, technological specializations, knowledge bases, business networks, industry clusters, entrepreneurial activities, innovative capabilities, built environments, customs, reputations, and histories. Guided by futures-literate economic strategists, these places will be better prepared to assemble the local resources through which they can respond to global change.

It was in the early 1900s that one of the forefathers of the planning profession, the unclassifiable Scottish polymath named Patrick Geddes, told planners to diagnose not just how a region fits together into an organic whole, but how it evolves. He proposed that regions were undergoing a profound evolution, leading them away from what he called "paleotechnic" civilization (an analogy with "paleolithic," referring to the old Stone Age) built on railroads, belching factories, and enormous industrial cities, and toward a finer "neotechnic" civilization of private automobiles, electrification, long-distance communication, and regional dispersal (Geddes, 1968/1914).

Now, almost a century later, regions are undergoing change that is, if anything, even more overwhelming. They need planners—including the particular types of planners I have called economic strategists—who can help inform communities about the global forces affecting their residents' livelihoods. We can certainly acknowledge Geddes's insight that good planning requires an appreciation of change. However, we can by now also recognize why his approach was so fundamentally wrong. There is not now, if there ever was, a single, massive, overarching evolutionary direction.

Rather, we confront multiple forms of capitalist transformation, technological revolution, paradigm shift, and sectoral dissolution. For a new generation of economic strategists, the premium is on having intellectual grounding that allows them to diagnose how these merge into a unique confluence of forces driving change in the locality. They can best obtain such knowledge through education that makes them futures literate while also offering them an array of more conventional professional skills. It is with such education that they might yet help their communities, not just to recognize emerging futures, but, perhaps, to actively shape them.

NOTES

1. It is to these colleagues that I owe my discovery of futures as a subject of study. I thank Ibrahim Jammal and Magda Cordell McHale, and my colleague in this collection, Sam Cole, for getting me interested in and encouraging me to pursue this exciting field.

2. For my now somewhat dated attempt to come to terms with one technological revolution, see Sternberg (1992).

3. Among the numerous works on the topic are Drucker (1993) and Kelly (1998).

REFERENCES

Drucker, P. F. (1993). *Post-capitalist society*. New York: HarperCollins.

Geddes, P. (1968). *Cities in evolution*. London: Ernest Benn. (Original work published 1914).

Kelly, K. (1998). *New rules for the new economy*. New York: Penguin Putnam.

Sternberg, E. (1992). *Photonic technology and industrial policy: U.S. responses to technological change*. Albany: State University of New York Press.

Sternberg, E. (1993). Preparing for the hybrid economy: The new world of public–private partnerships. *Business Horizons, 26* (6), 11–15.

Sternberg, E. (1999a). *The economy of icons: How business manufactures meaning*. Westport, CT: Praeger.

Sternberg, E. (1999b). Transformations: The forces of economic change. In K. Taylor and W. E. Halal (Eds.), *21st century capitalism*. Boston: St. Martin's Press.

28

Prophets of a High-Tech Age: Futures Studies through the Eyes of a Futurist

William E. Halal

Why does one become a futurist? My experience is that being a futurist is exciting, pioneering, but very difficult work. It involves taking constant risks by challenging the status quo with a vision of change, which may or may not earn one acclaim but is almost certain to meet a lot of criticism. In short, it means taking flak.

Then why study the future?

It seems to me that futurists are born with a hungry interest in where society is going. They understand in their bones that life has always changed enormously and that it is now changing far more dramatically and more rapidly than ever before. A few are dispassionate scholars or technicians, certainly, but most futurists are fascinated, ultimately, by the prospect of creating and living in a very different world.

That's why I have long been convinced that futurists are modern equivalents of the ancient prophets. Prophets of old were more concerned with religion, but mainly because that was the focus of change in biblical times. Today the focus is on the revolution in technology that is driving a new global order, and so futurists can be thought of as the prophets of this high-tech age.

This is not often stated because it is a sensitive issue. Proposing change is tough enough, but who would want to invite more criticism—and even scorn—

for professing to have special knowledge about how others should change to create a better future? This is a daunting role, so it is little wonder that most of us do not wish to suffer more abuse by claiming to be prophetic.

Yet I cannot shake the conviction that the past thirty years of my life have been devoted to exactly this type of work. Although I willingly pursued this path, in another sense it seems to have been thrust upon me by something bigger. I could attribute it to my innate curiosity, intelligence, rebelliousness, and countless other traits, but that doesn't fully explain it to my mind. On those occasions when I experience the thrill of discovery and am able to convey this successfully to others, I feel a great sense of mastery, of pioneering an unexplored frontier. One could call it many things—forecasting, strategy, institutional change—but my very being seems destined to explore the future.

A SHORT BIOGRAPHY

This all started while I was working as an aerospace engineer on the Apollo Program. I had obtained a B.S. in aerospace engineering at Purdue University, served as an Air Force officer in Europe, and then joined Grumman when it was awarded the NASA contract to build the lunar module. It was thrilling to see our first "spaceship" land on the moon, especially because I helped to design it in a small way. But still, I felt a keen need to become involved in something closer to the heart of life and American society.

When the student demonstrations erupted at the University of California, Berkeley in the 1960s, I was captured by the intellectually provocative spirit of the times. College students just did not act that way before, usually being more concerned with sex and beer parties than ending wars, overthrowing corruption, and transforming society.

I attended Berkeley for six exciting years, obtaining M.B.A. and Ph.D. degrees and a lasting fascination in the pivotal changes to a knowledge-based society. Gorging on a vast range of literature and ideas that were new to me, I was slammed by thunderbolts of insight. On the streets I was given glimpses into the arbitrary social structures defining how the world really worked. Even more marvelous was the realization that the entire system I had grown up in was poised for transformation. It was heady.

I vividly recall sitting in a dark movie house gripped by Stanley Kubrick's movie, *2001: A Space Odyssey*. There it was: the stark realization that life has progressed from a lifeless planet swirling in the tides of the Big Bang, to apes who stumbled onto the first tools, then to civilization, and now to voyages into space. How could one not be absorbed in this greatest adventure imaginable? This drama that swept up astronomy, biology, technology, culture, economics, society, and everything else into a great cosmic arc of life rushing to meet God?

That's when I knew I was a futurist.

MY GUIDING PERSPECTIVE:
THE LIFE CYCLE OF EVOLUTION

The idea that American society was entering a postindustrial era remains my guiding perspective, but I think this is more usefully understood from the bigger view noted already. Today's rush to a knowledge-based world is simply the present phase in that millions-of-years-long voyage from the origin of life to the birth of civilization, then passing through the agrarian, industrial, and knowledge revolutions, and eventually culminating in some type of advanced global order capable of colonizing deep space (Figure 28.1). It strikes me as little short of a miracle that our planet was merely a mass of hot rock several billion years ago, yet now we sit here comfortably pondering the meaning of this rise in consciousness and wondering where it will lead.

Applying my technical skills to understanding this grand phenomena, I came to the conclusion that the entire pattern of evolution can be best understood as forming a life cycle of the planet, what I have called the "Life Cycle of Evolution" (LCE). This cycle is similar to the life cycle of all

Figure 28.1
The Life Cycle of Evolution

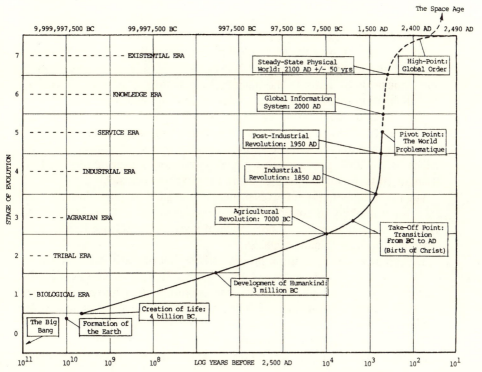

organisms, but vastly larger in scope and duration, comprising what I believe to be the characteristic path that life on Earth (and perhaps other planets) follows in its development.

This work produced a way to grasp the LCE in meaningful terms: a logarithmic graph able to collapse these vast time differences into a useful scale. The result, shown in Figure 28.1, reveals an S curve that many other scholars have tried to sketch in rough terms but have never been able to map precisely (Halal, 1990). This is not speculation but based on hard empirical evidence. The data points in Figure 28.1 are confirmed historical facts, except for the projection into the future, which is portrayed with a dashed line.

This is not the place to go into details, so I will simply sum up the major conclusions from this work that are more fully explained elsewhere (Halal, 1990).

The Planet Evolves through a Life Cycle

The evolution of the planet can be best understood as following roughly the same cycle of growth experienced by all organisms, humans, and other living systems: a period of slow formative development, followed by a period of accelerated growth, then passing through an inflection to decelerating growth, and finally culminating in a period of stable maturity. Although the LCE covers such a vast scale of time that it is almost incomprehensible, Figure 28.1 shows that it precisely fits the same S curve exhibited by all life forms.

Consider how the major phases of the LCE require time periods that differ by orders of magnitude. Evolution required billions of years from the origin of life to produce humans, then millions of years to found civilization, thousands of years to the industrial revolution, hundreds of years to the information revolution, and decades to unify the world.

The inflection point to decelerating growth seems to have been passed only recently, about 1975, when several indicators suggest that the rate of growth peaked and is now subsiding toward a period of stability. For instance, it is widely predicted that global population is expected to level off at about 10 to 14 billion people within the next few decades.

The major uncertainty involves projecting the LCE into the future. Physical growth is likely to continue its deceleration to a stable world, but who knows what could happen to the growth of knowledge and spirit, which are essentially infinite (Halal, 1998a)?

This entire cycle is a natural process arising out of the internal dynamics of the Earth as a living system, a huge organism in its own right: Gaia. The completion of earlier phases creates the conditions that make later stages possible—"push"—while the power of later phases is always present in some degree and serves to draw the system on to its conclusion—"pull."

The push of early phases is almost obvious, as in the striking sequence of agriculture paving the way for industrialization, and so on. The pull of later phases, however, is less obvious but especially intriguing. For instance, the point of rising inflection in Figure 28.1 coincides with the coming of Christ, Buddha, Mohammed, and other great prophets who can be understood historically as anticipating the final endphase of evolution into a spiritual age.

One useful aspect of the LCE is that it makes today's major trends come to life more vividly. The population explosion can be seen as the equivalent of a youth's accelerated growth into a fully developed body within a few short years. Likewise, today's exploding communication networks are not too different from the increased social and intellectual networks that guide the teenager's passage into maturity. And global diversity is much like the rich complexity of the fully developed human personality. Even the propagation of humans into deep space can be viewed as comparable to the propagation of a family through its offspring.

In sum, the world can be insightfully understood as a living organism undergoing a natural process of maturation as it evolves from a relatively harsh, youthful past into a far more sophisticated phase of adult maturity. Today the world is passing through a very difficult adolescence.

Evolution Proceeds from the Material to the Spiritual

There is also a rather precise direction to the LCE, moving from the most rudimentary, physical domain to the social, intellectual, and finally the spiritual domains. Evolution proceeds from the geological formation of the planet, to the creation of biological life, to humans working the soil, to the manufacture of goods, to the organization of complex social structures, to the management of knowledge, and now to shaping values, beliefs, and other transcendent concerns.

Thus, the most striking pattern displayed by all this change is that life progresses toward greater power, complexity, emotion, knowledge, awareness, choice, wisdom, ideals, and other facets of that ineffable quality comprising the human spirit. Moreover, this growing intensity of natural spirit seems to arise directly and naturally out of the process of living itself—push—as well as from some higher source—pull. To offer an analogy, just as a tree bears fruit, so life produces spirituality. Countless recognized scholars and philosophers agree (Sperry, 1988; Harman, 1988).

Please note that the spirit is not simply a state of bliss, but a more heightened, existential state of being that also includes painful experiences as people struggle to guide more complex matters. Life at advanced levels of evolution is more *intense*; it requires the careful use of more sophisticated capabilities to choose among a greater range of options in order to carry out grave new responsibilities. A good example is the power to control genetics now being conferred by biotechnology.

Despite all the controversy over the issue of spirituality, then, this mundane natural definition of spirituality is a demonstrable fact that should satisfy even positivists. Who could deny that there is far more human "spirit" in the world today than during the primitive stone age, and certainly before life existed at all. The Darwinian view offers only half of the story, merely explaining the mechanics of what happened rather than why it happened. Human behavior is motivated not only by basic needs for survival and physical gratification, but also by higher-order needs for community, personal achievement, and meaning that guide the actions of all people in everyday life:

- The visions that all business people today struggle with to inspire an enterprise.
- The *joie de vivre* that medicine increasingly understands to be the wellspring of health.
- The sense of union with a higher power that all religions have always fostered to provide meaning and purpose to life.

There seems little doubt that such spiritual phenomena exist, and the only serious questions are what causes this evolution of spirit, where does such metaphysical power come from, and where is it leading? That is, who is doing the pulling? The physical products of evolution are simply a manifestation of this creative energy that seems to flow from some poorly understood metaphysical domain, where it cascades down through the hierarchy of life in the form of thoughts, then behavior, and finally as physical artifacts.

The World Is Poised on the Brink of Maturity

The cycle described here arises out of the life of the planet, global forces far bigger than individual humans. In that sense, the evolution of a knowledge-based world is almost inevitable. Many scholars are critical of such deterministic views, and I certainly agree that the world can be changed by a wide range of human actions. But absent some major calamity, such as nuclear annihilation, the future is almost certain to be transformed by today's knowledge revolution because information networks are essential to contain the awesome complexity of a unified globe. This is the only direction in which further evolution makes sense.

Information technology is now the strongest force on Earth, primarily responsible for the collapse of communism, the restructuring of corporations and governments, and the general transformation of civilization into some new type of knowledge society. And what we have seen thus far is only the beginning. The really powerful technologies are likely to arrive during the next decade or so: interactive multimedia allowing almost anyone to work, learn, buy, sell, correspond, heal, pray, and otherwise interact with anyone else on Earth. This newfound ability to recreate human relationships at a distance through vivid, graphic electronic media will comprise one of the most significant advances in the life of the planet, electrifying the globe into a single, huge, thinking, more highly conscious organism.

However, this pivotal transformation can only be made by passing through a "crisis of maturity." The world is growing very rapidly to 10 billion or more people, most of whom are determined to live as comfortably as we do. This means a five- to tenfold increase in industrialization, material consumption, competition for scarce resources, cultural diversity, and environmental strain. China alone will likely triple the load on the environment. Thus, people in all nations must learn to manage the inevitable transition to a technological world of unfathomable complexity and change. We will have to create sophisticated institutions that decentralize control to ordinary people, resolve differences with our adversaries, develop modest but adequate lifestyles, design international information networks, cultivate our wisdom, and pray for spiritual unity. In short, we have to grow up and behave as responsible adults. There is no alternative.

Some Caveats

We all see these issues differently, but this view strikes me as the only reasonable way we can fully understand today's profound global changes. The LCE offers a plausible cosmology with greater explanatory power because it integrates the positivist view of science with the subjective nature of life.

However, I do not interpret my studies to mean that life will become utopian. For instance, I doubt that it is possible to halt today's march toward a five- to tenfold increase in industrial output. Many Americans may be ready to give up their luxuries, but try telling a Chinese or Mexican that growth is a bad idea. It seems to me that the challenge of sustainable development requires creating an ecologically benign technoeconomic system that can tolerate these far greater levels of global consumption.

I also wonder about the hope of achieving widespread social equality to bridge the gap between rich and poor. There seems little doubt that a knowledge society is empowering because anyone can gain access to power and wealth through information. The rapid rise of Japan, Korea, and Singapore, for instance, attest to the newfound possibilities for pulling any nation up by its bootstraps. However, many other people seem to lack such resolve. Just as we are facing the fact that many unfortunate souls seem unable to avoid living on our streets, the same may be true of entire societies—Somalia?—despite the best efforts of the world community.

I am not even convinced that the purpose of this journey can be universally described in laudable terms of improving human and social welfare. The broad focus of civilization as a whole may turn to such goals, but I am more impressed by the divergence of the human experience. People increasingly seek the most varied sources of fulfillment, ranging from scientific knowledge and devout religiosity to sexual fantasy, gratuitous violence, and even more bizarre behavior, which are all manifestations of the same creative spirit. In fact, it may be that the future will pit more intense values against one another violently, creating biblical-like battles between good and evil.

MY METHODS FOR STUDYING THE FUTURE

To operationalize this view, I've developed various methods over the years that sketch out the emerging role of business corporations and government, the advance of revolutionary technologies, and the shape of a knowledge-based world. Here are some of my more notable works.

Modeling: Beyond the Profit Motive

I am impressed with the enormous power for change posed by large corporations, the greatest economic engine in history. That's why my first major effort was to model the corporation as a socioeconomic system by accounting for all resource flows among investors, employees, customers, suppliers, communities, and other corporate stakeholders. The result was a dramatically different systems perspective that offers far more explanatory power than the old profit-centered model (Halal, 1977). For instance, I find there is no intrinsic conflict between profit and social welfare, leading to enormous possibilities for productive new synergies. The reality is that business can generally make more money by serving its constituencies and society better.

This work received prominent recognition, winning the 1977 Mitchell Prize and an award of $10,000, which would be equivalent to about $50,000 today. But I must admit to being disappointed upon seeing how difficult it is to alter the status quo. Here I had shown that a vast world of new economic possibilities lay unexplored, yet it seemed almost impossible to get businesspeople, politicians, and even futurists to show serious interest. I've done lots of consulting, speaking, and teaching, with doubtful impact in creating serious change.

This systems view of the corporation is gaining acceptance today, as prominently seen in the guiding philosophy of the Saturn Corporation, which could have been taken directly out of my writings. I helped Saturn in a very minor role, so I suppose my work has contributed in some way to today's progress. However, this incident and many other examples bear out another facet of the prophetic role that futurists usually play, often unwittingly.

We are primarily motivated by the obvious need for change, yet most other people simply do not see life in these terms. The result is a chronic problem in which futurists are usually marginalized or ignored. A few stars manage to break through this wall of indifference, such as Alvin Toffler and John Naisbitt. But to be frank, the biggest struggle most of us seem to face is that it's very hard getting people to listen.

I cannot help comparing this to the fate of many great prophets. For instance, St. John the Baptist spent most of his adult life wandering through deserts in communion with his God and telling others about the imminent coming of Christ, only to be so rejected that he eventually lost his head. Would John today be thought of as a futurist? Is there a difference?

Scanning: The New Capitalism

Undaunted, I went on to write my first book, which sketched out the new system of business, economics, and social institutions emerging for a knowledge-based world: *The New Capitalism* (Halal, 1986). I am a synthesizer, and so I aimed to integrate data from the scientific literature, the popular press, scores of interviews, and anything else of value I could find into a working whole. After struggling with this mass of information, patterns emerged to guide aggregating this data into clusters. The result was about fifty emerging trends, which in turn were aggregated to define major features of the new system.

Without thinking about it very much, I had invented a great methodology for defining emerging systems: (1) scan to create a database of emergent behavior, (2) cluster these data to identify trends, (3) cluster trends to define new concepts, and (4) integrate concepts to develop a framework grounded in empirical observations. This methodology remains one of my primary approaches to studying the future, used in many different projects with good success.

I have updated my original study of the new capitalism to produce other books—*Internal Markets* (Halal, 1993a), *The Infinite Resource* (Halal, 1998a), and *21st Century Economics* (Halal, 1998b)—as well as a practical guide for businesspeople and government administrators, *The New Management* (Halal, 1996). It was good to see that the trends and concepts identified many years earlier remained remarkably valid, although I could possibly reorganize them a bit. In fact, all of the features I predicted in 1986 to characterize the emerging economic system—revolutionary information technologies, intense global competition, entrepreneurial organizations, empowerment of workers, collaboration among all stakeholders, and so on—can vividly be seen today. This attests to the robust nature of such methods, but more important, it confirms the feasibility of doing rigorous future studies to identify emerging social systems.

Delphi: The George Washington University Forecast

Coming from an engineering background, I remain fascinated by technology, especially because it seems clear to me that all of this change is ultimately driven by the revolutionary technologies of today. About ten years ago I began conducting a Delphi Forecast of Emerging Technologies, which I have repeated roughly every two years. With four iterations now completed, this has blossomed into an international forecasting system that draws more attention than anything else I have done. The most recent results appeared in *The Futurist* (Halal, 1997) and produced the strongest response to any article ever published in this magazine.

The meaning of this success is not entirely clear, but I think it involves the fact that technology seems to transcend the controversies futurists get embroiled in over murky issues laden with emotional and ideological baggage, such as social institutions. It certainly helps now that anyone who hasn't been living in a cave starkly understands that we are rushing pell mell into a technology revolution that will alter the world. Guidance is clearly needed, and so people respond when it is provided.

Strategy: The WORLD 2000 Project

The practical side of future studies is its application to strategic planning, which I gave an interesting twist a few years ago when forming the WORLD 2000 Project. A conference I organized with Hazel Henderson (Halal, 1989) led to the idea of developing an international dialogue to help shape the new system that was emerging to govern a unified world. The phrase we coined to capture this idea was "strategic planning for the planet."

This turned into a provocative effort, producing a number of working conferences that engaged large numbers of people in articulating their hopes and fears for the future of the world, their best ideas, visions, and strategies for change, and so on. Various conferences were held, focusing on institutions, spirituality, space, and other topics. This project produced an ambitious "Global Strategic Plan," including a forecast of global supertrends, a most-plausible scenario, an analysis of major world issues, and strategies needed to get there (Halal, 1993b).

An Evaluation of Futures Studies Methodology

Such examples show that most of the prominent methods can produce good results. I do not think that the more exotic methods—cross-impact analysis comes to mind—are very useful, because they tend to overwhelm people with complexity and thus lose the face validity needed to help us understand the results.

While various methods are useful, I have to caution against the tempting faith in finding the "right method." My experience shows that the most brilliant methodology, the most accurate data, the most clever researchers mean little if not guided by an intuitive grasp of the complex forces for change and how they are likely to play out. Time and time again I have seen fine scholars struggle to make sense of future trends, only to produce an impressive compilation of facts that lacks meaning.

That brings me back again to the futurist as prophet. The description of the futurist as scientist misses the heart of the futurist's role. If there is one talent that is most essential it is that unique ability to actually envision the future in a realistic, tangible way that allows us to see possibilities before they arrive. No amount of data can do this. Without the subtle but essential ability to sense patterns, draw on insight, and exercise imagination, the future cannot possibly be understood. Without vision, all else is but wandering about aimlessly.

MY GUIDING VISION

The major trends identified in the WORLD 2000 study were integrated into a composite scenario to help visualize what the world should look like when it stabilizes into a coherent global order about the mid-twenty-first century. That scenario remains my best estimate of where we are heading. Of course, enormous challenges must be overcome and unexpected crises could deflect events into other directions, but the evidence indicates that a long-range trajectory of global development is moving rather clearly toward the following "central scenario."

The dynamics of an evolving global system should drive the planet toward a mature stage of development marked by a few dominant features at roughly the middle of the twenty-first century. World population should peak somewhere between 10 and 14 billion people who live mainly in knowledge-based societies, although some will still remain at the industrial or agricultural phases of development. This stable global population will interact through information networks to operate an advanced civilization that focuses on the pursuit of knowledge and major new endeavors like the serious exploration of deep space. Environmental pressures created by a resulting five- to tenfold increase in economic output will force technoeconomic systems to be designed so they are ecologically benign, sometimes only because of crashes in biological ecosystems. Society will work to curb the destructive tendencies of troubled or disaffected people with limited success, so occasional wars, crime, and other acts of violence will persist. Most nations should be part of a cohesive single community, but a decentralized global system of governance should also nourish a rich diversity of smaller subcommunities that possess the freedom to control their own affairs. These differences will be held together by a broadly shared international culture that agrees on a few essential matters, such as common standards of public behavior, the paramount role of human values and freedom, and a widely accepted set of general spiritual values, all of which will serve to unify the globe into a functioning whole.

This central scenario can be thought of as the "standard future" from which others may deviate, some being less desirable while others may be more desirable. Which of these variations is likely to occur is hard to say, but they should all share the same common features defining the emerging world order in general terms.

FUTURISM AND PROFESSIONAL LIFE

Although it should be clear that I am a committed futurist, I have to integrate this view into my professional life and the academic world, as most futurists must do. Even those free spirits who remain uncommitted to some institution have to cope with the realities of working effectively with a variety of authorities. I've always liked the way most futurists wear another hat as professors, businesspeople, consultants, or members of other professions.

I feel fortunate to have found a comfortable home for my work at George Washington University. While I am deeply involved as a futurist, I am also a normal, accepted member of a large professional faculty of business and government. I see little conflict between these two roles if one respects the demands of each and weaves them together, just as any professional might adopt a particular perspective. Thus, I teach mainstream courses (such as "Organization, Management, and Leadership") in our M.B.A. and other graduate programs, yet I've also been able to give them a strategic or future-oriented slant that is prized by most of my colleagues. Occasionally I offer a truly futurist course (such as "Emerging Technologies") that fits a special need well.

IMPLICATIONS FOR THE STUDY OF THE FUTURE

Looking back on the past few decades, my most striking impression is that the relationship between futurists and society has changed enormously. In the 1960s a few great futurists, such as Daniel Bell, Alvin Toffler, and Herman Kahn, captured attention by heralding the onset of bold changes in a distant future. Today average people well understand the very things we have been forecasting for so long: The technological revolution is obvious, big corporations and even governments are struggling to reinvent themselves, entire economic systems such as communism and the welfare state are being transformed, and the beginnings of a unified global order are at hand. In short, the future we have been envisioning and forecasting is almost here. Now the challenge is to help others make this understanding a reality.

As scholars, teachers, and scientists, we bear a special responsibility to conduct and explain our work carefully. We must make a point of avoiding grandiose, frightening, or unreasonable claims that often discredit bold ideas, but instead examine the limits of such concepts and the dangers that may result. For instance, I've recently been organizing "knowledge-sharing" conferences at the World Future Society and putting my Emerging Technologies Forecast on-line, which seem useful. If we can act more effectively, we could then assist policy makers and citizens in redefining the social order that is now failing.

I must admit, however, that the prospects for exerting such widespread impact do not look great. I'm not sure whether all the change we've just seen is a serious result of our guidance or just the natural flow of the LCE, in which case we are keen but unneeded observers. Even if we do have an impact, it may take such indirect forms that we don't hear of it. How many of the ancient prophets, such as John the Baptist, saw the fruit of their labors?

In another sense, I must admit that it doesn't really matter, because the entire odyssey I've travelled seems beyond me. I'm not entirely clear on what it means or where it will end, but am more impressed by the almost unpredictable, open-ended nature of the grand sweep of evolution. We may grasp a few broad outlines of the type I've sketched out, but the devil is in the details, the texture of everyday life, and especially the very different inner thoughts that will occupy our minds and souls in years to come.

At the time I started out on this path many years ago, for instance, I never would have imagined the accomplishments noted here. Bill Halal redefine the role of the corporation? Sketch out a new capitalism? Develop an international system for forecasting advanced technologies? Conduct strategic planning for the planet? Impossible! A silly dream!

Perhaps that is what we futurists have to grasp more fully. All these conflicting half-truths, all the successes and failures, all the varying perspectives, all of us—everything—are different faces of this same evolutionary flow of life, the same relentless search for meaning, the same spirit that energizes all. It is both humbling and elevating to be part of this great drama.

REFERENCES

Halal, W. E. (1977). Beyond the profit motive: The post-industrial corporation. *Technological Forecasting & Social Change, 12* (1), 13–30.

Halal, W. E. (1986). *The new capitalism.* New York: Wiley.

Halal, W. E. (Ed.). (1989). The global economy [Special issue]. *Futures, 21* (6).

Halal, W. E. (1990). The life cycle of evolution. *ICIS Forum, 20* (2), 28–42.

Halal, W. E. (1993a). *Internal markets.* New York: Wiley.

Halal, W. E. (1993b). WORLD 2000. *Futures, 25,* 5–21.

Halal, W. E. (1996). *The new management.* San Francisco: Berrett-Koehler.

Halal, W. E. (1997). Emerging technologies. *The Futurist, 31* (6), 20–28.

Halal, W. E. (1998a). *The infinite resource.* San Francisco: Jossey-Bass.

Halal, W. E. (1998b). *21st century economics.* New York: St. Martin's Press.

Harman, W. (1988). *Global mind change: The new age revolution in the way we think.* Indianapolis, IN: Knowledge Systems.

Sperry, R. (1988). Psychology's mentalist paradigm. *American Psychologist, 43,* 607–613.

Index

About the Editor
and Contributors

Ikram Azam is founder and director of the Pakistan Futuristics Foundation and Institute, Islamabad, Pakistan. He has been a civil servant since 1960. He has written numerous books, articles, and poems on future-oriented themes.

Wendell Bell is professor emeritus of sociology, Yale University, and, since 2000, senior research scientist in the Yale Center for Comparative Studies. He was a professor at Yale University from 1963 to 1995 and, before coming to Yale, was a member of the faculties of UCLA, Northwestern University, and Stanford University. During World War II he was a naval aviator and served a tour of duty in the Philippine theatre. He has been a futurist for about four decades, beginning with his research in the new states of the Caribbean. His most recent major work is the two-volume *Foundations of Futures Studies: Human Science for a New Era* (1997).

Peter Bishop is an associate professor of human sciences at the University of Houston, Clear Lake. He is on the faculty of the graduate program in studies of the future, where he specializes in techniques for long-term forecasting and planning. Dr. Bishop delivers keynote addresses and conducts seminars on the future for business, government, and not-for-profit organizations. He facilitates groups in developing scenarios, visions, and strategic plans for the future. Dr. Bishop's clients include IBM, Caltex Petroleum, Toyota Motor Sales, Shell Pipeline Corporation, the Defense Intelligence Agency, the Lawrence Livermore National Laboratory, the W. K. Kellogg Foundation, the Texas Department of Commerce, the City of Las Cruces, NM, and the Canadian Radio and Television Commission. Dr. Bishop has also worked with the NASA Johnson Space Center, where he designed a database interface used by hundreds of administrators.

Kuo-Hua Chen is associate professor in the Division of Futures Studies, Educational Development Center, Tamkang University, Taiwan.

Sam Cole is a professor in the Department of Planning (since 1983) and the Department of Geography (from 1993 to 1997) at the State University of New York at Buffalo, director of the Center for Regional Studies (from 1988 to 1993), and former president of the North East Regional Science Association. Prior to this he was at the Science Policy Research Unit at the University of Sussex. He has authored and edited several books on global models and futures scenarios, including *Models of Doom: A Critique of the Limits to Growth* (1973), *World Futures: The Great Debate* (1979), *Worlds Apart: Technology, Distribution and the International Economy, The Global Impact of Information Technology*, and *Global Models and Futures Studies*. He was a member of the executive council of the World Futures Studies Federation and is North American editor of the journal *Futures*.

Jim Dator is professor and head of the Alternative Futures Option, Department of Political Science, and director of the Hawaii Research Center for Futures Studies, Social Science Research Institute, at the University of Hawaii at Manoa. He is also codirector of the Space and Society Department, International Space University in Strasbourg, France. He was secretary general and president of the World Futures Studies Federation during the 1980s and early 1990s.

William E. Halal is professor of management at George Washington University, Washington, DC. He is an authority on emerging technologies, strategic management, and institutional and economic change, and has consulted to Fortune-500 companies and other organizations. He also worked on the Apollo program, served as a major in the U.S. Air Force, and spent years in industry and government. He is the author of five books and hundreds of articles, ranging from studies in scholarly journals to op-ed pieces in papers like the *New York Times*. Halal was awarded the 1977 Mitchell Prize for his article, "Beyond the Profit-Motive."

David Hicks is professor of futures education in the School of Education at Bath Spa University College, and recently described himself in the journal

Futures as "a teacher, writer, poet, nurturer of visions and radical educator." He directed the World Studies 8–13 curriculum project and the Centre for Peace Studies at the University College of St. Martin in Lancaster during the 1980s and then set up the Futures Project in 1989 to help students and teachers think more critically and creatively about the future. He is internationally recognized for his work on a global and futures perspective in the school curriculum and has lectured widely in the United Kingdom, Australia, Canada, and Italy. His most recent books are *Futures Education: The World Yearbook of Education 1998*, with Rick Slaughter (1998), *Visions of the Future: Why We Need to Teach for Tomorrow* (1995), *Educating for the Future: A Practical Classroom Guide* (1994), and *Preparing for the Future: Notes & Queries for Concerned Educators* (1994). He has recently carried out research projects on children's hopes and fears for the future, the importance of envisioning preferable futures, and educators' sources of hope in postmodern times.

Eva Hideg is associate professor at the Futures Research Department of the Budapest University of Economic Sciences. Beside teaching futures research, she is researching postmodern paradigms of scientific theory and the futures research application of models of chaos and evolution, as well as future orientation.

Jan Huston is a business consultant, president of the Institute for the Study of Evolving Systems (ISES), an associate at the Hawaii Research Center for Futures Studies, and an instructor of politics, law, and alternative futures at the University of Hawaii. Formerly he was the CEO of a computer arts firm and worked in government and as a writer. He is currently completing a book, *A Passion to Evolve*.

Sohail Inayatullah is a professor at the Center for Futures Studies, Tamkang University in Taiwan; an adjunct professor at the Faculty of Arts and Social Sciences, University of the Sunshine Coast in Australia; and a professor at the International Management Centres Association, University of Action Learning. Inayatullah is coeditor of the *Journal of Futures Studies* and associate editor of *New Renaissance*. He is on the editorial board of *Development, Futures and Foresight*.

Christopher Burr Jones is a visiting associate professor, M.S. Studies of the Future Program at the University of Houston, Clear Lake, and is secretary-general of the World Futures Studies Federation. The article was written while he was a professor of political science at Eastern Oregon University.

Ian Lowe is emeritus professor of science, technology, and society at Griffith University in Australia, where he was previously head of the School of

Science. He directed Australia's Commission for the Future in 1988 and chaired the advisory council that produced in 1996 the first national report on the state of the environment. He has a futures-oriented consulting company, Thinking Futures.

Peter T. Manicas has taught and published books and articles in a variety of disciplines in the social sciences and in philosophy. He is currently director of liberal studies and professor of sociology at the University of Hawaii at Manoa. Among his books are *Logic: The Essentials* (1968, 1976), *The Death of the State* (1974), *A History and Philosophy of the Social Sciences* (1987), *War and Democracy* (1989), and *Social Process in Hawaii: A Reader* (1995).

Mika Mannermaa has held several positions of a researcher, mainly in the Academy of Finland, and also acted as a futures consultant in several companies, municipalities, and ministries and for the government and the Parliament of Finland. His research areas include theory and methodology of futures research, paradigms in futures research, futures barometers, the relation between humanity and nature, the future of highly developed countries (information society), and the role of citizens' movements in shaping the future. Mannermaa is an author or coauthor of about 140 reports, books, and articles. He has also been a member of the council of the Finnish Society for Futures Studies and of the World Futures Studies Federation.

Oliver W. Markley is a registered professional engineer and social psychologist who has worked as a futurist for the majority of his professional career: for ten years at the Stanford Research Institute (now SRI International), where he was a senior policy analyst, principal investigator, and management consultant with SRI's Management and Social Systems Group, and for twenty years on the faculty of the graduate program in studies of the future at the University of Houston, Clear Lake (UHCL), where he taught courses in applied futures research, environmental scanning, visioning, and the facilitation of organizational change. He also codirected UHCL's Institute for Futures Research, which provides opportunities for students to work with faculty doing applied futures work for external clients. Dr. Markley has done management training and consulting for scores of organizations, both corporate (Apple Computer, Texas Instruments, Conoco, Amoco) and nonprofit (National League of Cities, EarthSave Foundation, Texas State Higher Coordinating Board, Houston Area Urban League), and is the coauthor of four books and author of several dozen articles on various aspects of forecasting, planning, futures research, and change management.

Eleonora Barbieri Masini has been professor of futures studies (social and human aspects) and human ecology at the Faculty of Social Sciences, Pontifical Gregorian University, Rome, since 1976. She is a member of the Club of Rome, former secretary general and president of the World Futures Studies Federation, coordinator of the "Futures of Cultures" project for UNESCO, member of the executive council of the Inter University Center at Dubrovnik, former chairman of the Futures Research Committee of the International Sociological Association, former president of the World Association for Science and Arts for Europe, and president of the Network WIN (Women's International Network) Emergency and Solidarity, sponsored by UNESCO and initiated with Rita Levi Montalcini, Nobel Prize for Neurobiology. Among her books are *Women, Households and Change* (1991), *Why Futures Studies?* (1993), and *The Futures of Cultures* (1994).

Graham H. May is principal lecturer in futures research and course leader of the master's degree in foresight and futures studies at Leeds Metropolitan University in the United Kingdom. He is author of *The Future Is Ours: Foreseeing, Managing and Creating the Future* (1996).

Erzsébet Nováky is head of the Futures Research Department, Budapest University of Economic Sciences, and the vice president of the Futures Research Committee, Hungarian Academy of Sciences. Her main research topics are the behavior of complex large systems, chaos and forecasting, future orientation of humans, education, and vocational training. She has published fourteen books, seventy-five articles, and two-hundred conference papers and working papers.

Reed D. Riner is professor of anthropology at Northern Arizona University. He has published on the epistemology and applications of futures research in *Futures, Futures Research Quarterly, Futurics, Human Organization, Current Anthropology*, and *City & Society*. He is former editor of *Cultural Futures Research*. He is the coordinator of and an instructor in the NAU Solar System Simulation, an Internet-mediated educational environment used by college classes nationally since 1990, and was honored by EduCom and CNI (1994) for the "most effective use of networked information in the classroom." He is also director of the "Flagstaff Tomorrow" project, an ongoing instructional exercise in ethnographic futures research and applied anthropology.

Anita Rubin works as a researcher with the Finland Futures Research Centre, Turku, Finland. Her current research theme is "Adolescents' Images of the Future." Ms. Rubin has presented over thirty papers at scientific conferences and seminars on futures issues, published twenty-five research reports and articles in scientific books and journals (in Finnish, English, and Swedish), and two books (in Finnish), and coedited two books (in Finnish). She has served as the secretary general of the Finnish Society for Futures

Studies, and was the assistant to the secretary-general and president of the World Futures Studies Federation. She was a member of the WFSF executive board.

Jordi Serra del Pino is the director of the Centre Catala de Prospectiva, head of projects at the Institute for Prospective and Strategic Studies, editor of the magazine *Papers de prospectiva*, and former member of the executive board of the World Futures Studies Federation. He has published many articles in *Futures, La Vanguardia, El temps, Àmbits, The Manoa Journal, New Renaissance*, and others.

Arthur B. Shostak joined the faculty of the Wharton School in 1961, where he taught courses in industrial sociology, management and society, and social problems. A member of the Drexel University faculty since 1967, he has introduced courses in futuristics, race and ethnic relations, urban sociology, and social implications of twentieth-century technology. Author, editor, or coeditor of twenty books and over 125 articles, his views on work issues have appeared in the *New York Times*, the *Wall Street Journal*, the *AFL-CIO News*, and elsewhere. He has served as a consultant to every level of government, Fortune-500 companies, and major labor unions. Since 1975 he has served as the adjunct sociologist for the Antioch College Degree Program at the AFL-CIO's George Meany Center for Labor Studies, Silver Spring, MD.

Richard A. Slaughter is foundation professor of foresight at Swinburne University of Technology and director of the Futures Study Centre in Melbourne. He is a consulting futurist who has worked with a wide range of organizations in many countries and at all educational levels. He is a fellow of the World Futures Studies Federation and a professional member of the World Futures Society. In 1997 he was elected to the executive council of the WFSF. In 2001 he was elected president. He is a prolific writer and holds several editorial positions. These include: consulting editor to *Futures* (United Kingdom), series editor for Routledge (London) for the *Futures and Education* series, board member of the *Journal of Futures Studies* (Taiwan), board member of *On the Horizon* (University of NC), board member of *Foresight* (United Kingdom), and series editor of *The Knowledge Base of Futures Studies* (Melbourne). He is coauthor of *Education for the 21st Century* (1993), author of *The Foresight Principle: Cultural Recovery in the 21st Century* (1995), editor of *New Thinking for a New Millennium* (1996), and coeditor of the *World Yearbook of Education 1998: Futures Education* (1998). He has also published a series of futures resource books. His most recent books are *Futures for the Third Millennium: Enabling the Forward View* (1999), and *Gone Today, Here Tomorrow: Millennium Previews* (2000).

Markku Sotarauta is a professor at the University of Tampere, Department of Regional Studies and Environmental Policy. He is a director of the Research Unit for Urban and Regional Development Studies. He specializes in strategic thinking, futures studies, communicative planning, and network management in promotion of regional and local development. He has written numerous articles on those topics, and has consulted to ministries, regions, cities, and municipalities.

Ernest Sternberg is associate professor and chair of the Department of Planning at the School of Architecture and Planning, State University of New York at Buffalo. His latest book is *The Economy of Icons: How Business Manufactures Meaning* (1999).

W. Warren Wagar is distinguished teaching professor of history at the State University of New York at Binghamton, where he has taught since 1971. In addition to futures studies, he teaches and publishes in the fields of comparative world history and modern European intellectual history. His futures books include *The Next Three Futures: Paradigms of Things to Come* (1991), *A Short History of the Future* (1999), and *Memoirs of the Future* (2001).

Paul Wildman specialized in futures studies, organizational development, and labor market programs as director of labor market programs in Queensland from 1989–1994. He then commenced as a lecturer at Southern Cross University (SCU). At SCU he helped develop and lecture in futures studies, the only on-line master's specialization in futures studies in Australia. Presently he is fellow in futures studies at the International Management Center University. He also lecturers part time, consults in the futures field, and has an extensive publishing record in the futures studies, organization, and community development fields, having published some sixty articles, contributed chapters, two books, and a CD-ROM.

Kaoru Yamaguchi is a professor in the Department of Management Sciences, Osaka Sangyo University, Japan. His main areas of research are information economics, system dynamics, and futures studies.